PUBLIC HISTORY FOR A POST-TRUTH ERA

Public History for a Post-Truth Era explores how to combat historical denial when faith in facts is at an all-time low. Moving beyond memorial museums or documentaries, the book shares on-the-ground stories of participatory public memory movements that brought people together to grapple with the deep roots and current truths of human rights abuses. It gives an inside look at "Sites of Conscience" around the world, and the memory activists unearthing their hidden histories, from the Soviet Gulag to the slave trade in Senegal. It then follows hundreds of people joining forces across dozens of US cities to fight denial of Guantánamo, mass incarceration, and climate change.

As reparations proposals proliferate in the US, the book is a resource for anyone seeking to confront historical injustices and redress their harms. Written in accessible, non-academic language, it will appeal to students, educators, or supportive citizens interested in public history, museums, or movement organizing.

Liz Ševčenko is the Founding Director of the Humanities Action Lab, currently homed at Rutgers University-Newark, and was the Founding Director of the International Coalition of Sites of Conscience. She organizes coalitions for historical memory and redress, combining the visions and forces of people working in public history, social movements, and transitional justice. She lives in Brooklyn.

Global Perspectives on Public History
Edited by Dr. Kristin O'Brassill-Kulfan, Rutgers University

This series explores the work of public historians and the contested histories they engage with around the world. Authored by both scholars and practitioners, volumes focus on cases where complex histories and diverse audiences meet and examine public representations of history. The series aims to link professional discussions of different historical methodologies with broader dialogues around commemoration, preservation, heritage, and interpretation in diverse geographical, cultural, social, and economic contexts. The co-existence of both global and regionally specific volumes in the series highlights the wide range of innovative new projects and approaches on offer. These books will provide students, researchers, and practitioners with new case studies and helpful analytical tools to confront the (mis)representations of history they encounter in their work and as members of 21st-century communities.

Contested Commemoration in US History
Diverging Public Interpretations
Edited by Melissa M. Bender and Klara Stephanie Szlezák

Public in Public History
Edited by Joanna Wojdon and Dorota Wiśniewska

Public History in Poland
Edited by Joanna Wojdon

Public History for a Post-Truth Era
Fighting Denial through Memory Movements
Liz Ševčenko

PUBLIC HISTORY FOR A POST-TRUTH ERA

Fighting Denial through Memory Movements

Liz Ševčenko

Routledge
Taylor & Francis Group

NEW YORK AND LONDON

Cover image: Dasha Nagorodnyuk, courtesy Humanities Action Lab

First published 2023

by Routledge
605 Third Avenue, New York, NY 10158

and by Routledge
4 Park Square, Milton Park, Abingdon, Oxon, OX14 4RN

Routledge is an imprint of the Taylor & Francis Group, an informa business

© 2023 Liz Ševčenko

Library of Congress Cataloging-in-Publication Data
A catalog record for this title has been requested

ISBN: 978-1-032-02922-1 (hbk)
ISBN: 978-1-032-02921-4 (pbk)
ISBN: 978-1-003-18582-6 (ebk)

DOI: 10.4324/9781003185826

Typeset in Bembo
by KnowledgeWorks Global Ltd.

For Hugo and Margot

CONTENTS

ACKNOWLEDGMENTS

This is a book about the power of coalitions: about the work of hundreds of people across dozens of countries over two decades. But many played critical roles that don't come through in the narrative.

First, the people who worked in the central offices of the coalitions described in the book, coordinating members' collective work and individual projects, and shaping the ideas and frameworks within which we collaborated. After Ruth Abram and I got it off the ground, the International Coalition of Sites of Conscience was coordinated by an incredible team including Sylvia Fernández, Heidi Karst, Ereshnee Naidu, Max Novichenko, Olga Rudenko, and Vivien Watts. Bix Gabriel came up with the idea for a memory project around Guantánamo and built its foundations. The Humanities Action Lab (HAL) was brought from scattered inspiration to an organized coalition through the astounding energy, intellect, and commitment of Julia Thomas. Shana Russell, who managed States of Incarceration (SOI) and the Rikers Public Memory Project, and Aleia Brown, who managed Climates of Inequality (COI), brought their experience and creative brilliance as historians and organizers to reshape HAL's priorities and practices. Margie Weinstein managed all aspects of HAL while I was on leave writing and later homeschooling my kids during COVID lockdown, including guiding our coalition through the pandemic.

There are over 1,000 faculty, students, issue organization leaders, and scholar-advisors, who together created the HAL participatory memory projects described here. For the GPMP, see https://gitmomemory.org/about/traveling-exhibit/#students; for SOI, see https://statesofincarceration.org/university-partners; and for COI, scroll down to "Contributors" within each local story: https://climatesofinequality.org/local-stories/.

HAL got off the ground thanks to the vision and support of individual people working in big institutions, who put their resources into the idea: Elazar Barkan invited the GPMP to come to Columbia University; David Scobey and then Laura Auricchio brought HAL into being at The New School; Tim Raphael opened the door for HAL to come to Rutgers University-Newark; and Chancellor Nancy Cantor made it happen.

The book itself was also a group effort. The American Academy in Rome provided astoundingly generative space, intellectual community, and confidence to get the first draft on paper. But it was my mother Nancy Ševčenko and mother-in-law Holly Wallack who made it possible for me to use the Academy's space, designed around its single fellows, by coming and taking care of my kids for weeks at a time. Further, they both offered me space in their homes – and more fun time they spent with my kids – to finish. I thank my mother in particular for providing support on every level, from close readings of the text to long walks away from it.

Mike Frisch was the first person to believe the book worthy of publishing, the first to read drafts, and gave critical feedback that was absolutely instrumental in the book's basic shape. When other obligations avalanched and my confidence dwindled, I would not have kept going without the coaching and careful reading from Jana Lipman, Martha Miller, and Rachel Seidman. The book's final form is due to the superhuman efforts of Annie Anderson and Kristin O'Brassill-Kulfan. Annie conducted research on critical points around incarceration, immigration, and other issues and wrote key portions presenting it; did incredibly detailed fact checking; and ensured all the footnotes were there and correct. Kristin, editor of this series at Routledge and a faculty lead in the Humanities Action Lab, took on way more than she bargained for with this project, especially since I was completely inexperienced with any aspect of writing a book. She gave extremely generously of her very limited time, supporting every single aspect from the overall framing to footnotes.

Most importantly I thank my husband Josh Wallack, who suggested I apply to the American Academy and sacrificed sleep and sanity to make it possible for me to go, and my kids, Hugo and Margot, who cheered me on the whole way, and asked all the right questions.

INTRODUCTION

The last straw, for me, was when Trump denied the rain. Video of his inauguration speech, broadcast to millions of people around the world, showed dignitaries huddling under umbrellas, and water streaming from his lapels. "You know," he said that evening, "I looked at the rain, which just never came. It's like God was looking down on us."[1] I remember obsessively puzzling over why he didn't just say rain was good luck, like people do at weddings. Why couldn't he leave the rain alone – let observable reality be – and shape what it signified? God could still have been credited for blessing the new Presidency, but I wouldn't have to doubt my own eyes (wait, was it actually raining? Does drizzle count?). Masha Gessen, a journalist who fled Putin's Russia, spelled it out for me, and for millions of stunned Americans and frantic fact checkers: "Lying is the message. It's not just that both Putin and Trump lie, it is that they lie … to assert power over truth itself." Trump, Gessen explained patiently, "is not making easily disprovable factual claims: he is claiming control over reality itself."[2]

I was no stranger to political lies. I had spent the last 20 years learning from activists trying to reclaim truths of state violence, suppressed by governments but spoken by people, from secret prisons in Argentina to the Soviet Gulag in Russia. They had turned the tide in their countries by exposing incontrovertible evidence: exhuming bodies of people the state claimed were never killed, recording testimonies about former prisons the state denied existed. But Trump's seemingly innocuous fib about the weather in my own country shook me. If our President could deny the rain falling from the sky, what else could he make disappear – from our present, and from our violent past?

The President may have made a rainless reality official, but he was brought to power by millions of people who also denied observable changes in the

DOI: 10.4324/9781003185826-1

natural world. Despite a massive surge in hurricanes, wildfires, and floods, and a whole new profession of "climate communicators" working to explain them, after Trump's election, Americans' belief in human-caused climate change became increasingly determined by their partisan identity.[3] By 2018, Republicans were barely half as likely to believe global warming was happening than Democrats: only an estimated 52% of registered Republican voters compared to 91% of Democrats.[4]

Such aggressive denial of visible evidence has sustained violence not only to the planet but also to its people. New technologies and communications allowed individuals to document and disseminate forensic evidence of state-sanctioned violence. Clear videos of Michael Brown, Eric Garner, and other Black men being murdered by police in broad daylight circulated, uncensored, to millions of people. Crisp audio recordings of Trump boasting about sexual assault were heard equally widely. But these exposures did not guarantee accountability: most police officers were not convicted; Trump was elected President of the United States.

Four years later, the US was living under such a divided reality that the government was unable to achieve a peaceful transfer of power. On January 6, 2021, a mob of people stormed the Capitol building because they did not accept the truth of the election results. The insurgents may have been extreme in their tactics, but their understanding of truth represented huge portions of the population. A poll conducted in the aftermath of the January insurrection found that 67% of Republican voters nationwide viewed the 2020 presidential election as invalid.[5]

The total rupture of the connection between truth, evidence, and accountability inspired panicked political commentators and philosophers to herald a "post-truth era." This book asks what this rupture bodes for how we understand our history: how Americans can collectively confront our violent past, and explore how it continues to shape us, when we are this divided about the world we see with our own eyes in the present day.

The Democratic response to Trump-era denial has been to double down on truth. After centuries of refusing to heed citizens' calls to officially reckon with the past, an explosion of initiatives across multiple levels of the US State is finally launching official investigations into histories of discrimination and violence. US cities from Evanston, IL to Amherst, MA, and states from California to New Jersey, initiated truth commissions, reparations programs, and other initiatives to expose historical harms and redress their legacies. Even the federal government advanced a federal bill to study reparations, more than three decades after its introduction, as well as a new bill calling for a US Truth, Racial Healing, and Transformation Commission.[6] In so doing, the US finally joined hundreds of other governments around the world – from new democracies like South Africa to long-standing ones like Canada – who launched official investigations into historical abuses, recognizing that peace in the present depended on reckoning with violence in the past.

Reparations programs and truth commissions in the US have incredible potential to generate transformative public policies that understand, and undo, structural racism. But they rely on a faith that historical truth has its own power to combat denial and bring about accountability: that if we produce the evidence, people will believe in it, and act on it. It's a risky strategy, since however incontrovertible the evidence may seem, this truth about our history exists only on one side of the aisle. Not one Republican congressperson has signed on to either of the federal bills. The change in presidential administrations between Trump and Biden did not change the country's deeply rooted culture of denial. Now more than ever, as reams of psychological research have demonstrated, more facts don't change people's minds.[7] Any attempt to assert historical truth needs to take this state of mind seriously.

We are not going to be able to teach our way out of this. More and better history books, museum exhibits, and documentaries are not going to make the difference. Time-limited truth commissions can't wrap up reckoning in a bow. Even media focused on winning "hearts and minds" has to struggle to reach its audience. But staring our history full in the face shouldn't be paralyzing. Instead, we can draw energy from where real change is happening, in the dynamic, collective action of social movements. From this, we can develop an approach to dealing with the past that's powerful for the moment we're in: participatory public memory.

Participatory public memory initiatives mobilize thousands of people from disparate locations and perspectives to grapple with historical denial together. A participatory public memory process applies the logics and modes of social movements to the ways we deal with the past. And it invites social movements to use understandings of the complex origins of current problems to shape effective strategies. This process opens a public sphere in which diverse participants wrestle with a social issue, engage in debate across differences on its causes and consequences, and collaborate on interventions. These interventions range from museum exhibits to mass protests. But they share a commitment to an ongoing, dynamic process of connecting past and present: exploring the deep roots of current crises, and shaping solutions. This pursues public history as more than a catalyst for civic engagement, but as its own form of active participation for social change.

Tracing the Path to the "Post-Truth Era"

In 2016, "post-truth" was named Word of the Year by the Oxford English Dictionary (OED). This reflected a massive spike in public anxiety about truth. The term had been around for a few years: the OED traced the first usage to 1992; Ralph Keyes' *The Post-Truth Era*, the first book to claim the term, was released in 2004.[8] But Trump's election sent the term's use soaring. In 2018 alone, at least a dozen books were released with "post-truth" in the title, and publications from the mainstream media to scientific journals were flooded with analyses of the concept.[9]

Anti-racist critics set straight that claiming post-truth as a new thing is a mark of white privilege. While the experience of someone in power denying the basic material realities you see, feel, and know every day might be deeply disorienting to those who have been historically supported by the cultural consensus of what's true, it's horribly familiar to those who have not. As cultural studies scholars Robert Mejia, Kay Beckermann, and Curtis Sullivan argue, "In demarcating 2016 as the beginning of our post-truth era, [post-truth criticism] effaces the epistemological, ontological, and axiological danger experienced by people of color throughout American history."[10] In the US, truth has been an exclusive privilege of whiteness since the nation's founding, when the authors of the Declaration of Independence declared their "self evident" truth that all men were created equal while enslaving Black people. As historian Ibram X. Kendi argues, "the heartbeat of racism is denial,"[11] and more specifically, that "part of America is denying all of what is part of America."[12] For example, American historians have persistently described slavery as "the nation's most enduring contradiction," a "paradox," and a "blatant inconsistency," as opposed to confronting it as fundamental to "who we are."[13] But Kendi cites 2016 as a moment of crisis not so much for truth, as for denial, as Trump's overt celebration of white supremacy meant that "no president has caused more Americans to stop denying the existence of racism than Donald Trump."[14]

Whatever we believe is distinctive about the place and time we find ourselves in, it represents a particular "regime of truth," in the words of philosopher Michel Foucault.[15] While in every truth regime, power has defined the relationship between truth, evidence, and accountability, in each the notion of historical truth itself has been eroded and fortified in different ways, shaped and reshaped to address or elude past harms. Exploring battles for historical truth and its relationship to accountability is critical for devising strategies to confront historical denial and pursue justice moving forward.

I began my public history career in the mid-1990s, in the midst of a worldwide celebration of the inherent power of historical truth. Starting after the end of the Cold War, dozens of countries around the world emerging from dictatorships – such as South Africa after apartheid and Chile after the ouster of Augusto Pinochet – championed a truth regime change. They organized highly publicized truth commissions, in which hundreds of people shared testimony of their former regime's repression, backed by new data from researchers, while thousands more watched on TV. Truth commissions were based on the belief that airing evidence of past abuses would ensure they would never recur, placing tremendous faith in the independent power of truth to create a culture of accountability. But these new monuments to truth were built on shifting sands.

One force weakening the truth's stable foundations came from deconstructionists, a group of European philosophers in the 1960s and 1970s, who held a very different theory of what kind of truth could take on totalitarianism. Seeking to bust up the "grand narratives" that undergirded state power, deconstructionism decoupled text from referent, representation from reality, in an effort to expose the subjectivity of any statement, and therefore remove the absolute authority behind truth claims that legitimized totalitarian regimes. Deconstructionism is important to the disintegration of truth not because Putin or Trump read Derrida – and not even because deconstructionists should be blamed for eroding truth – but because of how far its ideas spread from their original source and intent. Millions of people involved in analyzing or creating narratives, whether in museums or movies, educated any time after the 1980s or 1990s – myself included – knowingly or unknowingly embraced some ideas of subjectivity and the importance of narrating from multiple perspectives. Then, in 1987, the cracks in deconstructionism's moral foundations widened with the revelation that one of its leaders, Paul De Man, had written anti-semitic propaganda for Nazi publications in his youth, lied about his financial dealings, and cheated on his wife. Placed in the wrong hands, an ideology that suggested, as *New York Times Magazine* editor James Atlas put it, "language and literature can never be put in the service of truth because it is impossible to define what the truth is,"[16] could unintentionally weaken the link between truth and accountability, and offer a weapon to denialists.

In the sciences, the integrity of truth was undermined through intentional assault. Several scholars trace the disintegration of scientific authority and belief in scientific facts back to the 1950s and 1960s, when the tobacco industry deliberately deceived the public about the health hazards of smoking.[17] The industry's disinformation tactics – and its consequent dilution of science into mere spin – profoundly shaped the next generation's public discourse and inaction on climate change. As Naomi Oreskes and Erik M. Conway argue in *Merchants of Doubt*, starting in the 1990s, fossil fuel industries funded a small group of scientists to flood the media with misinformation, and an army of pundits to parrot it, creating the impression of a genuine division within the scientific community on the reality of climate change and undermining public confidence in scientific evidence.[18] The Yale Program on Climate Change Communication discovered that between 2008 and 2012, as information about climate change and its human causes was ever more widely accessible, public concern actually dropped by more than 10%. Analysis revealed this was due to political pundits talking about climate change *more*, but in polarizing ways, linked to political partisanship. As a result, people's beliefs about climate change became increasingly determined by their political affiliation.[19]

In politics and policy, journalists point to the War on Terror as a key turning point for truth. After 9/11, the US government launched a sprawling, violent, and ultimately failed enterprise from a single falsehood: that Iraqi strongman Saddam Hussein had weapons of mass destruction. The majority of the American public, at the time believing this to be true, supported the operation. *New York Times* journalist Ron Suskind recounted an exchange he had with a senior Bush advisor in the summer of 2002, in which, when Suskind presented him with material evidence contradicting claims a US official made about Iraq, the official responded,

> People like you are still living in what we call the reality-based community. You believe that solutions emerge from your judicious study of discernible reality. That's not the way the world really works anymore. We're an empire now, and when we act, we create our own reality.[20]

For Suskind, this laid the foundations for the total collapse of truth that would come later. Looking back on the Bush Administration in 2017, he reflected, "I think we understand more deeply some of the innovations of those in power in that period in terms of separating public dialogue from agreed-upon, discernible reality."[21]

These episodes illuminate some of the precedents for the idea of "post-truth," and demonstrate how far the problem has metastasized beyond the OED's definition. While the OED defined "post-truth" as "relating to or denoting circumstances in which objective facts are less influential in shaping public opinion than appeals to emotion and personal belief,"[22] as philosopher Vittorio Bufacchi observes, it has come to represent something more profound: post-truth "doesn't simply deny or question certain facts," he writes, "but it aims to undermine the theoretical infrastructure that makes it possible to have a conversation about the truth."[23] Returning to journalist Masha Gessen's explanation, Trump didn't simply use his power to assert his own version of the truth, but "to assert power over truth itself" by systematically destroying people's belief that there was a truth out there to be found, one that existed separately from people's beliefs or from manipulation by his enemies.[24] Trump's signature approach was to publicly and openly make claims that could easily be proven false with a quick Google search or one's own eyes, and inspire millions of his followers to support them as true. Followers did not always support falsehoods because they actually believed them to be true; as some studies suggest, many upheld disprovable claims in order to demonstrate their allegiance to the President and his politics.[25] Progressives were not immune to partisan truth-making either. In the world of electoral politics, truth was fully wrested from what traditionally defined it, such as documentation and evidence: "Partisanship has been revealed as the strongest force in U.S. public life" *Vox* reporter David Roberts declared, summing up his analysis of voter data days after Trump's election, "stronger than any norms, independent of any facts."[26]

Yet this period has also seen unprecedented protest against historical denial. If looked at from the vantage point of its massive social movements – by some accounts the largest in US history[27] – this period could instead be described as a "pro-truth era." People whose lived experiences had long been officially denied, for whom the rejection of observable reality did not begin with Trump, organized to reaffirm truth and its power to bring accountability. The Black Lives Matter movements were propelled by the practice of documenting police violence against Black people on cell phones and publicizing it on social media. The #MeToo movements, calling out abuses of power that were undocumentable, elevated testimonies of sexual assault as truth. These demands extended to historical truths, as calls to remove Confederate statues and other racist symbols in the American landscape erupted in every corner of the country. And now even segments of the US government, heeding generations of activists, have begun promoting truth and accountability in unprecedented ways, through a proliferation of truth commissions and reparations programs.

These movements to win justice and redress for historical harms are wielding truth as their main weapon. They reflect continued faith that evidence has its own power, unchecked by any official regime, to catalyze collective movements for justice. The federal reparations bills begin by presenting "evidentiary documentation" and "facts."[28] Congresswoman Barbara Lee, who with Senator Cory Booker introduced the proposal for a Truth, Racial Healing, and Transformation Commission, announced her hopes to "educate and inform the public" about what really happened in American history, to ensure people "reject the big lie of white supremacy."[29]

But historical truth may not have the power and meaning proponents of truth commissions uncritically accord it. The same social media technologies that circulated evidence of racial violence and fostered solidarity to fight it also created insulated online communities, each governed by its own truths, each with its own authorities and systems for validating what is true. The most recent truth regime left scorched earth, leaving little to recover. This barren terrain sets a new context for historical denial, where there is nothing real out there to deny. This poses a greater challenge for rebuilding a society that is accountable to its history, requiring new strategies for dealing with the past, and new approaches to public memory.

Challenges for Public Memory in a Post-Truth/Pro-Truth Era

Formulating these new approaches requires rethinking the role and relationship of different levels of historical truth: individual historical facts; the narratives that connect facts together; and the umbrella frameworks that synthesize narratives into a way of explaining the world.

What Is the Role of Historical Facts?

Journalists responded to Trump by assembling an army of fact checkers, doubling down on notions of objective truth. Activists pressed for the installation of dash- and body-cameras to document civilian-police encounters; when those aren't there, people diligently video the daily violence law enforcement for so long dismissed as subjective recollections. Those who preserve the past – historians, archeologists, legal investigators – should follow suit in this push for documentation. If we abandon all faith in historical evidence, we will have no foundation for examining and reexamining the past now, or in future generations. We will have erased any possibility of understanding how we got here. This era too shall pass, and we should hold steady through it. So facts still matter.

But facts aren't enough. They don't work to convince people of realities that run counter to what they already believe. As science journalist Simon Oxenham writes, "not only can misinformation often spread faster and wider than the truth... but even worse, combating misinformation with evidence can often have the complete and utter opposite of the desired effect." Reams of research reveal that "repeating that a claim is false can actually leave an even stronger impression that the claim is true."[30] Historical reckoning won't be won through a battle of truth claims alone.

What Is the Role of Stories?

The emerging field of "narrative change" is based on the idea that public opinion will not be shifted by better facts, but by better stories. Narrative change has had strong supporters among legal advocates and policy makers who came to understand that their arguments and policies, their attempts to change structures behind the scenes, could not be sustained without a wide constituency of people who understood and supported what they were trying to do. In other words, policy change required cultural change; a change in the narratives people use to understand their lives and make decisions about their future.[31] To create these narratives, compelling stories of individuals, not systems, ones that emphasize universal human experience over partisan political affiliation, can bring people around better than bullet-pointed facts can.

While proponents of narrative change aren't arguing that facts work, their premise is still that people just need to see or hear the "right" things in order to change their minds. This implies that racism and other ideologies, in the words of political philosopher Tommie Shelby, "continue to be widely held largely because of widespread ignorance, faulty reasoning, and failures to appreciate relevant evidence" so that "all mistaken beliefs can be effectively combated through criticism and intellectual training alone."[32] This faith in the power of teaching and truth ignores the "possessive investment in whiteness" explored by American Studies scholar George Lipsitz.[33] White people, for example, have a possessive investment in historical narratives that describe wealth as something all people have had equal access to, something those who have it earned through hard work.[34] Historical facts, or even compelling human stories, that contradict those narratives – such as stories of slavery, or discriminatory practices carried out by the Federal Housing Authority, or predatory lending by banks – may provide new information and insight, but do not disturb our possessive investment in narratives of equal opportunity.[35]

That investment is psychological, as well as material. Public historian Julia Rose applies psychoanalytic research to historic site interpretation. She recognizes that simply proving a fact will not persuade those who have deep reasons to reject it, and argues that public historians must take this rejection seriously, offer space for it, and mobilize creative strategies to engage it. Rose studied the resistance of both visitors and volunteers at a Louisiana plantation historic site to accept new information that enslaved people lived and worked there, despite the physical evidence around them at the site. Rose suggests that when people are confronted with a fact that radically disrupts a larger truth that has guided their life – for instance, that they live in a country built on equal opportunity – they experience something similar to a death. As they process and mourn the passing of their previous understanding of their world, they experience stages of grief, including denial and anger. Public historians, Rose argues, must create space and time for visitors and other stakeholders to process these assaults to their worldview.[36]

This suggests that in addition to learning new facts and hearing compelling human narratives, public memory projects need to invite people to reflect deeply on how their position shapes the way they understand these facts and narratives. This reflection would not only include how their life experience has shaped their understanding, but what possessive investment they have in that understanding: how it has worked for them, or against them. Participatory public memory requires understanding of the process by which people assimilate new facts and stories, and requires new strategies to support and shape that process.

What Is the Role of Explanatory Narratives and "Umbrella Frameworks"?

Public memory projects, especially collectively created ones, need to grapple with how to help people make sense of the past, by putting together pieces of evidence into a coherent picture of why their world is as it is. Narrating history through individual human stories is often critiqued for extracting the experience of one individual from the larger system that shapes it, obscuring the structural issues and the scope of the problem. Explanatory historical narratives can help people see how individual acts of cruelty, perhaps incomprehensible on their own, are part of a larger system that can explain their origins and impetus, and can identify who and what should be held accountable. This kind of narrative can demonstrate that broad inequalities we see now are the legacy of a long history, and how individual phenomena we observe are cogs in a larger machine. Yet such umbrella frameworks can also force complex histories into self-justifying explanations. Deconstructionists had observed how totalizing narratives, for instance, ones that recounted world history as a series of steps leading inevitably to successful communism – supported the totalitarian regimes that produced them.

Public historians assume our job is to explain. But some historians of mass atrocities, like the Holocaust and repression in Stalinist Russia, argue otherwise. These scholars observed how frequently the scale and scope of the violence they study inspire disbelief, seeming to defy explanation. Holocaust historian Saul Friedlander critiques the assumption that the main purpose of historical analysis should be "to domesticate disbelief, to explain it away."[37] Instead, he argues this disbelief should be embraced, since in some contexts, rejection of horrific events is the only way to truly understand their truth. Soviet historian Alexander Etkind further reflected:

> Remembering the Soviet terror often entails disbelief that such things could have happened. This is a productive feeling, but the least appropriate response to it would be a redemptive narrative that demonstrates the functionality of terror... Writing history does not imply resolving its warped contradictions in a smooth, functional narrative.[38]

Then should we refuse to "domesticate disbelief"? The danger is that we're not ready for the wilds; that without an explanation, our only recourse is denial. In Russia, Masha Gessen suggests, vast public historical denial took place not so much because people couldn't face the explanation for what happened; but because they couldn't face the possibility that what happened was unexplainable:

> The truth was too primitive and too bloody. The regime had attacked its citizens for no imaginable reason and was beating them, torturing them, and executing them... Looking at truth would have been akin to staring down the barrel of a gun, so one tried to steal oneself away.[39]

There may be elements of every history that defy explanation. In some contexts, is denial more effectively combated through a public memory project that refuses to explain?

Four Truths for Navigating a New Truth Era

I've been seeking a public memory approach that can navigate a new truth era - one that embraces post-truth realities but retains a pro-truth politics. The South African Truth and Reconciliation Commission (TRC) created a taxonomy of truth that provides a helpful starting point. With the benefit of decades of critique exposing its exclusionary practices, its limited impacts and unintended consequences, and its failure to bring about effective reconciliation or redress, the South African TRC might seem a poor choice of inspiration.[40] But to work through our current clashes over the integrity of historical truth itself, the Commission's definitions may provide a guide.

Established in 1995, just after the end of apartheid, the TRC's charge was to help South Africa move forward from its repressive past to a strong multiracial democracy, by inviting victims of gross human rights violations under apartheid to testify publicly about their experiences, and inviting perpetrators to testify to their actions in exchange for amnesty from prosecution. The Commission needed to acknowledge the radically different life experiences and perspectives of its deeply divided society, while maintaining the integrity of its investigation of abuses under apartheid. To do so, it declared that it "rejects the popular assumption that there are only two options to be considered when talking about truth – namely factual, objective information or subjective opinions."[41] Instead, the Commission identified four distinct "notions of truth": forensic truth, or the material evidence of violence; narrative truth, or the description of the violent event; dialogic truth, or the exploration of multiple perspectives on the same event; and finally, community, or healing truth, or a collective acknowledgment of the larger story of what happened and its implications. This compartmentalization can provide a productive starting point for confronting the past across deep divides.

Forensic Truth

The Commission defined "forensic truth" as "bringing to light factual, corroborated evidence."[42] It was charged with making "findings on particular incidents and in respect of specific people. In other words, what happened to whom, where, when and how, and who was involved?"[43] Commissioners recognized, citing Canadian historian and politician Michael Ignatieff, that in this they could only hope to "reduce the number of lies that can be circulated unchallenged in public discourse," making it "impossible to claim, for example, that: the practice of torture by state security forces was not systematic and widespread; that only a few 'rotten eggs' or 'bad apples' committed gross violations of human rights."[44] The Commission believed it had a responsibility to make the individual facts add up to certain larger, collective facts, which would provide an unassailable foundation for all further understanding. This suggests that public memory projects, no matter how multi-vocal, may similarly take responsibility for transparently naming and asserting, as the TRC did, certain "contexts, causes and patterns" as "givens."[45]

Personal/Narrative Truth

The Commission separated forensic truth from "personal and narrative truth," to provide, in South African Archbishop Desmond Tutu's words, "everyone… a chance to say his or her truth as he or she sees it."[46] As the Commission explained, "The stories told to the Commission were not presented as arguments or claims in a court of law. Rather, they provided unique insights into the pain of South Africa's past" and "sought to contribute to the process of reconciliation by ensuring that the truth about the past included the validation of the individual subjective experiences of people who had previously been silenced or voiceless… to recover parts of the national memory that had hitherto been officially ignored."[47] This elevated "perceptions, stories, myths and experiences" to truth, but, by relieving such stories of the burden of proof, allowed them to fully express the knowledge they contained.[48] Public memory projects can similarly facilitate and promote diverse personal narratives in all their complexity as their own form of truth, with their own standards and integrity that complement, but are distinct from, forensic truth.

Social/Dialogue Truth

The Commission's report claimed that "it was in its search for social truth that the closest connection between the Commission's process and its goal was to be found."[49] The Commission cited Justice Albie Sachs' definition of social truth – also referred to as "dialogue" truth – as "the truth of experience that is established through interaction, discussion and debate." Dialogue truth was forged through "participation and transparency" in "an environment in which all possible views could be considered and weighed, one against the other."[50] It described "the process whereby the truth was reached," which was "itself important because it was through this process that the essential norms of social relations between people were reflected. It was, furthermore, through dialogue and respect that a means of promoting transparency, democracy and participation in society was suggested as a basis for affirming human dignity and integrity."[51] For public memory projects, this suggests that dialogue should not be understood as something that's merely back-end, or only a means to an end. For example, the collaboration between students and people with direct experience should not be understood simply as a means of producing a more representative or informative exhibit panel. Nor should it be understood only as a by-product, or side benefit, for instance as episodic public programming that takes place around the exhibit. Instead, it should be structured and evaluated as an ongoing process of participation that should enact, as the TRC wrote, the "essential norms of social relations between people" that the project is trying to envision.[52]

Healing and Restorative Truth

This last notion of truth about the past was the one most closely connected to the future, and to justice. Like social truth, restorative truth described a collective process, not a static piece of knowledge. It described the nexus between knowledge of the past and its concrete application in the service of future justice. This truth "places facts and what they mean within the context of human relationships – both among citizens and between the state and its citizens... a truth that would contribute to the reparation of the damage inflicted in the past and to the prevention of the recurrence of serious abuses in the future."[53] It could be called, less poetically, "policy truth," since in the South African context it was articulated specifically for/as policy recommendations for everything from police reform to school curricula.

Public memory projects that aren't run by governments don't have the mandate to make government policy. But they nevertheless have great potential to promote restorative truth. The Commission argued that the foundation of restorative truth was acknowledgment, which it defined as "placing information that is (or becomes) known on public, national record." The Commission explained, "It is not merely the actual knowledge about past human rights violations that counts; often the basic facts about what happened are already known, at least by those who were affected. What is critical is that these facts be fully and publicly acknowledged."[54] In contexts where governments and other institutions of power refuse to fully acknowledge past wrongs, public memory projects can take the lead. Further, they can establish a link between past, present, and future policy, illuminating how policies of the past have shaped social realities and human experiences of the present, and how policy decisions we make now will shape the same in the future. In this way, public memory projects can help stoke a policy imagination, and inspire people to harness all three other truths to take intentional and specific action.

Notes on Professional Fields, Perspectives, and Position

"In societies where everything works," observed journalist Anne Appelbaum, "it is very difficult to meet extraordinary people. In societies where nothing works... extraordinary people abound."[55] The man who inspired Appelbaum's insight was historian Viktor Shmyrov, whom I began working with in 1999, after he had gone to incredible lengths to save an abandoned Stalinist labor camp. This book describes and analyzes projects through the extraordinary people propelling them. This is not just because I love and admire so many of them, nor is it a narrative device to make things more lively for readers. It's mainly because I recognize that public memory and public policy, starting with individual exhibits or legislation, are the result of sometimes deliberate, sometimes more random, decisions of individuals, and I think it's important to analyze them that way. The projects described in this book are all circumscribed by the emotional and political experience of whoever was in the room to create them, not least myself – as expansive as our vision, and as limited as what and who we knew.

I was brought up in a house of historians who didn't talk much about their own past. My father was full of silences about his own childhood in Warsaw during World War II, made worse by all the talking he did with other grownups in languages I couldn't understand. We lived in Cambridge, Massachusetts, a town full of white liberals who loved condemning Southerners' racism but stayed real quiet about the home-grown kind. So denial is in my DNA, something I've struggled with all my life. Perhaps in response, I found my way to a cacophonous style of doing history, bringing people together to talk to each other, build community and pursue shared visions. My first exhibit, in my first public history class at Yale, was collaboratively created by four generations of alumni from the local Hillhouse High School, who each contributed their own objects and captions, before coming together to meet each other for the first time and see the collective exhibit at the New Haven Public Library.

After graduation, while working for Charas, a community arts organization led by Puerto Rican activists fighting gentrification and displacement on the Lower East Side of New York, I experienced the potential of memory projects as organizing tools. I created pop-up collective memory mapping events that invited residents of "Loisaida," as organizers dubbed the neighborhood, to mark their memories and celebrate their roots there, as they mobilized to defend their rights to stay there amidst rising rents and property seizures.[56] From that point forward, community organizing and mobilizing public memory were inextricably linked for me. My work evolved in generations, each project incubating the germ of the next one, which I would spin off once it was ready to live on its own. I brought the Lower East Side mapping project to the Lower East Side Tenement Museum, where then-President Ruth Abram invited me to help her pursue more examples of memory projects for social change by organizing the International Coalition of Sites of Conscience, which then grew into its own organization; a decade later, Coalition members and staff brought their experience to bear on the struggle to close Guantánamo, by launching the Guantánamo Public Memory Project; that project's translocal participatory public memory strategy established the idea for the Humanities Action Lab, which went on to organize the other projects the book describes.

I write neither detached academic analysis nor personal memoir. The projects and movements I describe are all ones in which I was directly involved. On one level, the book is an organizational history, tracing the creation and development of the two coalitions I coordinated – the International Coalition of Sites of Conscience and the Humanities Action Lab (HAL) – and three of HAL's initiatives – the Guantánamo Public Memory Project, States of Incarceration, and Climates of Inequality. But these specific projects are only relevant as windows onto the larger questions this book grapples with. I do not claim that they are the best models of participatory public memory, but I only feel comfortable writing about what I've seen myself. I hope this vantage point can complement the wealth of literature from scholars who have closely studied and richly theorized memory, museums, and heritage; transitional justice; and social movements.

For the projects in this book, I write from the perspective of a coordinator, not a creator. I stood at the center of a changing group of extraordinary people, all coming together to clash and challenge each other to create different ways of knowing and acting on the past and the future. I witnessed people's moments of shock, self-reflection, and inspiration; and experienced plenty of my own. I observed how people from diverse perspectives each confronted the histories that were new to them, as I did myself; we shared reflections about the causes and consequences of our own denial and that of the groups of which we each were a part.

This book speaks from and to a wide variety of professional fields and academic disciplines. In fact, it argues that anyone interested in how confronting the past can activate change for the future must look beyond their own fields; a wealth of tools and knowledge already exist, but are often found in the least expected places. The case studies described here involve people working in public history and public policy; transitional justice and historic preservation; heritage and human rights; museums and movement organizing. The stories suggest what can be achieved when elements from each of these approaches are combined and recombined to address the unique challenges of different times and places. Participatory public memory projects are related to memorial museums in their desire to build empathy and inspire conscience; but they break down the barriers between curator and visitor, spilling far outside the confines of an exhibition. They are related to transitional justice in their commitment to historical accountability; but they spill outside the confines of court cases and policy reform to build a lasting culture of human rights. They are related to social movements in their commitment to participation and mobilization, but seek long-term narrative change that can support movements' immediate policy goals. The book also seeks to integrate models and lessons from a variety of cultural and political contexts around the world, to provide a flexible collection of tools that can be adapted in different situations.

I write from the perspective of someone deeply implicated in, but differentially impacted by, the social issues the projects described in this book were trying to address. I have never been in a refugee camp; I have never been incarcerated; I have never lost my home or my health to climate or environmental hazards. I was trained as a historian and have had a long-standing personal obsession with historical denial and accountability. Yet over the course of my career I found myself repeatedly stunned by new revelations of things about the past that I had not known. These things were not particularly hidden; they were publicly accessible to me and to anyone else. They were things I had never bothered to – or had refused to – look for, or listen to. As Ta-Nehisi Coates described his response to the election of Donald Trump, "I was shocked at my own shock."[57] I have tried to be reflective about the ways I have participated in the large-scale historical denial, and its consequences, this book explores; and use that reflection to think seriously about how participatory public memory can address that for me and others like me.

Preview of Chapters

The historical denials explored in this book take two forms. Both represent refusals to accept responsibility for past harms. The first is denial that harms took place in the past at all – for instance, the Argentinean state denying it knew the whereabouts of thousands of young people who had disappeared, when in fact it had tortured and killed them in secret sites hidden throughout its major cities. The second is denial that inequality or injustice in the present *has* a history, that it is rooted in structures and systems that were constructed long ago, sustained over time, and in which the society is now deeply invested – so eradicating it won't be easy. This denial manifests not so much as direct erasure, but a stubborn orientation to the present, or very recent past, that keeps deeper history, and its lessons, in the dark. It's not only propagated by those who silence the past to maintain the status quo, but by those who seek change. Too often they miscalculate how deep the problems run – or just don't want to face it – and get stuck. President Obama tried to "close Guantánamo" without confronting our century of investment in exploiting this space outside of US law; the base remains open today. Some criminal justice reformers tried to end mass incarceration without addressing its deep roots in structures of racial control; the US remains a world leader in incarceration. Several US administrations have tried to save the planet by getting all countries to reduce their emissions, without owning up to our historical responsibility for creating the crisis in the first place. The global temperature continues to rise.

The stories of public memory projects in this book and how they contested these forms of denial are rooted in particular places and times. They are told in chronological order, from just after the end of the Cold War, through the end of the Trump Administration. They explore how the specific contours of historical denial in each country and community shaped policy and the political culture that supports it. They also demonstrate how the specific contours of combating that denial were born in a particular moment, shaped by particular assumptions, and how they seized particular opportunities that moment presented.

Chapters 1 and 2 profile the people who first came together to found the International Coalition of Sites of Conscience in 1999 and the specific challenges each brought with them that year. Through their experiences, the chapter describes the historical events that had been denied – from the internment of Japanese Americans to the disappearance of 30,000 Argentinians to the genocide of millions of Bangladeshis – as well as the consequences of that denial in their societies, and the innovative ways each sought to build social movements for public memory. These chapters locate these local struggles in the context of larger national and global trends in truth, memory, and accountability at the turn of the millennium, such as the founding of the International Criminal Court; the proliferation of truth commissions and transitional justice; the embrace of the idea of "memory" or "*memoria*" as democratic, activist counterweights to "heritage" and "*patrimonio*"; and the mandates for public accountability in the US through "civic engagement."

Chapter 3 analyzes three distinct ways founding members worked with memory, and how we integrated them into a shared idea for "Sites of Conscience." Each way bridged the past, present, and future, but represented different ideas of the relationship between memory and accountability. The first was memory as *reconnecting* the past and the present, demonstrating that the past was relevant in the present day, and mining history as a source of ideas for how to confront parallel contemporary challenges. In this framework, people in the present were not held responsible for what happened in the past, but for learning from its successes and failures to forge a better future. The second was memory as *reminding* societies of the people still suffering now from the legacies of what happened in the past. In these contexts, the struggle was to defy any official attempts to bury past abuse in false closure, by keeping victims at the center of public attention as "present," in both senses of the word: as in the current moment, and as living among us. The third framework stressed memory as a means to achieve *redress*, identifying current inequalities or abuses as a direct result of the past, and demanding compensation for their harms.

The chapter shares the deep debates sparked by connecting these three concepts of memory, around questions such as: Does working with memory imply that a problem is now "history"? Does looking too far back distract attention from the present? What does it mean to be "political"? Is addressing issues the same as advocacy? This chapter combines discussion of these theoretical issues with descriptions of the strategic process by which they were integrated to form the foundation of a working coalition. It describes how Sites of Conscience, while emerging from the fields of transitional justice, heritage, and museums, and a growing global "transnational memory culture"[58] ultimately forged approaches that pushed against their evolving norms.

Chapter 4 tries to take stock of how that approach fared over time. First, it discusses these sites' attempts to define and measure success, and some of the immediate impacts Sites of Conscience made on their societies' relationship with the past. Jumping ahead 20 years, it concludes with how the ideas Sites of Conscience promoted were coopted and perverted to support three "post-truth" regimes: Trump's vision of "very fine people on both sides," muddying moral understanding of violence around public memory of the confederacy; Argentinian President Mauricio Macri's revision of the history of state terrorism around what critics call the *teoría de los dos demonios* (theory of two demons); and Russia's "hybrid history" around Stalinist terror and the Gulag, in which multiple narratives collide and contradict to create general confusion.

From there, the book returns to the US to explore the potential of participatory public memory during three regimes of truth and denial – the administrations of George W. Bush, Barack Obama, and Donald Trump – around three of America's most contested issues: Guantánamo's "state of exception," mass incarceration, and climate change. Policies and protest around these issues have been fundamentally shaped by denial of their deep historical roots, but in different ways. Chapters 5–7 focus on the US naval base at Guantánamo, a place most people will never see. Chapter 5 tracks how wider public attention on the site has focused and faded at startling speed, while people who actually witnessed the place maintain completely divergent memories through communities closed to the public and to each other – from Cuban refugees held behind barbed wire to US military "Guantanamigos" who held barbecues on the beach. Chapters 8–10 focus on the carceral state created by America's prison boom and how it has divided Americans into two nations, one whose daily life is dominated by living in, visiting, or working in prison, and the other that doesn't know where the nearest prison is. Chapter 11 explores the most totalizing denial of all: the denial of climate change, a phenomenon posing an existential threat to all of us. This chapter explores how climate change is shaped not just by a denial of science, but of history and racism: a refusal to acknowledge and repair generations of actions that have deeply harmed the planet, and have placed low-income earners and BIPOC communities on the front lines of "natural" disasters.

In each of these sections, the book tells the stories of how hundreds of students, activists, and scholars organized collective actions that sought to simultaneously confront the past, present, and future of these issues. Participatory public memory takes the force of denial seriously, and admits it cannot be contested solely by stating truths legitimized by a small group of elite experts. A participatory public memory process applies the logics and modes of social movements to the ways we deal with the past, and invites social movements to use understandings of the complex origins of current problems to shape effective strategies.

First, participatory public memory projects invite all participants to serve simultaneously as authors and audience, continuously teaching and learning from each other. The projects described in this book were created through a process of dialogue and exchange among hundreds of people from dozens of cities, representing a wide variety of knowledge and experience. For example, Chapter 7 recounts how students who had never heard of Guantánamo learned from people who had been there; people who had served at GTMO in the 1960s learned from those who had been held there in the 1990s; scholars of 19th-century American empire learned from lawyers of habeas corpus; museum curators preparing to host the project learned from the students. Together, this entire group took responsibility for teaching a wider public what they learned from their own life, the research they conducted, and from each other, by collaborating to create a traveling exhibit on GTMO's history and the questions it raised for them.

Second, participatory public memory works in coalitions, bringing together people from diverse geographic contexts into a collection of locally controlled initiatives. Chapter 10 details how the States of Incarceration project invited teams of students, people directly impacted by incarceration, and historical and legal experts in 20 cities to explore the roots of mass incarceration in each of their localities. Students in New Orleans and North Carolina traced a historical trajectory from slavery to convict leasing to mass incarceration through an exploration of how incarcerated laborers worked their land and built their roads. To understand high rates of incarceration among Native Americans in their state, the University of Minnesota team started with the Dakota Wars and the ideologies and technologies of settler colonialism. Four of the local teams – in New Jersey, Arizona, Florida, and Texas – chose to focus on immigrant detention, which as a new criminal approach to immigration policy has produced a massive detention apparatus within the prison boom. While the teams together formulated collective questions, their diverse answers emerged organically from their local contexts, creating much richer and more complex genealogies of incarceration than any central scholarly committee could have developed. In an age of one-size-fits-all approaches to criminal justice reform, these diverse local histories suggested new locally responsive policy solutions.

Finally, participatory public memory projects seize their political moments. They recognize that shifting political landscapes present fleeting periods of possibility for new thinking and action; they look for cracks and try to mobilize memory to pry them open. Projects begin by looking for new urgent concerns around which public conversation is coalescing, even and especially when that conversation is deeply contested. They seek openings in how publics and policy makers are willing to see them, and build on momentum that's growing for change, mobilizing memory to push this momentum further.

To highlight these strategies, each section of the book begins with a chapter describing the context for memory for each project, demonstrating how each of the memory projects could only have started in the particular moment it did. Chapter 4 describes how the Guantánamo Public Memory Project was launched in June 2009, five months after Obama declared his intention to "close Guantánamo," when the tiny base and questions about how it defined and delivered national security dominated the media. Chapter 8 sets the scene for States of Incarceration in 2014, in a moment when leaders of both political parties were discussing criminal justice in a way unthinkable just a few years before: as a failed system that had harmed people, disproportionately people of color, and that needed to be reformed. Public interest was accompanied by a whole landscape of organizational and financial resources – reporters, lawyers, funders, campaigns – on which the project relied for support. Chapter 11 describes a moment of shift in the mainstream climate movement, toward recognition of the environmental justice movement and "frontline" communities as critical political constituencies, and the openings that created for a public memory project on the climate crisis to center issues of justice.

The book's appendix speaks more explicitly to practitioners – whether they are museum professionals, community organizers, or educators – about the concrete tools the stories of the book suggest. These include:

- *Collaborative curation*: what does it look like to actually "make history" together?
- *Designing memory coalitions*: why and how should people build public memory movements through coalition?
- *Working translocally*: how and why should we link local stories into collective memory movements?
- *Choosing institutional locations*: what are the opportunities and challenges of working with and within universities, museums/heritage bodies, advocacy organizations, state entities, or grassroots groups?

I hope that digging deep into the stories of these struggles to combat historical denial, situated in their own particular circumstances, can help you reflect on your own context, wherever and whenever you are reading this, and identify specific strategies to suit your own time and place.

Notes

1 Transcript, "The Trump Inaugural Balls," Anderson Cooper 360 Degrees, *CNN*, January 20, 2017, http://transcripts.cnn.com/TRANSCRIPTS/1701/20/acd.02.html
2 Masha Gessen, "The Putin Paradigm," *The New York Review of Books*, December 13, 2016, http://www.nybooks.com/daily/2016/12/13/putin-paradigm-how-trump-will-rule/
3 Anthony Leiserowitz, Edward Maibach, Connie Roser-Renouf, Seth Rosenthal, Matthew Cutler, and John Kotcher, *Politics & Global Warming, October 2017*, Yale University and George Mason University (New Haven, CT: Yale Program on Climate Change Communication, 2017), https://climatecommunication.yale.edu/publications/politics-global-warming-october-2017/
4 "Democratic and Republican Views of Climate Change (2018)," https://climatecommunication.yale.edu/visualizations-data/partisan-maps-2018/, visualization generated from Matto Mildenberger, Jennifer Marlon, and Peter Howe, "The Spatial Distribution of Republican and Democratic Climate Opinions at State and Local Scales," *Climatic Change* (2017).

5 Jonathan Easley, "Majority of Republicans Say 2020 Election Was Invalid: Poll," *The Hill*, February 25, 2021, https://thehill.com/homenews/campaign/540508-majority-of-republicans-say-2020-election-was-invalid-poll

6 Rachel Treisman, "In Likely First, Chicago Suburb of Evanston Approves Reparations for Black Residents," *NPR*, March 23, 2021, https://www.npr.org/2021/03/23/980277688/in-likely-first-chicago-suburb-of-evanston-approves-reparations-for-black-reside; Philip Marcelo, "A Price Tag on Trauma? College Town Weighs Black Reparations," *AP News*, March 10, 2021, https://apnews.com/article/race-and-ethnicity-massachusetts-c54f6419bf59017ab-28956d35981a55e; Emily Hoeven, "California Launches Reparations Task Force," *CalMatters*, June 2, 2021, https://calmatters.org/newsletters/whatmatters/2021/06/california-reparations-task-force/; Rodrigo Torrejon, "'Say the Word': Hundreds Gather with N.J. Social Justice Leaders to Call for Reparations Bill," *NJ.com*, June 19, 2021, https://www.nj.com/essex/2021/06/say-the-word-hundreds-gather-with-nj-social-justice-leaders-to-call-for-reparations-bill.html; Nicholas Fandos, "House Panel Advances Bill to Study Reparations in Historic Vote," *New York Times*, April 14, 2021, https://www.nytimes.com/2021/04/14/us/politics/reparations-slavery-house.html; "H.Con.Res.100 – Urging the Establishment of a United States Commission on Truth, Racial Healing, and Transformation," Congress.gov, June 4, 2020, https://www.congress.gov/bill/116th-congress/house-concurrent-resolution/100/text

7 Elizabeth Kolbert, "Why Facts Don't Change Our Minds: New Discoveries about the Human Mind Show the Limitations of Reason," *The New Yorker*, February 27, 2017, https://www.newyorker.com/magazine/2017/02/27/why-facts-dont-change-our-minds; Julie Beck, "This Article Won't Change Your Mind: The Facts on Why Facts Alone Can't Fight False Beliefs," *The Atlantic*, March 13, 2017, https://www.theatlantic.com/science/archive/2017/03/this-article-wont-change-your-mind/519093/ Thank you to Kristin O'Brassil-Kulfan for these references.

8 Ralph Keyes, *The Post-Truth Era: Dishonesty and Deception in Contemporary Life* (New York: St. Martin's Press, 2004).

9 See, for example, Lee McIntyre, *Post-Truth* (Cambridge, MA: The MIT Press, 2018); Mikael Stenmark, Steve Fuller, and Ulf Zackariasson, eds., *Relativism and Post-Truth in Contemporary Society: Possibilities and Challenges* (Cham, Switzerland: Palgrave Macmillan, 2018); Ilan Z. Baron, *How to Save Politics in a Post-Truth Era: Thinking Through Difficult Times* (Manchester: Manchester University Press, 2018); Steve Fuller, *Post-Truth: Knowledge as a Power Game* (London: Anthem Press, 2018).

10 Robert Mejia, Kay Beckermann, and Curtis Sullivan, "White Lies: A Racial History of the (Post)Truth," *Communication and Critical/Cultural Studies* 15, no. 2 (2018): 113.

11 Ibram X. Kendi, "The Heartbeat of Racism Is Denial," *New York Times*, January 13, 2018, https://www.nytimes.com/2018/01/13/opinion/sunday/heartbeat-of-racism-denial.html

12 Ibram X. Kendi, "Denial Is the Heartbeat of America," *The Atlantic*, January 11, 2021, https://www.theatlantic.com/ideas/archive/2021/01/denial-heartbeat-america/617631/

13 James Oliver Horton and Lois E. Horton, *Slavery and Public History: The Tough Stuff of American Memory* (Chapel Hill: University of North Carolina Press, 2009), vii.

14 Ibram X. Kendi, "Is This the Beginning of the End of American Racism?" *The Atlantic*, September 2020, https://www.theatlantic.com/magazine/archive/2020/09/the-end-of-denial/614194/

15 Michel Foucault, "The Political Function of the Intellectual," *Radical Philosophy* 17 (Summer 1977), https://www.radicalphilosophy.com/article/the-political-function-of-the-intellectual

16 James Atlas, "The Case of Paul De Man," *New York Times*, August 28, 1998, https://www.nytimes.com/1988/08/28/magazine/the-case-of-paul-de-man.html

17 See McIntyre, *Post-Truth*; Naomi Oreskes and Erik M. Conway, *Merchants of Doubt: How a Handful of Scientists Obscured the Truth on Issues from Tobacco Smoke to Climate Change* (New York: Bloomsbury Press, 2010).

18 Oreskes and Conway, *Merchants of Doubt*.

19 Matto Mildenberger and Anthony Leiserowitz, "Public Opinion: Is There an Economy-Environment Tradeoff?" Yale Program on Climate Change Communication, August 8, 2017, http://www.climatecommunication.yale.edu/publications/public-opinion-economy-environment-tradeoff/

20 Ron Suskind, "Faith, Certainty and the Presidency of George W. Bush," *New York Times*, October 17, 2004, https://www.nytimes.com/2004/10/17/magazine/faith-certainty-and-the-presidency-of-george-w-bush.html?mtrref=www.google.it&gwh=9FA7547ED643CECC6B2AAB9109344FBB&gwt=pay

21 Zach Schonfeld, "The Curious Case of a Supposed Karl Rove Quote Used on The National's New Album 'Sleep Well Beast,'" *Newsweek*, September 8, 2017, http://www.newsweek.com/national-sleep-well-beast-karl-rove-662307

22 "Word of the Year 2016," Oxford University Press, https://languages.oup.com/word-of-the-year/2016/#:~:text=After%20much%20discussion%2C%20debate%2C%20and,to%20emotion%20and%20personal%20belief'.

23 Vittorio Bufacchi, "Truth, Lies and Tweets: A Consensus Theory of Post-Truth," *Philosophy and Social Criticism* 47, no. 3 (2021): 349.

24 Gessen, "The Putin Paradigm," http://www.nybooks.com/daily/2016/12/13/putin-paradigm-how-trump-will-rule/

25 Beck, "This Article Won't Change Your Mind."

26 David Roberts, "Everything Mattered: Lessons From 2016's Bizarre Presidential Election," *Vox* November 30, 2016, https://www.vox.com/policy-and-politics/2016/11/30/13631532/everything-mattered-2016-presidential-election

27 Larry Buchanan, Quoctrung Bui, and Jugal K. Patel, "Black Lives Matter May Be the Largest Movement in U.S. History," *New York Times*, July 3, 2020, https://www.nytimes.com/interactive/2020/07/03/us/george-floyd-protests-crowd-size.html

28 "H.R.40 – Commission to Study and Develop Reparation Proposals for African Americans Act," Congress.gov, January 4, 2021, https://www.congress.gov/bill/117th-congress/house-bill/40/text

29 Congresswoman Barbara Lee, "Representative Barbara Lee and Senator Cory Booker Reintroduce Legislation to Form Truth, Racial Healing, and Transformation Commission," February 25, 2021, https://lee.house.gov/news/press-releases/representative-barbara-lee-and-senator-cory-booker-reintroduce-legislation-to-form-truth-racial-healing-and-transformation-commission

30 Simon Oxenham, "When Evidence Backfires," Big Think, April 15, 2014, http://bigthink.com/neurobonkers/when-evidence-backfires

31 Hans Hansen, *Narrative Change: How Changing the Story Can Transform Society, Business, and Ourselves* (New York: Columbia University Press, 2020); Corinne Squire, *Stories Changing Lives: Narratives and Paths Toward Social Change* (Oxford: Oxford University Press USA – OSO, 2020) See definitions and approaches to narrative change among advocacy organizations: https://www.socialchangeinitiative.com/narrative-change; https://www.opportunityagenda.org/approach/communications-culture-narrative-change; https://communitychange.org/portfolio/narrative-change/

32 Tommie Shelby, "Ideology, Racism, and Critical Social Theory," *Philosophical Forum* 34, no. 2 (Summer 2003): 184–5.

33 George Lipsitz, *The Possessive Investment in Whiteness: How White People Profit from Identity Politics* (Philadelphia: Temple University Press, 1998).

34 Mejia et al., "White Lies."
35 Ibid.
36 Julia Rose, *Interpreting Difficult History at Museums and Historic Sites* (Lanham, MD: Rowman & Littlefield, 2016).
37 Saul Friedlander, *The Years of Extermination: Nazi Germany and the Jews* (New York: HarperCollins, 2007), xxvi.
38 Alexander Etkind, *Warped Mourning: Stories of the Undead in the Land of the Unburied* (Stanford: Stanford University Press, 2013), 12.
39 Masha Gessen, *The Future is History: How Totalitarianism Reclaimed Russia* (New York: Riverhead Books, 2017), 144.
40 See, for example, Elizabeth Stanley, "Evaluating the Truth and Reconciliation Commission," *Journal of Modern African Studies* 39, no. 3 (September 2001): 525–46; Mahmood Mamdani, "Amnesty or Impunity? A Preliminary Critique of the Report of the Truth and Reconciliation Commission of South Africa (TRC)," *Diacritics* 32, no. 3–4 (Fall-Winter 2002): 32–59; Rina Kashyap, "Narrative and Truth: A Feminist Critique of the South African Truth and Reconciliation Commission," *Issues in Criminal, Social, and Restorative Justice* 12, no. 4 (2009): 449–67; Josh Bowsher, "The South African TRC as Neoliberal Reconciliation: Victim Subjectivities and the Synchronization of Affects," *Social & Legal Studies* 29, no. 1 (2020): 41–64; Jonathan Tepperman, "Truth and Consequences." *Foreign Affairs* 81, no. 2 (2002): 128.
41 Truth and Reconciliation Commission of South Africa Report, Volume 1, http://www.justice.gov.za/trc/report/finalreport/Volume%201.pdf
42 Truth and Reconciliation Commission of South Africa Report, Volume 1.
43 Ibid.
44 Ibid.
45 Ibid.
46 Ibid.
47 Ibid.
48 Ibid.
49 Ibid.
50 Ibid.
51 Ibid.
52 Ibid.
53 Ibid.
54 Ibid.
55 Anne Applebaum, "A City Where People Won't Forget," *New Statesman*, July 31, 1998, 24+.
56 Liz Ševčenko, "Making Loisaida: Placing Puertorriqueñidad in Lower Manhattan," in *Mambo Montage: The Latinization of New York City*, eds. Agustín Laó-Montes and Arlene Dávila (New York: Columbia University Press, 2001).
57 Ta-Nehisi Coates, *We Were Eight Years in Power: An American Tragedy* (New York: One World, 2017), 336.
58 Amy Sodaro, *Exhibiting Atrocity: Memorial Museums and the Politics of Past Violence* (New Brunswick: Rutgers University Press, 2018).

PART I
Sites of Conscience

This section explores the different strands of knowledge and experience that came together to shape "Sites of Conscience," and the strategies they suggest for public memory projects. Projects emerged from diverse parts of the world, grappling with transitions in distinct political and cultural contexts, including post-Thatcher England; post-apartheid South Africa; and post-communist Russia. And they emerged from divergent fields of practice: legal campaigns; truth commissions; democracy movements; and traditional heritage and historic preservation. The International Coalition of Sites of Conscience integrated varying approaches and built on a number of trends that came together at the turn of the millennium. The foundation of the International Criminal Court in 1998 and the maturing of "transitional justice" as a field and practice represented a new international responsibility for holding nations accountable for past crimes. US and European museums and heritage sites were being reshaped by a newfound sense of accountability of another sort: to diverse publics and their demands for engaging with a past that addressed their experiences and concerns. Understanding the growth of individual Sites of Conscience in this specific historical context can provide perspective on how to develop memory strategies suited to our own time. The story of the formation of the International Coalition of Sites of Conscience also suggests the potential for multi-sited memory coalitions, and strategies for building collective memory movements.

Chapters 1 and 2 introduce the individuals who founded Sites of Conscience, and the dramatic political, cultural, and disciplinary challenges they faced, tracing the path each leader forged to open their sites. Chapter 3 extrapolates from these individual narratives a taxonomy of approaches to public memory projects and how project founders wove these approaches together in

DOI: 10.4324/9781003185826-2

various ways. Chapter 4 explores the strategic decision to come together as a coalition; how the group defined its criteria and boundaries; and the impact their union made on their individual work. The section concludes with a look at three of the founding projects' memory contexts, in the US, Argentina, and Russia, and how they fared 20 years later, questioning whether the Coalition's insistence on multiple perspectives and dialogue on the past as the foundation of cultures of democracy and human rights left sites' histories vulnerable to future denial and repression.

1

SNAPSHOTS FROM MEMORY MOVEMENTS AT THE TURN OF THE MILLENNIUM, ALBUM 1

Heritage and Human Rights in New York, Nottinghamshire, Buenos Aires, and Cape Town

My first training in museum work was from a social movement organizer. In the US, in the 1990s, this was unusual. Ruth J. Abram strode into the history museum field straight from leading campaigns for women's rights and civil rights, for which she had often used history as a model and inspiration. In the 1970s, she mobilized over 100 women's organizations, representing a diversity of racial backgrounds and wildly differing political approaches to form the National Women's Agenda, by pointing to the policy change achieved when radically different women's groups joined in coalition during the Progressive Era. A decade later, she decided to explore how she could bring a social change agenda to history, by founding an unconventional model of a historic site museum, the Lower East Side Tenement Museum, in 1988. At a time when the missions of US history museums were almost universally described in terms of what piece of the past they preserved, not why, Ruth grounded her museum in its social goal: "to promote tolerance and historical perspective."[1] "What got you interested in preservation?" the National Trust for Historic Preservation later asked her. "I wasn't," she answered. "What I was interested in was the relationship between history and social change."[2]

Most US history museums at the time maintained a firewall between past and present, believing the barrier essential for survival. Overt discussion of contemporary issues, or contemporary implications of the past, was too often labeled "political" or "advocacy." And "the last thing that a public historian wants to be called is an 'advocate,'" Martin Melosi, then president of the National Council on Public History confirmed in his 1993 annual address. "To gain a reputation otherwise is to lose face, or worse yet, to lose work."[3] While Melosi's address was ultimately encouraging his colleagues to find a way past this resistance, he was accurately describing the state of the field.

DOI: 10.4324/9781003185826-3

From my time at the Tenement Museum in the 1990s, I remember countless conversations with other museum leaders who claimed, with a willful misreading of the law, that they would be considered a lobbying organization and lose their non-profit tax status if they invited their audiences to discuss current questions. I was puzzled at the persistent conflation of discussing contemporary issues and advocating for specific policies. Particularly frustrating to me was the underlying assumption that historical interpretation could and should be neutral, and that neutrality was only possible with the distant past.

Neither did the Tenement Museum find acceptance among those who embraced being "political." Immigrant service and advocacy organizations, understandably, given the attitude of most museums, could not imagine how a history museum could be relevant to them. They were unwilling to spend any of their precious time and resources participating in planning initiatives based at a museum.

By the late 1990s, ten years after the Tenement Museum's founding, Ruth realized that being caught between two worlds – history and advocacy – could leave the Museum without funding or friends from either, endangering its ability to achieve its mission. The challenge required creative organizing. Ruth's true art form, and her main mode, was building coalitions for change. "We are not going to win unless we work as a coalition," she wrote in 1976, when organizing the National Women's Agenda. "[W]e can achieve most anything if we can see our way clear to join forces."[4] She was certain there must be people in other parts of the world who believed history museums had a role to play in contemporary conflicts, helping divided societies come together to address them, without serving as propaganda machines. She asked me to help find out.

Sending out faxes to a short list of museums across the world, composed somewhat haphazardly through pre-internet research and word-of-mouth references, she asked if recipients believed their museums had a "social mission." Based on the responses, we invited nine sites – including the Gulag Museum in Russia, the District Six Museum in Cape Town, and the Liberation War Museum in Bangladesh – to meet and share their experiences, and explore forming an alliance. Before any coalition-building could begin, we had to physically get people around a table, and Ruth's first strategy was to make that table as appealing as possible. She applied for a week-long residency at the Rockefeller Foundation's Bellagio conference center, a sprawling villa and gardens nestled on the top of a hill overlooking Lake Como outside of Milan. The site brought luxury, natural beauty, and global legitimacy.

My main job was to get participants from the airport to the conference center on time. Each had traveled from a different maelstrom of political transition in their country – one they both reflected and had helped bring about. To move the transitions forward and make them stick, they all needed to puncture decades of historical denial that had thwarted change: from the shared experience of poverty in England, one of Europe's wealthiest nations, to the particular persecution of Czech Jews during World War II, and recognition of the very existence of individual "disappeared" people in Argentina. Each brought bags full of different worries that shaped different approaches to what they came to recognize as common challenges.

Heritage for the Have-Nots: Confronting Class in the US and England in the Clinton–Blair Era

Lower East Side Tenement Museum, US

I flew in early, carrying my own concerns. As the newly appointed and awkwardly titled "Director of the Usable Past" at the Tenement Museum, I was charged with exploring how every aspect of the museum – from tours to the website to the gift shop – could address contemporary issues in our neighborhood and beyond. I had no peers in the museum field in this particular position. But the idea of crossing the threshold between past and present was gaining support. By the late 1990s, voices at the top of US museum leadership were calling on their constituencies to reimagine the role of museums. Beyond their 19th-century identity as a keeper of relics, and even beyond their hard-fought 20th-century identity as trusted educational institutions, museums could serve as centers for active exchange on issues that matter outside their walls. The American Association of Museums – then the largest field-defining entity in the US museum world – was developing the ground-breaking publication *Mastering Civic Engagement: A Challenge to Museums*, based on a vision of the museum as "a center where people gather to meet and converse... and a participant in collaborative problem solving. It is an active, visible player in civic life, a safe haven, and a trusted incubator of change."[5] The Ford Foundation, one of the largest private funders of US museums, articulated its own vision of the civic museum space, celebrating "a growing number" of cultural institutions who "are moving to claim an active, intentional role in public dialogue around the kinds of contemporary issues that provoke multiple viewpoints."[6] These leaders were far from responsible for introducing these ideas, which came from practices pioneered from the bottom. But the voices from the top opened new possibilities.

For the museum and heritage field, it was an era rich in proclamations but poor in practice. The highly visible Enola Gay debacle of 1994 struck fear into the hearts of museum professionals across the country. The Smithsonian's National Air and Space Museum decided to create an exhibit around the plane that dropped the atomic bomb on Hiroshima, proposing text exploring how the decision was made and the debate over nuclear weapons it inspired. The proposed script caused such a furor among veterans' groups and public officials – who claimed it dishonored American veterans and minimized

Japan's role as an aggressor in World War II – that the Smithsonian was threatened with a congressional inquiry and funding cuts, and battled negative headlines for months. In 2003, conceding defeat after nearly a decade of discussion, the Smithsonian elected to display the remains of the plane with almost no context or commentary.[7]

The impact of this object lesson far outweighed that of any rhetoric urging museums to take on "tough stuff." Opening dialogue on most "issues that provoke multiple viewpoints" was almost impossible without getting into questions of historical responsibility. And Americans, the Enola Gay incident confirmed, would go to great lengths to avoid such questions. "Opening dialogue" translated to seeking controversy; controversy could have serious material consequences.

In the midst of this, the Tenement Museum sought out points of controversy, tuning its stories to debates of the day.[8] In 1994, it opened its first exhibit on immigration and working-class life on the Lower East Side, on the crest of a rise in anti-immigrant and anti-welfare sentiment. Two years later, in 1996, President Bill Clinton signed a welfare reform bill that crippled social support, and the Illegal Immigration Reform and Immigrant Responsibility Act, which made it significantly easier to deport people and more difficult for people in the US illegally to obtain legal status. The bills rode in on more than a decade of debate over "responsibility," about who was deserving of sanctuary and support, based on racialized rhetoric around "illegals" and "welfare queens."

Against this backdrop, the Tenement Museum recreated the home of Adolfo and Rosario Baldizzi, who came from Palermo, Sicily, and lived in the building in the early 1930s. They had managed entry despite the 1924 National Origins Act, which all but barred immigration by people from races the government considered inferior, including Italians. Shortly after arriving, they went on the dole, benefitting from a New York welfare program that laid the foundation for our current welfare state. The Baldizzis, then, were, in the terms of the mid-1990s, a family of illegals and welfare queens.

The Museum sought to use stories of the past, like that of the Baldizzis, to build empathy in its majority-white visitors – huge numbers of whom had Irish, Italian, or Jewish immigrant ancestors – for immigrants arriving in the US at the time, who were largely people of color. The storylines of families we developed didn't seek to establish a line of continuity or accountability between past and present. Visitors came from a single moment in time (the present) and entered a single frozen moment in the past (1935), recreated in an elaborately detailed apartment stage-set, including period furnishings, decorations, and cooking utensils. But by revealing parallels between people in two far-flung moments in time, the Museum sought to expose the racialized language and false frameworks supporting current punitive immigration and social welfare policy. We hoped to inspire visitors to think: we wouldn't support laws that kept grandma out because she wasn't worthy of being here, or laws that would have her starve, would we?

The Museum used time travel to take on one of the most contested concepts in the neighborhood and the nation in the late 1990s: "sweatshops." At the time, the Lower East Side was littered with more than 500 garment shops, 75% of which the Department of Labor classified as sweatshops. The vast majority of their workers were immigrants. Solutions to the problem were hotly contested. In some instances, when the Department of Labor sought to protect abused workers by shutting shops down, the workers themselves picketed in protest, demanding their jobs back. The question of what system for making the clothes on our backs would be most fair and functional was a question that implicated everyone: every visitor arrived at the museum wearing clothes bearing tags that told the story of their creation.

Just a few years earlier, the Smithsonian Institution had produced an exhibit titled "Between a Rock and a Hard Place: A History of American Sweatshops, 1820-Present" on the history of the garment industry, which became an Enola Gay redux, inspiring a major uproar among labor unions and clothing manufacturers alike. At issue was how the word "sweatshop" was defined, how pervasive labor abuse was in the garment industry, and whose responsibility it was to combat the problem, rooted in extremely heated debates about these same questions in the present day.[9] Unions and international labor organizations were clashing with big brands over how clothing should be produced. The Tenement Museum believed history could be productively brought to bear on the conflict, but through a more participatory and smaller scale approach.

Scanning the list of historical tenants at 97 Orchard Street, the building the Museum inhabited, staff found Harris and Jennie Levine, who ran a small garment-making shop out of their apartment in 1897 – the very type of space the word "sweatshop" was, in that period, coined to describe. The Levines were Eastern European Jewish immigrants, people visitors could identify with as struggling. But they were also small business owners, manufacturing bosses some visitors might view as exploiting workers, while other visitors would identify with them as striving for the upward mobility they deserved, and that America was supposed to reward them with.

By skipping back a whole century – eliding the development of mass production and its extreme labor exploitation, and the rise and fall of labor unions – and by focusing on the ambiguous moral position of the bosses of a mom-and-pop shop, the Museum was able to engage a wide range of stakeholders then locked in the bitter conflict over sweatshops. This became my first big assignment in political organizing in a museum setting: I was charged with inviting workers, contractors (bosses), manufacturers, retailers, members of labor unions and human rights organizations, government inspectors, and journalists to tour the unrestored Levine apartment. We invited them first in caucus groups of the same profile, sharing information our researchers had uncovered about the family and its garment shop, and asking for their feedback on the issues and experiences the Museum could explore in the exhibit to provide perspective on the conflicts in the garment industry today.

Using the feedback from the caucus groups, the exhibit team developed a draft narrative and mock-up recreation of the Levine apartment and garment shop and invited representatives from each caucus group – totaling about 20 people – to the museum for a day-long summit to review them and discuss lessons for the garment industry past and present. Out of the summit, the group developed a report identifying ways the different sectors could collaborate to improve working conditions in the local garment industry. To share these ideas with a larger public, the Museum conducted audio recordings of representatives from each group about their perspectives on the critical challenges of the present-day industry and integrated them into the final exhibit. Over the following year, nearly a dozen industry organizations brought their members or staff to visit the Levines and hear the audio "conversation" among workers, bosses, manufacturers, and inspectors; Museum staff used the audio as a starting point for dialogues we facilitated among Museum visitors on the role and responsibility of consumers.[10]

Across the Atlantic, an analogous historic site was emerging in a parallel political context. When I first learned about plans to preserve and interpret a 19th-century workhouse in England, I thought I'd found a sister site for confronting class. Together, our countries had witnessed the punitive Reagan–Thatcher regimes fall and be replaced by a Clinton–Blair era rhetorically warmer to labor, creating a conducive cultural climate. The proposed Workhouse Museum would explore England's history of poverty and responses to it, using this history to humanize social welfare policy from the Victorian era through the present. Exhibits would show the impact of this policy on the lives of individual men and women by recreating their living quarters at different moments in time – the same strategy as the Tenement Museum. From this emotive starting point, it would open new conversations about how English people should live together and support each other today.

I quickly came to appreciate how different, in fact, our contexts were, and how different were the challenges to our sites.

The Workhouse, England

Leigh Rix spoke the Queen's English, wiped clean of regional and class inflections. He arrived for our meeting in Bellagio crisp, pressed, and organized, but sweating a little. His third daughter was to be born sometime that week, so he feared he might have to leave the meeting at a moment's notice. And, after a quiet career preserving landscapes and sites of gentility, he had been recently charged by the British National Trust with getting Britons to talk about poverty. The Trust was founded in 1895 to preserve the heritage and natural sites of England, Wales, and Northern Ireland. One hundred years on, it was largely known as a safety net for fallen manses, taking over the estates and gardens of lesser nobility and preserving them for public use. By the time Leigh arrived at Bellagio, the Trust was managing about 500 historic sites; the effect was a heritage landscape celebrating the beauty and wonder of bygone British wealth as a foundation of national culture and character. Although the Trust was not a state institution, managing this much property, it played a significant role in defining the UK's historical identity. As its centenary neared, it did some soul searching, having become as a *Guardian* journalist wrote in 1995, "acutely sensitive to the accusation that it preserves only the lives of the rich, and a sugared, sanitised version at that."[11]

Leigh came to the National Trust as it decided to turn its attention to preserving the lives of the poor. Although it had for some time interpreted servants' quarters in many of its historic houses, domestic labor did not represent the experience of the majority of the Trust's middle- and upper-class visitors. But the landscape was littered with buildings that had shaped what it was like to live in poverty – and debates about who was responsible for it – for over a century. These were workhouses, hulking structures that loomed at the outskirts of every town, to house people who could not support themselves. They were designed as deterrents to the "undeserving poor," environments so bleak and punishing that only the truly needy would submit to living in them.[12] While the Poor Law that underpinned workhouses was abolished in 1948, the institutions loomed in the imaginations of British citizens, whether or not they had ever set foot in one. As National Trust Project Researcher Susanna Smith later explained, "Being 'sent to the workhouse' has passed into our national memory as a serious threat."[13] Immortalized in Charles Dickens novels and local lore, the menace of the workhouse shaped ideas of poverty as personal rather than systemic failure, and social welfare as supporting the "undeserving," for generations, creating deep silences and shame. This shame had only grown more acute in the last few decades: during Leigh's lifetime, Margaret Thatcher and her Conservative government were accused of pursuing a deliberate "strategy of inequality" through the 1970s and 1980s; the number of people living in poverty in the UK grew from 5 million to nearly 14 million.[14]

But a new day was dawning in Britain: the Conservative party had fallen, replaced by a New Labor government dedicated to a new concept: "social inclusion." At the end of 1997, it created a Social Exclusion Unit, which charged every sector of the state – including museums and heritage sites – to come up with new policies and practices to address inequality and marginalization. The National Trust embraced the state's social inclusion project, taking on the task of redefining what counted as British heritage. It decided it wanted a workhouse. This was an unusual move, not just because it was a different type of property, but because the Trust typically took over properties in response to requests to save them, later coming up with a narrative containing lessons the property could teach people about British heritage. In this case, it decided to seek out a property that would support the heritage lessons it wanted to teach. The Trust set about looking for the best-preserved workhouse, the one – of the hundreds scattered across the country – that could best tell the story of Britain's struggle over social welfare.

The Workhouse in Southwell, a town in Nottinghamshire, smack in the center of England, opened in 1824, was one of the country's earliest, pioneering a system, introduced nationally in 1834, that would become the norm in Britain for decades to come. The "New Poor Law," and the buildings that enforced it, were constructed around a new vision of individual and social responsibility and accountability. The operating principle was that there was a difference between the "blameless poor" – otherwise described as the "old and infirm" – and the "idle and profligate" – anyone who was able-bodied but unemployed. The British state would not hold itself accountable to the "idle and profligate." Each locality was required to set up a workhouse, at a distance from its communities, to remove its indigent from society. Buildings were designed to segregate people by sex and age, in both indoor sleeping areas and outside work yards. Children remembered glimpsing their mothers over the tops of high walls, unable to go to them. Workhouses were technically not prisons; if an "inmate," as residents were called, found a job outside, they were free to leave. But the houses' environments were made so punitive that people would turn to them only as a last resort.[15]

The workhouse system was done away with in 1948 as part of a massive expansion of the British welfare state, which included establishing the National Health Service and abolishing the Poor Law.[16] The National Health Service took over workhouses and repurposed them as hospitals, orphanages, and mental health institutions. But the buildings retained the shame of the systems they were built to enforce. *Guardian* reporter Maev Kennedy remembered that in the 1960s, her great-aunt was admitted to a hospital that had once been a workhouse, where she died. "It was an ordinary geriatric hospital by then, but it was the old workhouse. The shame was still so intense that some members of the family could not speak of it."[17]

Acquiring the workhouse at Southwell, and preserving it with the same care as a manor, not only acknowledged the workhouse system as a shared experience critical to British heritage and identity, but broke more than a century of silence by opening a space for public discussion. The Southwell workhouse provided particularly rich opportunities to reflect on changing ideas of social welfare, as it was used from 1824 through the end of the 1970s and thus had witnessed generations of experiences of poverty and responses to it. In addition to preserving the building as it would have been experienced just after its opening, the Trust recreated a "bedsit," or shared temporary housing for homeless women from the 1970s. Leigh and the Trust envisioned the project as an opportunity to open dialogue on social welfare and collective responsibility in Britain moving forward, by "offering the chance to debate a range of definitions of and solutions to poverty."[18]

The center of this effort was a concluding exhibit titled "What Now? What Next?" The exhibit included a number of stations, offering comparisons between the workhouse system and the present day. Similar to the Tenement Museum, the Workhouse used a common memory and historical experience to establish parallels between different moments in time – the present day and 1824 – and build greater empathy for people today. The most prominent piece of the exhibit was an installation titled "where would people from the work-house be today," featuring life-sized cutouts of people that were literally cut in half, with one-half dressed in 1830s clothing, and the other in modern-day attire. No representation of the generational impact of Britain's 19th-century social welfare policy was on display, and no exploration was offered of how a person today might be impoverished because her ancestor was denied access to advancement. While National Trust officials hoped to "stimulate individuals to take some kind of action," they made it clear from the beginning that the museum would not seek to establish accountability for cruelties of the past. "It is not our place to judge or pronounce," a spokesperson affirmed.[19]

Campaigns for Accountability: Memory Movements in the Era of Transitional Justice

Strategies like the Workhouse's and the Tenement Museum's represented the outer edge of what was possible in terms of addressing contemporary issues within the context of their countries' traditional heritage fields in the late 1990s. In these contexts, drawing connections between past and present was novel and risky. But in the same historical moment, in other parts of the world, memory-based social movements were emerging that treated the past and the present as continuous and inextricable, identifying museums as important vehicles for establishing historical accountability.

Memoria Abierta, Argentina

My main memories of Patricia Tappatá de Valdez, Argentinian human rights activist, are of waiting. Patricia talked fast, thought faster, and demanded immediate action, but she was not to be rushed. Especially not through break-fast. Breakfasts during the many group meetings I staffed were often followed by me piling participants into a bus to get somewhere on time – to the con-ference center, to important meetings with local dignitaries, to the airport. In an exasperated retort to one of my tentative requests that she get on the bus with the others, she explained her refusal. While directing El Salvador's truth commission and the Human Rights Department of the National Conference of Bishops in Peru, she had given birth to a succession of four daughters, all of whom had to be dressed, fed, and packed off to school before Patricia could start her day. Now that they were grown, no one was going to tell her to hurry up and finish her toast, especially not someone her daughters' age. I waited for her outside while the bus idled.

Patricia came to the Coalition's founding meeting in Bellagio from Buenos Aires. During the military dictatorship of the 1970s and 1980s in Argentina, she explained to us, more than 30,000 people were "disappeared" and countless more detained and tortured for supposed sedition, many of them youth. The violence and repression infested the everyday landscape, hidden in plain sight: torture took place in private homes, in the back of auto repair shops, the basements of police stations.[20] Mothers of the disappeared began organizing to call for investigations into what happened to their children by occupying public spaces, most famously the Plaza de Mayo in Buenos Aires, holding giant photographs of their sons and daughters. In 1983, democracy was restored in Argentina. But the mothers remained; until the truth of their children was discovered, they would continue their protest.[21] In response to pressure from the mothers and others, that year the new government formed the world's first major truth commission, an official body charged with formally investigating mass human rights abuses of the former regime.[22]

The Commission's report, *Nunca Mas* (Never Again), issued in 1984, was a wild success, becoming a national bestseller when it was published as a book. The report served as the foundation of trials for high-ranking officials, convicting over half the junta; such public accountability for authoritarian abuses represented another first watched closely by countries around the world. But the military had ceded power only after granting itself amnesty, and it threatened the fragile new government with a coup if trials continued. In 1986, the government abandoned the project of holding perpetrators accountable, and military personnel who had ordered or carried out torture settled back into daily life, living and working side by side with the families of victims.

Argentina's experience informed and inspired countries around the world navigating a new world order. Through the 1980s and 1990s, dozens of repressive governments gave way to democracies, creating a worldwide need for new processes to guide societies from one system to the other. A new field of international law emerged, and developed a variety of tools for confronting the past – from truth commissions to prosecutions – collectively named "transitional justice." The field claimed origins in the Nuremberg trials – the title of the Argentine Commission's report, "Never Again," was a phrase coined as a response to the Holocaust. But since Nuremberg, through the Cold War, historical accountability had been held hostage. Both sides of the iron curtain feared that reckoning with past abuse would destabilize the regimes built on its legacies: denial was required to maintain the Cold War's international order. But as the iron curtain began to fall and new democracies proliferated around the world, legal scholar Naomi Roht-Arriaza explains, finally "investigation of the past would not necessarily entail alignment with one superpower, or aid and comfort to the other."[23]

This post-Cold-War wave of transitional justice rolled in with a new enthusiasm for international judicial cooperation in investigating past atrocities. Perhaps recognizing that the shocking genocides in the Balkans and Rwanda in the early 1990s were in part legacies of the Cold War's international order, the United Nations invited the new international community to repair the damage of the old by creating an International Criminal Tribunal for ex-Yugoslavia in 1993, and one for Rwanda in 1995. By 1998, nations around the world came together to establish the International Criminal Court (ICC) in recognition of other "unimaginable atrocities that deeply shock the conscience of humanity," to prosecute genocide, crimes against humanity, and war crimes anywhere in the world and to "put an end to impunity for the perpetrators of these crimes and thus to contribute to the prevention of such crimes."[24] The establishment of the ICC marked a watershed moment in a growing international commitment to building cultures of accountability. By the end of 2002, the year the treaty establishing the court took effect, 85 states had ratified it. The US, unwilling to submit to global standards of justice that could charge US nationals, did not.[25] But in the rest of the world, the time was ripe for reckoning.[26]

As the ICC declared states' obligation to prosecute perpetrators of mass crimes, the United Nations (UN) established a duty to publicly remember those crimes. In 1997, UN Special Rapporteur Louis Joinet examined the causes and consequences of impunity for perpetrators of human rights violations for the UN Commission on Human Rights. Based on his findings, he developed a set of principles, including a new set of rights countries wishing to combat impunity must uphold, which were updated by Diane Orentlicher, then the United Nations Independent Expert on combating impunity, in 2005. At the core of these "Joinet/Orentlicher" principles were "the right to know," and its corollary, "the duty to preserve memory." The "right to know" established that:

> Every people has the inalienable right to know the truth about past events concerning the perpetration of heinous crimes and about the circumstances and reasons that led, through massive or systematic violations, to the perpetration of those crimes. Full and effective exercise of the right to the truth provides a vital safeguard against the recurrence of violations.[27]

And the "duty to preserve memory" is:

> ...the State's duty to preserve archives and other evidence concerning violations of human rights and humanitarian law and to facilitate knowledge of those violations. Such measures shall be aimed at preserving the collective memory from extinction and, in particular, at guarding against the development of revisionist and negationist arguments.[28]

While the principles were non-binding, by using the language of rights and duties, they established memory for accountability as an international human right, and established international norms for its preservation and promotion.

By the late 1990s, transitional justice, and enthusiasm for confronting the past as the key to building democracy, was sprouting in every corner of the globe.[29] But while nations around the world were rushing to apologize, confront, and commemorate, for Patricia Tappatá de Valdez and fellow Argentinians who sought accountability for the abuses of the military dictatorship, the bloom was already off the rose. As one of the first countries in the world to try high-ranking officials, and to hold a truth commission, it was also one of the first to experience the limitations of both justice mechanisms. Patricia and fellow activists believed that without holding all perpetrators accountable, not just a handful at the top, "Never Again" could never be achieved in Argentina. But they also recognized that individual accountability would not prevent future abuses without a collective, participatory effort to reckon with the past. Patricia had seen a generation emerge after the release of the truth commission's *Nunca Mas* report, and witnessed how little the report did to build public memory of the dictatorship and its consequences, despite being so widely read in the 1980s. The young people she worked with in the late 1990s, she told us, had frighteningly little knowledge of the brutal regime they had been born in. So by the time Patricia arrived in Bellagio, she was looking for another way.[30]

The year before our meeting, Patricia had joined with nine groups, a mix of popular protestors and academics, who were organizing into a coalition dedicated to building comprehensive archives of the dictatorship and raising public awareness of what happened during those years. Patricia became its founding director.[31] When Patricia accepted our meeting invitation, her coalition was called "Proyecto Recordar" ("Project to Remember"); by the time she arrived in Bellagio, it had renamed itself "Memoria Abierta" ("Open Memory"). Across South America, the term *memoria* was inspiring a new movement, emerging from democracy campaigns, connoting a reckoning with recent human rights abuses combining legal and cultural strategies. Over the next decade, the concept of *memoria* inspired a proliferation of museums across South America, from an Espacio para Memoria y Derechos Humanos (Space for Memory and Human Rights) in Buenos Aires, to the Museo Nacional de la Memoria y los Derechos Humanos (National Museum of Memory and Human Rights) in Chile, interpreting the Pinochet era, to the Museo de la Memoria de Uruguay (Uruguay Museum of Memory).[32] Memoria Abierta assumed a leading role in this larger movement.

Memoria Abierta's members came from the same circles as prosecutors and others pursuing legal accountability and worked closely with them. As they campaigned for prosecutions, they prepared the ground with what would be needed the moment trials resumed. Sufficient evidence had to be gathered, and through that long and painstaking process, public awareness and support needed to be maintained in order to sustain pressure on authorities to open the widest possible investigation and see all the cases through. During the period of amnesty, when perpetrators of torture and disappearances lived with impunity down the street from families still seeking their loved ones, the strategy of *memoria* – especially oral histories – was the only means of collecting evidence of atrocities and who was responsible. *Memoria* activities built renewed public pressure for prosecutions, which were reinstituted in 2003. And it strengthened prosecutors' cases, since they could draw on evidence Memoria Abierta's members had collected over the years, including clues that pointed them to buried sites of detention and allowed them to conduct forensic investigations to uncover them. But the material was activated for much more than identifying immediate individual culpability.

Memoria used many of the same tools that the traditional institutions of *historia* or *patrimonio* (heritage) did, such as building archives, conducting oral histories, developing exhibits, and preserving sites. But whereas Argentina's heritage offices at the time focused on preserving Buenos Aires' beaux-arts architectural gems, and other artifacts accepted as defining the nation, they did not adopt the Joinet/Orenlichter principle that "A people's knowledge of the history of its oppression is part of its heritage."[33] Memoria Abierta sought to build a new and lasting public memory of the atrocities in Argentina's recent history that would become part of the country's understanding of its heritage. In the city of Buenos Aires, state terrorism did not operate through one site, but through a kind of urban infrastructure of torture and detention, a dense, interconnected network snaking just under the city's visible surface like gas lines. Making this vast system visible to the city's residents – to reveal that almost everyone had been living right next to or on top of sites of brutal violence – was critical for demonstrating how state terrorism functioned, and how citizens' silence enabled it. Through new archives, events, digital mapping, memorialization of sites, and a traveling exhibit, Memoria Abierta fought to ensure that certain truths could no longer be denied.[34] The *memoria* movement's integration of legal accountability and public memory was critical to the success of both – not only in Argentina, but also in other countries it inspired. Argentina's activists opened the door for historical accountability to take hold around the world.[35]

District Six Museum, South Africa

Next to Argentina, the country most frequently held up as defining transitional justice as a global practice is South Africa. There the transition was different; thus, so was the form of transitional justice. The new democratic South African government that rose in 1994 acknowledged that the country could not build a lasting democracy without collectively reckoning with its past. As happened in Argentina, the South African military only agreed to relinquish power if they were granted total amnesty, narrowing the path to reckoning. But in Argentina, the military's negotiating hand was weaker, opening space for activists to push past the country's early truth commission and hold individual perpetrators criminally accountable. In South Africa, by contrast, ending apartheid depended on military cooperation.[36] Thus, South Africans went all in on a Truth and Reconciliation Commission (TRC). The TRC would investigate and document the mechanisms of apartheid's racist repression through a massive public process of collectively sharing memories of violence and its impact, granting amnesty to perpetrators of violence during the apartheid era who testified to their actions.

The TRC sought to create a broader societal accountability by engaging as many South Africans as possible in extensive public testimony and published reports. State-sponsored memorials and museums were a critical part of the strategy, which focused on researching history, sharing it publicly, and inviting people to reckon with it together. A mad rush ensued to memorialize people and places around the country associated with the anti-apartheid struggle, to create a visual landscape and public culture that would support the values of the new South Africa. In 1997, the nation's new Department of Arts and Culture established the Robben Island Museum in the island prison where Nelson Mandela and other leaders of the anti-apartheid struggle were held. Robben Island soon became South Africa's most famous place to remember and repudiate the old regime.[37] But while South Africa's focus on reconciliation was celebrated the world over, it was deeply criticized at home for refusing to dismantle the legacies of racial power and privilege, ignoring the unique experiences of women, and therefore not actually shepherding the country out of a racial caste system and the patriarchy that undergirded it.[38] The critique found strong expression in an oppositional memory movement, challenging official state commemorations of the death of apartheid, championed by the District Six Museum in Cape Town.

South Africa had declared apartheid "history" just five years before Sandra Prosalendis, the District Six Museum's first director, introduced herself as "Sandy" at the Bellagio meeting. Just a few months before she arrived in Bellagio, Robben Island was named a World Heritage site.[39]

But Sandy represented a radically different project. The District Six Museum Foundation was formed in the late 1980s as part of the anti-apartheid movement, and sponsored exhibits and events around the city as part of a campaign to protest and resist policies of forced removals under apartheid. The District Six Museum did not simply commemorate the anti-apartheid struggle by representing the memory of a movement, as did sites that opened after apartheid was over, like Robben Island; it was a memory movement itself. Where most post-apartheid museums drew a sharp line between the evils of the past and hopes for the future, the District Six Museum was an ongoing campaign, evolving with, and helping to evolve, its society.[40] It mobilized memory for material redress, by fighting to get one colored community's land back from the white government that took it.

District Six had been a thriving, culturally diverse working-class neighborhood in Cape Town. But in 1966, it was declared a "whites only district" under the apartheid government's Group Areas Act. Over 60,000 residents classified as non-white were forced from their homes, displaced to far-flung areas lacking the cultural and infrastructural support of their centrally located neighborhood. In 1968, the government began demolishing the neighborhood, and by 1982, bulldozers had flattened the whole district into a wasteland of empty red dust. The plan was to build a new community, for whites.

While ex-residents could not stop the destruction of their neighborhood, they vowed to stop the destruction of its memory, and preserve the memory of its destruction, by preventing any new building. In 1987, a group of activists formed the "Hands Off District Six Campaign" to organize protests reminding Cape Townians and all South Africans of what had been lost, and to call for the neighborhood not to be rebuilt until apartheid was dismantled and democracy was restored. One of the campaign's first acts, in its first year, was to establish the District Six Museum Foundation. As former director Valmont Layne remembered, "Participants realized that memory was the most important weapon they had and that they needed to organize around a way of remembering District Six and keeping it alive."[41]

The empty land was the first memorial to District Six. "The landscape as it exists," Layne wrote in 2008, "as a space of absence, has its own message; it is a huge scar in the center of the city, and it speaks volumes."[42] The stories of the scar were shared through exhibits and events the Museum Foundation created around the city as part of the Hands Off campaign, recovering the community's history and heritage of democratic organizing, civic participation, and multicultural coalition – acting as a precedent for the vision many anti-apartheid activists shared for a new South Africa.

In 1994, the District Six Museum found a permanent home in a former Methodist Church, while around it, the country began its transition out of apartheid and into democracy. Although the TRC forum allowed for many more stories to be shared than in individual legal cases, it remained limited in time and scope, restricting itself to "gross human rights violations," which it defined as murder, abduction, and torture. This left out the sexual violence that shaped many women's experiences under apartheid, as well as the day-to-day repression and abuse that was the reality for the vast majority of citizens. And while it included a Committee on Reparations and Rehabilitation, which, in 1998, published bold recommendations in the TRC's report, the government slow walked their implementation.[43] Recognition and restitution for "ordinary" abuses legalized under apartheid needed to be won by more popular social movements, using alternative forms of storytelling and public memory.

The year the District Six Museum opened, the new South African government passed the Restitution of Land Rights Act, allowing people who had been displaced by the Group Areas Act to make land claims. While other entities like the District Six Beneficiary Trust, established in 1997, focused on the mechanics of the claims process, the Museum, as Valmont Layne described it, "create[d] the memorial framework" for it.[44] The Museum began by covering the floor of its new space with a giant map of the former neighborhood, and inviting the thousands of people who had lost their homes and community to "return" to it. Ex-residents were invited to place themselves back in the neighborhood by marking their memories on the map – where they lived, worked, played – and sharing their individual stories of daily life. An installation meant to last two weeks became a lasting, evolving portrait of the neighborhood, using narrative to rebuild what had been destroyed.[45] But these stories were much more than symbolic: the process of gathering and reconnecting with former neighbors and sharing what they had lost, both emotionally and materially, served as a critical catalyst for organizing a land reparations movement that succeeded in winning property titles back for many displaced people. The Museum became a place for education on the claims process, and even held one of the land courts that granted title back to displaced residents.[46]

Meanwhile, the official memorialization boom was in full swing. While proliferating state-sponsored initiatives drew a stark line between past and present, seeking to contain the racism and inequalities of the apartheid era in museums in order to disempower them, the District Six Museum called attention to continuities between the old and new South Africas.[47] It persisted in its oppositional stance to the state, eschewing most government funding and official heritage status in favor of an identity as a "community museum." The term sounded cozy and quaint, but actually represented a commitment to maintaining the museum as a space for ongoing, democratic contestation.[48]

This applied as much to the land claims as to the curatorial process; indeed, the two were inextricably intertwined. The initial proposal for implementing land claims was to combine all claims into a single development plan for the neighborhood. This reflected a significantly less democratic process than the one envisioned by ex-residents connected to the Hands Off campaign and the Museum, one that did not reflect the diversity of individual stories that continued to layer the memory map. After strong organizing and protests, in 1997, the original proposal was revised and the Museum hosted a special session of the Land Claims Court to recognize individual claims. In 1998, the Museum hosted a public signing of an agreement between the city and the newly created District Six Beneficiary Trust, "aimed at facilitating a difficult land-restitution process involving many stakeholders."[49]

The Museum next highlighted new forms of displacement and erasure. As the area's real estate value skyrocketed, development exploded and working-class non-white Cape Townians were again excluded from the larger district. The Museum and many ex-residents believed the new neighborhood should honor the heritage it bequeathed the new South Africa, the heritage that helped bring about the transition to democracy and the restitution itself. Again, this was not a memorial to the past with no material function in the present, but a thriving community that carried on the neighborhood's activist, working-class, multi-cultural legacy.[50] This legacy would be competing with a destructive continuity from the apartheid era: gentrification arising from new outside investment and the opening of markets – all of which privileged white South Africans whose wealth was owed to generations of apartheid. The Museum and the Beneficiary Trust worked with ex-residents to create an agreement called the "Social Compact," a set of principles to which each claimant would sign on that would attempt to carry on the values of the old District Six including guidelines "for security of tenure, for the responsibility not to speculate on property, for the integration among poorer tenants and wealthier homeowners, and among Muslims, Christians, and Hindus."[51]

~

Energized by examples like Argentina and South Africa, transitional justice spread like wildfire across the world. By 2001, human rights scholars Ellen Lutz and Kathryn Sikkink heralded a "justice cascade," in which historical accountability engulfed global politics, and transitional justice mushroomed, as legal scholar Ruti Teitel later put it, "from the exception to the norm to become a paradigm of rule of law," and even "the persistent discourse of the final years of the twentieth century."[52] Spanning almost every continent, countries from Chile to Sierra Leone undertook truth commissions, public apologies, reparations, and other official means of reckoning with violent histories.[53] The stage was set for Sites of Conscience, as many parts of the world saw, in the words of sociologist Amy Sodaro, "a new temporal orientation toward the past in political and social life."[54]

But if officially confronting the past was becoming a requirement for political legitimacy in some democracies, it remained a pipe dream in others. Transitional justice required a firm and final rejection of an authoritarian regime for a democratic one: its mechanisms did not readily apply to long-standing liberal democracies like the US, and couldn't find foothold in shifting political sands like Bangladesh. Memory leaders from such contexts faced a different set of challenges, and despite each seeming unique and unrelated, found ways to support each other through them.

Notes

1 Ruth J. Abram, "Kitchen Conversations: Democracy in Action at the Lower East Side Tenement Museum," *The Public Historian* 29, no. 1 (Winter 2007): 59–76.
2 Sophia Dembling, "Ruth Abram: Explaining Today Through Stories of Yesterday," National Trust for Historic Preservation, November 19, 2014, https://savingplaces. org/stories/ruth-abram-explaining-today-stories-yesterday#.XpR5nMhKg2w

3 Martin V. Melosi, "National Council on Public History President's Annual Address: Public History and the Environment," *The Public Historian* 15, no. 4 (Autumn 1993): 10–20.

4 Cynthia Harrison, "Creating a National Feminist Agenda: Coalition Building in the 1970s," in *Feminist Coalitions: Historical Perspectives on Second-Wave Feminism in the United States*, ed. Stephanie Gilmore (Urbana: University of Illinois Press, 2008), 29.

5 American Association of Museums, *Mastering Civic Engagement: A Challenge to Museums* (Washington, DC: American Association of Museums, 2002), 9.

6 Barbara Schaffer Bacon, Cheryl Yuen, and Pam Korza, "Animating Democracy: The Artistic Imagination as a Force in Civic Dialogue," Americans for the Arts, 1999, https://www.animatingdemocracy.org/sites/default/files/documents/reading_room/Animating_Democracy_Study.pdf

7 Neil A. Lewis, "Smithsonian Substantially Alters Enola Gay Exhibit After Criticism," *New York Times*, October 1, 1994; Edward Tabor Linenthal and Tom Engelhardt, *History Wars: The Enola Gay and Other Battles for the American Past* (New York: Metropolitan Books, 1996). *The Journal of American History* devoted much of its December 1995 issue to the Enola Gay exhibit controversy. See "History and the Public: What Can We Handle? A Round Table about History after the *Enola Gay* Controversy," *The Journal of American History* 82, no. 3 (December 1995): 1029–1144.

8 Charles Hardy III, "Lower East Side Tenement Museum," *The Journal of American History* 84, no. 3 (December 1997): 1009–13; Margaret Garb, "Review of the Lower East Side Tenement Museum," *Journal of Urban History* 26, no. 1 (November 1999): 108–11; Mort Sheinman, ed., *A Tenement Story: The History of 97 Orchard Street and the Lower East Side Tenement Museum* (New York: Lower East Side Tenement Museum, 1999). For more on the museum's history and evolution, see Russell A. Kazal, "Migration History in Five Stories (and a Basement): The Lower East Side Tenement Museum," *Journal of American Ethnic History* 34, no. 4 (2015): 77–93; Shira Kohn, "Review: Lower East Side Tenement Museum," *The Public Historian* 30, no. 4 (November 2008): 157–9; Adam Steinberg, "What We Talk About When We Talk About Food: Using Food to Teach History at the Tenement Museum," *The Public Historian* 34, no. 2 (Spring 2012): 79–89; Andrew Urban, "Under One Roof," *The Public Historian* 40, no. 4 (2018): 169–76; Hakim Bishara, "After Layoffs, Tenement Museum Union Files Complaint With National Labor Relations Board," *Hyperallergic*, July 31, 2020; R. E. Fulton, Erin Reid, Jackie Wait, and Daniel Walber, "'We are Workers in a Workplace Who Have Rights': Unionization, COVID-19, and the Place of Labor at the Lower East Side Tenement Museum," interviewed by Andy Urban, *The Public Historian* 43, no. 2 (May 2021): 81–102.

9 Laura Hapke, *Sweatshop: The History of an American Idea* (New Brunswick: Rutgers University Press, 2004).

10 Liz Ševčenko, "The Power of Place: How Historic Sites Can Engage Citizens in Human Rights Issues," ed. Liam Mahony, New Tactics Project of the Center for Victims of Torture, 2004, https://www.sitesofconscience.org/wp-content/uploads/2012/10/Members_member-Benefits_005.pdf; Liz Ševčenko, "Dialogue as a Resource for Heritage Management: Stories from Sites of Conscience," in *Consensus Building, Negotiation, and Conflict Resolution for Heritage Place Management: Proceedings of a Workshop Organized by the Getty Conservation Institute, Los Angeles, California, December 1-3, 2009*, eds. David Myers, Stacie Nicole Smith, and Gail Ostergren (Los Angeles: The Getty Conservation Institute, 2016), https://www.getty.edu/conservation/publications_resources/pdf_publications/pdf/consensus_building.pdf

11 Maev Kennedy, "Unlocking the Memories of Terror Within These Walls," *The Guardian*, October 21, 1995. For the National Trust's later shift toward inclusive storytelling and accountability, see Alison Oram and Matt Cook, *Prejudice and Pride: Celebrating LGBTQ Heritage* (Warrington, UK: National Trust, 2017); "Challenging Histories Public Programme 2017-19," National Trust, https://www.nationaltrust.org.uk/features/how-we-are-challenging-our-history; Irene Galea, "The Diversity Decade: How Heritage is Spanning Differences in 2020," National Trust for Canada, May 1, 2020, https://nationaltrustcanada.ca/online-stories/the-diversity-decade-how-heritage-is-spanning-differences-in-2020; Sally-Anne Huxtable, Corinne Fowler, Christo Kefalas, and Emma Slocombe, eds., "Interim Report on the Connections Between Colonialism and Properties Now in the Care of the National Trust, Including Links with Historic Slavery," National Trust, September 2020, https://nt.global.ssl.fastly.net/documents/colonialism-and-historic-slavery-report.pdf; Sam Knight, "Britain's Idyllic Country Houses Reveal a Darker History," *The New Yorker*, August 16, 2021.

12 Susanna Smith, *The Workhouse Southwell* (National Trust Books, 2006); Simon Fowler, *The Workhouse: The People, the Places, the Life Behind Doors* (South Yorkshire: Pen & Sword History, 2014); Peter Higginbotham, *Workhouses of London and the South East* (Gloucestershire: The History Press, 2019).

13 Susanna Smith, "'Back to the Workhouse': Poverty from the Past Serving the Present," *Museum International* 53, no. 1 (2001): 21–4.

14 Richard Sandell, "Museums as Agents of Social Inclusion," in *Museum Studies: An Anthology of Contexts*, ed. Bettina Messias Carbonell (Malden, MA: Wiley-Blackwell, 2012), 563. Sandell is drawing on the work of the book *Britain Divided: The Growth of Social Exclusion in the 1980s and 1990s*, eds. Alan Walker and Carol Walker (London: Child Poverty Action Group, 1997).

15 Smith, "Back to the Workhouse."

16 Higginbotham, *Workhouses of London and the South East*; "1940's Origins of the Welfare State," The National Archives, https://www.nationalarchives.gov.uk/cabinetpapers/alevelstudies/1940-origins-welfare-state.htm; Paul Spicker, "British Social Policy, 1601-1948," http://www.spicker.uk/social-policy/history.htm. The British National Assistance board was also established in this moment.

17 Kennedy, "Unlocking the Memories of Terror Within These Walls."

18 Charlotte Crow, "Richer for Poorer," *History Today* 52, no. 3 (March 2002), 3.

19 Ibid.

20 Max Page, ed., *Memories of Buenos Aires: Signs of State Terrorism in Argentina* (Amherst: University of Massachusetts Press, 2013).

21 Marguerite Guzman Bouvard, *Revolutionizing Motherhood: The Mothers of the Plaza de Mayo* (Lanham, MD: SR Books, 2004).

22 Uganda held the world's first truth commission in 1974, and Bolivia the second in 1982. Because neither produced a final report, they did not set the global precedent that Argentina's did. See Kathryn Sikkink and Carrie Booth Walling, "Argentina's Contribution to Global Trends in Transitional Justice," in *Transitional Justice in the Twenty-First Century: Beyond Truth Versus Justice*, eds. Naomi Roht-Arriaza and Javier Mariezcurrena. (Cambridge, UK: Cambridge University Press, 2006).

23 Naomi Roht-Arriaza, "The New Landscape of Transitional Justice," in *Transitional Justice in the Twenty-First Century: Beyond Truth Versus Justice*, eds. Naomi Roht-Arriaza and Javier Mariezcurrena (Cambridge: Cambridge University Press, 2006), 3.

24 "Rome Statute of the International Criminal Court," United Nations, July 17, 1998, http://legal.un.org/icc/statute/99_corr/cstatute.htm

25 As of this writing, the US has still not signed on to the ICC. Jamie Mayerfeld, "Who Shall Be Judge?: The United States, the International Criminal Court, and

the Global Enforcement of Human Rights," *Human Rights Quarterly* 25, no. 1 (February 2003): 93–129; Jason Ralph, *Defending the Society of States: Why America Opposes the International Criminal Court and Its Vision of World Society* (Oxford: Oxford University Press, 2007); Lee Feinstein and Tod Lindberg, *Means to an End: U.S. Interest in the International Criminal Court* (Washington, DC: Brookings Institution Press, 2009); Andrea Betti, "'Slay This Monster': The United States and Opposition to the Rome Statute on the International Criminal Court," *Human Rights Review* 17, no. 4 (2016): 417–38; "States Parties: Chronological List, UN Treaty – Rome Statute of the International Criminal Court," International Criminal Court, https://asp.icc-cpi.int/en_menus/asp/states%20parties/Pages/states%20parties%20_%20chronological%20list.aspx

26 For more on the evolution of the landscape of political opportunity that gave rise to the transitional justice trend, see Kathryn Sikkink and Carrie Booth Walling, "Argentina's Contribution to Global Trends in Transitional Justice," in *Transitional Justice in the Twenty-First Century: Beyond Truth Versus Justice*, eds. Naomi Roht-Arriaza and Javier Mariezcurrena (Cambridge: Cambridge University Press, 2006), 301–24.

27 Diane Orentlicher, "Promotion and Protection of Human Rights: Report of the Independent Expert to Update the Set of Principles to Combat Impunity," United Nations, February 8, 2005, https://undocs.org/E/CN.4/2005/102/Add.1

28 Ibid.

29 Ruti G. Teitel, "Transitional Justice Genealogy," *Harvard Human Rights Journal* 16 (2003): 71. See also Ruti G. Teitel, *Globalizing Transitional Justice: Contemporary Essays* (New York: Oxford University Press, 2014).

30 Kathryn Sikkink and Carrie Booth Walling, "Argentina's Contribution to Global Trends in Transitional Justice," in *Transitional Justice in the Twenty-First Century: Beyond Truth Versus Justice*, eds. Naomi Roht-Arriaza and Javier Mariezcurrena (Cambridge: Cambridge University Press, 2006), 301–24.

31 Marí a Laura Guembe, "Challenges on the Road to Memory," *The Public Historian* 30, no. 1 (February 2008): 63–71.

32 Liz Ševčenko, "Sites of Conscience: Reimagining Reparations," *Change Over Time* 1, no. 1 (Spring 2011): 6–33.

33 Orentlicher, "Promotion and Protection of Human Rights."

34 Guembe, "Challenges on the Road to Memory."

35 Kathryn Sikkink and Carrie Booth Walling, "Argentina's Contribution to Global Trends in Transitional Justice," in *Transitional Justice in the Twenty-First Century: Beyond Truth Versus Justice*, eds. Naomi Roht-Arriaza and Javier Mariezcurrena (Cambridge, UK: Cambridge University Press, 2006).

36 Kathryn Sikkink and Carrie Booth Walling, "Argentina's Contribution to Global Trends in Transitional Justice," in *Transitional Justice in the Twenty-First Century : Beyond Truth Versus Justice*, eds. Naomi Roht-Arriaza and Javier Mariezcurrena (Cambridge, UK: Cambridge University Press, 2006).

37 Heidi Grunebaum, *Memorializing the Past: Everyday Life in South Africa After the Truth and Reconciliation Commission* (New Brunswick, NJ: Transaction Publishers, 2011).

38 Mia Swart and Karin van Marle, *The Limits of Transition: The South African Truth and Reconciliation Commission 20 Years on* (Leiden: Brill Nijhoff, 2017); Rina Kashyap, "Narrative and Truth: A Feminist Critique of the South African Truth and Reconciliation Commission." *Contemporary Justice Review: CJR* 12, no. 4 (2009): 449–67; Brandon Hamber, "Dealing with the Aftermath of Political Violence in South Africa: Evaluating the Impact of the Truth and Reconciliation Commission." *Aggressive Behavior* 27, no. 3 (2001): 183.

39 "Robben Island," United Nations Educational, Scientific and Cultural Organization, https://whc.unesco.org/en/list/916/

40 Ciraj Rassool and Sandra Prosalendis, *Recalling Community in Cape Town: Creating and Curating the District Six Museum* (Cape Town, South Africa: District Six Museum, 2001); Charmaine McEachern, "Mapping the Memories: Politics, Place and Identity in the District Six Museum, Cape Town," *Social Identities* 4, no. 3 (October 1998): 499–521.

41 Valmont Layne, "The District Six Museum: An Ordinary People's Place," *The Public Historian* 30, no. 1 (February 2008): 57.

42 Ibid., 58.

43 Mia Swart and Karin van Marle, eds., *The Limits of Transition: The South African Truth and Reconciliation Commission 20 Years on* (Leiden: Brill Nijhoff, 2017); Deborah Posel and Graeme Simpson, *Commissioning the Past: Understanding South Africa's Truth and Reconciliation Commission* (Johannesburg: Witwatersrand University Press, 2002).

44 Layne, "The District Six Museum," 61.

45 Leslie Witz, Gary Minkley, and Ciraj Rassool, "Sources and Genealogies of the New Museum: The Living Fossil, the Photograph, and the Speaking Subject," in *Unsettled History: Making South African Public Pasts*, eds. Leslie Witz, Gary Minkley, and Ciraj Rassool (Ann Arbor: University of Michigan Press, 2017), 197–203.

46 Layne, "The District Six Museum," 61.

47 Charmaine McEachern, "Working with Memory: The District Six Museum in the New South Africa," *Social Analysis* 42, no. 2 (July 1998): 48–72; Annie E. Coombes, *History After Apartheid: Visual Culture and Public Memory in a Democratic South Africa* (Durham: Duke University Press, 2003).

48 Ciraj Rassool, "Community Museums, Memory Politics, and Social Transformation in South Africa: Histories, Possibilities, and Limits," in *Museum Frictions: Public Cultures/Global Transformations*, eds. Ivan Karp, Corinne A. Kratz, Lynn Szwaja, and Tomas Ybarra-Frausto, with Gustavo Buntinx, Barbara Kirshenblatt-Gimblett, and Ciraj Rassool (Durham: Duke University Press, 2006), 286–321.

49 Ciraj Rassool, "Making the District Six Museum in Cape Town," *Museum International* 58, no. 1–2 (May 2006): 9–18.

50 Bonita Bennett, Chrischené Julius, and Crain Soudien, eds., *City-Site-Museum: Reviewing Memory Practices at the District Six Museum* (Cape Town: District Six Museum, 2008).

51 Layne, "The District Six Museum," 62.

52 Ellen Lutz and Kathryn Sikkink, "The Justice Cascade: The Evolution and Impact of Foreign Human Rights Trials in Latin America," *Chicago Journal of International Law* 2, no. 1 (2001): 1.
Teitel, "Transitional Justice Genealogy," 71 and 85.

53 Teitel, *Globalizing Transitional Justice*; Roht-Arriaza and Mariezcurrena, eds., *Transitional Justice in the Twenty-First Century*.

54 Amy Sodaro, *Exhibiting Atrocity: Memorial Museums and the Politics of Past Violence* (New Brunswick: Rutgers University Press, 2018), 4.

2

SNAPSHOTS FROM MEMORY MOVEMENTS AT THE TURN OF THE MILLENNIUM, ALBUM 2

Truth without Accountability in Bangladesh, Czech Republic, Russia, the US, and Senegal

Achieving state-sanctioned investigations, legally binding accountability, or even consensus on the basic outlines of historical abuse remained exceedingly difficult in many parts of the world, especially those where societies remained deeply divided and the "transition" from dictatorship to democracy was incomplete or unclear. The meeting at Bellagio included leaders mired in this level of struggle for historical accountability from radically different contexts: the scrappy Liberation War Museum in Bangladesh; the dissident-led Gulag Museum and the state-funded Terezín Memorial in post-communist Eastern Europe; the massive US National Park Service; and the physically tiny but globally symbolic Slave House in Senegal. Before coming together, none would have seen they had much in common, least of all the political contexts in which they worked. But they shared cultures and structures that blocked historical accountability so completely that a memory movement might be the only mechanism for collectively confronting authoritarian or repressive pasts, and modeling a democratic future.

Liberation War Museum, Bangladesh

Akku Chowdhury had two pieces of business in Italy: gaining recognition for genocide, and gelato. They were not actually unrelated: both pursued international support for creating a democratic, secular culture in Bangladesh. At our meeting, Chowdhury sought to advance a nascent struggle over the memory of the Liberation War of 1971, and win recognition for the killing of massive numbers of Bengalis by the Pakistani army as a crime against humanity. But while in the country, he also collected ingredients and recipes for Italy's most delicious frozen confection, with an eye to revolutionizing refreshment in

DOI: 10.4324/9781003185826-4

Dhaka, and furthering Bangladesh's capitalist economic development through a new chain of gelaterias.

Akku owned several Pizza Huts in Dhaka, and he believed in the positive effect of Western franchises on an Islamic society. Akku saw recognition of genocide as a precondition for post-war economic development, a view he shared with other Bangladeshi business leaders. In 1972, as Bangladesh's new democratic constitution was being written, the Agrani Bank took out an ad in the "'genocide issue' of *Banglar Bani*, a leading Bengali newspaper," featuring the beautiful face of a victim with the words: "Bengal's muted sobs want to say, 'never again genocide.'"[1] Immediately after the war, many in the business class supported public acknowledgment and repudiation of the violence Bangladeshis had suffered, believing the brand new nation's political and economic stability required that it define itself against the abuses of the past. But within a few years, the democratic constitution was scrapped and the memory of past violence suppressed.

Akku was one of eight people who came together in 1994 to found the Liberation War Museum, which opened its doors two years later. Members of Dhaka's educated middle class, including a medical doctor, a member of parliament, and a theater director, the seven men and one woman were young "freedom fighters" in the bloody battle for Bangladesh's independence in 1971. By the 1990s, they were all active in the Awami League, a democratic political party struggling to bring about the vision for Bangladesh they had fought the war for: a secular, parliamentary democracy built on religious diversity, and broad civic participation. The country they lived in now was plagued by sectarian violence and Islamic extremism. Although they were neither historians nor museum professionals, they shared a deep concern about historical denial; they believed their country's problems were rooted in the erasure of public memory of the Liberation War.

Like so many 20th-century conflicts, the War was rooted in colonial political geography. After India gained its independence from Britain, its northeastern and northwestern corners were carved out to create a Muslim homeland, divided into two parts, to be called East and West Pakistan. They were separated by thousands of miles, and by significant cultural and linguistic differences. All that united them was Islam. West Pakistan was the seat of political and economic control, and imposed its language and customs on East Pakistan, fueling calls for autonomy over the subsequent decades, which gained greater inspiration in the late 1960s from the global youth movement. In December 1970, the Awami League gained significant power in East Pakistani elections. To suppress the threat that growing Bengali nationalism posed to West Pakistan's authority, the Pakistani Army launched a campaign of violence so massive in scope and so systematic – including mass executions and the rape of thousands – that many would describe it as a genocide. Of those that survived, millions were displaced.[2]

What East Pakistani resistors called a "people's army" of "freedom fighters" waged a brutal war for independence, culminating in a secular, parliamentary democracy based on international human rights principles. But in the chaos of armed conflict, the Awami League was unable to lay a foundation of democratic culture strong enough to support its fragile constitution. Like Argentina and South Africa, Bangladesh was forced to build its new government on total amnesty for the military it defined itself against. Many clamored for war crimes trials, creating further internal conflict. At this moment, in the early to mid-1970s, it was an all-or-nothing choice: the "third ways" of truth commissions and restorative justice were not yet widely recognized alternatives. With no means to fully reckon with the trauma its people had just experienced, repudiate the structures and cultures that created it, or facilitate a national process to address tensions between the multiple competing factions that emerged from the Liberation War, Bangladesh's democracy crumbled. In 1975, martial law and military rule was imposed. In 1982, the constitution and all political parties were suspended, and in 1988, Islam became the state religion.[3]

Military rulers spun a history of the War designed to create a political culture that would support their rule. Their narrative celebrated the War as a military victory achieved by a small set of leaders, as opposed to a popular victory against tyranny achieved collectively by the people, the origin story of many secular democracies. The military relationship with the past required impunity; the democratic narrative required accountability. As Akku later wrote,

> ...people asking for the trial and punishment of war criminals were subjected to all sorts of harassment including a legal charge slapped on them for being "anti state" elements. It was a time when the history books were being written for schools that avoided the heroic part of our liberation forces or the barbarism of the perpetrators of the Genocide, the Pakistan Military and their local collaborators. ... A generation grew up in Bangladesh not knowing the true history of the birth of the nation.[4]

In 1990, a new student movement emerged to unify what had been a fractured opposition to military rule. In 1991, diverse political parties came together to restore parliamentary democracy in Bangladesh. Three years later, Akku and his colleagues formed the Liberation War Museum Trust in the hope of helping ensure this time democracy stuck. They sought to build a democratic memory movement in the country, one that would invite as many citizens as possible to participate in shaping a historical narrative of civic participation, thus building a historical identity and performing it at the same time. The Museum conducted this work as part of a new campaign for accountability that, in the post-Cold-War era of transitional justice, took a different shape than the campaign for war crime trials of the 1970s. Calls for accountability had been revived immediately after the restoration of democracy, with the opening of the Gono Adalat, or "People's Court" in 1992; but this was a partisan performance of mock trials, strongly opposed by the government, and without any legal standing.[5] It was down to the Museum to build a collective space to confront the past.

Trustees began by calling their Museum a "citizen's museum," and asking people to donate artifacts and oral histories of their experiences.[6] In the narrative they constructed, the War was won by ordinary people who came together to combat human rights abuse and establish representative democracy. They dedicated a portion of the exhibition to acknowledging women's widespread experience of rape and celebrating their resistance, an intervention that had become a hallmark of the early democracy movement.[7] In the coming years, they further emphasized memory as a collective civic project through a youth oral history program that invited school children in Dhaka and remote rural villages to interview their elders about their experiences in the War. The interviews were not professionally managed to produce reliable legal or historical evidence, but the process was designed to allow young people to learn that independence was not due to a small group of military leaders, but to all the country's citizens. The Museum published children's accounts of the interviews in a magazine, which it then distributed to the countryside, allowing young people and their families in isolated areas to read parallel stories from others in different parts of the country. Finally, each year the Museum hosted a massive Freedom Festival, reporting that it brought together 15,000 students from over 200 schools who had participated in the oral history program.[8]

While the Museum's greatest strength was its participatory process of national narrative construction, this was also its greatest weakness. It had no foundation of legal or historical evidence to build on, and did not itself follow norms of historical or legal objectivity. The artifacts were described by the ordinary people who donated them; "oral histories" were conducted by children, and further filtered through their written summaries. The kind of evidence on which truth commissions, tribunals, or other official mechanisms for accountability were based was missing. In the country's highly polarized context, the project was easily dismissed as narrowly partisan.

The Museum began to seek forensic evidence of the War's atrocities it hoped would be indisputable. Five years after its founding, it began identifying and exhuming mass graves, at first in and around Dhaka. The first was discovered accidentally, during construction for a mosque. The second was found in the underground tanks of an abandoned pump house. Barely two weeks before Akku arrived in Italy, he oversaw the exhumation of over 5000 bones and 70 skulls, most of which had been severed from the neck with a sharp instrument, or struck by something heavy.[9] But there were killing fields all over the country: as the oral histories started coming in, some stories pointed to possible locations. Over the next two decades, the Museum would excavate over 20 of them.

But the truths of what happened during the Liberation War remained deeply contested. The estimate the Museum promoted was that the Pakistani Army and its collaborators murdered over 3 million civilians and raped at least 200,000 women. The Museum fought hard for the violence to be acknowledged as a genocide, as opposed to a crime against humanity, a war crime, or any other atrocity, but the United Nations, as well as the US, which had supported the Bangladeshi fight against Pakistan, refused to. While the evidence from killing fields and widespread collective memory made mass violence indisputable, the specific numbers were easily contested; and the campaign for recognition of genocide got tangled up in global debates over the technical definitions of the term.[10]

Denied external support for genocide claims, the Liberation War Museum focused instead on its citizen movement to remember the country's violent past. With over 200 schools engaged across the country and thousands of participants at the annual freedom festival, it enacted the democratic participation it believed was necessary for preventing future violence, a strategy that would form an important inspiration for other Sites of Conscience.

From the Deep State to Street Protests: Memory and Democracy Building in Post-Communist Cultures

Perhaps the most closely watched transitions to democracy in the 1990s were in Eastern Europe and the former Soviet Union. New liberal democracies were emerging all across the region, buoyed by a common narrative about tearing down regimes based on denial and replacing them with "open societies" that would puncture denial through dialogue and debate. But the foundational tools of transitional justice would not be used here. After living through repression fueled and justified in part by official histories, "truth commissions," which produced a new state-sponsored, singular historical narrative, were unappealing.[11] Reckoning with the past required different types of memory movements from those organized in the Global South. The strategies developed in post-communist contexts would intertwine with others to shape the concept of Sites of Conscience and their role in the world.

Terezín Memorial, Czech Republic

Jan Munk was a man who took the long view. He responded to adversity with a resigned shrug and a warm smile. He provided an essential pragmatic counterweight to the rushed idealists in the rest of the group at Bellagio. He'd stayed silent through a particularly animated discussion around how our new museums could inspire a new global human rights consciousness, finally interrupting with: "But who is going to cut the grass?"

This wasn't a purely rhetorical question. The memorial site Jan managed – a sprawling former internment camp for Jews in the Czech Republic – did in fact have an enormous amount of grass, grass Jan had spent considerable energy trimming, to respect and make visible what had happened on the ground beneath. Terezín Memorial had been around longer than any other site represented around the table at Bellagio: nearly a half-century, the same age as Jan when he met us. Without a plan for long-term maintenance, Jan reminded us, all of our newly opened sites – and the ideals they represented – would wind up shaggy and neglected.

Terezín Memorial was preserved as a museum immediately after World War II, in 1947. Although it was associated with the Holocaust, Munk had only recently, in 1991, managed to open the first exhibit to mention Jews. He did it not through a massive and urgent public movement, but by leading a very small group of quiet, dedicated people, and by biding his time.

It is difficult to imagine how one would talk about Terezín during the War without talking about Jews. In 1940, one building, known as the Small Fortress, an 18th-century military installation, was converted into a Gestapo prison for political prisoners. The entire rest of the town of Terezín was evacuated by the Nazis in 1941 to establish a ghetto and concentration camp for Jews from surrounding Bohemia and Moravia, and later for Jews from other Nazi-occupied territories. At its height in 1942, nearly 60,000 Jews were held there. Thousands died from malnutrition, disease, or abuse; others were transported to death camps like Auschwitz. Terezín had a long history of false representation: in 1944, Nazis welcomed the Red Cross to the camp, displaying it as a "model Jewish settlement"; they also made a film about the camp promoting the health and success of the ghetto system.

Jan didn't need the state to tell him the story of Jews in Terezín. Both his parents were sent there in 1941, before being shipped to Auschwitz-Birkenau and other camps. Remarkably, they survived, and Jan was born in Prague in 1946. One year later, the official erasure of their experience began. After the War, civilians were invited to move back to Terezín, papering over the traces of the Jews held there before them. The Small Fortress building, not used to imprison Jews exclusively, as opposed to the entire surrounding town, which was, became the synecdoche for the story of Terezín. As sociologist Alena Heitlinger explains, the fortresses' "duality of purpose, and the fact that the town of Terezín was returned to civilian use after the end of World War II, made it relatively easy for the communist authorities to downplay the Jewish character of Terezín, and to lump prisoners from the Small and the Big Fortresses together as undifferentiated 'victims of fascism.'" [12]

In 1947, the Czech government passed an act to establish a "Memorial of National Suffering," in the Small Fortress, which officially opened as the "Museum of Oppression" in 1949. By 1952, a permanent exhibit on the Jews of Terezín was approved. But it was soon crushed by the weight of Cold

War political culture, which required totalizing narratives of a unified class struggle, or communist opposition to Naziism. The singular suffering and resistance of a persecuted minority had no place in a story of shared experience. As Jan explained, soured external relations with Israel and internal political trials "eventually made any presentation of Jewish persecution undesirable."[13] Throughout the communist period, sociologist Alena Heitlinger found, "Czech and Slovak school textbooks also did not use the word 'Jew,' not even in connection with the Shoah."[14] Academic and popular histories based national outrage on the figure of 360,000 Czechoslovak Nazi victims; but as Heitlinger observed,

> Rarely, however, and practically never when the relevant text is aimed at a wider audience, do we encounter the information that 240,000 to 255,000 of the total number of victims were persons of Jewish origin who constituted the majority of the Jews of the pre-war [Czechoslovak] republic.[15]

> This was the deeply dissonant reality for caretakers of many Holocaust memorials in communist Europe.

Throughout the 1960s and 1970s, Memorial staff and scholars struggled to install an exhibit there telling the story of Jewish persecution. In the early 1970s, a building in the town of Terezín became available for the museum's use; an ideal spot to tell the story of the Jewish ghetto. But, according to Jan, because they did not want to ban a Ghetto exhibit outright, state authorities installed their own exhibit in the space, entitled "Permanent Exposition of a History of the National Security Forces and Revolutionary Tradition of North Bohemia," ensuring that, in fact, the story of the Terezín as a ghetto would not be told in Terezín.[16] Despite this, the staff continued to conduct research on Jewish life and develop ideas for exhibiting it, with faith in a different future. So when Czechoslovakia's "Velvet Revolution" came, and the communist regime fell in 1989, they were ready. Jan was appointed director in 1990. A sociologist who was active in the Jewish community, he immediately put all the staff's decades of work into action. In the space of a year, he finally opened the Ghetto Museum, a half-century in the making. In addition to opening more identity-based, democratic discourse, the transition to democracy thawed relations both with Israel and Jewish tourism markets, inspiring new investment in Jewish memory sites. The Museum opened just in time for a visit from Israel's President Chaim Herzog in 1991.[17]

By the time Jan arrived in Bellagio in 1999, he had produced an avalanche of exhibits for the Museum. His team opened four separate permanent exhibitions, on music, fine art, literature, and theater in the Terezín Ghetto.[18] In a style parallel to the Tenement Museum's, it also constructed a replica of Ghetto barrack life, featuring packed triple bunk beds bearing Jews' personal belongings. For Jan, it wasn't a moment too soon: on the dark side of the new democracy, Jan saw neo-Nazi and racist nationalist movements growing. These movements, he later wrote, "may seem to be insignificant today in terms of their member count or political influence, but we know that circumstances could arise which could change this very quickly... what will be important is whether people will realize at that point what it is actually all about and what the threat is."[19]

Terezín's truths emerged from their communist chrysalis only when external conditions supported their life. But for the Gulag Museum in Russia, where memory thrived during the anti-communist movement, the final fall of the wall presented as many closings as openings.

The Gulag Museum at Perm-36, Russia

By the time I met him, Viktor Shmyrov had died twice. After each heart attack, he remembered floating happily away, only to have the voice of his wife and professional partner, Tatiana Kursina, call him back to earth. Russians were still refusing to reckon with the Gulag system that had killed millions of their friends and family, she reminded him. Until these dead were acknowledged, he had to stay alive.

Viktor and Tatiana had recently opened the only museum in a former Soviet prison camp, in a small town in the Perm region called Kuchino. Perm-36, as it was known, was one in a network of thousands of such camps spread across nine time zones, collectively referred to as the Gulag, after the Russian acronym for the "Main Administration of Corrective Labor Camps" that controlled it. Exploding in the 1930s, the Gulag served as both forced labor and social control, disappearing millions of people for any infraction against the state, major or minor, real or invented, to mine gold, cut timber, and build dams and canals, to grow the Soviet empire. After Stalin's death in 1953, Khrushchev shrank the system dramatically, and many Russians considered it closed. But the system remained a vital instrument of political repression through the late 1980s.[20] Viktor had been part of the struggle for democracy during that last decade, and with the fall of the Soviet Union and the Communist Party in 1991, he turned to building a lasting democratic culture, one based in a strong public memory of what can happen when democracy dies. That past, and potential future, would be expressed through the crumbling barracks and barbed wire that remained from Perm-36.

At our meeting in 1999, Viktor was most excited about the road. He had news of a new highway that would cut the time it took to get to Perm-36 in half. The whole way the Gulag worked was to build a system of repression that was far away and couldn't be seen; making it even more difficult to remember. So the road sounded to the rest of us like a great improvement; until Viktor explained that cutting the journey in half meant from four hours to two. And this was the journey not from Moscow, but from Perm, a medium-sized city, but hardly on the forefront of Russian public discourse. In the best case, a trickle of deeply dedicated visitors would come to the site to stand in Gulag prisoners' shoes.

Many scholars and journalists have described the period of Stalinist terror as unknowable.[21] Its scope was so vast, its violence so capricious, and its motivations so muddy that no one knew where to start trying to understand it. In the period before Stalin's death alone, over 20 million people were killed.[22] In particular, historian and memory scholar Alexander Etkind argues, the lack of clear lines between victims and perpetrators was deeply confusing – creating a simultaneous sense of collective guilt and victimhood:

> Though in every singular act of torture or murder the victim and the executioner were separated by an enormous distance, the fact was that a little later, in several months or years, the executioner would likely become a victim of the same treatment. This rotation makes it very difficult to reach any historical, philosophical, or theological – in fact, any rational – understanding of these events.[23]

After Stalin's death, Nikita Khrushchev and subsequent leaders officially dismantled the Gulag system and repudiated the worst of its violence. But the camps continued. Viktor, who came of age in the 1960s, had seen a new generation of dissidents, advocating for democracy and human rights, sent to camps as political prisoners. The practice only ended with Perestroika, when Gorbachev approved the release of political prisoners in 1987. That same year, a small group of young intellectuals formed a group called "To Keep Alive the Memory of the Victims of Repression," later renamed Memorial. Their initial goal was to create a monument to the victims of state terror. From the very beginning, they were attacked by the state: arrested for gathering signatures in support of the monument, and for leading a silent march for the idea. So by the time Memorial held its founding conference, its goals for remembering the past were inextricably intertwined with goals for change in the future. As journalist David Satter observed, "Memorial was also for a time, the only vehicle in the country for expressing political opposition other than the Democratic Union, the small, self-proclaimed political party. The political potential of Memorial was becoming obvious."[24] Branches of Memorial had proliferated across the country. In addition to advocating for the monument, Memorial's founding platform included publishing the *Gulag Archipelago* of Alexander Solzhenitsyn and freeing some dissidents that were still imprisoned.[25]

Thus, in Russia, the movement for democracy was waged in large part as a movement for memory. As in the case of the District Six Museum, the Memorial movement was not commemorating a bygone system, but activating the memory of that system to mobilize people around current political change, in order to eradicate it and prevent its recurrence in another form. With the movement's first goal achieved – the fall of communism – Memorial needed to evolve to build a post-Soviet society. As it turned out, popular energy around remembering Soviet terror was highest when the system was weakening, but still in place.

Whereas in South Africa the restoration of democracy triggered a rush to memorialize, in Russia, once the immediate goal of democracy was won, memory was quickly forgotten.[26] Memorial continued its work; but memory was no longer a popular movement. Scholars of post-Soviet culture have attributed Russians' turn away from remembering state terror to the great cultural shock brought about by the transition from communism to capitalism, a rupture that turned people's worlds upside down overnight and forced their focus onto everyday survival.[27] Journalist Anne Applebaum observed," During the late 1980s, when perestroika was just beginning, Gulag survivors' memoirs sold millions of copies, and a new revelation about the past could sell out a newspaper."[28] But in the mid-late 1990s, "in the scramble to make a living, the subject has simply dropped out of most people's line of vision. There are almost no monuments, few museums, only a handful of interested historians."[29] By 1997, just before Viktor came to Bellagio, his colleague Lev Rozgon had summed it up this way to Applebaum: "People don't want to hear any more about the past… People are tired of the past."[30]

Absent popular pressure, the state did its part to close the books: police archives were not opened; no formal investigations were launched. Etkind and journalist Masha Gessen, among others, attribute this to the chaos prosecutions would wreak, with such a huge proportion of citizens playing the role of both perpetrator and victim; there seemed to be no one outside of the system, no way to excise the tumor of repression.[31] As a result, former Soviets were left to build a new society with no common understanding of what happened to them. For Etkind, even in 2013,

> the only certainty about the Soviet catastrophe, apart from its massive scale, is its very uncertainty. We do not have anything like a full list of victims; we do not have anything like a full list of executioners; and we do not have adequate memorials, museums, and monuments, which could stabilize the understanding of these events for generations to come.[32]

In this context, Perm-36 had a special role to play. It was not a manufactured memorial, but evidence of the system and how it worked. Perhaps most important, it was one of the few camps that stayed open past the purported restoration of "normalcy" after Stalin's death, becoming one of the country's main political prisons. While ruins of Stalin's labor camps littered the landscape, Perm-36 stood strong: a new maximum-security section for political dissidents was added as late as 1980, and the camp did not close until the end of 1987. Perm-36 testified to the endurance of the Gulag system, and the ways repression can evolve and take different forms through different regimes. This was a particularly important lesson for post-Soviet society.

Viktor was a leader in the Perm chapter of Memorial, which, in 1992, was given responsibility for preserving the camp. By 1994, it managed to establish a Museum organization capable of receiving and managing funds. While local residents had stripped the camp of most of its material, including destroying buildings, by 1998, the Museum had recreated two of the barracks. And it had begun collecting artifacts from farther-flung camps with even less possibility of visitorship.

In addition to being so far from the nearest city, the camp was in hostile territory. The community of Kuchino was dominated by camp guards and their families. Despite the blurred lines of Russian repression, a stark division between prisoners and guards remained. Recognizing the need for some form of reconciliation, and for a collective investment in the project, Viktor and his colleagues reached out to local guards to participate in ex-prisoners' pilgrimages to the camp. Some did, though the interactions were uneasy.

The main task for Viktor and his colleagues was not only to remember totalitarianism, the only system most Russians had ever known; but to teach democracy, to build a lasting culture of democracy that would serve as the bulwark against totalitarianism in any new forms. Museum directors brought students through the cells and work yards, and they discussed the human experience of living there and how the camp fit into the larger system of Soviet repression. Using the history of the camp and interviews with their own families, students conducted workshops to define their vision of democracy and identify how they could promote it. In the "I Have Rights" program, students were asked to write or draw their associations with the word "freedom" on a large piece of construction paper and pin it up on a wall. Students then debated each other's concepts of freedom, and, reflecting on the lessons from the camp and their own families, they debated what it takes to support and protect those visions of freedom. With programs like these, the Gulag Museum would be a training site for a new citizenry that could sustain a democratic society, a place to practice how to debate, question, and organize to address the challenges this society would face.

Official Heritage Wrestles with Reparations: Slavery, Truth, and Accountability in the US and Senegal

Mixed in with the movement leaders, human rights activists, and pioneering private museum directors who first gathered in Italy were two people representing national governments; governments that would not have described themselves in transition. In the absence of truth commissions or legal prosecutions, official state heritage bodies are the closest thing nations have to arbiters of historical accountability. International heritage organizations, led by collections of national governments, can provide external pressure and establish criteria for "outstanding universal value," in the terms of UNESCO's World Heritage Program.[33] As the international movements for accountability gained strength, and the US refused any obligation to them, the heritage bodies of the US and Senegal navigated contrasting paths. Where the US National Park Service offered truth in lieu of accountability, the Slave House, a World Heritage Site run by the Ministry of Culture in Senegal, demanded accountability as a prerequisite for truth.

National Park Service, US

In the process of organizing the conference, the person I feared meeting the most was Marie Rust, Director of the Northeast Region of the US National Park Service. While the Park Service is best known for natural sites like the Grand Canyon, it is also the United States' official heritage body. It's charged with telling the official story of the country to its citizens, which includes deciding what buildings, fields, and factories are worthy of preservation as American heritage. Marie oversaw over 200 historic and natural sites and nearly 1,000 landmarks, from Maine to Virginia, including the Statue of Liberty and Ellis Island, commanding a budget of over 200 million dollars and a staff of thousands. I braced myself, anticipating such a powerful bureaucrat would throw her weight around. As it turned out, she had little weight to throw, but used it brilliantly: the tiny hand I shook in greeting belonged to a diminutive woman in her 70s, wearing black leather pants and a smooth silver beehive that nearly doubled her height. Teetering in her stilettos, she affected a frailty that obscured her power. As we picked our way across the cobblestones, she leaned on my arm and described the small revolution she was starting in the Park Service.

Marie was the sole representative of the US government to this international group. As the rest of the world was embracing a new era of conscience and accountability, the US remained one of the few countries refusing to join the International Criminal Court. Calls for reparations for slavery, Jim Crow, or any of the manifestations of America's structural racism had never been heeded.

On one significant occasion, the US government admitted wrongdoing, and submitted to demands for reparations: for the internment of Japanese Americans during World War II. After the bombing of Pearl Harbor, the Roosevelt administration enacted a series of measures to control suspected "enemy aliens," focusing on people of Japanese descent, constructing a series of "relocation centers." More than 110,000 Japanese Americans, most of whom were native-born US citizens, were forced from their homes to camps in remote locations, such as the Manzanar War Relocation Center in the desert of Independence, California.[34]

As early as 1969, survivors of Manzanar began making what would become an annual pilgrimage to the site that continues to this day. Ritual returns to camp sites, and demands for their preservation, became a critical component of a larger national campaign for the recognition of the violation of Japanese Americans' civil rights and its long-term consequences.[35] In 1972, Manzanar was named a California Historical Landmark; in 1985, it won the higher status of National Historic Landmark.[36] In 1988, President Ronald Reagan signed the Civil Liberties Act, establishing a reparations package for internees that included both material reparations, in the form of a $20,000 payment to eligible victims, as well as symbolic reparations, in the form of an official government apology. The Act also created a public education fund "so as to prevent the recurrence of any similar event."[37] This included federal support for the preservation of camp sites.[38]

Marie Rust brought us big news from the US government. In 1992, Manzanar had been designated a National Historic Site, the highest level of government recognition and support, to be administered by the National Park Service.[39] Park staff were now in the process of building its interpretive center – the place that would tell the public the story of what happened there and why it mattered – which would open in 2004. The person to lead the charge had just been named, which I imagined would be someone active in the redress movement, or someone who had led the pilgrimages that maintained Manzanar's memory. Instead, Marie proudly proclaimed it would be the white man who had most recently served as superintendent of the Grand Canyon. I was horrified. But Marie explained that within the logic of the Park Service, this meant they were putting their best man on the job. The Grand Canyon superintendent had more responsibility and accountability than any other in the country. His appointment signaled that this site of national cruelty would be accorded the same value as its most prized natural treasure. Although Manzanar was outside Marie's Northeast region, so was not under her care, she hoped it could pave the way for confronting dark histories in her territory. Hers, after all, was the soil of American slavery.

By the time of the Bellagio meeting, the slavery reparations campaign was already centuries old; but at the end of the 1990s, the US government remained unmoved. Representative John Conyers Jr.'s "reparations bill" – a proposal merely to form a commission to study the issue – had been introduced and rejected for ten years straight. There was no federal mandate to acknowledge and repair the harms of slavery. Instead, what grew in the late 1990s was a state-sponsored celebration of Americans' success in resisting or rejecting it.

In 1998, Congress passed the National Underground Railroad Network to Freedom Act, creating a "Network to Freedom" in the Park Service with the mission to "honor, preserve and promote the history of resistance to enslavement through escape and flight, which continues to inspire people worldwide," by identifying, preserving, and interpreting sites associated with the Underground Railroad.[40] The National Park Service's first African American director, Robert Stanton, appointed by President Bill Clinton the year before, presided over the network's first event in the fall of 2000.[41] Although it refused to support research on reparations, Congress commanded the Park Service to study places where Americans might remember the Civil Rights Movement, such as the Selma to Montgomery trail, Little Rock High School, and Martin Luther King, Jr.'s birthplace, church, and gravesite in Atlanta.[42] These sites, which were in fact places of state repression, were to be held up as symbols of resistance, helping to portray Americans as a people who rejected racist policies. While NPS's chief historian argued that at the new Little Rock Central High School National Historic Site, "There is no way to sugarcoat the racism that drove white citizens of Little Rock to protest the desegregation of their Central High School," the park was not established to reckon with this racism or its legacies. Instead, its mission was to celebrate America's history of anti-racism, to "interpret [Central High School's] role in the integration of public school and the development of the Civil Rights movement in the United States."[43]

In this moment of the late 1990s, then, the focus of Park Service system-wide attention on racism was to establish anti-racism as a fundamental piece of American heritage and identity. Foregrounding resistance and leadership is critical for a public memory of the Civil Rights Movement that can build a civic culture around resisting oppression. But in the absence of any official reckoning with the racist structures that requires that resistance, the Park Service's anti-racist national identity was being built on a false foundation.

Establishing new sites like Little Rock, especially when they celebrated American moral progress, was fresh and exciting work that brought the Park Service, and its Congressional supporters' happy headlines. Dismantling denial operating at existing historic sites, where racism had long been erased, was a much harder grind. One lightning rod became Civil War battlefield sites. According to Dwight Pitcaithley, who served as the Park Service's chief historian starting in 1995, before he came on "the NPS avoided all mention of the causes of the war in its exhibits, films, and publications."[44] In 1998 – the very same year the new African American director of the Park Service was publicly championing the creation of a new American public memory of resistance to slavery – a group of Civil War battlefield site superintendents held a small internal meeting in Nashville to discuss how they might, for the first time, mention slavery in their historical explanations of the Civil War. The meeting became a news story, prompting an avalanche of protest letters, many of which, Pitcaithley recounts, condemned the Park Service for daring to "change history so that it is politically correct."[45]

Within this fraught landscape, Marie Rust saw possibilities popping up. But she also saw that to coalesce these possibilities into a movement with any force, she'd have to transform the structure surrounding them. NPS history staff as a whole was neither ready nor willing to reckon with America's history of racial violence. A later study found an entrenched culture of "fixed and fearful interpretation," a "tendency toward 'defensive history' that seems to stem from a certain timidity in the face of controversy or criticism."[46] Further, the administrative structure of the Park Service's vast bureaucracy didn't have procedures for confronting denial. It had a mechanism for acquiring new properties, but not for breaking silences at its existing ones. "Unlike for the various components of our physical plant," one administrator explained, "there is no administrative system that requires and enforces the periodic maintenance and replacement of our intellectual infrastructure."[47] So for instance, there was no established path for opening new narratives at plantation sites about enslaved peoples on the land they worked; or about genocide and resistance of Native Americans at forts and missions, or, for that matter, on any of the lands originally theirs. But here too Marie saw cracks that might be widened with more support.

The moment required unequivocal, strong direction, which was just Marie's style. She supported site leaders moving in the right direction, like at the Hampton National Historic Site, an early 19th-century estate in Maryland, who had uncovered slave quarters there and were exploring how to integrate them into a tour that had completely erased the human cost of the opulence in which visitors delighted. And she laid down the law with anyone dragging their feet, like the superintendent of Independence National Historical Park in Philadelphia, who tried to duck openly discussing the enslaved people who had worked the land right across from the Liberty Bell as the American Revolution was being fomented.[48]

The Park Service armed itself to the teeth with sanctioned scholarship and primary sources for its tentative ventures into confronting slavery and its legacies. Pitcaithley was ultimately able to build public support for Civil War battlefield reinterpretation by arguing that "As a society, we cannot afford to let our federal agencies promote interpretations of the past that are no longer accepted by the scholarly community," and insisting that "the revised or new exhibits and publications clearly reflect the scholarship of secession over the past decade."[49] In this framing, accountability begins with a truth sanctioned by a body of experts; this truth was a prerequisite for identifying who should be held responsible and how. But in Africa, where the trauma of slavery originated, the Maison des Esclaves flipped the script: accountability must come first. The truth would follow.

The Maison des Esclaves (Slave House), Senegal

As Marie Rust struggled to open tiny slave outbuildings on massive plantation sites in the US National Park Service – no more than architectural footnotes acknowledging slavery – Eloi Coly, her counterpart at Senegal's Ministry of

Culture, sat on a booming slavery tourism industry. In the few years before Eloi met Marie in Bellagio, the number of middle-class African American leisure travelers — a demographic the Park Service labored to attract — visiting West Africa exploded.[50] As Salamishah Tillet argues, these were "African American heritage tourists who feel compelled to travel to Africa in order to supplant the national amnesia of slavery in the United States and locate alternative ancestral origins."[51] Millions of visitors turned to one small site, known as the Maison des Esclaves, or the Slave House, as a rare material remnant of the entire slave trade.

The Maison des Esclaves sits on Gorée Island, about a 20-minute ferry ride from Senegal's capital city of Dakar. The whole island is just over a tenth of a mile square, dominated by a large fort, crisscrossed by a few winding, carless streets lined with low, late 18th- and early 19th-century houses. One of these is the Slave House. It is tiny compared to the vast burden of history it bears: standing just two stories tall, it fronts a small courtyard that could maybe fit two Fiats. The house is dwarfed by the massive Cape Coast Castle complex in Ghana, whose dungeons held more than a thousand people at once. But Cape Coast lay several hours on questionable roads from the Ghanaian capital of Accra, difficult for dignitaries to make a brief stop at during tours of the region. Gorée, by contrast, was a quick ride from Dakar on a cheap and accessible ferry. Thus, while Cape Coast may have welcomed more tourists year over year, the Maison des Esclaves became the preeminent symbolic site of sorrow and reckoning for the centuries-long brutality and legacy of slavery.[52] It was central to the Gorée Island World Heritage Site, granted that status by the United Nations Educational, Scientific and Cultural Organization (UNESCO) over 20 years before our Bellagio meeting. This was the highest international recognition that could be awarded a historic site, one none of the other sites present at Bellagio enjoyed.

The personal scale and intimacy of the Slave House highlights the individual human cruelty of this vast global system. Tours usher visitors to the dank, dark rooms on the lower floors, less than 300 square feet each, and describe how men and women were segregated and shackled as they awaited the ships that would transport them into American slavery. Enslaved people were then brought out into the courtyard, while merchants standing on the upper balconies negotiated their sale. Once sold, people were marched one by one through a small opening at the back of the courtyard and directly onto a ship bound for the Americas. Tours referred to this portal as the Door of No Return.

The Door became perhaps the principal global site of mourning and reckoning for the Atlantic slave trade for international dignitaries. Nelson Mandela came in 1991, one year after his release from prison; in a widely circulated story, he spent a few minutes alone in the space tours described as a punishment cell, emerging visibly shaken. Pope John Paul II visited in 1992 to make a formal apology for the slave trade on behalf of the Catholic Church.[53]

One year later, President George Bush, the first sitting Republican President to visit Africa at all, came to Gorée to give a spirited condemnation of slavery, stopping short of apologizing for the US role in it.[54] In 1998, the year before Eloi Coly came to Italy, President Bill Clinton peeked through the Door of No Return and, upholding American tradition, did not apologize; though he had recently apologized for the internment of Japanese Americans and for the Tuskegee Experiment. He instead admitted, "America's struggle to overcome slavery and its legacy forms one of the most difficult chapters of that history."[55] Most days, Eloi tried not to get trampled by the 300 or so tourists, mostly Americans and Europeans, disgorged from the Dakar ferry twice each day to cram into the Slave House's tiny courtyard. The best Eloi could do was bark from a bullhorn, and manage their moment at the Door of No Return, which stood at the end of a narrow passageway requiring visitors to line up single file.

Eloi had arrived in Bellagio at a moment when the question of who spoke for the site, and who the site spoke for, was at the center of a global controversy over historical truth and accountability for slavery.[56] The site was backed by national and international governments, sharing Gorée Island's World Heritage Site status. Despite this thick officialdom, the sole "voice" of the site – the person who gave every tour – was Boubacar Joseph N'Diaye, a single impassioned individual who lacked any of the formal training that would make him recognized as a historian by Senegalese or world heritage bodies. But N'Diaye had saved the Slave House from ruin. This earned him the right to be its storyteller, nominally and nervously monitored by Eloi in his position as official heritage arbiter at the Ministry of Culture.

N'Diaye grew up hearing the residents of Gorée discuss the island's role in the Atlantic Slave Trade, and noting how accounts of the site – oral and textual, Senegalese and European – clashed.[57] Once Senegal won independence in 1960, N'Diaye saw a chance to secure the site's truth. In 1962, he opened the doors of the house as the Maison des Esclaves. At that time, almost no other state historic sites commemorated slavery in West Africa; Cape Coast Castle in Ghana didn't open until 1970. Alex Haley's bestselling novel *Roots*, which broke open popular discussion of the slave trade, wouldn't be published for more than a decade. Too few historians anywhere researched the Atlantic Slave Trade for it to constitute a recognized field.

In the decades that N'Diaye grew the Maison des Esclaves into a global pilgrimage site, academic research on the slave trade had also developed. N'Diaye's narrative centered on the story of how 15 million Africans had been sold into slavery from the site. But evidence mounted that neither the House, nor the island of Gorée, nor indeed the entire Senegambia region, played as significant role in the Atlantic slave trade as N'Diaye, or even UNESCO claimed, having granted the island World Heritage status as the "largest slave-trading centre on the African coast."[58] In 1995, US historian Philip Curtin publicly called out the Slave House as a "hoax" in a post on the H-Net Africa listserv, an early online forum for scholars of the slave trade.[59] Curtin's post was picked up in an article in *Le Monde* in 1996, from which it sparked controversy in academia and the media. The stakes were high: for the sanctity of memory in the African diaspora, for the Senegalese tourism industry, and for the perennial struggle for accountability. That same year, UNESCO doubled down on the Slave House, launching a partnership with the World Tourism Organization for a Program for Cultural Tourism on the Slave Route in Africa, in which the Slave House would be prominently featured.

The facts, as American and European historians had come to understand them, were these: first, the entire Atlantic slave trade sold just over 12 million people during its entire history, only 6% from the Senegambia region.[60] The "Slave House" was constructed for a merchant family called Pépin between 1780 and 1784, in the final years of the French slave trade, suggesting that even if it had been wholly dedicated to exporting enslaved people, it could not have exported very many. While families like the Pépin would certainly have owned people as slaves, historians argued that based on other such houses, the rooms N'Diaye identified as holding cells for hundreds of enslaved people would have been living quarters for a handful. Perhaps most devastating to the emotional meaning of the Slave House was the argument that the "Door of no Return" was never crossed by any enslaved people at all, as the rocks beneath it would have prevented any ships from coming near. Any people sold into slavery from Gorée, historians contended, were more likely to have been held and resold in one of the forts or other structures on the island. The academic historical community's most recent accounting estimated between 30,000 and 40,000 traded from the island during its entire history. Most of those enslaved from the region would have been traded from two other nearby ports.[61]

The Senegalese government responded quickly to Curtin's accusation by convening a conference of Senegalese and European academic historians one year later, in 1997, to settle the question of the Slave House's integrity. Two main messages emerged from the conference proceedings and publication: history and memory were two separate things with two separate values, and the Slave House had value both for its history and its memory. Mbaye Gueye of Cheikh Anta Diop University in Dakar sought to reestablish the House's historical value through his discovery of new evidence from an archive in Nantes that over 100,000 slaves had been sold from Gorée between 1763 and 1775.[62] Eloi's superior at the Ministry of Culture, Hamady Boucoum, described N'Diaye as "the main architect of the defense of the memory of the Atlantic slave trade, the man most fervent and unrelenting against any revisionism."[63] But conference convenors gently pried data-based truth from N'Diaye's narrative, commending him for "leading a fine battle of Memory," as philosopher Djibril Samb put it, despite being "not exactly one of us, the academic community."[64]

The question was, what truth did data on the slave trade produce, given the context of its production? The narrative of the Slave House was primarily produced for European and American tourists: visits to the site were not a regular part of Dakar school curricula, and few locals visited. According to Dalla Malé Fofana, "coverage of high-profile visitors to the House of Slaves is the only occasion for this part of our history to be mentioned in the media."[65] The imperial histories of the people and institutions producing the knowledge shaped the knowledge produced, and its legitimacy in colonies living with imperial legacies. As Samb, the editor of the conference publication, noted in the introduction, "it is absolutely necessary to leave behind the European and general western perspective. An African perspective must be laid out, not only on the basis of a rigorous historiography, but also by becoming fully aware that the history of the Slave Trade has not yet been written and that it will only be done to the highest standard by Africans, not because they are professionally superior to their western colleagues, but because they are called to it by their relationship to the history of the Slave Trade, as well as its place in African history."[66]

And what did data really do? As philosopher Achille Mbembe contended on the H-Africa listserv, in response to Curtin's 1995 post, "It isn't possible to comprehend the significance of Gorée for African-Americans if one considers it only a matter of numbers."[67] Many scholars and others facing the total erasure of Black experiences and voices in historical archives of the Atlantic slave trade have produced a different intellectual tradition of historical truth, what Saidiya Hartman calls "critical fabulation," which aims "to imagine what cannot be verified... a history of an unrecoverable past; it is a narrative of what might have been or could have been; it is a history written with and against the archive."[68] Bocoum asserted that "the discourse commemorating this function of the island [the slave trade] has never claimed to obey the rules of academic knowledge production and, consequently, cannot be measured by this yardstick."[69]

In fact, in some ways, it was the very lack of verifiable data and material remains that defined the slave trade and its legacies; that was part of what should be remembered and preserved. Poet and novelist Dionne Brand reflected on the Door for her own life in the Caribbean and Canada, in full knowledge of the controversy over authenticity. For Brand,

> The door exists as an absence. A thing in fact which we do not know about, a place we do not know. Yet it exists as the ground we walk....
> One does not return to the diaspora with good news from the door except the news that it exists and that its existence is the truth.[70]

Dalla Malé Fofana, who first saw the Door on a school trip, explains that for locals,

Both the place and the events of the slave trade haunt the Senegalese

> cultural memory, ... [the Door of No Return] is... an image that we carry within us, defining us as Senegalese.[71]

This haunting was internalized through the sound of Ndiaye's storytelling; Fofana remembers growing up with his "firm and strong voice re-telling his well-known narration that educated locals know so well even without having been there."[72]

Western-defined forensic truth barely made a dent in the story of the Slave House. After the release of countless media articles on the controversy, a full publication of the conference proceedings, and articles by other academic historians, the official interpretation of the Slave House did not change. UNESCO's World Heritage designation and description remained intact, and N'Diaye continued his tours. Guidebooks and academic articles continued to embrace the Slave House's importance in the history of slave trade, whether statistically or symbolically.[73]

This was perhaps a reflection of how weak specific truth claims are, in the absence of accountability. In Argentina and Bangladesh, forensic truth was the prerequisite for establishing accountability; if the bodies, or the records, were uncovered, the perpetrators could be prosecuted. For N'Diaye and other defenders of the Slave House, accountability for the larger crime of the Atlantic Slave trade was required for any specific smaller truth claims to be taken seriously. "The world has never come to terms with the enormity of this evil," N'Diaye told a *New York Times* reporter in 1998. "The perpetrators have never been held to account. Others may not be able to bear hearing what happened here, but I will be talking about it until I die."[74] Until recognition of the slave trade was linked to accountability, there was no point in quibbling over the details. As Eloi explained in a 2013 interview, "Two thousand slaves, or two million slaves, it's the same, it's the same exactly in terms of principle."[75]

~

Bonding together participants' radically different experiences and visions for memory – born from liberal democracies and Islamic states, transitional justice and traditional heritage, grassroots movements, and government projects – would take intense organization and force of will. Ruth ran the meetings with a drive that puzzled conference center staff, accustomed as they were to guests enjoying lingering lunches and extended coffee breaks. We spent each long day listening intently to each other, straining through struggles with English and accents, to understand the specific historical denial we each grappled with, and our radically different ideas for facing it.

Over the course of the week, and for decades afterwards, our approaches collided and intertwined around three key ideas – memory, dialogue, and action – and how they could combine to build lasting cultures of conscience. After dinner each night, Ruth and I huddled in an office we commandeered from one of the center staff and typed up our notes, teasing out ideas, conflicts, and connections. We would not leave without a collective vision, and an agreement to work together. We had six days.

Notes

1 Nayanika Mookherjee, "'Never Again': Aesthetics of 'Genocidal' Cosmopolitanism and the Bangladesh Liberation War Museum," *The Journal of the Royal Anthropological Institute* 17, no. s1 (2011): S79.

2 Caitlin Reiger, "Fighting Past Impunity in Bangladesh: A National Tribunal for the Crimes of 1971," International Center for Transitional Justice, July 2010, https://www.ictj.org/sites/default/files/ICTJ-BGD-NationalTribunal-Briefing-2 010-English.pdf

3 Srinath Raghavan, *1971: A Global History of the Creation of Bangladesh* (Cambridge: Harvard University Press, 2013). Raghavan writes of this fraught moment: "The prolonged liberation war also created the cauldron in which the witches' brew of post-independence politics came to a boil. The tensions between the army and the civilian leaders, between the Awami League and the leftist parties, between the variety of militias, and between the various factions of the Awami League all germinated during those nine months in 1971. In effect, the liberation war created the background conditions for the collapse of democracy in Bangladesh."

4 Akku Chowdhury, "A Citizen's Effort," *The Daily Star*, March 26, 2010, http://archive.thedailystar.net/magazine/2010/03/04/anniversary.htm; Brandon Hamber, Liz Ševčenko, and Ereshnee Naidu, "Utopian Dreams or Practical Possibilities? The Challenges of Evaluating the Impact of Memorialization in Societies in Transition," *International Journal of Transitional Justice* 4, no. 3 (November 2010): 397–420.

5 Reiger, "Fighting Past Impunity in Bangladesh."

6 Chowdhury, "A Citizen's Effort."

7 Nayanika Mookherjee, *The Spectral Wound: Sexual Violence, Public Memories, and the Bangladesh War of 1971* (Durham: Duke University Press, 2015); Mookherjee, "'Never Again,'" S82.

8 Chowdhury, "A Citizen's Effort."

9 Akku Chowdury, "Keeping the Spirit of the Liberation War Alive," *The Daily Star*, March 26, 2009, https://www.thedailystar.net/news-detail-81320

10 Sarmila Bose, "The Question of Genocide and the Quest for Justice in the 1971 War," *Journal of Genocide Research* 13, no. 4 (November 2011): 393–419. Bose writes: "Over time, the claim of 'genocide of three million' took on the status of a sacred *mantra* in the popular telling and political culture of Bangladesh, the ritual chanting of which signals a particular political allegiance. It acquired a political meaning in Bangladesh that has little to do with the definition of genocide in international law or the veracity of the casualty figure of three million."

11 Ruti G. Teitel, "Transitional Justice Genealogy," *Harvard Human Rights Journal* 16 (2003): 79.

12 Alena Heitlinger, "Politicizing Jewish Memory in Postwar Czechoslovakia," *East European Jewish Affairs* 35, no. 2 (December 2005): 135–53.

13 Jan Munk, "The Terezín Memorial in the Year 2000," *Museum International* 53, no. 1 (2001): 17–20.

14 Heitlinger, "Politicizing Jewish Memory."

15 Ibid.

16 Jan Munk, "The Terezín Memorial: Its Development and Its Visitors," *Museum Management and Curatorship* 17, no. 1 (1998): 3–19.

17 Ibid.

18 Munk, "The Terezín Memorial in the Year 2000."

19 Jan Munk, "Activities of Terezín Memorial," *The Public Historian* 30, no. 1 (February 2008): 78. This wording is taken from an unpublished earlier version in my files, in his original English before it was edited by journal staff, which I think reflects Jan's speech and intention better.

20 Anne Applebaum, *Gulag: A History* (New York: Doubleday, 2003).
21 Alexander Etkind, *Warped Mourning: Stories of the Undead in the Land of the Unburied* (Stanford: Stanford University Press, 2013); Masha Gessen, *The Future Is History: How Totalitarianism Reclaimed Russia* (New York: Riverhead Books, 2017); David Satter, *It Was a Long Time Ago, and It Never Happened Anyway: Russia and the Communist Past* (New Haven: Yale University Press, 2012).
22 Applebaum, *Gulag: A History.*
23 Etkind, *Warped Mourning*, 8.
24 Satter, *It Was a Long Time Ago*, 38.
25 Ibid.
26 Ibid, 40.
27 Gessen, *The Future Is History*; Satter, *It Was a Long Time Ago.*
28 Anne Applebaum, "A City Where People Won't Forget," *New Statesman*, July 31, 1998, 24–5.
29 Ibid.
30 Ibid.
31 Gessen, *The Future Is History*; Etkind, *Warped Mourning*; Daniel Chirot, Gi-Wook Shin, and Daniel Sneider, eds., *Confronting Memories of World War II: European and Asian Legacies* (Seattle: University of Washington Press, 2014).
32 Etkind, *Warped Mourning*, 10.
33 "Policies Regarding Credibility of the World Heritage List," World Heritage Policy Compendium, United Nations Educational, Scientific and Cultural Organization, https://whc.unesco.org/en/compendium/100
34 "Japanese-American Internment During World War II," National Archives, https://www.archives.gov/education/lessons/japanese-relocation; "A Brief History of Japanese American Relocation During World War II," National Park Service, https://www.nps.gov/articles/historyinternment.htm; Roger Daniels, Sandra C. Taylor, and Harry H. L. Kitano, *Japanese Americans: From Relocation to Redress*, rev. ed. (Seattle: University of Washington Press, 2001).
35 Alice Yang Murray, *Historical Memories of the Japanese American Internment and the Struggle for Redress* (Stanford: Stanford University Press, 2008).
36 "Park Statistics," Manzanar, National Park Service, https://home.nps.gov/manz/learn/management/statistics.htm.
37 Eric K. Yamamoto and Liann Ebesugawa, "Report on Redress: The Japanese American Internment," in *The Handbook of Reparations*, ed. Pablo De Greiff (Oxford: Oxford University Press, 2006), 257–83.
38 Yang Murray, *Historical Memories.*
39 "Park Statistics," Manzanar, National Park Service.
40 "National Underground Railroad Network to Freedom," Network to Freedom, National Park Service, https://www.nps.gov/orgs/1205/index.htm
41 "Our History," Network to Freedom, National Park Service, https://www.nps.gov/orgs/1205/our-history.htm
42 "Recent Theme Studies," National Historic Landmarks, National Park Service, https://www.nps.gov/subjects/nationalhistoriclandmarks/recent-theme-studies.htm. According to the NPS, "In 1999, the US Congress directed the National Park Service to conduct a multi-state study of civil rights sites to determine their national significance. NPS partnered with the Organization of American Historians to develop an overview of civil rights history entitled, Civil Rights in America: A Framework for Identifying Significant Sites (2002, rev. 2008). The framework recommended that a National Historic Landmarks theme study based on provisions of the Civil Rights Act of 1964, the Voting Rights Act of 1965, and the Fair Housing Act of 1968 be prepared to identify potentially nationally significant sites related to desegregation of schools, public accommodations, voting rights, housing, and equal employment."

43 Dwight T. Pitcaithley, "The National Park Service and the Civil Rights Movement: Remembering a Difficult Past," *Juniata Voices*, 2005, https://www.juniata.edu/offices/juniata-voices/past-version/media/2005-dwight-pitcaithley.pdf; "Management," Little Rock Central High School, National Park Service, https://www.nps.gov/chsc/learn/management/index.htm.

44 Dwight T. Pitcaithley, "Public Education and the National Park Service: Interpreting the Civil War," *Perspectives on American History*, American Historical Association, November 1, 2007, https://www.historians.org/publications-and-directories/perspectives-on-history/november-2007/public-education-and-the-national-park-service-interpreting-the-civil-war#note4. See also J. Christian Spielvogel, *Interpreting Sacred Ground: The Rhetoric of National Civil War Parks and Battlefields* (Tuscaloosa: University of Alabama Press, 2013).

45 Pitcaithley, "Public Education and the National Park Service."

46 Anne Mitchell Whisnant, Marla R. Miller, Gary B. Nash, and David Thelen, "Imperiled Promise: The State of History in the National Park Service," Organization of American Historians, https://www.oah.org/site/assets/documents/Imperiled_Promise.pdf. See also James Oliver Horton, "Slavery in American History: An Uncomfortable National Dialogue," in *Slavery and Public History: The Tough Stuff of American Memory*, eds. James Oliver Horton and Lois E. Horton (New York: The New Press, 2006), 35–56, and Gary B. Nash, "For Whom Will the Liberty Bell Toll? From Controversy to Cooperation," in *Slavery and Public History: The Tough Stuff of American Memory*, eds. James Oliver Horton and Lois E. Horton (New York: The New Press, 2006), 75–102.

47 John H. Sprinkle, Jr., "Planned Obsolescence: Maintenance of the National Park Service's History Infrastructure," *The George Wright Forum* 34, no. 3 (2017): 254–60.

48 Whisnant et al., "Imperiled Promise"; Nash, "For Whom Will the Liberty Bell Toll?"

49 Pitcaithley, "Public Education and the National Park Service."

50 Bayo Holsey, *Routes of Remembrance: Refashioning the Slave Trade in Ghana* (Chicago: University of Chicago Press, 2008); Paulla A. Ebron, "Tourists as Pilgrims: Commercial Fashioning of Transatlantic Politics," *American Ethnologist* 26, no. 4 (1999): 910–32.

51 Salamisha Tillet, "In the Shadow of the Castle: (Trans)Nationalism, African American Tourism, and Gorée Island," *Research in African Literatures* 40, no. 4 (Winter 2009): 122–41.

52 Katharina Schramm, *African Homecoming: Pan-African Ideology and Contested Heritage* (Walnut Creek: Left Coast Press, 2010); Holsey, *Routes of Remembrance*.

53 Howard W. French, "Gorée Island Journal; The Evil That Was Done Senegal: A Guided Tour," *New York Times*, March 6, 1998, https://www.nytimes.com/1998/03/06/world/goree-island-journal-the-evil-that-was-done-senegal-a-guided-tour.html

54 Bradford Vivan, "The Paradox of Regret: Remembering and Forgetting the History of Slavery in George W. Bush's Gorée Island Address," *History and Memory: Studies in Representation of the Past* 24, no. 1 (Spring-Summer 2012): 5–38.

55 William J. Clinton, "Remarks at Gorée Island, Senegal," April 2, 1998, The American Presidency Project, https://www.presidency.ucsb.edu/documents/remarks-goree-island-senegal

56 Charles Forsdick, "*Cette île n'est pas une île*: Locating Gorée," in *At the Limits of Memory: Legacies of Slavery in the Francophone World*, eds. Nicola Frith and Kate Hodgson (Liverpool: Liverpool University Press, 2015), 131–53.

57 A French guidebook from 1958 (Gilbert Houlet's *Afrique Occidentale Française: Togo*), discovered by historian Ralph A. Austen, mentioned the house and what Houlet

described as local rumors of its role in the slave trade, along with a French historian's refutation. Austen notes that: "The early history of this tradition remains to be written. The oldest reference known to me cites the historian Raymond Mauny as casting doubt on some of the stories connected to the house." Ralph A. Austen, "The Slave Trade as History and Memory: Confrontations of Slaving Voyage Documents and Communal Traditions," *The William and Mary Quarterly* 58, no. 1 (January 2001): 230.

58 "Island of Gorée," United Nations Educational, Scientific and Cultural Organization, https://whc.unesco.org/en/list/26/

59 Philip Curtin, "Gorée and the Atlantic Slave Trade," H-Africa Discussion Log, H-Net, August 2, 1995, https://lists.h-net.org/cgi-bin/logbrowse.pl?trx=vx&list=H-Africa&month=9508&week=a&msg=5uc1rZuh%2bRt64hicbL9PYw&user=&pw=

60 Ana Lucia Araujo, "Welcome the Diaspora: Slave Trade Heritage Tourism and the Public Memory of Slavery," *Ethnologies* 32, no. 2 (2010), 151; David Eltis and David Richardson, *Atlas of the Transatlantic Slave Trade* (New Haven: Yale University Press, 2010), 15.

61 Araujo, "Welcome the Diaspora."

62 French, "Gorée Island Journal."

63 "B. J. Ndiaye, Curator of Landmark in Slave Trade, Dies at 86," *New York Times*, February 18, 2009, https://www.nytimes.com/2009/02/19/world/africa/19ndiaye.html

64 Austen, "The Slave Trade as History and Memory"; Djibril Samb, ed., *Gorée et L'esclavage: Actes du Seminaire sur "Gorée dans la Traite Atlantique: Mythes et Réalités"* (Gorée, 7-8 Avril 1997) (Dakar, 1997).

65 Dalla Malé Fofana, "Senegal, the African Slave Trade, and the Door of No Return: Giving Witness to Gorée Island," *Humanities* 9, no. 3 (2020): 57.

66 Austen, "The Slave Trade as History and Memory."

67 Achille Mbembe, "REPLY: Gorée and the Atlantic Slave Trade," H-Africa Discussion Log, H-Net, August 8, 1995, https://lists.h-net.org/cgi-bin/logbrowse.pl?trx=vx&list=H-Africa&month=9508&week=b&msg=/tRDDwFfRZ54HMgfWFbUXw&user=&pw=

68 Saidiya Hartman, "Venus in Two Acts," *Small Axe* 12, no. 2 (June 2008): 1–14.

69 Forsdick, "Cette île n'est pas une île."

70 Dionne Brand, *A Map to the Door of No Return: Notes to Belonging* (Toronto: Doubleday Canada, 2001). See also Fofana, "Senegal, the African Slave Trade, and the Door of No Return."

71 Fofana, "Senegal, the African Slave Trade, and the Door of No Return."

72 Ibid.

73 "Island of Gorée," United Nations Educational, Scientific and Cultural Organization; Regis St. Louis, "Île de Gorée: The Perfect Dakar Day Trip," Lonely Planet, August 29, 2018, https://www.lonelyplanet.com/articles/ile-de-goree-day-trip-dakar

74 French, "Gorée Island Journal."

75 Transcript, "Sunday Spotlight, History of Gorée Island," This Week with George Stephanopoulos, ABC, July 7, 2013.

3
DEFINING MEMORY, DIALOGUE, AND ACTION

The debates began in the morning and continued deep into the night. This was because the issues ran far deeper than typical discussions among museum professionals, around exhibit design techniques or archival practices. We shared a commitment to building lasting cultures of democracy and human rights, and were trying to figure out how. We knew this could not be achieved through new laws or political structures alone: it could only be maintained over time by a well-rooted civic culture that supported them. But, coming from such diverse contexts and histories, we had different ideas of the kind of society we each sought to build, and what was required to build it. What does a culture of democracy and human rights look like? What is required to create and sustain it? At the heart of these debates were different definitions of three key concepts, and how they could come together to build collective conscience: memory, dialogue, and action.

Memory

Members of our group came to the table with three different notions of memory: memory as *reconnecting* distinct moments in the past to the present; memory as *reminding*, or raising public awareness of people still suffering or resisting, and problems still unresolved; and memory as *redress*, or correcting the contemporary legacies of past abuses. The collision of those ideas gave rise to critical questions, such as: when is it right to remember – is it ever too soon? How far back should we remember – does distant history offer useful perspective or dangerous distraction? How should the focus of memory evolve over time, as the legacies of the past continue to evolve, and new problems arise?

DOI: 10.4324/9781003185826-5

Memory as Reconnecting Past and Present

Sites like the Workhouse, the Tenement Museum, and those in the US National Park Service – those that did not emerge from social movements – connected the past to the present through snapshots of particular moments in time. Like at the more traditional sites in their countries – such as manors in England, or mansions in Virginia – history at these new Sites of Conscience was not a continuum that flowed into the current day. It was "back then," something to be viewed at a safe distance. What made "conscience" heritage different was its insistence on drawing explicit comparisons between past and present, naming contemporary contested issues, and demonstrating that history was a valuable resource for addressing them. This comparative study of how different people in different moments debated similar questions to the ones we struggle with today can yield great insights. Studying the unintended consequences of other generations' policy solutions can give us a glimpse of our own possible futures, and studying how others organized and resisted exploitation can provide models and inspiration for how we can make change.

Among middle-class museum goers in the US and Britain, the more distant past could provide a safer starting point for dialogue on highly contested current issues than anything in living memory. The Workhouse's "What Now, What Next?" exhibit, with its section on "Then and Now" contrasting how people at the Workhouse in the 19th century would be assisted in contemporary Britain, elided the more charged debates of recent decades, between Conservative and Labor approaches to welfare. Similarly, when the Tenement Museum sought to open discussion of the highly charged issues of sweatshops, immigrant labor, and consumer capitalism, it invited its visitors to a frozen moment in time a whole century ago. The 1897 recreation of the Levine family's small garment shop opened up space for open debate over the knotty problem of who was responsible for current abuse within the garment industry's complex chain of worker, contractor, retailer, and consumer. Like at the Workhouse, the discussion may have been possible because by focusing only on the two moments of the 1890s and 1990s, the exhibit avoided fraught questions of legacy, continuity, and accountability for what happened in between, including the rise and fall of labor union power.

In new states emerging from transitions, official heritage was used to draw a firm line between old and new regimes. Here the history being discussed was more recent, but still needed to be kept at a safe distance, through imposed division. As discussed in the previous chapter, in South Africa, most official heritage projects in the years immediately following the fall of apartheid presented the racist system as firmly in the past, on the other side of an impermeable divide. Similarly, in Eastern Europe, almost no Holocaust sites explicitly acknowledged contemporary racism or xenophobia in their countries. Terezín was a bold exception, calling out the rise in violence against Roma people and racism toward African Immigrants. But Terezín did not portray these wrongs as direct descendants of Nazi-era anti-semitism, so much as a parallel phenomenon, a separate specimen that one could more easily analyze with the benefit of hindsight. This past was highly relevant for the present as a cautionary tale, but did not bleed into the present. To speak of legacies or vestiges might empower the ghosts of the past.

The "reconnecting" approach to memory reaps lessons from the past, while avoiding accountability for it. By looking to the past as a source of comparisons, instead of continuities, people in the present can ignore the ways the legacies of historical abuses or inequalities live on in their lives, and how they may still be profiting, or suffering, from them.

Memory as Reminding

In places where perpetrators of recent abuses had not been held to account, the struggle was to break down the walls erected between present and past, to defy any official attempts to place violence in the past, and bury it in false closure. Here memory was about *reminding* people of unresolved issues: The goal was to keep them at the center of public attention as completely present and unresolved.

The Argentinean memory movement, for one, was a direct response to the blanket amnesty the Menem administration believed was necessary in order to achieve a peaceful transition to democracy. Until every person who was disappeared was found, and until every person responsible for their disappearance was brought to justice, all the disappeared must be asserted as "present," in both senses of the word: in the current moment, and living among us.

When there is no division between past and present, it's never "too soon" to remember. Patricia Valdez later explained, "In Argentina, the Madres said that they made memory from the very beginning when they used the images to find the disappeared. When they tried to create international awareness of the issue, this use of memory is memory action. It's not that you should wait until the problem is over to think about memory action."[2]

If national heritage bodies sought solace in the distant past, *memoria* and other initiatives who defined memory as "reminding" resisted veering too far from the present. Public attention needed to remain laser-focused on the urgent issues at hand, the people hurting now, without wandering into a wilderness of century-old context and muddy causality. "Memory Action" was extremely effective at keeping public attention and pressure on victims of recent violence to win legal accountability for them.

Further, since the primary goal of memory action was justice won through official state mechanisms – such as prosecutions and truth commissions – it needed to work within the structures and limits of those mechanisms. Transitional justice focused on political and economic reforms achievable in the short-term period of transition, such as better police education, a more independent judiciary, or even financial reparations to individual victims of state crimes. Geared to get the new state up and running, transitional justice mechanisms often focused on the near past, whose wrongs could be righted in the near future. Knottier problems with deeper histories – things like generational income inequality and structural racism – were not its primary remit.

In Argentina, the focus on prosecutions set narrow parameters for the history under their official investigation. The history began only when the abuses being addressed first became visible in their current form, and only considered stories directly related to them. In Memoria Abierta's campaign to reopen prosecutions, "*memoria*" meant the period of state terrorism, from 1976 to 1983, and its specific abuses. It did not include calls to remember longer life histories of people with experiences outside of this time or theme, such as those of European immigrants coming to Buenos Aires in the 1930s, or people who were not directly involved as victims or perpetrators. Developed as a necessary strategy, this approach produced particular public historical narratives: in many *memoria* reports and museums, the repressive regime and the widespread culture of silence that sustained it seemed to appear out of nowhere in the 1970s, with no roots or antecedents. Academic historians might analyze how such violence became possible and identify its deeper roots in Argentine society, but the *memoria* movement would maintain its focus on bringing to justice those who were still living among them.

Memory as Redress

Memory for redress seeks to quantify the material consequences of past abuses, and restore some measure of what has been lost. Memory for redress does not seek to keep the past alive as a presence, but rather as an absence. What the past has robbed from the present must be remembered until it is returned. For example, the Hands Off District Six campaign fought to keep the bulldozed empty land in the middle of Cape Town that had once been District Six undeveloped, to maintain public memory of the deep loss and harm to the thousands of people scattered in townships.

Memory for redress focuses simultaneously on collecting evidence for material claims – documenting who lost what – and building the collective momentum for individuals to make such claims. Restoring the community's memory was part and parcel of restoring the community's material assets. By inviting ex-residents to come together around the map of the destroyed District Six, for instance, the District Six Museum not only helped ex-residents identify their individual losses, but galvanized a successful movement for reparations.

If sites dedicated to "reminding" grappled with how far back to remember, those employing "redress" memory had to decide how far forward to extend their focus. Museums like District Six emerged to remember a particular event or system in the past: the racist Group Areas Act and its human cost, in the destruction of a community and its culture. That event formed the site's main "problem"; its history would focus on the events for which it sought account-ability. But the legacies of the original problem evolved with each passing day, into new issues site founders never could have foreseen. Cape Town's rapid gentrification, which displaced poorer residents of color, was driven by generational wealth disparities created by apartheid. While this displacement was driven by the veiled racism of market forces instead of the open racism of law, it remained rooted in the same apartheid system. Yet given that it was not directly connected to the Group Areas Act, were Museum founders responsi-ble for mobilizing memory to address this new displacement too? Should they create new exhibits about generational wealth and homeownership? When should site museums' historical narratives end? Or should they ever?

Dialogue

Founding sites' emphasis on dialogue – on connecting people to each other through open discussion – distinguished them from the growing numbers of memorial museums emerging around the time of the Bellagio meeting, which focused on connecting visitors to historical figures through exhibition design.[3] But meeting participants were deeply divided on their definitions of dialogue and its role in building a culture of human rights. Ideas included dia-logue as truth-telling; as integrating multiple narratives; and as an exchange of views from different perspectives. Whereas everyone arrived with their own notions of "memory," "dialogue" was not a familiar or important concept for everyone. It was a mainly US import, initially championed at the meeting by Ruth and me, grounded in liberal ideas of the public square as the foundation of democracy. Those participants who had experienced "open" debate as a fallacy, constrained by the powers controlling who got to speak and for whom, pushed back. The result was a more variegated approach to dialogue shaped and reshaped through vigorous debate. Core questions included: was dialogue antithetical to truth-telling? Would "multiple perspectives" lead to moral rel-ativism, and historical revisionism? Among whom should dialogue be held?

Dialogue as Truth-Telling

For Memoria Abierta, as in other places fighting against denial, the main goal for "dialogue" was to get people to speak the truth – to inspire many people to tell their stories of state terrorism and insert them into the public discourse. For some, this meant breaking silence for the first time, sharing things they had seen, heard, or experienced first-hand, but were afraid to talk about. For others, this meant hearing and repeating a truth about the dictatorship they had never known before, whether its scope in statistics or its impact on a single individual. The primary aim of dialogue was not to open debate or engage multiple perspectives, but to assert long-suppressed facts and establish a new common understanding of the recent past.

Not long after 9/11, I brought Patricia to visit one of the first public oral history booths erected by StoryCorps, installed near ground zero. I asked if she could imagine a booth on every corner in Buenos Aires, inviting people across the city to break the silence that had oppressed them for so long. Patricia was appalled. What many American museum professionals were celebrating as a great democratization of oral history, Patricia saw as a dangerous corruption of truth. Such open sharing involved no process for verifying the accounts people gave of their experience, leaving them vulnerable to denial, and no mechanism for protecting the people who came forward, leaving them vulnerable to retributive violence. This would not fly where she was from.

In many of the Bellagio meeting participants' contexts, dialogue that encouraged exchanging interpretations of the past – airing different "sides of the story" – was code for denial and historical revisionism. People who had battled so hard to establish basic truths, like that 30,000 people were disappeared by the state in Argentina, or 6 million Jews were murdered by the Nazis, feared "dialogue" would once again call these facts into question. A democratic culture, they stressed, must be built on a foundation of accurate understanding of abrogations of democracy in the past, how they came to be, and how they were ultimately combatted. Shared knowledge and consensus about the past were vital; the risk of revisionism was deeply dangerous for accountability.

On the other hand, when the Liberation War Museum invited school-children across Bangladesh to interview their family members about their experience in the War, they knew these testimonies, taken by children in an unsupervised setting, would never be included in any future tribunal. But the founders believed the experience for both the young interviewer, hearing stories often for the first time, and for the older family members, were equally critical for building public awareness of what happened and commitment to dealing with its legacy. And, as it turned out, several of the interviews conducted by children yielded specific information that led investigators to uncover new mass graves.

Dialogue as Democratic Practice

For US and British participants, a culture of democracy was built more on the way people grappled with the truth than on the specific truth they grappled with. In their vision, a democratic culture capable of stopping human rights abuses before they started required a citizenry capable and comfortable with questioning what they were told, and with engaging with each other across differences, in a peaceful and productive way. A dogmatic approach, even if the content was right, would fail to get through to people or change their behavior. Thus historic sites should put their energy into giving museum visitors the opportunity to participate in open debates, and engage critically with the past, through dialogues with other visitors, between visitors and victims, or between stakeholders from conflicting perspectives.

The western liberal ideal of dialogue as democracy – the belief that deliberative debate and civil discourse form the foundation of free societies – was enjoying a global revival. The fall of communism ignited an explosion of international democracy-building initiatives – supported by private foundations like the Open Society Institute and federally funded US organizations like the United States Institute of Peace and the National Endowment for Democracy – who launched research and projects that trained students, teachers, and other citizens raised in totalitarianism to question and debate. This same funding supported the educational activities of many of the founding Sites of Conscience.

OSI and NED supported the Gulag Museum and its vision of dialogue as democratic practice. Founders of the Museum had been at the forefront of democracy movements in the 1980s. Given the particular nature of Soviet totalitarianism, their main demand was the right to dissent: the right to disagree with the regime and speak openly about their disagreement. A decade after the fall of the Soviet Union, former dissidents were realizing that while the political and economic systems had toppled like a house of cards, the totalitarian culture that had supported them remained extremely strong. Through youth programs like the "I Have Rights" workshops, the Museum sought to create a training site for a new citizenry that could sustain a democratic society, a place to practice how to debate, question, and organize to address the new challenges the society would face in the future.

Likewise, the Liberation War Museum sought to impart information about the democratic ideals of Bangladesh's founding, in a format and setting that would model secular democratic practices. LWM's mobile museum drove into schoolyards and invited students to come out of the classroom to engage in participatory activities with Museum staff. The space and pedagogy introduced a different culture of learning from that traditionally practiced in Bangladeshi classrooms, where teaching was organized around central control and rote memorization. In addition to introducing a new subject matter, then, the Museum was part of a wider effort for educational reform critical for developing the democratic culture the Museum seeks to promote.[4]

The emphasis on dialogue at these sites distinguished them from the growing numbers of memorial museums emerging around the time of the Bellagio meeting.[5] The main strategies of these museums, which over the next decade would solidify into norms and expectations, lay primarily in their exhibition design: devices like, as Amy Sodaro catalogues them, narrative panels, audio of victim's testimony, recreations, and other "experiential techniques and affect to make visitors feel that they have had a personal experience of the past that will shape their present moral sensibility."[6] These devices built empathy by inviting visitors to put themselves in the shoes of those who had lived through the history they were learning about – people who they would never actually meet, through an experience that focused on engagement between visitor and exhibition, not between visitors. Site directors gathered at Bellagio shared a commitment to creating spaces in their countries for people to exchange personal memories with each other, and grapple together with their real-life, present roles in the unfolding legacies of the events museums commemorated.

This strategy was much more politically challenging than even the most immersive exhibit, even – or perhaps especially – in the US. In the country that claimed to model open dialogue, much of the heritage field remained nearly as resistant to questioning and debate as a Soviet classroom. Most US historic sites turned to dialogue only as a defensive tactic, a measure of last resort: sites should open dialogue on contested issues only when it would be more controversial to stay silent; dialogue was not something to seek out proactively. Back home, Ruth Abram had urged her peers to place dialogue at the center of historic sites' mission and activities: rather than laying low, they should set out to find the faultlines. They should actively seek out the most contested issues challenging their societies, and serve as a resource for address-ing them. Achieving this would require as much reeducation as anywhere in the Eastern bloc.

Non-US meeting participants challenged this type of dialogue, asking whom it should involve. Was it a tool for radical reconciliation, between victims and perpetrators, bridging polarized groups in a divided society? Or meant for building a more sophisticated and nuanced understanding among an open-minded centrist majority, leaving out people at either extreme of the spectrum who would never be persuaded from their poles?

Dialogue as Multiple Narratives

For the District Six Museum, dialogue meant opening space for a wide range of individual stories to create a multi-faceted portrait of the past. The Museum had grown out of a wider anti-apartheid movement in South Africa whose vision of democracy centered around values of racial inclusion and equality. As official memorials proliferated to individual, well-known heroes of the anti-apartheid struggle – Nelson Mandela, Desmond Tutu, Steve Beko, and others – District Six's neighborhood narrative celebrated the cumulation of small stories of hundreds of ordinary people. The form of the museum – its mechanisms for collecting and sharing new stories on an ongoing basis, such as its floor map and the oral history collection – supported this vision of dialogue and democracy. Stories placed in the museum are restored to the nation and its narrative over time.

The Tenement Museum was experimenting with another form of dialogue, that was as much about reflection on one's own power and position in relation to immigration – a sort of dialogue with the self – as it was about an exchange with others. In its "Around the Kitchen Table" program, after a museum tour, a facilitator began by asking people in a small group to reflect on their own personal experiences and how they might have shaped how they viewed the world. The facilitator then invited people to reflect on the personal experiences they heard from others in the group and imagine how those must have shaped their own worldviews. Only after that would participants be invited to discuss any point of disagreement.[7]

These forms of dialogue were radically different from dialogue as truth-telling. Facilitators were not asked to establish or mediate forensic truths. The goal was to get everyone to understand that different people's life experiences shaped different visions of reality, and to argue from a point of empathy. This dialogue allowed everyone to have their own truths; to get to any point of peace or consensus, here the most important thing was to accept that what you believed to be truth was in fact shaped by your own life experiences, just as it was for others who believed a different truth.

Would this mean that everyone's truths were equally valid? A core ongoing debate was around whether humanizing all actors – perpetrators, victims, bystanders, and the many ordinary people who fell between these categories – in order to understand them, could be distinguished from condoning their actions. Would taking their humanity seriously always amount to excusing what they did? Or could it provide a more sophisticated framework for identifying how individuals come to commit abuses, without requiring absolution? As with many aspects of dialogue, multiple perspectives could be more easily entertained in societies where a basic moral consensus was stronger. For those who had seen torturers reintegrated into society, or architects of violence like Stalin be rehabilitated as cherished historical icons, "humanizing" threatened to weaken the moral bulwark against perpetrators, casting doubt on whether they were "all bad," and strengthening the possibility they could be reinstated as role models.

Action

Founding members also vigorously debated the role they should play in collective action. For many, memory work was not meant simply to inspire a separate form of protest, but was the actual focus or vehicle for it. In Russia during Perestroika, for instance, remembering the Gulag was an explicitly political act; Memorial was the first, and for a brief time, the only organized movement for democracy in Russia. Remembering was political because of what it signified, and because of the repressive reaction from the state it provoked. In other contexts, memory constituted action for accountability. In

Buenos Aires, unearthing a clandestine detention center was not a historic preservation project, but the start of a legal case. In Cape Town, remembering where one's house was in the old District Six was the first step in making a claim to a parcel of land as reparations. Confronting the past was participation in legal, political, and social change.

For entities run by the state or representing national heritage, the issue was more fraught. Arguing for a specific policy change would violate their vision of democratic culture, which required creating a space for public debate and disagreement. Terezín Memorial had spent its first 50 years having its history instrumentalized to inspire collective allegiance to the state, with Jews and gentiles alike painted as equal victims of Nazi persecution. For Jan Munk, a post-communist heritage site's first obligation was to avoid being prescriptive. And for traditional heritage bodies like the US National Park Service or the British National Trust, raising questions about contemporary issues and facilitating discussions on them was a big enough step; appearing to advocate a specific policy solution was a third rail. Marie Rust was fully accountable to a Congress deeply divided on policy issues; her sites could encourage visitors to vote, but not advocate for anything specific that represented a partisan stance. The National Trust was still tiptoeing away from its celebration of Britain's ruling class; to maintain this precarious progress, Leigh Rix needed to reassure Trust leadership that "It is not our place to judge or pronounce."[8]

Underlying these debates about promoting action were different ideas of what it meant to be "political," and whether or not it was a bad thing. Jan Munk of Terezín Memorial and Viktor Shmyrov of the Gulag Museum had waited for decades for their history to be released from the prison of state politics, so it could breathe free on its own terms. To them, being political meant forcing facts into a narrow narrative to support the state's agenda; even one as absurd as a story of the Holocaust with no Jews. Those who had seen basic facts of the past seized and distorted by the state had developed more objectivist views of history: they believed there were stable truths about the past that could be politicized, their meaning denied or distorted to serve narrow ends. In Eastern Europe, this view led to a rejection of truth commissions, with their emphasis on testimony and consensus narratives, in favor of a heavy investment in opening public access to archives, to a truth unmediated by the state or individual narrators.[9] The American public historians who worked for Marie in the National Park Service were also bound by a need to prove their objectivity. While they might embrace their historical work for the US government as "public service," they worked hard to avoid being called "political": after decades struggling for professional recognition and legitimacy in the face of derision from academic historians, being called "political" meant hackneyed, and endangered their careers.[10]

By contrast, Sandy Prosalendis of the District Six Museum had recently emerged from a Truth and Reconciliation process structured around the idea of multiple truths – from forensic to dialogic – that continually challenged each other. District Six's "community museum" and memory movement was, like Terezín and Memoria Abierta, challenging its state's official narrative. But District Six community leaders understood politics simply as a structure of power. From that perspective, there was no "staying out of politics." It was not that the District Six Museum was "objective" while the New South African heritage agencies were "political," or vice versa: both were equally political, they just had different agendas. Struggling myself with how to interpret American social policy at the Lower East Side Tenement Museum, I also felt that memory projects had an obligation to historical truth, but that they should pursue it by being transparent and self-reflective about what their politics were – about their perspective, the participants in their construction, and their intentions. To claim to "not be political" simply meant to obscure one's politics and deceive the public.

Creating a Hybrid Framework

To define our common vision and unique approach to each other, and legitimize them to the outside world, we needed a name. Drawing from Amnesty International's term "prisoners of conscience," Ruth proposed, "Sites of Conscience," and all agreed. The group then worked on a definition, to be both descriptive and aspirational. From their distinct perspectives on memory, dialogue, and action – and the debates they sparked – founders developed a set of collective principles.

Memory: Sites of Conscience would "draw connections between past and present" and "interpret history through site." This last harnessed the power of specific places of past struggle as both irrefutable evidence and irreplaceable emotional experiences. With this principle, the group could also advocate for the long-term preservation of this evidence, not only the construction of memorials.

Dialogue: Ruth initially proposed a collective principle to "stimulate dialogue on pressing social issues." For her, dialogue was inherently positive, the essential foundation of a culture of human rights. She sought to distinguish Sites of Conscience from linear museum narratives and static monuments which, though they might make certain truths unassailable, risked relegating the problems they represented to the past, signaling that they were safely resolved. But other founders had seen that without a statement of values, "dialogue on pressing social issues" could be undertaken for practically any purpose, including ones that undermined the social goals of the sites. So they insisted that dialogue should be framed with a moral imperative, to "promote democratic and humanitarian values." As vague and varied as the meaning of those terms were, they established some shared responsibility for pursuing specific ethics and resisting moral relativism.

We later added a pledge to affirm the forensic truths of what happened at our sites, while opening dialogue on their contemporary implications. Site museum leadership should decide what was and what was not up for debate. This ensured that the basic facts of what happened would not be called into question.

Action: The group did not initially include a shared principle on action as part of its founding documents. But several members argued that advocating for dialogue alone could imply that talk was as good as action, distracting from or diluting calls for real change. By 2001, the group agreed on a compromise commitment that Sites would "share opportunities for public involvement" in the issues the site addressed. In this way, without having to instrumentalize the past to advocate for any particular political position, Sites of Conscience could provide their visitors with information on avenues of action available to all citizens, from voting to volunteering, as well as how other organizations were tackling current problems from a variety of perspectives.

Carving Out a New Field

Founding Sites of Conscience came from a variety of sectors and fields of knowledge: transitional justice; history and heritage; social movements. They also represented a variety of ways of governing, or managing, memory: they were variously overseen by heritage, human rights, military, and tourism branches of government. The Coalition could have organized itself within one of the arenas from which its founding members came: there was an affinity group around sites of atrocity within the International Council on Museums; the International Center for Transitional Justice was developing a Monuments and Memorials program. But neither international transitional justice nor heritage organizations, nor any of our domestic democracy movements, provided the necessary support for Sites of Conscience to operate in the way the founders foresaw. Founding Sites of Conscience saw a strategic need to open a new professional space, defined by a hybrid framework that combined strengths from our constitutive fields.

Transitional Justice

Transitional justice included several approaches Sites of Conscience could draw from. First, its main goal was accountability. It pursued knowledge about the past not for any broad humanistic purposes, but specifically in order to pursue justice and social reconstruction. Second, it acted with the sanction of the state (though most often only in response to pressure from civil society), and was an important way for the state to publicly assume responsibility for past abuses. But transitional justice, in that moment in its historical development, had several political and structural limitations that Sites of Conscience sought to exceed.

First and most importantly, as discussed earlier, during this time, most transitional justice processes had a severely restricted view of history, what sociologist John Torpey derided as a "tendency to view the past as having begun only the day before yesterday."[11] Riding the post-Cold-War wave of enthusiasm for individual human rights and liberal democracy, instead of grappling with deeply rooted structural inequality, the main goal was often to overturn the policies of a prior regime that had been in power for a decade or two.[12] For this goal, the recent past was most relevant, histories the citizenry could remember first hand. Truth commissions were themselves short term, usually lasting around four years, since their effectiveness and legitimacy depended on their ability to deliver conclusions quickly. To meet this time limitation, they needed to restrict the number and scope of victims they could include. Further, truth commissions and prosecutions circumscribed which kinds of stories officially counted: testimonies had to adhere to certain legal standards, even though the purpose of transitional justice was to introduce a toolbox of accountability measures much wider than criminal law, to give deeply divided societies more options for dismantling cultures of impunity. Finally, truth commissions were limited in public engagement and legacy. While the testimonies themselves were broadcast on national television, the final product of most early truth commissions was a lengthy written report, which risked winding up nothing more than a doorstop. Despite efforts to promote and disseminate the reports widely, they often remained in the specific form of a book (or dense downloadable pdf), limiting engagement to people who read, reading alone.

Transitional justice rubrics also limited how Sites of Conscience were categorized and understood. In the late 1990s, transitional justice professionals were starting to consider memorialization as an important part of their work. But to fit it into one of the field's existing categories, they described memorialization as a form of reparations called "satisfaction," or "symbolic reparations." In contradistinction to material reparations, such as financial compensation to victims, "symbolic reparations" included official apologies and other forms of public recognition. "Symbolic reparations" forced the more dynamic and iterative process of public memory into a legal framework designed for closure and fixed outcomes, as though memory were a discrete object or good.[13] Sites of Conscience leaders believed societies needed memory measures that would be ongoing, and iterative. Sites of Conscience then could not, in that moment anyway, be accommodated fully in the field of transitional justice.

Heritage and Memorial Museums

Sites of Conscience sought to draw on several important facets of traditional heritage practice. Heritage took the long view, planning for the preservation of historic material for centuries to come, through a constantly changing contemporary context. Sites of Conscience, too, sought to provide space for societies to continually draw new lessons and understandings from their histories; and to engage ever-expanding swaths of citizens. That space must not limit the types of stories that "counted," as a truth commission did, but must continually learn from new aspects of a historical experience that had not come to light. In particular, Sites of Conscience sought to create a space for new generations to identify and share what their country's violent past means to them and what they would do with its lessons – a past they most likely knew little about, but which nevertheless profoundly shaped their life experience and their understanding of the world.

Heritage practices also suggested a different physical treatment of sites than transitional justice. Legalistic mechanisms defined sites as crime scenes, places with short-term utility as sources of evidence. Teams of forensic archaeologists and lawyers were sent in to extract proof: find the bones, or instruments of torture, or secret prisons, to prove who did what to whom as quickly as possible so the society can learn what happened and move on. Heritage site managers, by contrast, imagined sites as spaces for long-term memory and reflection. They were concerned with how to uncover the site's buried knowledge; but equally, with when and where to let it be – when to refrain from digging, disturbing, or restoring to prove what happened, and instead create a space for people to reflect and mourn.

Heritage practices also offered broader ways for people to exchange stories about the past than transitional justice, including more process-oriented story-sharing, focused less on evidence and more on building relationships and mutual understanding, such as story circles or mutual interviews. Heritage professionals collected farther-ranging narratives, including aspects of life that might not fit into an official inquiry's categories of relevance, yet could yield critical insights into the roots of violence and how to prevent it.

But for different reasons, both the heritage and museum fields had their own limitations for Sites of Conscience. In that moment in its historical development, the heritage field was ill equipped to seek accountability. Official national and international agencies that defined and governed heritage consistently distanced themselves from unresolved questions of justice and ongoing campaigns for legal or financial redress. In addition to being ingrained in the professional culture of such agencies, the aversion to accountability was codified in innumerable ways, including through the criteria for which sites would be preserved; processes for developing what stories would be told and how; and training for interpreters.

Memorial museums were developing myriad strategies for immersing visitors in the past through creative exhibit design, far more effective for building empathy than the fat texts of truth commission reports.[14] However, emerging from art historical traditions of display, museums often focused on facilitating engagement between the visitor and the exhibit. Sites of Conscience instead drew on democracy movements, so prioritized engagement among visitors, to enact the democratic participation required to put empathy into practice and build a culture of human rights.

Social Movements

The modes and structures of social movements – mobilizing a diverse mass public, raising public awareness, creating a sense of solidarity, inspiring action – provided critical tools for Sites of Conscience. Individually and collectively, Sites of Conscience worked to seize what social movement theorists call "political opportunity structures" – the conditions conducive to collective mobilization – and create their own.[15] But as the District Six Museum and the Gulag Museum experienced, social movement strategies are often modeled around intense campaigns with short term goals. Once the campaign is won or lost, the energy and engagement dissipates. Sites of Conscience needed to integrate social movement strategies with heritage and transitional justice strategies to sustain long-term memory movements that transcended short-term political objectives. Sites should become spaces for training and education on how to act on a wide variety of issues, as they emerged over time.

Governance

Creating and naming Sites of Conscience as a new category was also important for helping us – and others who would come after us – navigate basic questions around how sites should be governed, and what their political place should be within a society. In many countries, potential Sites of Conscience were tossed around different ministries and sectors of government like a hot potato, not recognized as the responsibility of any of them. In Argentina, much early memory work was led through the Ministry of Justice and its Secretary of Human Rights, though many of the main secret detention sites were still managed by the entities that originally exploited them, such as the Navy or the city police. That made the ongoing memorial activities and forensic work both painful and awkward. In Chile, sites that had been abandoned by Pinochet's secret police were by default the responsibility of the Ministry of Public Lands, whose main portfolio was public housing. In Liberia, the prison where President Ellen Johnson Sirleaf was detained remained under the Ministry of the Interior, which ran the country's prisons.[16] And in the US, for over a century, government-run historic sites were managed by the Department of the Interior and its National Park Service, whose original mandate was the preservation of natural resources. In societies confronting past abuse, who (which agency or group) should govern and manage the sites of that abuse on a daily basis is not just an administrative question. The administration of heritage sites determines levels of financial support, symbolic importance, and characterization: managing a site in a justice ministry situates it as a symbol of human rights; the same site, if managed by a parks department, presents as a natural resource; if by a corrections bureau, as part of the prison system. In other words, administration determines the place of a site's stories, and the lessons they hold, in the nation's larger infrastructure. The title "Sites of Conscience" established a distinctive category, at the intersection of justice, heritage, and public space, making the case for administrative oversight that would respect its hybrid role in society.

Building a Movement

Why Work Together?

Serving as a Site of Conscience was radical in every context in 1999, though for different reasons. The US National Park Service had exponentially more money than any of the sites around the table, but it faced an extremely conservative organizational culture. The Gulag Museum, on the other hand, could be raided or shut down any day of the week. No matter their status, everyone at the table needed support that would allow them to take risks. This clear shared need made it possible for our motley crew to come together as equals.

Why Work in Coalition?

All of us who came together in Bellagio could have written up notes from our discussions, published our presentations, made a listserv (it was 1999 after all), and begun to meet annually. This would have founded a membership association, not a movement. To create a new culture and practice of memory outside our individual sites, and strengthen it as a force for puncturing the historical denial that undergirded systems of oppression around the world, we needed something more. The founding group of nine sites could not support its individual members or its collective vision alone. It needed to grow in breadth and depth – to demonstrate that many communities across the world embraced the concept, and that it could be applied and adapted in many different contexts.

Who Should Work Together?

Initial participants were limited to those Ruth had heard of, or that we researched, or were referred to us by funders and scholars. But as an experienced organizer, Ruth recognized that it was critical to have representation as diverse as possible from the founding. Otherwise, the movement would never have the collective knowledge and broad-based legitimacy it needed to advance. It is extremely difficult, if not impossible, for a narrow group to launch a movement and then invite different types of participants to join later, once the frame is set. This is something any movement-builder knows, but many heritage professionals didn't.

We tried our best to compose as diverse a group as possible, focusing both on geography, and on different institutional contexts, with extremely different relationships to power. Memoria Abierta and the Liberation War Museum were tiny, volunteer-run civil society organizations that for years had labored in explicit opposition to the state; the US National Park Service was the official public heritage body for the largest economy in the room. It also represented a country that had a significant hand in just about every human rights abuse the others were now recovering from, from trading slaves in Africa to training torturers in Argentina. The government entities in charge of some sites and their resources also varied widely. The budget of the Maison des Esclaves, or indeed, of the entire Senegalese Ministry of Culture, was likely less than what the Park Service spent on staples; Terezín Memorial was technically subject to the Czech state, but Jan Munk raised at least half his budget from US and international Jewish organizations, which he could spend quite autonomously.

The group's greatest diversity lay in the sites' wildly differing histories, which defied all categorization. Were these all sites of atrocity? That designation would require us to draw equivalencies between the struggles of immigrants to New York (Tenement Museum) and those of Jews during the Holocaust (Terezín Memorial). And looking ahead, only sites that articulated clear victims and villains would be able to join. Were all the histories recent? That would have excluded the Maison des Esclaves or any other sites remembering the slave trade. Were they all remembering events their nations had collectively repudiated, about which some narrative consensus had emerged? That would have excluded any sites still struggling to get a history recognized, like the Liberation War Museum.

Ruth understood this movement needed to be defined on the actions participants committed to taking, not on anything essential about their sites. It should be possible for anyone recovering history to help build a new global culture of heritage for human rights, whether a museum about daily life in a tenement, or a killing field marking mass atrocity. To support this big a tent, our coalition must be founded on a firm set of principles practiced across all member sites, however varied their contexts. Founders crafted and signed on to three: to interpret history through site; stimulate dialogue on pressing social issues and promote democratic and humanitarian values; and to share opportunities for public involvement in the social issues raised.

How Should Standards Be Enforced?

Also key to the coalition's success, we determined, was striking a balance between inflexibility on standards, and flexibility on how they were met. Being uncompromising, even exclusionary, about the principles and practices that defined Sites of Conscience was critical. While we might not have the perfect recipe for how to produce "conscience," we knew it did not come naturally; setting standards ensured participating sites would put in the tremendous effort, creativity, and vigilance it required. If expectations were loosened, or exceptions easily made, then the values that bound us would be eroded, and the group would lose the collective force that each member, and the movement as a whole, so desperately needed. The founding members set up an accreditation process, to which they themselves agreed to submit every five years, structured around the founding principles.

This commitment to standards produced some awkward results. For example, for many years, Auschwitz was not a Site of Conscience. For most people learning about the Coalition for the first time, Auschwitz seemed to be the ultimate expression of the term Sites of Conscience. As several scholars have noted, the Holocaust came to define historical violence and set the standards for how societies should confront it, creating norms for everything from prosecutions to memorial design.[17] But in the Coalition's early years, while various private, German-run and funded teen camps on tolerance proliferated around the Polish site, its state-controlled museum had no interest in opening dialogue on its country's most contested contemporary issues. Excluding the most recognized site in the most recognized human rights history was a major risk for the movement. Auschwitz's absence from the list provoked constant questions and doubt among funders and potential new members. But that provided valuable opportunities to articulate the concept of Sites of Conscience and what those that committed to such practices had the unique potential to do.

If losing Auschwitz was awkward, the commitment to clear, written standards, and a transparent process for reviewing whether sites met them, bolstered the Coalition's budding reputation. Soon after its founding, some museums began to seek membership in order to gain the imprimatur of "conscience" while pursuing quite opposite goals. In 2002, the Coalition was approached by a new museum in Hungary called the House of Terror, located in a former detention center run by Nazis and then communists, dedicated to memorializing the repression of both regimes; so seemingly similar to many current Coalition members. But the museum was the brainchild of rightist leader Viktor Orbán, who over the next two decades would all but dismantle the country's democracy to create a brutal authoritarian regime. Inside, it was half-horror show, sensationalizing torture devices, and half blunt propaganda.[18] Becoming a Site of Conscience would have raised the local legitimacy of its version of the past and the political conclusions it heavily implied. If Sites of Conscience had been defined as places where atrocities took place, this museum would definitely have been held up as a model. Bringing it into the fold would have opened the movement to the millions of other sites around the world that instrumentalize the past for propaganda purposes. But comparing the site's practices to the standards for Sites of Conscience made it immediately clear that the Coalition was not for them.

Equally critical to the success of the movement was staying wide open to the variety of different ways sites could meet the standards. The standards should pose no financial or structural obstacles to sites that wanted to meet them, like requiring that sites have a particular type of governance or staffing. Meeting them should be a pure matter of commitment and creativity. In fact, the Coalition sought to cultivate as many different individual expressions of the shared values as possible. For example, given the deep tensions over definitions of "dialogue," the Coalition celebrated – by financially supporting and publicly promoting – a variety of strategies grounded in different historical traditions of exchange and deliberation. These involved differing rules of engagement between people, and differing physical environments to nurture the exchange. A new South African partner, Constitution Hill, designed conversations about the new South African constitution around the tradition of lekgotla, derived from a Botswana tradition of public gathering and decision-making led by a village elder. Lekgotla traditionally have firm rules about letting every participant have their say and speak fully, while coming to a conclusion at the end. Constitution Hill's lekgotla invited school children to gather outdoors in a wide public plaza in front of the Constitutional Court, where an adult facilitator would lead them in discussions about rights and responsibilities of South African citizenship.[19] At the Tenement Museum, dialogues were called "Kitchen Conversations," held in a small, low-ceilinged room in the historic tenement, with snacks and drinks running down the length of a formica-topped kitchen table surrounded by well-worn, mismatched chairs. A trained facilitator established ground rules, like not interrupting, but after initial introductions, anyone could jump in, as one would at a family dinner. The conversation was organized to build understanding and empathy, not to arrive at a specific conclusion.[20] In other national contexts, the dialogue strategy was designed to disrupt traditional modes: the Liberation War Museum in Bangladesh insisted that rural students come out of their rigidly organized classrooms to roam the mobile museum and exhibits in the open school yard.[21]

Who Makes Decisions and Who Pays?

The founders also had to design how they would work together. For its first five years, the Coalition was coordinated from within the Tenement Museum, before becoming a legally independent organization. Founding members formed a steering committee, which became the Board of Directors, to set strategic priorities and review the budget for the Coalition's collective work. Member sites were independent entities who raised and managed their own budgets and activities. But by joining the Coalition, they were allowing a larger entity to speak for them. For the most part, this strengthened their local status, positioning themselves as part of a global force. But one false word or move from the Coalition office in New York could upend a member's fragile standing in their own context – another reason hammering out precise language about the defining features of Sites of Conscience was critical.

As the Coalition grew, it began charging modest membership fees tiered according to an organization's budget and what part of the world it came from. The founding members who made up the Board were not expected to contribute funds beyond that. So the majority of funding came from US-based foundations, whose diversity reflected the Coalition's hybrid identity, from cultural funders within the Ford Foundation to human rights foundations like Open Society and the Oak Foundation. With the support of Tenement Museum staff, Ruth and I raised funds for any collective activities of the Coalition. By 2004, we sought to decentralize leadership by naming Regional Coordinators, who managed subsidiary budgets and activities to support new sites in their orbits.

Once the Coalition grew to include hundreds of sites, the intensive accreditation process became unwieldy. We replaced it with a grant program to seed projects at member sites that demonstrated Sites of Conscience activities in as many different ways and contexts as possible. Applications were reviewed by peer member sites for how well they fulfilled the founding principles. Awardees' projects were promoted extensively so others could learn from them. In this way the grant program served as a much more generative, less exclusionary means of assessment, providing an internal and public forum for elaborating and strengthening our core definition.

~

On the last evening of the week in Bellagio, Ruth gathered everyone together in a lushly appointed but intimate room in the villa to sign a Founding Declaration. The delegates had come to Bellagio with very different levels of power, traditionally defined. But they came together as equals to this meeting, and discovered that to achieve what each of us was trying to do locally, we needed each other. As mismatched as we were, they had more in common with each other than they did with others in their own national and professional contexts. We all defied common understandings of heritage and human rights in our own countries, and fell outside existing international professional communities, such as transitional justice and heritage, that might have provided a network of peers.

I created a document with a fancy font that spelled out the principles we had worked so hard to hammer out, with room for nine signatures. Honestly, I thought it was a bit much. But Ruth could see that we were founding a movement in that small room, one that would grow to include many others, and that a written declaration provided the firm foundation it needed to build on. She framed a copy and hung it in her office, where she told the story behind it to everyone she received.

After Bellagio, Ruth gradually turned over leadership of the Coalition to me, though she remained a constant support and guide. As new sites entered the Coalition, representing new stories and contexts, our debates continued – over approaches to memory, and its relationship to accountability; approaches to dialogue, and its relationship to truth; and approaches to action, and its relationship to democracy. Integrating new members and their unique practices provided ongoing, productive challenges to the collective framework. The next chapter shares how the principles fared in practice over time: where the standards supported sites through devastating political and social challenges, and where they failed them. It explores how we began developing ways to test what worked, what didn't, and why.

Notes

1 Amy Sodaro, *Exhibiting Atrocity: Memorial Museums and the Politics of Past Violence* (New Brunswick: Rutgers University Press, 2018).
2 Patricia Valdez, statement made during workshop at "Remembering Guantánamo: 1898-Present," University of Memphis, June 2009.
3 Sodaro, *Exhibiting Atrocity*; Paul Williams, *Memorial Museums: The Global Rush to Commemorate Atrocities* (Oxford: Berg, 2007); Silke Arnold-de Simine, *Mediating Memory in the Museum: Trauma, Empathy, Nostalgia* (Houndmills: Palgrave Macmillan, 2013).
4 Brandon Hamber, Liz Ševčenko, and Ereshnee Naidu, "Utopian Dreams or Practical Possibilities? The Challenges of Evaluating the Impact of Memorialization in Societies in Transition." *The International Journal of Transitional Justice* 4, no. 3 (2010): 410.
5 Sodaro, *Exhibiting Atrocity*; Williams, *Memorial Museums*; Arnold-de Simine, *Mediating Memory in the Museum*.
6 Sodaro, *Exhibiting Atrocity,* 24–5.
7 Ruth J. Abram, "Kitchen Conversations: Democracy in Action at the Lower East Side Tenement Museum," *The Public Historian* 29, no. 1 (Winter 2007): 59–76.
8 Charlotte Crow, "Richer for Poorer," *History Today* 52, no. 3 (March 2002), 3.
9 Ruti G. Teitel, "Transitional Justice Genealogy," *Harvard Human Rights Journal* 16 (2003): 79.
10 Denise D. Meringolo, *Museums, Monuments, and National Parks: Toward a New Genealogy of Public History* (Amherst: University of Massachusetts Press, 2012).
11 John Torpey, "Introduction: Politics and the Past," in *Politics and the Past: on Repairing Historical Injustices*, ed. John Torpey (Lanham, MD: Rowman & Littlefield, 2003), 8.
12 Paige Arthur, "How 'Transitions' Reshaped Human Rights: A Conceptual History of Transitional Justice." *Human Rights Quarterly* 31, no. 2 (2009): 321–67.
13 Sebastian Brett, Louis Bickford, Liz Ševčenko, and Marcela Rios, "Memorialization and Democracy: State Policy and Civic Action," International Center for Transitional Justice, June 2007, https://www.ictj.org/publication/memorialization-and-democracy-state-policy-and-civic-action. Several scholars later argued against categorizing symbolic reparations in contrast to material reparations for a variety of reasons, including that any material reparations are in any case symbolic, as they can never compensate for what victims have lost. See Claire Moon, "'Who'll Pay Reparations on My Soul?' Compensation, Social Control and Social Suffering," *Social & Legal Studies* 21, no. 2 (2012): 187–99; Brandon Hamber, "Narrowing the Micro and Macro: A Psychological Perspective on Reparations in Societies in Transition," in *The Handbook of Reparations*, ed. Pablo de Greiff

(Oxford: Oxford University Press, 2006), 560–88; Kris Brown, "Commemoration as Symbolic Reparation: New Narratives or Spaces of Conflict?" *Human Rights Review* 14, no. 3 (2013): 273–89; Kevin Hearty, "Problematising Symbolic Reparation: 'Complex Political Victims,' 'Dead Body Politics' and the Right to Remember," *Social & Legal Studies* 29, no. 3 (2020): 334–54; Ereshnee Naidu, "Symbolic Reparations: A Fractured Opportunity," Centre for the Study of Violence and Reconciliation, 2004, https://www.files.ethz.ch/isn/104771/symbolicreparations.pdf

14 Sodaro, *Exhibiting Atrocity*, 24–5.
15 Sidney G. Tarrow, *Power in Movement: Social Movements and Contentious Politics*, Rev. & updated 3rd ed. (Cambridge: Cambridge University Press, 2011).
16 Liz Ševčenko, "Sites of Conscience: Reimagining Reparations," *Change Over Time* 1, no. 1 (Spring 2011): 6–33.
17 Daniel Levy and Natan Sznaider, *The Holocaust and Memory in the Global Age* (Philadelphia: Temple University Press, 2006).
18 Sodaro, *Exhibiting Atrocity*, 58–63.
19 Churchill Madikida, Lauren Segal, and Clive van den Berg, "The Reconstruction of Memory at Constitution Hill" *The Public Historian* 30, no. 1 (February 2008): 17–25.
20 Abram, "Kitchen Conversations."
21 Hamber et al., "Utopian Dreams or Practical Possibilities?"

4

ASSESSING IMPACT

This chapter first charts how Sites developed in the few years after founding the Coalition, locally and across their regions. It then explores the Coalition's first attempts to design ways to measure impact. While the founding years were spent defining shared goals, the following period focused on defining shared metrics of success. Just as founders blended a variety of approaches in creating their sites, so did they need to draw on multiple means of assessing them. Combining evaluation strategies from museums, holocaust education, peace-building, and other fields, the Coalition struggled to identify ways to hold itself accountable and learn from its experiments, while creating data-based insulation against future political climates that might be more hostile. The chapter's last section skips ahead two decades to explore how the principles of Sites of Conscience fared through right-wing political turns in three contexts – the US, Argentina, and Russia – where national leaders used the founding principles of Sites of Conscience against them. These stories raise questions about what public memory projects need in order to weather political storms and survive over the long term.

Local Impact

When the founding members of the Coalition gathered in 2004, five years after the first meeting in Bellagio, we had each made significant progress. We convened not at a conference center, but at one of our member sites – Terezin Memorial in Cezch Republic – where we met under the pitched beams of an attic room in the former ghetto. This was in part to celebrate that Terezin had at long last opened a permanent exhibit in the Ghetto Museum.

DOI: 10.4324/9781003185826-6

Memoria Abierta had continued to make the vast system of secret detention centers visible to the residents of Buenos Aires, including through an online, interactive map called "Topografía de la Memoria," which identified dozens of former secret detention centers around the city hidden in plain sight, from gas stations to private homes. Many of the sites had been destroyed, but they were represented by digital architectural recreations based on oral histories. "Topografía" carefully mapped the administrative system that oversaw the centers, demonstrating the level of coordination among what might otherwise seem a disparate scattering of back rooms. People visiting the map could locate the sites that had operated closest to where they lived and worked and hear the stories of survivors who had been detained there. This work helped visitors learn how state terrorism functioned, and how citizens' silence enabled it. Memoria Abierta also supported efforts to physically unearth these buried histories. For example, research conducted by Memoria Abierta and others revealed that buried beneath a massive overpass was the basement of a federal police building, "Club Atletico," that had detained and tortured around 1,500 people before being razed to build the highway. In 2002, after the site was digitally represented on "Topografia," the city government began excavations, uncovering a layer of underground chambers containing objects used for torture.

The most significant site in the city – what Patricia Valdez used to call "our Auschwitz" – was the Escuela Mecánica de la Armada (ESMA), a naval academy whose sprawling campus took up acres of land smack in the middle of Buenos Aires. Behind its gates, over 5,000 people were secretly detained and disappeared. In 1999, the building was still occupied by the Navy. Memoria Abierta began holding conversations among victims called "The Museum We Want," which created both the vision and the political will to imagine the ESMA as a Site of Conscience.[1] In 2004, President Nestor Kirschner ordered the Navy to withdraw from the building and declared the ESMA a "Space for Memory and for the Promotion and Defence of Human Rights," which would include a museum interpreting what happened there, as well as offices for human rights organizations.[2]

In Russia, the Gulag Museum had managed to lobby UNESCO to nominate Perm-36 for inclusion on its World Monuments Watch list. This meant that the United Nations (UN) identified this tiny, remote site in the Ural Mountains as critical not only to Russian heritage, but to the heritage of the world. It also indicated that the site was in urgent need of preservation, providing the Museum with international leverage to argue for more funding. The Gulag Museum's greater challenge was building popular interest in the site and its grim history. Even after the construction of the new road from Perm, the Museum still only welcomed a few thousand people each year. Viktor Shmyrov and his colleagues started to develop a new approach: to turn the camp into a destination for young people. For ten months of the year, Kuchino was a grim, grey, snow-covered landscape. But in the summer, for a brief moment, the ground turned green and lush. The Museum designed a festival named Pilorama, after the sawmill prisoners used at the camps to process timber.

Pilorama became Perm's Burning Man. Thousands of young people camped out in the fields and woods around the site, lugging acoustic guitars, booze, and other universal trappings of youth movements. Beside a festival of rock concerts, film screenings, plays, and poetry readings, the Museum offered lectures and discussions by democracy advocates, including former political prisoners, on "difficult themes in Soviet history, and the development of democracy."[3] While many of the young people skipped the lectures, they could not be at the festival without connecting to what Perm-36 was and the project of remembering it. The Gulag Museum had made memory cool again.

At the US National Park Service, Marie Rust's tool for change was federal policy. Marie reported how she returned home from the Bellagio meeting determined to translate the Coalition's ideas to the hundreds of US historic sites in her system's care, and connect them to other like-minded initiatives emerging in the agency, such as the NPS Advisory Board's *Rethinking the National Parks for the 21st Century*.[4] In 2001, she convened a national meeting in New York, joined by Ruth and me, that included the superintendents of a variety of potential NPS Sites of Conscience, including Manzanar and some of the Civil War battlefields that had been such lightning rods for controversy. Titled "The National Park Service and Civic Engagement," the convening emerged with a vision statement supporting parks to "connect the heritage of the nation to its contemporary environmental, social, and cultural issues" since "Parks serve as important centers for democracy and as places to learn and reflect about American identity and the responsibilities of citizenship." By the end of the workshop, "participants proposed that the NPS implement civic engagement throughout its parks." "Let this be the beginning of a significant shift in the way we do business," Marie declared.[5] The meeting sparked a movement within the agency, and by 2003, the Director of the National Park Service made "civic engagement" a mandate for every site. Ultimately defined more as community consultation for land use, as opposed to public dialogue around contested issues, this "director's order" nevertheless articulated a new level of state accountability to diverse publics for what kind of history the state preserves.

In Bangladesh, the Liberation War Museum survived even as the transitional justice process that gave rise to it began to fail, suggesting that in some cases Sites of Conscience could be more durable than other mechanisms for accountability. In 2009, it seemed the Museum and its supporters had fulfilled their ultimate goal to win official justice for the victims of the Liberation War, with the establishment of the International Crimes Tribunal, an official war crimes court. But the Tribunal was discredited from the start. International human rights organizations such as Human Rights Watch deemed it politically motivated, partisan, and illegitimate.[6]

Yet while the Tribunal faltered, the Museum thrived. Just after the Awami government took power in 2008, it allotted a larger piece of land on which the LWM could design a new facility, purpose-built for the museum, with technology and amenities it never had in the original building it had adapted. LWM also opened a Center for the Study of Genocide and Justice in order to research and document claims outside of the Tribunal, and place them in the context of other genocides.

The other sites had good news to share as well. The Workhouse opened to the public in Spring 2002, and was heralded for moving the definition of British heritage, as defined by the National Trust, "towards a consideration of the lives of ordinary people rather than of the gentry in their grand houses."[7] In Cape Town, when a developer sought to build luxury apartments over a historic burial ground for unnamed slaves, political prisoners, and other marginalized people, the District Six Museum was ready. Building on the success of Hands Off District Six, it launched Hands off Prestwich Place in 2003, mobilizing to address unresolved legacies of apartheid, especially the ways the market replaced legal discrimination. And the Tenement Museum had expanded its "Around the Kitchen Table" program to engage hundreds of Americans in personal discussions on immigration every week.

Regional Impact

As the founding group had hoped, joining as an international coalition helped legitimize the individual member sites in their local contexts. Now, we sought to widen that support to the many other efforts emerging in each place, by creating regional coalitions of sites remembering related histories, opening public conversation about the past and its contemporary legacies in every corner of the country or region, building a much stronger overall culture of human rights. I raised funds from the National Endowment for Democracy for founding members to lead the regional coalitions, which would also provide local sites with more tailored support through a peer network of museums confronting similar questions and audiences, and would decentralize Coalition leadership, which was essential for its long-term growth and stability. Mirroring the strategy of the international coalition, regional networks engaged any projects willing to commit to the shared Sites of Conscience principles, allowing them to amplify the voice of each individual institution and foster broader public awareness and dialogue in each of their societies.

Latin America

Memoria Abierta began tracing the system of state terror beyond the capital city into the suburbs. On a peaceful leafy street in nearby Moron, a lovely house known as Mansion Sere mysteriously burned to the ground toward the end of the dictatorship. Oral histories and legal testimonies revealed that hundreds of people had been kidnapped, blindfolded, and taken there to be tortured. The city decided to excavate the abandoned lot, revealing evidence of electrocutions and imprisonment. The site joined a growing number of others in the suburbs that the city designated as official historic sites, expanding the visible landscape of memory.

Memoria Abierta also brought together and supported efforts to remember state terrorism in other countries of Latin America and the Caribbean. While each country's history and experience were unique, there were parallels and connections between the repressive regimes, and similar sociological and psychological responses of their citizenry. As new democracies, all also shared similar goals for activating memory to prevent future abuse. The network grew to include over 40 sites in 12 countries, including other sites of torture and detention like Villa Grimaldi in Chile, archives on the conflicts in Guatemala, museums, like the Museum of Memory in Uruguay and the Center for Memory, Peace and Reconciliation in Columbia, and national coalitions like the Never Again Citizens Movement in Peru. The *memoria* movement began to be institutionalized across the continent.

Russia

Starting around 2003, Viktor Shmyrov and Tatiana Kursina of the Gulag Museum at Perm-36 began stitching together a network of museums remembering the Gulag and Stalinist repression across the massive swath of the globe once controlled by the Soviet Union. Whereas state terrorism in Argentina was hidden in plain sight, the Gulag functioned by dispersing people to remote corners of the country. Connecting people striving to save Gulag history across the vast geography that had been designed to divide them, and connecting tiny amateur memory efforts with established museums, was critical to building a solid foundation for Gulag memory, one that could endure the severe and violent challenges widely anticipated to come. But while the Gulag Museum enjoyed unusual support and protection from its regional government, this was hardly true in other parts of Russia. The Museum was therefore in a strong position to lead a national charge for public remembrance of Soviet terror as a coherent, empire-wide phenomenon.

Viktor and Tatiana struggled with how to build a collective national consciousness of places spread across eleven time zones. Some were near large cities, like Krasnoyarsk, with existing museums and cultural professionals who could manage new collections or exhibitions. But even those in urban centers were politically and culturally isolated; simply put, few people cared. Speaking in 2004 of the Tomsk Memorial NKVD Prison Museum, Boris Trenin, head of the Tomsk branch of Memorial, lamented, "I have the impression that now there are two people to whom this museum is necessary, me and the director, Vasily Khanevich."[8]

Compounding the challenge of building a coherent national network was that the most important Gulag centers were at the ends of the earth. Places where, in the early and mid-2000s, personal e-mail had not yet penetrated, internet access was scarce as sunshine, and faxes were communal. Preserving these places was left to the last man standing. I first met Ivan Panikarov, Director of the Kolyma Gulag Museum, in July 2006 at a Lukoil summer corporate retreat center we had rented space in, an hour or two outside of Perm. The Ford Foundation had granted us enough money to fly him and a handful of other representatives of Gulag museums to host the first gathering of museums remembering Soviet repression across Russia, organized by Viktor and Tatiana.

Before the meeting began, Ivan and I went for a walk on the lush lawns of the center's grounds. The first thing I noticed about him was the numbers tattooed on his fingers. These, it turned out, were the dates of his time in the Gulag, a memory he, like other *zeks* (prisoners), was determined to physically inscribe on his person. The second thing I noticed was his bare feet, which he dug greedily into the grass. When I gently inquired whether he might like to fetch his shoes before entering the conference room for the start of the sessions, he shot back, "I'm from Magadan. I can do whatever the f – I want and I'm not putting on shoes until I have to go back."[9]

Ivan's toes had not felt grass for a long time. He had traveled thousands of miles to make it to the green part of Siberia. Magadan is a moonscape; a vast expanse of permafrost, made habitable only through extreme determination or desperation. Running through it is the Kolyma River, containing a treasure of gold, which labor camps were set up to mine starting in 1932. At its height in 1952, nearly 200,000 people were taken from their homes and families, imprisoned for minor infractions or politics, and shipped thousands of miles to mine gold in Magadan. Ivan was one of them.

In the group of university-educated historians and museologists gathered, it was not only Ivan's lack of shoes that made him stand out. He had taken a different path to this place. After his release from the camps, Ivan, like many others, had nowhere to go back to and no easy way to get back; so he decided to stay. He began work as a truck driver. Over the years, as he drove his loads along the roads of Magadan, he passed hulking ruins of Gulag camps, their memories abandoned to the snow. He began stopping and picking up things he found on the ground, determined that they should not be lost. Bringing them back to the home he shared with his wife, he piled them in corners, as she got more and more exasperated by the clutter. One day he returned home to find them gone. As he told the story, his wife handed him a set of keys. "Here are the keys to your museum," she announced, giving him the address of a storage space where she had moved all the material. Thus was founded the Kolyma Gulag Museum, with Ivan Panikarov as its first director.

Recognizing the extreme conditions for Russian historical memory, and the extraordinary people who overcame them, required an expansive definition of museum, museum director, and museology. The Russian network created a Summer School of Museology at Perm 36, to help people like Ivan find effective strategies for communicating histories of Soviet repression, and, most urgently, for engaging their communities in recognizing and combating its contemporary legacies, the new forms of state repression and totalitarian popular culture that were growing around them. In other words, to train a new brand of museum director who was simultaneously a history educator and democracy movement organizer.

The Coalition soon had regional networks in every part of the world its founding members represented. The Liberation War Museum created an Asian Sites of Conscience network; the Slave House and District Six Museum organized an African network. These were sometimes less cohesive in terms of shared histories and goals, but they were nevertheless important vehicles for supporting local sites to pursue the Coalition's shared mission. Overall, regional networks enabled a flowering of diverse memory initiatives that a central administration – especially one based in the US – never could have.

Evaluating Sites of Conscience

As Sites of Conscience labored in their local contexts, memorializing atrocities grew into a global trend, fueling a "memory boom."[10] Confronting historical violence had become a new norm for fledgling democracies, imperative for demonstrating political legitimacy on the world stage.[11] And that history was expanding in scope: growing numbers of truth commissions, especially those in post-colonial African contexts, recognized the need to examine "historical antecedents" to recent violence.[12] Most importantly for Sites of Conscience, truth commission reports, alongside recommendations for police reform, anti-corruption measures, and the like, increasingly mandated memorials as a staple of their standard reform package, making it a nearly rote step in the transition process. The International Center for Transitional Justice started a Monuments, Memorials, and Museums program, later renamed Truth and Memory. In the cultural sector, pockets of the international museum and heritage fields began identifying themselves as agents of human rights. In 2003, UNESCO, the UN body that oversees the World Heritage program, adopted a "Strategy on Human Rights" to promote human rights and human rights education in all of its activities. The International Committee on Museum Management of the International Council on Museums (ICOM), the world's leading international museum association, issued a "Declaration of Museum Responsibility to Promote Human Rights," in 2009.[13] By 2018, ICOM proposed a wholesale revision of the very definition of what a museum is, declaring that any new definition "should be clear on the purposes of museums, and on the value base from which museums meet their sustainable, ethical, political, social and cultural challenges and responsibilities in the 21st century."[14]

Saving or creating spaces to remember painful pasts was becoming uncritically accepted. While this had the advantage of making the once inscrutable work of Sites of Conscience legible and supported, it also risked hollowing out their challenging core into empty symbols that allowed new governments to check the required reckoning box without doing the deeper societal work. It was time to get real data on what was required for creating Sites of Conscience, and what the impact could be. It was time to learn what worked and what didn't.

Searching for strategies to evaluate their impact, Sites of Conscience once again found themselves betwixt and between. Traditional museum evaluation of the time focused on learning outcomes, assuming a division between author/curator and audience. That didn't apply to most Sites of Conscience, which were more often participatory experiences in which those directly affected were deeply involved in creating the site as well as consuming it. Meanwhile, the emerging evaluation mechanisms for transitional justice were geared to measure impacts of structural reforms, like reduction in incidents of police violence, not new narrative frameworks about the value of human rights. The closest analog to evaluations of Sites of Conscience might have been studies of Holocaust or peace education, but these again assumed a division between educator and learner, and usually took place in a classroom or other neutral setting, not in a place of memory, leaving the significance of the setting unexplored. The coalition therefore had to create another hybrid framework to measure the impacts of its hybrid methodology.

The central question was what role Sites of Conscience could be expected to play in societal transformation: transformation of public consciousness, the narratives that expressed it, the policies that enacted it, and the practices that sustained it. Many site directors reported that armchair assessors – such as private funders or government supporters – made the mistake of using long-term indicators to assess a short-term experience. This mismatch of indicators to impact led to false conclusions: saying the recurrence of genocide in Rwanda proves that Holocaust museums failed gives the site too little agency; saying disappearances in Argentina have not recurred because of the strength of the country's memorials gives them too much agency, implying impact can be achieved by the very existence of the site. In both cases, the specific strategy of a site and its specific impact were left unanalyzed.[15]

Coalition members recognized that a new set of measures was needed to evaluate the effectiveness of Sites of Conscience, and around 2008, we developed a set of specific impact goals that could be achieved in a single visit to a site, conceived of as part of an interconnected set of forces fostering a broader culture of human rights. As published later, these were:

- *New information:* a Site of Conscience seeks to offer multiple perspectives on history and memory as a tool to dismantle myths, and explore the diversities of ethnic or political identities. Did participants identify new perspectives on the past or on their relationship to others?

- *Change of opinions:* did participants think differently about the contemporary issues the site raised as a result of their experience at the site? Did something they saw or heard change their mind about a specific policy or other question?

- *Emotional understanding of human consequences:* a Site of Conscience provides a visceral connection to the past. Did participants express empathy for the people they learned about at the site, and make a human/emotional connection? Did they articulate new ideas about a group of people, or become sensitized to something?

- *New relationships and collective conscience:* a Site of Conscience seeks to inspire dialogue and sharing of perspectives, create shared awareness of hidden aspects of the past, and communicate a collective sense of social responsibility. Did the program build new communication among participants in the program? Did it create a new shared understanding of something?

- *Critical thinking and engagement:* a Site of Conscience seeks to provide citizens a space for open debate and questioning, a one-day model of the kind of engagement they hope to foster in the larger society over the long term. Did participants indicate they felt free to express things they had not expressed in other forums? Did the program provoke participants to ask questions and engage in discussion among themselves? Even a small doubt or question raised can be an indicator of new critical thinking.

- *New understanding of civic agency and personal responsibility:* a Site of Conscience seeks to inspire participants to act as a result of the visit. Did participants articulate an understanding of their personal potential and responsibility to support the construction of democracy?[16]

Site directors involved in creating the indicators also recognized the need to measure how a person's engagement with a Site of Conscience was connected to other policies and practices that shaped their lives. Additional questions critical for measuring the success of single site visits included: "Is the experience at the site effectively connected to/supporting other opportunities for democratic engagement and tolerance-building? Is it integrated with the education system? Does the Site directly collaborate with or support other initiatives pursuing social reconstruction (for instance, truth commissions, judicial processes, or police education)?"[17]

The study focused on three radically different sites in radically different contexts – Italy, Chile, and Bangladesh. But all of them offered programs for young people in partnership with local schools that explained their nations' histories of violence, and analyzed the cultural assumptions about racial, religious, or political differences that supported human rights abuse. The programs hit all the targets for short-term impact: students learned new things about their societies and embraced new values of human rights and diversity. One Santiago school plagued with bullying and xenophobia even reported incidents of violence between students decreased.

But how these experiences might connect to broader, long-term processes of social change remained blurry. The challenge to finding that connection was in large part a logistical and financial one: the obvious ways for sites to have a deeper impact, such as having a longer term, sustained collaboration with schools, were too expensive for sites to provide. So were longitudinal studies of how people's engagement with a site amplified or challenged the influences of other institutions and processes in a transition. Recommendations included greater financial investment in programming and its assessment, and collaboration among sites and other institutions to analyze how their impacts interacted.

Meanwhile, a deeper confusion remained about how to define success in the first place, unresolved from the Coalition's founding debates. Assessing a site's effectiveness in societal transformation depended on what kind of society the site directors wanted to see, but how did each site define a healthy culture of human rights? This debate also involved questions about sites' relationship to state narratives and nation-building projects in times of transition. Should sites present unifying narratives that bring previously divided societies together, or does that risk denying minority experiences? Should they serve as a bridge between community and state concerns, a forum for multiple voices and perspectives? Or should they present strong counter-narratives with a narrow, unwavering focus on a single voice that has been denied?

It was impossible and unhelpful to pursue a single answer to these questions across the vast variety of contexts in which Sites of Conscience were working – from Brazil to Bangladesh, from religious sectarianism to state terrorism, from government memorials to community museums. But by resisting strict and categorical mandates around the details of implementing dialogue and truth on the ground, the Coalition may have left public memory of some histories vulnerable to the one thing none of the sites wanted: more denial.

How the Hybrid Framework Held Up: The Post-Truth Blow

However closely Sites of Conscience might have analyzed the impact of individual programs – did a visit to Villa Grimaldi equip Santiago students to fight bullying in their classrooms? Did interviewing a parent about the Liberation War give Bangladeshi youth a new appreciation for democracy? – the real test came when the world swung right, and hit hard.

In 2015, nearly two decades after its founding, the Coalition included over 250 sites, ranging from tiny archives to massive state-sponsored museums, from South America to South Asia to the Southern US. Separately, in regional collectives, and as an international movement, they were mobilizing their communities – in many diverse ways – around the integrated ideas of memory, dialogue, and action.

But by around 2015, post-truth cultures were growing globally, cohering into a shared weapon of anti-democratic, right-wing regimes in several parts of the world. These cultures took different forms in different languages and places; but in each case, authoritarian leaders coopted the original ideas of memory, dialogue, and action – particularly notions of multiple perspectives as critical to democratic culture – and turned them inside out, creating conditions that threatened to immobilize the force of Sites of Conscience. Snapshots from Argentina, Russia, and the US reveal what can happen when memory is untethered from truth; when dialogue is untethered from justice; and when action is untethered from dialogue.

Argentina: Los Dos Demonios

In December 2016, after a razor-thin runoff, Argentinians installed their first democratically elected rightist president since 1916, and the first rightist to assume power since the military dictatorship. President Mauricio Macri made it clear he believed in facing the nation's violent past head on. Drawing on the discourse Memoria Abierta and other human rights groups had spent three decades popularizing, he declared, "it hurts to recognize things, but that's what makes you grow."[18]

But while he used the same language of reckoning as Memoria Abierta had, the "things" Macri called on Argentinians to recognize were different from those Patricia fought to surface. Where Memoria Abierta and other groups publicly paraded portraits of disappeared youth, Marci argued these were not the only people to suffer during the 1970s. As one of his administration's first acts, just over a month after assuming power, his new Minister of Human Rights welcomed a group of "victims of terrorism" – family members of Argentinian military personnel who had been killed by guerillas during the military dictatorship. Soon after, the government hosted a conference for "victims of the guerrilla." The Macri administration also resurrected a long-discredited term – "dirty wars" – for the decades of dictatorship, which had been identified for the last 30 years as the "period of state terrorism," or the "military dictatorship." "Dirty wars," by contrast, implied a messy period of diffused violence in which it was hard to see through the fog who was doing what to whom – but a period that was nonetheless a war, requiring extraordinary measures to secure the peace.

This framing was called out by human rights activists as the "teoría de los dos demonios," the "theory of the two demons." It drew a moral equivalency between the violence of the movements seeking to overthrow the military dictatorship and the repression of the Argentinean state against a wide swath of the population. The Macri government was resurrecting the strategy of denial that had dominated Argentina's first pass at social reconstruction in the 1980s, immediately following the restoration of democracy, when President Carlos Menem used it to justify a blanket amnesty to "all sides" of the conflict, and asked the nation to move on. The memory movement in Argentina spent the next two decades combating this refusal to reckon with the past, finally overturning the amnesty in 2003. It seemed the "dos demonios" theory had been debunked.

But Macri brought it back, in a post-truth version: rather than erasing facts of the past, or introducing counter-claims, he cast doubt on the meaning of facts themselves. He began by questioning the foundational forensic truth of the memory movement: the number of disappeared. For many Argentinian memory activists, the number 30,000 is akin to the number 6 million for the Jewish diaspora. Memory activists had spent decades documenting individual disappearances and any piece of evidence related to it. But given the nature and strategy of the repression, the evidence was still incomplete. So in the end, the number 30,000 was not, in fact, precise, but an estimate based on the mountain of documentation they had amassed.[19] This was the very example Patricia Valdez gave in our earliest conversations in 1999 about the perils of "dialogue": that if "multiple perspectives" was introduced as a value in Argentina, it would serve as an invitation to call the fundamental truths of state violence into question. The Macri administration honed in on that weakness. The Minister of Culture began giving his own figures to the press and on social media, claiming that families of the disappeared had exaggerated the numbers to claim reparations.[20] But Macri's main strategy was not to dispute the numbers themselves, rather to discredit the importance of numbers at all. "It doesn't happen through the numbers," he claimed. "I have no idea (how many there were). It's not a debate I'm going to get into. If there were 9,000 or 30,000, if they are the ones that are written on a wall or if there are many more, it's a discussion that doesn't make sense."[21]

The crack Macri made in the foundation of 30,000 allowed him to dismantle the major institutions of memory established by the Kirchner administration, without admitting it. Under the Kirchners, the ESMA – the massive former detention center transformed into a multi-purpose campus – was entirely supported by the state, within the budget of the Ministry of Human Rights, demonstrating the centrality of the values of memory and justice to the nation. Macri's Ministry, while it kept workers at the ESMA's museum and cultural center on salary and kept the lights on, stopped all funds for the activities and supplies the museum required to welcome and engage visitors. Similarly, in October 2016, the budget for the National Memory Archive – the repository for much of the evidence supporting the 30,000 claim – was slashed by more than half.[22] Macri defended this as part of a campaign of "de-ideologization" of Argentinean public culture, which also included replacing the Presidents featured on Argentine bills with the country's unique wild animals. Leftist memory activists were "ideological"; his administration was not.

While Macri was dismantling the institutions that reminded Argentineans what happens when they abandon democracy, he was dismantling the institutions of democracy itself. He crushed dissent against his economic austerity measures by criminalizing public protests against layoffs. As Marci weakened the constitutional right to political protest through amendments rammed through while Congress was on holiday, a prominent Indigenous activist was detained for her protest activities. The arrest was condemned by the UN Working Group on Arbitrary Detention; one alarmed commentator described it as the "use of executive presidential power to take the first political prisoners in Argentina since the apparition of Democracy in the mid-1980s."[23]

Russia: "Hybrid History"

Reality can be controlled through single false claims, or by an avalanche of contradictory ones. As the communist era receded in Russia, the new government gauged what position it should take in relation to the Soviet past, and began cloaking its intentions in a memory policy formed from conflicting, continuously shifting decrees. In 2009, President Medvedev created a commission designed to "counteract attempts to falsify history to the detriment of the interests of Russia," critiqued by liberal leaders as a tool for the official rehabilitation of the Soviet past.[24] But the following year, Medvedev appointed a human rights advisor, Mikhail Fedotov, who announced he would present the President with a multi-faceted plan to rid the country of "totalitarian thinking" – soon to be shorthanded as "the de-Stalinization" program – through memorials and reparations for victims of Stalinist repression. The project aimed at no less than "to surmount the remnants of totalitarianism in society and in practice – in other words, to modernise consciousness," but without being "at war with the image of Stalin." "No one is touching him," Fedotov insisted.[25]

Russia's public memory policy was part of a broader national project of "hybrid" or "non-linear" warfare, terms developed to describe the nation's military strategy in Ukraine. "Hybrid warfare" is not waged between two sides, but involves engaging multiple players of different shapes and sizes – national armies, splinter local guerrilla groups, foreign funders – forming constantly shifting alliances with and against each other. It is supported by a communications strategy that avoids a single message from a single authority; instead, it produces what Soviet-born British journalist Peter Pomerantsev describes as a "contradictory kaleidoscope of messages to build alliances with quite different groups. ... The result is an array of voices, all working away at Western audiences from different angles, producing a cumulative echo chamber of Kremlin support."[26] By 2015, Historian Irina Scherbakova from Memorial warned that this new truth regime – in which citizens are caught in a maelstrom of overlapping and conflicting narratives – was perverting public memory. "Like we have a 'hybrid war' in Ukraine," she explained, "we have a hybrid history policy."[27] As scholar Maria Tumarkin lamented, "If there are some relatively stable tropes of memory-work, some patterns and idioms of collective working-through of the past we have come to expect, Russia defies them all."[28]

A presidential Committee on Historical Memory, during a meeting attended by President Medvedev, called for a state-sponsored campaign to construct memorials to victims of political repression across all eleven time zones, and establish new national days of remembrance. But this enthusiasm for memorialization focused on those who died, without getting into who killed them. As Medvedev's appointee Fedotov argued, the campaign should "emphasise not the fault of our forebears," but instead "on honouring and committing the memory of the victims of the regime to eternity."[29] When Memorial argued that real "de-Stalinization" of Russian consciousness could only be achieved together with legal accountability for state crimes, Medvedev demurred.

Putin further wrenched apart the connections between crime and criminal accountability in the Russian memory landscape by restoring an ode to Stalin in the Moscow Metropolitan Station, arguing that "the excessive demonization of Stalin is… one of the ways to attack… Russia"[30], while also supporting monuments to victims of Stalinist purges. At the opening of one such monument in 2017, Putin declared, "This terrible past must not be erased from our national memory and cannot be justified by anything," but, "It doesn't mean demanding accounts be settled."[31]

Putin's strategy worked well. As researchers from the Levada Center steadily polled citizens' perspectives on Stalin starting in 2001, they saw a steady decline in the association of the dictator with crimes against Russian citizens. They observed the public's sense of Stalin's responsibility devolving over three periods: "one defined by negative perceptions (2001–2006), one defined by indifferent attitudes (2008–2012), and one defined by positive assessments (2014–2018)."[32] By 2016, while 62% still agreed Stalin was "a cruel, inhuman tyrant, guilty of the deaths of millions of innocent people," the majority also credited him with defeating the Nazis, for which 85% judged he played a positive role in Russia's history, and 57% agreed he was "a wise leader who brought greatness and prosperity to the USSR."[33] But the trend toward acceptance of Stalin was characterized as much by confusion as conviction, mainly over the question of accountability. Analyzing fluctuations and contradictions in survey responses over the past two decades, researchers wrote, "It is worth noting that the number of respondents who struggled to answer increased in relation to all positions, although… only in relation to Stalin's culpability in the Purges and the Great Terror."[34]

It was this "hybrid history" that killed the Gulag Museum at Perm-36. In March 2015, after a protracted battle, the Perm provincial government confiscated the Museum's property and dismissed its staff. The activities of the museum were increasingly incompatible with the political culture of the Putin regime; in particular, the stories of repression of Ukrainians and other nationalists challenged the narrative underlying Russia's annexation of Crimea. Rather than closing the museum down, the Perm authorities took over governance of it. While they invested considerable funds to improve the site's facilities, the renovations included a complete replacement of the core exhibit and its narrative. Renaming the Gulag Museum from the "Memorial Center of the History of Political Repression Perm-36," as it was originally called, to "The Museum of the History of Camps and Workers of the Gulag" they revised the site's core interpretation to stress what the new exhibition director called "our region's contribution to victory,"[35] namely the role of camp labor in timber production during WWII, portrayed as fueling the victory against Nazi Germany. This re-presented the camp as an appropriate and important war effort. The new museum opened on July 9, 2015. "Glory to the heroes," Perm's Minister of Culture said in his opening speech. "Glory to those who fought, who laid down their lives in the name of our great victory and the preservation of our country."[36]

The new administration ended both the message and modes of the Gulag Museum: both its narratives about democracy, and its activities modeling democratic participation. The new, Putin-aligned Perm regional governor cut off funding for the free-wheeling Pilorama human rights and cultural festival, putting it out of business.[37] The new museum also ended participatory programs like "I Have Rights," the youth workshops in which students interviewed their own families about the Gulag, and then developed their own definitions of democracy and what they could do to protect it. The original museum leaders tried to keep the educational programs alive off the original site by forming a separate non-governmental organization, called the "Commemorative Centre of History of Political Repressions 'Perm – 36,'" but in April 2015, the Russian government categorized it as a "foreign agent."[38]

United States: "Many Sides, Many Sides"

One of President Trump's strongest public statements in support of white supremacy during his first year in office was made as an argument for multiple perspectives in US history. In August 2017, a series of public protests and counter-protests over whether or not to remove a statue of Robert E. Lee from a public park in Charlottesville, VA – one of a host of clashes over public memory of the Confederacy erupting across the country – ended in Ohio white supremacist James A. Fields Jr driving a car into a group supporting the removal of Lee's statue, killing Heather Heyer and injuring dozens of others.[39] "We condemn in the strongest possible terms this egregious display of hatred, bigotry and violence on many sides, on many sides," Trump said in a short statement. Critics blasted his words as devoid of "the absolute moral clarity that we need from the President of the United States at times like this," as Scott Jennings, a former special assistant to President George W. Bush, said. Joe Biden tweeted simply: "There is only one side."[40]

While politicians from the left and right immediately repudiated the moral (and implied historical) equivalency of "many sides," Trump was drawing on "civic dialogue" frameworks that had grown in popularity over the last decades. That popularity was driven in part by the Coalition of Sites of Conscience itself, celebrating multiple perspectives on US history. For example, the Minnesota Historical Society's Historic Fort Snelling, the site of Dakota concentration camps and mass death in 1862–1863, had long been interpreted as a "place of pride" in the pioneer spirit of its white settlers, while Dakota historians like Jim Anderson protested, "This is a place where there should be a holocaust museum for the Dakota."[41] When the Fort joined the Coalition in 2011, a panel designed to introduce the site's new interpretive approach to visitors explained,

> For many, Historic Fort Snelling is a place of pain and grief. For others, it is a place of pride. ... By joining the International Coalition of Sites of Conscience... we began a big shift. More complexity, more sides to the story.[42]

Promoting "more sides" had dangerous implications in a country where, as a Public Religion Research Institute poll conducted in May 2017 found, 52% of white working-class people "believe discrimination against whites is as big a problem as discrimination against blacks and other minorities." Among working-class Americans aged 65 and older, nearly six in ten held that view.[43]

By calling out Trump's language so strongly, critics expressed new recognition that the President's statement on "many sides" was in fact a way of supporting only one. While political analysts lamented increased polarization of the US electorate, Trump goosed them into drawing a clearer rhetorical line between multiple perspectives and moral relativism. "Though it was hardly his intention," Ibram Kendi observed, "no president has caused more Americans to stop denying the existence of racism than Donald Trump."[44] Kendi argues that Trump's loud celebration of white supremacy coupled with his repeated insistence that he is "the least racist person there is anywhere in the world" laid bare the ways American racism depends on its denial, and galvanized people to address it.

In the museum field, La Tanya S. Autry and Mike Murawski launched the hashtag #MuseumsAreNotNeutral, calling upon the field to recognize that "white supremacy thrives within this tyranny of the universal, the neutral, the apolitical, the fair and balanced, and the objective."[45] In 2018 Congress established a 400 Years of African American History Commission to "acknowledge the impact that slavery and laws that enforced racial discrimination had on the United States."[46] This opened a window for reckoning: in 2019, the House bill to study the case for reparations, raised repeatedly by John Conyers since 1989, was reintroduced after a decade-long silence under Obama (who opposed it), with a record number of signatories. For the first time in its history, the bill was voted out of committee. As federal bills progressed, the years that followed saw an explosion of reparations programs in cities and states across the country.

As the conditions for real historical reckoning ripened, public awareness of the bifurcation of historical memory in the US was growing rapidly. As historian Jill Lepore noted in 2017, "the more polarized our politics has become, the more polarized our past."[47] In January 2020, the *New York Times* published a study revealing that textbooks, created by the same publisher, contained different accounts of US history for schools in Texas than in California, catering to the political cultures of each state. While slavery itself was narrated fairly consistently, interpretation of its legacies and the continuous replication of structural racism – in the demise of Reconstruction, or redlining – differed in significant ways. For instance, the California textbook described racially discriminatory housing practices that shaped the post-war suburban landscape, while the Texas one did not.[48] As growing numbers of voices on the left condemned the idea that "many sides" of historical understanding – and its moral implications – could coexist, the sides just grew stronger apart.

Back in 2009, when the existence of member Sites of Conscience seemed secure, I and my colleagues in the New York office wrote that many members – this was especially true of those from the US and Western Europe – were "highly dismissive of any attempts to convey a meta narrative, arguing that sites should strive to be inclusive spaces for dialogue from multiple perspectives, in which ideas can be contested in an ongoing way, building critical thinking and popular cultures of democracy." Viktor Shmyrov and Tatiana Kursina of the Gulag Museum, Patricia Valdez of Memoria Abierta in Argentina, and others had tried to warn the rest of the Coalition – including and especially Americans – about how precarious their success was, and how an emphasis on multiple perspectives only placed Sites of Conscience at greater risk. They argued that "democracy cannot exist without justice based on a single incontrovertible truth, and that dialogue on the past can expose hard-won facts to corruption and denial, and degenerate into an all-permissive moral relativism."[49] We only half listened.

These reflections are by no means meant to argue that individual Sites of Conscience are responsible for the post-truth blow to public memory of historical violence and its legacies in their countries. But several Sites were not strong enough to endure it. Why not? The post-Cold-War global discourses the Coalition embraced – of confronting the past, bringing divided societies together in dialogue, and highlighting multiple perspectives – were strong enough to become standards, reaching the ears of national leaders like Putin, Macri, and Trump. But the original intentions of these discourses were vulnerable to perversion, especially once societies moved on from the social movements or moments of political transition from which Sites originally emerged. Did Sites' promotion of dialogue and multiple perspectives lay the seeds of their destruction? Or should Sites have been even more forceful and expansive with these values, working more closely with enduring social institutions, as opposed to short-term campaigns or transitional structures, to root these values deeply in their societies and ensure they would flourish over the long term? In other words: was there too much dialogue, or too little?

Notes

1 "Meeting 'The Museum we want,'" Memoria Abierta, http://memoriaabierta.org.
ar/wp/el-museo-que-queremos/
2 "ESMA Site Museum – Former Clandestine Centre of Detention, Torture, and Extermination," United Nations Educational, Scientific and Cultural Organization, https://whc.unesco.org/en/tentativelists/6248/
3 "Auschwitz Exhibition at Perm-36 Gulag," Auschwitz-Birkenau Memorial and Museum, http://auschwitz.org/en/museum/news/auschwitz-exhibition-at-perm-36-gulag,610.html
4 "Rethinking the National Parks for the 21st Century," National Park Service, July 2001, http://npshistory.com/publications/npsab/rethinking-nps-21st-century.pdf
5 "The National Park Service and Civic Engagement: The Report of a Workshop Held December 6–8, 2001, in New York City," National Park Service, https://www.nps.gov/civic/about/civic.pdf
6 "Bangladesh: Azam Trial Concerns," Human Rights Watch, August 16, 2013, https://www.hrw.org/news/2013/08/16/bangladesh-azam-trial-concerns#; Christof Heyns, "UN Human Rights Experts Urge Bangladesh to Ensure Fair Trials for Past Crimes," *UN News*, February 7, 2013, https://news.un.org/en/story/2013/02/431482-un-human-rights-experts-urge-bangladesh-ensure-fair-trials-past-crimes
7 David Ward, "National Trust Recreates Workhouse Experience," *The Guardian*, October 24, 2001, https://www.theguardian.com/uk/2001/oct/24/davidward
8 Satter, *It Was a Long Time Ago*, 43.
9 Ivan Panikarov in discussion with the author, July 2006.
10 Arnold-de Simine, *Mediating Memory in the Museum*; Williams, *Memorial Museums*; Sodaro, *Exhibiting Atrocity*; Yifat Gutman, Adam D. Brown, and Amy Sodaro, eds., *Memory and the Future: Transnational Politics, Ethics and Society* (Houndmills: Palgrave Macmillan, 2010).
11 John Torpey, *Making Whole What Has Been Smashed: On Reparations Politics* (Cambridge: Harvard University Press, 2006); Jeffrey K. Olick, *The Politics of Regret: On Collective Memory and Historical Responsibility* (New York, Routledge, 2007).
12 Whereas in 1994 the South African Truth Commission's investigations started with events from the 1960s, in Sierra Leone, the truth commission charged in 2000 with confronting the conflict that ravaged the country starting in 1991 began its research nearly two centuries earlier, in 1808, when the British first occupied the territory and divided existing communities. In 2008, the Liberian Truth and Reconciliation Commission released a report on the series of brutal conflicts from

1979 to 2003, concluding that "the atrocities were the result of complex historical and geopolitical factors," including the slave trade. Executive Summary and Priority Recommendations, "A House with Two Rooms: Final Report of the Truth & Reconciliation Commission of Liberia Diaspora Project" (Minneapolis: The Advocates for Human Rights, 2009), https://www.trcofliberia.org/resources/reports/final/volume-three-7_layout-1.pdf

13 https://www.corteidh.or.cr/tablas/r35236.pdf

14 Standing Committee for Museum Definition, Prospects, and Potentials, International Council of Museums, December 2018, https://icom.museum/wp-content/uploads/2019/01/MDPP-report-and-recommendations-adopted-by-the-ICOM-EB-December-2018_EN-2.pdf

15 Brandon Hamber, Liz Ševčenko, and Ereshnee Naidu, "Utopian Dreams or Practical Possibilities? The Challenges of Evaluating the Impact of Memorialization in Societies in Transition," *International Journal of Transitional Justice* 4, no. 3 (November 2010): 397–420.

16 Ibid.

17 Ibid.

18 Javier Aceves, "Buzzfeed Interviewed Argentine President Mauricio Macri," *Buzzfeed*, August 10, 2016, https://www.buzzfeed.com/javieraceves/entrevista-buzzfeed-macri?utm_term=.wrP22Vejb#.fcjZZgdyx. Translation mine. Original: "Lo hemos podido enfrentar con coraje, porque duele reconocer las cosas, pero es lo que se hace crecer."

19 Kathryn Sikkink and Carrie B. Walling, "Argentina's Contribution to Global Trends in Transitional Justice," in *Transitional Justice in the Twenty-First Century: Beyond Truth Versus Justice*, eds. Naomi Roht-Arriaza and Javier Mariezcurrena (Cambridge: Cambridge University Press, 2006), 301–24.

20 Arturo Desimone, "The War on Memory Begins in Argentina," Open Democracy, March 23, 2016, https://www.opendemocracy.net/en/democraciaabierta/war-on-memory-begins-in-argentina/; Milton Läufer, "Trivializing Tragedy," *Guernica*, March 3, 2016, https://www.guernicamag.com/milton-laufer-trivializing-tragedy/

21 Aceves, "Buzzfeed Interviewed Argentine President Mauricio Macri." Translation mine. Original: "No tengo idea (de cuántos fueron). es un debate en el que yo no voy a entrar. Si fueron 9,000 o 30,000, si son los que están anotados en un muro o si son muchos más, es una discusión que no tiene sentido."

22 "La Preocupación de las Abuelas," *Página 12*, February 22, 2017, https://www.pagina12.com.ar/584-la-preocupacion-de-las-abuelas

23 Desimone, "The War on Memory Begins in Argentina"; Luis Andres Henao, "UN Panel Tells Argentina to Release Activist Milagro Sala," *AP News*, October 28, 2016, https://apnews.com/3463e634d0ca4fa5811491b603c28879/un-panel-tells-argentina-release-activist-milagro-sala

24 Pål Kolstø, "Dmitrii Medvedev's Commission Against the Falsification of History: Why Was It Created and What Did It Achieve? A Reassessment," *The Slavonic and East European Review* 97, no. 4 (October 2019): 738–60.

25 Susanne Sternthal, "Let history be judged: the lesson of Perm-36," openDemocracy, January 6 2012, https://www.opendemocracy.net/en/odr/let-history-be-judged-lesson-of-perm-36/; Thomas Grove, "Russia Must Exorcise Stalin's Legacy – Kremlin Aide," Reuters, December 6, 2010, https://www.reuters.com/article/idINIndia-53388420101206.

26 Peter Pomerantsev, "How Putin Is Reinventing Warfare," Foreign Policy, May 5, 2014, http://foreignpolicy.com/2014/05/05/how-putin-is-reinventing-warfare/

27 Roland Oliphant, "The Growing Struggle in Russia About Historical Memory and Stalin," *The Telegraph*, May 6, 2015, http://www.telegraph.co.uk/news/worldnews/europe/russia/11585936/The-growing-struggle-in-Russia-about-historical-memory-and-Stalin.html

28 Maria M. Tumarkin, "The Long Life of Stalinism: Reflections on the Aftermath of Totalitarianism and Social Memory," *Journal of Social History* 44, no. 4 (Summer 2011): 1047.

29 Sternthal, "Let history be judged." See also Maria Mälksoo, "In Search of a Modern Mnemonic Narrative of Communism: Russia's Mnemopolitical Mimesis During the Medvedev Presidency," *Journal of Soviet and Post-Soviet Politics and Society* 1, no. 2 (2015): 317–39.

30 Dmitriy Skulskiy, "When Memorials Cease to Commemorate: The Museum of the History of Political Repression in Tomsk as a Place of Non-Patriotic Remembering," Museum and Society 17, no. 3 (November 2019): 422–36.

31 Andrew Osborn, "Putin Opens Monument to Stalin's Victims, Dissidents Cry Foul," Reuters, October 30, 2017, https://www.reuters.com/article/us-russia-putin-monument/putin-opens-monument-to-stalins-victims-dissidents-cry-foul-idUSKBN1CZ256

32 "The Perception of Stalin," Levada Center, April 17, 2018, https://www.levada.ru/en/2018/04/17/the-perception-of-stalin/

33 "Stalin," Levada Center, June 10, 2016, https://www.levada.ru/en/2016/06/10/stalin-2/

34 "The Perception of Stalin," Levada Center.

35 Robert Coalson and Mikhail Danilovich, "Revamped Perm-36 Museum Emphasizes Gulag's 'Contribution to Victory,'" Radio Free Europe/Radio Liberty, July 25, 2015, http://www.rferl.org/a/russia-perm-gulag-museum-takeover-contribution-to-victory/27152188.html

36 Ibid.

37 Dmitriy Romendik, "Closure of Stalin-Era Gulag Museum Near Perm Raises Specters of Past," Russia Beyond, August 23, 2014, https://www.rbth.com/society/2014/08/23/closure_of_stalin-era_gulag_museum_near_perm_raises_specters_of_past_39225.html

38 "Russia: Government Against Rights Groups," Human Rights Watch, February 1, 2016, https://www.refworld.org/docid/56b453ce4.html

39 Sasha Ingber, "Neo-Nazi James Fields Gets 2nd Life Sentence for Charlottesville Attack," NPR, July 15, 2019, https://www.npr.org/2019/07/15/741756615/virginia-court-sentences-neo-nazi-james-fields-jr-to-life-in-prison

40 Dan Merica, "Trump Condemns 'Hatred, Bigotry and Violence on Many Sides' in Charlottesville," CNN, August 13, 2017, https://www.cnn.com/2017/08/12/politics/trump-statement-alt-right-protests/index.html

41 Nick Coleman, "Elders Met Where Rivers Meet Genesis and Genocide are Whitewashed," *The Alley Newspaper,* July 5, 2010, http://alleynews.org/2010/07/elders-met-where-rivers-meet-genesis-and-genocide-are-whitewashed/

42 Steph Chappell, "The Mystery of State Historic Preservation Office and the Nonprofit (aka MN History Society): Understanding the Senate's Article 2 Sections 68, 69, and Others," Minnesota House of Representatives, May 6, 2021, https://www.house.leg.state.mn.us/comm/docs/uF6T2QsTX0eiqA9fV3vgEg.pdf

43 Philip Bump, "How to Understand Trump's Condemnation of 'All Types of Racism,'" *The Washington Post,* August 12, 2018, https://www.washingtonpost.com/news/politics/wp/2018/08/12/how-to-understand-trumps-condemnation-of-all-types-of-racism/?noredirect=on&utm_term=.6d9fba812094

44 Kendi, "Is This the Beginning of the End of American Racism?"

45 Mike Murawski, "Museums Are Not Neutral," Art Museum Teaching, August 31, 2017, https://artmuseumteaching.com/2017/08/31/museums-are-not-neutral/

46 "H.R.1242 – 400 Years of African-American History Commission Act," Congress.gov, January 8, 2018, https://www.congress.gov/bill/115th-congress/house-bill/1242/text?overview=closed&r=58

47 "Americans Aren't Just Divided Politically, They're Divided Over History Too," NPR, May 23, 2017, https://www.npr.org/2017/05/23/529634859/americans-aren-t-just-divided-politically-they-re-divided-over-history-too
48 Dana Goldstein, "Two States. Eight Textbooks. Two American Stories," *New York Times*, January 12, 2020, https://www.nytimes.com/interactive/2020/01/12/us/texas-vs-california-history-textbooks.html
49 Hamber et al., "Utopian Dreams or Practical Possibilities?"

PART II

Guantánamo Public Memory and Reckoning with "Who We Are"

In January 2009, on his second day in office, President Barack Obama signed an executive order to "close Guantánamo." Since 2002, "Guantánamo" – shorthand for the military base in Cuba holding hundreds of "enemy combatants" from George W. Bush's War on Terror – had become an international symbol of torture, detention, and the failure of American democracy. "Is this who we are?" Obama demanded.[1] The question is real, but Obama posed it rhetorically, urging Americans not to look.too hard for an answer: we should "look forward as opposed to looking backwards," he insisted, when it came to abuses at Guantánamo and elsewhere.[2]

Members of the International Coalition of Sites of Conscience realized immediately that Obama's declaration to "close Guantánamo" opened tremendous possibilities for deep reckoning, up against massive forces of forgetting. They had long experienced how, as historians Manfred Berg and Bernd Schaefer observe, calls like Obama's to "let bygones be bygones and look towards the future" are "standard rhetorical features in the discourse of denial."[3] Members came together over the next few years to bring all their international experience with memory, dialogue, and action to build public memory of this place and the lessons of its long history.

Officially known as the US Naval Station at Guantánamo Bay, or GTMO, this tiny spot in Cuba was a battleground for American identity and values long before Obama challenged, "Is this who we are?"[4] What most Americans imagine as a remote tangential outpost, a place few could locate on a map, has been in fact an integral part of American politics and policy from the War of 1898 through the "War on Terror" and beyond. The unique qualities of the site – its legal ambiguity, political isolation, geographic proximity, and architectures of confinement – have been used and reused to detain people who

DOI: 10.4324/9781003185826-7

fall between the boundaries of legal protections and political imperatives. Its detention infrastructure was laid long before 9/11 and used repeatedly: for suspected enemy spies in the Cold War, for more than 20,000 Haitian refugees subject to the first mass screening for HIV, and for more than 30,000 Cuban rafters rescued at sea and then held while President Clinton renegotiated immigration laws.

GTMO has been forgotten, remembered, and forgotten again at startling speed. In the ten years preceding 9/11, GTMO was "closed" three times, each to great public fanfare. After each closure, the base quickly reopened to detain a different group of people. This section explores Guantánamo's unique history of public attention and forgetting, the consequences for public policy, and the various attempts to remind Americans of this place and its people. It is grounded in the idea that GTMO, while situated in the Caribbean, is a central, not a peripheral piece of the US as an empire; integral, not exceptional, to American democracy. Reframing GTMO as essential to American historical identity changes both how we remember its place in the American past, and how to confront its future.

This section traces how the history of Guantánamo has been fundamentally shaped by its denial: how the swift erasure of each era in GTMO's history has enabled, and determined, each new one. It explores struggles to tell GTMO's story in real time: who spoke about what was happening at GTMO, as it was happening; who listened; and who tried to silence the speakers. Finally, it describes a national movement to remember Guantánamo, and in so doing, reframe "who we are." The project inspired a new strategy of participatory public memory, focused on the specific challenges of American historical denial.

A note on terminology: The US naval station at Guantánamo Bay, Cuba is often referred to as "Guantánamo" by politicians, the press, and the public. In fact, Guantánamo is a city in Cuba over a dozen miles from the military base. The base has also been nicknamed "Gitmo," based on its military abbreviation, GTMO. I will generally use "Guantánamo" when referring to the base as a symbol or set of ideas; and "GTMO" when referring to the 45-square-mile territory.

5

HOW GTMO'S HISTORY HAS BEEN SHAPED BY DENIAL

Public Memory and Public Policy in America's State of Exception

I forgot all about Guantánamo. This erasure has haunted me all my professional life. I first learned about it in 1996, when I started working at the Lower East Side Tenement Museum. Day after day, giving tours of the Museum's recreated apartments in the stifling summer heat, I repeated stories of immigrant families who lived in the building a century earlier, like the Eastern European Rogarshevskys. Our job was to connect these stories with those of immigrants today. Another guide was on my heels with another group, preparing to tell the same story; so I had to make sure to time my narrative exactly the same on every tour and get out of the way. The moment the first line of sweat trickled down my back was my cue to give the closing story of "contemporary relevance": about Haitians held at GTMO. Just as European Jews like Abraham Rogarshevsky, who had tuberculosis, were depicted as physically diseased and discriminated against as ethnically polluting, so had the US government recently detained Haitians with HIV seeking asylum, refusing to let them into the country. I repeated the story of Haitians at GTMO on those tours at least once a week for more than five years.

The story was intended to build empathy for new immigrants among Museum visitors, who were predominantly white, descendants of the European immigrants celebrated in the museum. Many of them were appalled to find "their" families' neighborhood taken over by new generations with different complexions; the Lower East Side was then dominated by immigrants from Asia and the Caribbean. By raising awareness of the struggles of new immigrants, and drawing parallels to those of visitors' beloved ancestors, we all hoped to, in the words of the Museum's then mission, "promote tolerance and historical perspective." To help Museum staff with this task, our communications director invited a number of immigrant journalists, including

DOI: 10.4324/9781003185826-8

Garry Pierre-Pierre, who then covered Haitian issues for the *New York Times*, to come on a tour and offer ideas. It was Garry who suggested using our tours to raise awareness about Haitians' struggle against discriminatory immigration policies.

I was at the Tenement Museum on September 11, 2001. Together with the rest of the staff, I watched the towers fall. We opened our doors to the flood of people staggering up Allen Street covered in white dust flecked with red blood, offering them water and a place to sit before continuing their miles-long walk to home and safety. Some of them told us they saw body parts fall from the sky. I remember thinking, for this violence, massively disproportionate violence will be unleashed; we are a vengeful nation, and we're going to do very bad things to whomever we choose to blame. Within a week, every corner of New York City, from bodegas to the airports, became blanketed with posters reading "Never Forget," with images of the Twin Towers. By April 2002, a plane full of men from Afghanistan, captured as "enemy combatants," landed at the US naval base in Guantánamo Bay, Cuba, inaugurating a new regime of state-sanctioned torture and indefinite detention that included hundreds of men never charged with any offense.

In seven years of the Bush War on Terror, all the time watching relentlessly repeating images of shackled men in orange jumpsuits, I never once connected that Guantánamo with the one I spoke about every week on my tours. In 2009, I got the news that our new President Barack Obama declared he would close Guantánamo while at work in the offices of the International Coalition of Sites of Conscience. I was running the organization at the time, supporting societies to confront the most difficult places in their pasts. Following the model members had taken with their own sites, confronting this place would require exploring what had happened at Guantánamo since the day it opened. At that time, I believed that opening was in 2002. While pitching the idea of a project to remember Guantánamo to Aryeh Neier, then President of the Open Society Foundations, he suggested I talk to one of his colleagues, since, he explained, she worked there as a translator when Haitian refugees were there in the 1990s. I actually asked him, "What refugees?"

In the years I spent amplifying other people's memories, I had buried my own. It was deeply chilling for me to realize I could be guilty of this forgetting. It was doubly frightening because I knew what the consequences of forgetting were: that's why I had devoted my working life to pushing other people to reckon and remember. I now saw that denial had whole new dimensions I needed to learn about – from blunt force to subtle stealth – that would require whole new strategies to confront.

In 2013, when over 100 men imprisoned at Guantánamo staged a hunger strike, they had no way of knowing that exactly 20 years earlier, Haitians held at Guantánamo had done the same, to call attention to their indefinite detention. The erasure of the memory of those Haitians allowed new people – this time men from Afghanistan – to be detained there indefinitely again. I hadn't spoken with Garry Pierre-Pierre since 1996, but because his name repeated, I remembered him. I asked if he would help make sure no one else forgot this history again, through a Guantánamo Public Memory Project.[5]

This chapter considers how the history of Guantánamo has been fundamentally shaped by its denial: how the swift erasure of each phase has enabled each new one. In this way, it will suggest the deep consequences of forgetting Guantánamo for American politics, culture, and identity.

How GTMO's History Can Show Us "Who We Are"

GTMO was born at the turn of the 20th century, from the clumsy coupling of two contradictory ideas of America in the world. When the US leapt in to help Cubans drive the Spanish from the island in the War of 1898, the American government cast itself as a force that rejected old-world colonialism and championed independence, promising both Cuba and its own citizens that it would respect Cuban sovereignty. But America's political and economic ruling class still believed the country had rights and responsibilities to dominate the world; so even once the Spanish were defeated, it was not willing to relinquish control of the island. After occupying Cuba for a few years, the US government extracted a host of concessions from Cuban leadership as a price of independence, modeling the dissonant mash-up of freedom and unfreedom that would characterize US neocolonialism for more than a century to come. This included a 1903 lease of 45 square miles around Guantánamo Bay that recognized "the ultimate sovereignty of the Republic of Cuba" while simultaneously granting the US "complete jurisdiction and control."[6] This effort to smash together two contradictory ideals created a third space – what legal scholars have called a "legal black hole" – in which no country's laws applied.[7] The lease was not intentionally designed to create a legal back hole, and for most of GTMO's first hundred years, confusion about whose laws prevailed at the site arose from time to time, around questions of what rights workers there had, or what should be the citizenship of people born there. Those disputes were resolved through individual court cases that often contradicted each other in their interpretation of the broader issue.[8] But once later US administrations discovered GTMO's loophole, they realized it created an ideal place to detain people, and the problems they posed, outside of US laws and public scrutiny.

With some exceptions for imprisoning suspected Cuban spies without trial in the 1950s and 60s, the US government would not intentionally use GTMO to avoid US law until 1981; and one could argue it stumbled upon the idea. That year President Reagan declared an exodus of tens of thousands of Haitians in makeshift boats heading for Miami a threat to US "welfare and safety," and initiated a policy of interdicting people at sea. First, Haitians were held on aircraft carriers floating in the Caribbean. For over ten years, they were offered cursory asylum screenings on these floating islands that no lawyers could access. Only 8 of about 23,000 were granted asylum in the US.[9]

The potential of the legal black hole was not fully exploited until the early 1990s, when President George H. W. Bush ordered tens of thousands of Haitian refugees fleeing to the US by boat to be interdicted at sea. In the Fall of 1991, two of the floating asylum courts – Coast Guard cutters carrying close to 500 refugees who had suffered harrowing sea journeys – entered Guantánamo Bay so that medical personnel could attend to them. The refugees were "housed" on the open cutter decks, in the full sun. Commander George Walls remembered he was summoned to GTMO after the current base Commander sent "a duress message saying, 'Look, we have got all these people. It's 100 degrees down here, they are living on these steel flight decks. We have got to do something.'"[10] The Coast Guard had to find a place to move the people; so they brought them to shore. The base did not want for housing: it included a whole replica of small-town America for its military personnel, including bungalows on cul-de-sacs, backyards, and swimming pools. But these were not intended for refugees. Only then did the idea of building barracks at GTMO – the structures that would lay the literal foundation of all that was to come – emerge.

Base authorities scrambled to stand up a sprawling tent city to house more than 20,000 people on a base equipped to handle no more than 5,000. GTMO was conveniently located near the path refugees were sailing from Haiti to Miami, but Haitians could also have been brought to Florida bases like Krome. GTMO was key as a place that was not US soil and therefore outside the protection of US asylum law. When it was discovered that some of the refugees had contracted HIV, since the US had passed a law barring people with HIV from entering the US, they were held in indefinite detention. After a massive legal battle and social movement, Guantánamo was declared "closed" in 1993. But in fact, the mandate was merely to move the refugees to US soil, keeping the legal black hole – and the right to use it – intact.[11] Just one year later, the tent city reopened with more elaborate infrastructure.

When more than 30,000 Cuban refugees streamed from the country, hoping to immigrate to the US, President Clinton feared their arrival en masse in Miami would stoke anti-immigrant sentiment and turn constituents against him. So he ordered them to be interdicted at sea and brought to what he called a "safe haven" at GTMO. This bought his administration time to debate and revise its immigration policy. The refugees could be detained indefinitely, this time not only outside of US law, but without any US law to guide their future. But after another massive campaign, GTMO was "closed" again in 1996; again, the people were released, while detention facilities and the legal black hole remained.[12] Just six years later, seeking a place to manage the "unprecedented threat" of Islamic terrorism, George W. Bush sent the first "enemy combatants" to GTMO, initially to Camp X-Ray, a structure first built to imprison Haitian refugees deemed disruptive to the tent city.[13]

The majority of the American public could not see what was happening on the base in Cuba. But even for people living there, its topography and evolving built environment created multiple blinders and blocks that obscured the view of the whole for those occupying any one part of it. The US-controlled territory consisted of two swaths of land on either side of the wide waters of Guantánamo Bay. On one side was the naval base, where after World War II, a community was constructed for thousands of service people and their families, a replica of an American suburb, replete with bungalows with manicured yards, swimming pools, a movie theater, and eventually a McDonald's, which residents remembered as "Mayberry."[14] For several generations, service people and Cubans passed freely back and forth through the gates; Cubans coming in to work, US service people leaving for leisure in Caimanera and other nearby towns. But after the base severed its relations with the rest of Cuba in the early 1960s, "Mayberry" became surrounded by a "cactus curtain" of barbed wire and land mines. To keep their jobs, Cuban workers had to move to the base and live out their lives behind the barbed wire, prohibited from visiting the rest of the island.[15] These workers' children were born on the base, confined to the tiny community behind the cactus curtain. GTMO-born Dennis Miller described the extent of his isolation to journalist Carol Rosenberg,

> I would love to see what it's like on that side, where my parents came from… I don't know what a river is like. I saw it from a distance but I've never put my finger in it and felt how cold it is.[16]

The refugee camps were constructed decades later, on the opposite shore, at a considerable remove from the main naval community, starting in the early 1990s. Parts of the camp infrastructure were elaborated after 2002 into the prisons of the Guantánamo Bay Detention Camp, a geographically small but morally significant slice of the base the world came to call "Guantánamo." The navy community did not have free access to the detention camp, which was run by the Joint Task Force (JTF), a different military administration made up of people from all other branches. As we'll see later, this division inspired one JTF interrogator to propose constructing a replica of a detention cell in a museum on the navy side, to show navy families what it was like behind the prison gates. And even within the detention facilities, there were invisible places: "black sites" for top secret operations, hidden from the majority of JTF service people.[17]

America's aggressive amnesia about Guantánamo's long history has sustained this "legal black hole" for generations. The failure of legislators, policy advisors, and grassroots advocates alike to recognize and analyze GTMO's history – and its denial – has severely hampered efforts to close the site and end its practices.

In 2009, when President Obama declared through an executive order that GTMO would be closed within a year, he ignored the depth and breadth of Guantánamo's roots. As the deadline for closing Guantánamo passed and it remained open, political reporters and policy wonks puzzled over why. The dominant explanations centered on the politics of his particular presidency. Some pointed to his inability to win over conservative members of Congress who were unwilling to accept detainees in their own states or to relinquish GTMO as a symbol of their commitment to national security; others blamed a lack of real commitment to human rights. Commentaries persistently discussed GTMO as though it had been constructed out of whole cloth in 2002.[18]

For years, on each anniversary of Obama's executive order, a pile of articles would reiterate some variation on the theme that GTMO should be able to be closed, were it not for the conflict within the current government, or the pre-dilections of this particular president. Dozens of organizations and coalitions of organizations, from legal advocates to church groups to artists, organized a movement to "close Guantánamo," staging public protests, theatrical die-ins, and lobbying local representatives, all focusing exclusively on GTMO's people and policies since 9/11.[19] As the years dragged on, GTMO remained open and active as ever, but once again faded from public consciousness. The stream of articles slowed to a trickle, until they became little more than dutiful annual acknowledgments that people were still trapped there. What had been constant protests dwindled in size and frequency to little-noticed events marking the anniversary once each year. In the "close Guantánamo" movement, most organizations' messaging and strategy were designed as a rapid action to topple something believed to be already precarious, not a long-haul effort to uproot a deeply entrenched system. After a decade of grueling, emotionally wrenching work with no yield, many on the front lines began to burn out and move on to other issues. Obama's failure to close Guantánamo had become the main narrative of the place, its primary public memory.

With a strong understanding of GTMO's past, those looking to close Guantánamo would have approached the problem as one more like racism – something deeply embedded and systemic throughout American culture and institutions – and less like a stand-alone policy that can be simply reversed. Commander Jeff Johnston, stationed at GTMO, stated the truth others either didn't appreciate or preferred to deny: "Guantánamo is now part of who we are."[20]

To identify how GTMO is part of who we are requires identifying its place in American history. There are different ways to historicize GTMO, with different implications for how to address the place and its policies today. For historian Jonathan Hansen, "the history of the Guantánamo naval base exposes a fundamental paradox at the heart of American national identity between liberty and coercion."[21] Hansen's framing echoes debates in the historiography of American slavery, and the divergent ways Americans understand our history of slavery: as a historical exception to the nation's essential commitment to freedom, a shameful digression on the road to fulfilling the promise of the Constitution; or, as a foundational repression that was always and continues to be required to sustain its version of empire, capitalism, and democracy.

One way to categorize Guantánamo, then, is as a "peculiar institution," a tiny, specific site with a bizarre legal structure inherited from an outdated territorial agreement, which provides a loophole in democratic regulations that may have been abused for too long, but once exposed can be quickly stitched up. After all, the lease with Cuba was designed with military control of the Caribbean basin in mind, not to provide the US with an escape from its laws and democratic institutions. Only when GTMO's strategic naval importance waned after the Cold War, was the "legal black hole" discovered as its primary value. One way to understand how GTMO became an extralegal detention facility, then, is as a historical accident.

Alternatively, Guantánamo's use as a legal black hole can be understood as integral to the history of American democracy, an essential safety valve for its regular functioning. Political philosopher Giorgio Agamben has categorized GTMO as a "state of exception," in which an authoritarian government rules by making a state of emergency permanent, under the pretext of indefinite unusual circumstances, to enable "the physical elimination not only of political adversaries but of entire categories of citizens who for some reason cannot be integrated into the political system."[22] During GTMO's first decades, American democracy had its own mechanisms for excluding entire categories of citizens, limiting who could enter the country, and who could vote in it, by race. But as the US legal system developed greater checks against racial exclusion in voting and immigration during the 1960s, GTMO represented an alternative for maintaining it. Reagan's command to interdict Haitians at sea followed a Supreme Court decision calling out the INS for racist enforcement of immigration laws, in violation of the 1965 Immigration Act. The US legal system, his administration was told, was no longer a place to make immigration policy based on race. But GTMO was. Once the legal black hole was identified as a strategic asset, it became as valuable to the US government as Guantánamo Bay's location had once been to the military.

Americans' denial of Guantánamo as integral to "who we are" is bound up in our nation's vigorous refusal to identify as an empire. "Until recently," noted American Studies scholar Amy Kaplan in 2003, "the notion of American imperialism was considered a contradiction in terms, an accusation hurled only by left-wing critics."[23] Even within the academic community, scholars reeling from the horrors they were hearing about and trying to make sense of it had to demand that GTMO be recognized as an imperial instrument. Reflecting on 100 years since 1898, in the late 1990s and early 2000s, a crop of books by a new generation of historians tried to reframe American history as a history of empire.[24] When GTMO reopened in 2001 as an extrajudicial prison, the idea of American empire was just beginning to take hold. Kaplan used her 2003 Presidential Address to the American Studies Association to urge her colleagues to understand GTMO as an "imperial location," and asserted in a subsequent article that "the legal space of Guantánamo today has been shaped and remains haunted by its imperial history."[25]

But even scholars of empire grappled with whether GTMO was a "peculiar institution," or integral to "who we are." Scholars of the Caribbean despaired that even Kaplan, though she situated GTMO in US imperial history, still framed it as distinctive. Literary critic Jana Evans Braziel, citing histories of US intervention in Haiti, lamented in 2006 that "Kaplan codes Guantánamo as exceptional," when instead its recent history was only "manifesting a twenty-first century culmination of a nineteenth century trajectory."[26] Building on this work, by 2011 historian Jonathan Hansen could confidently describe GTMO as an exceptional tool for a consistent project:

> The United States has been an expansionist, imperialist nation from its inception... for over a century Guantánamo provided the laboratory and staging area where US imperial ambition could be implemented beyond the scrutiny of the American public and the constraint of US law.[27]

While these scholars' sphere of influence was small, the fact that people who did this for a living had serious trouble deciding whether and how Guantánamo was part of "who we are" points to the uphill battle for the larger public. Interpreting GTMO's lawlessness as a historical accident, as opposed to a strategic asset that has been deliberately developed over time, matters for current policy. Refusal to reckon with GTMO's history and its relationship to the history of American democracy – a refusal made by both beltway pundits and grassroots activists – had significant consequences for the effort to close it. Most fundamentally, without history, there can be no precise public, or public policy, definition of "closing Guantánamo." Does "closing Guantánamo" mean closing the current facilities, for instance, relocating all the "enemy combatants," but maintaining the right to detain others indefinitely there, outside of US law? Does it mean closing the legal black hole, somehow requiring US law to apply throughout the base, despite the fact it is Cuban sovereign territory? Or does it mean ceding American control, decommissioning the entire base, and giving the land back to Cuba?

How the Need for Closure Keeps GTMO Open: Cycles of Remembering and Forgetting

Ronald Aubourg worked as a translator for Haitian refugees trapped on the base in the early 1990s. In the summer of 1993, he celebrated with thousands of others when Judge Sterling Johnson ordered the HIV camps closed.

"We are singing," refugee leader Vilsaint Michel told a reporter, "because the United States is finally showing that they are a democracy."[28] Back in Brooklyn, Aubourg moved on to address the myriad other struggles Haitians were facing in New York City and elsewhere. When in 2002 he learned that "enemy combatants" were being held at GTMO, he told me, he was surprised and confused. "When I heard this through the news, I said, 'Not again.' … Haitians are out… It was closed. I was shocked. I thought it was closed."[29]

Any dream of permanently closing Guantánamo has only grown more distant over time. In 2007, even after the elaboration of the War on Terror detention center, a major new facility was constructed to house up to 20,000 potential future refugees. Both the Obama and Trump administrations held regular training exercises at GTMO simulating how to deal with a sudden migrant crisis, through a military unit specially dedicated to "migrant operations" – Joint Task Force MIGOPS – though in 2017 an Immigration and Customs Enforcement (ICE) spokesman claimed the agency "does not have any plans to use this facility for any new/additional detention."[30] In March 2011, the Obama administration upheld the use of GTMO for detainees to be held indefinitely, but pursued an aggressive strategy to try and transfer individual detainees. When President Obama left office, only 41 of the total 780 post-9/11 detainees remained on the base. But by repeating the strategy used in 1993 to release Haitians – of focusing on the people, not the principle – Obama not only did not close GTMO, but left it wide open. In 2016, Donald Trump promised to "load [GTMO] up with some bad dudes."[31] In January 2018, as one of his first acts as President, Trump signed an executive order reversing the one Obama issued, affirming the prison should stay open indefinitely, and maintaining the US's option to detain people there in the interests of national security. Although civil liberties lawyers lamented the order for its symbolism and potential to inspire more terrorists, it did not in fact change GTMO's status or role; it just stated them more honestly.[32]

Each of the times GTMO was "closed," public attention – and celebration – focused on freeing the individual group then held there, not on preventing the site's capacity to detain others in the future. Each new use of GTMO came as a surprise; each time, GTMO's legal black hole needed to be re-explained. As Aubourg's story demonstrates, confusion about what closing means – and the consequent erasure of Guantánamo from public consciousness – can plague even those who were directly involved in previous struggles to close Guantánamo. Former Commander Jeff Johnston observes that after each "closing," "everyone says, 'That's it! Gitmo's done! We're out of here!' Then something comes along – racial fears, fears of communism, Castro, the cold war, revolution in Haiti, terrorism, you name it – and someone says, 'Hey, use Gitmo!'"[33]

This section looks more closely at the series of Guantánamo's openings and closings from 1993 through 2002 and asks: who knew at the time? Who forgot? Who tried to remember? What difference did it make?

1993: Haitian Refugees

The tens of thousands of Haitians who set out to sea on makeshift boats in 1991 were fleeing political persecution after a military coup that overthrew President Aristide put pro-democracy activists, or anyone suspected of sympathizing with Aristide, in danger. By this time, the US executive branch had a firm commitment to turning Haitians away. Because this practice had been called out as flagrantly racist and repeatedly blocked by US courts, the presidency avoided scrutiny and sanction by processing asylum seekers at GTMO. Without access to lawyers, the vast majority of Haitians were denied asylum, and were returned to Haiti. Starting in 1992, those who were found to have "credible fear" were then subject to a second screening: for HIV. In 1986, the US had passed a law prohibiting anyone found to be HIV positive from immigrating to the US, and fears were particularly focused on Haitians: Three years earlier, the CDC had singled out Haitians as one of four "H"s, or high-risk groups, together with "homosexuals," fueling what Paul Farmer calls an "epidemic of discrimination" against Haitians and Haitian Americans.[34] HIV-positive Haitians granted asylum could not be sent back to Haiti; so the INS declared that they would be held at GTMO indefinitely while the US government determined their fate.

In the years that followed, a movement to release them began to build from several starting points. Haitian artists spoke to the trauma of their refugee experience, and condemned the racism and injustice of their detention and deportation. Some popular musicians, including a Rara band whose members had been held at GTMO before being returned to Haiti, wrote songs specifically citing "Guantánamo" as a critical point of betrayal and pain.[35] Others, including rasin mizik ("roots music") bands like RAM, addressed the overall experience of displacement of which GTMO was a part. In 1995, international star Wyclef Jean performed a remix of "Guantanamera" with Celia Cruz at the Bouyon Rasin (Roots Soup) music festival celebrating the restoration of Aristide. With the trauma of detention so fresh for his Haitian audience, a trauma Cubans were then still experiencing at GTMO, scholar Jana Braziel characterized the performance as "a cross-cultural, cross-national articulation of resistance between Cuba and Haiti, between Cubans and Haitians, to U.S. imperialism in the Caribbean."[36]

On another front, a major legal battle was waged in New York, initiated by a group of law students led by Harold Koh, a Yale Law professor. (Koh would later serve in the Obama Administration, urging the President to close Guantánamo; he knew what it took having tried before.[37]) Lawyers and advocacy groups worked tirelessly at the base to support refugees individually. But given the confusion about the very relevance of the law, a major part of the campaign was fought through public opinion. The most powerful component of this was initiated by refugee leader Yolande Jean in January 1993, when, recognizing that all progress was stalled on the legal front, she organized a hunger strike. Major US newspapers carried stories nearly daily throughout the winter and spring of 1993.

On February 14, after hearing of the hunger strike, Jesse Jackson flew to GTMO with a band of media in tow to help frame Haitian detention for the American public as an unequivocal moral issue: "Good will defeat evil, right will defeat wrong," he told the *New York Times*. He also framed the situation as a collective responsibility, offering to join the strikers in solidarity. Finally, he equated the hunger strikers with historical martyrs who defied unjust laws. "Jesus the Christ fasted, Mahatma Gandhi fasted, Dr. Martin Luther King fasted and for the next week I will join you in this fast until you are free."[38] In March, on the day before a scheduled meeting between Clinton and Aristide, a major protest took place outside the US State Department's Manhattan passport office on Fifth Avenue, at which Jackson was a prominent presence. He was arrested together with two other leaders, an act that assured greater media exposure. Privileged progressives organized allied public events. In April, at least six universities across the country staged solidarity hunger strikes to draw further attention to the issue. At Columbia, students formed an organization called the Coalition to Free the Haitian Refugees, and erected a tent to represent the tent cities at GTMO. During the Oscars, Susan Sarandon and Tim Robbins spoke about the detained Haitians and demanded that Clinton close Guantánamo; their words reached over 45 million Americans.[39] In April, Yvonne Jean was released as part of an initial settlement, and spoke on the *Phil Donahue Show* about those still trapped, together with Susan Sarandon and Jesse Jackson.

In June, US District Court Judge Sterling Johnson declared the Haitian refugee tent city "an HIV prison camp" and ordered it shut. The ruling upheld every legal claim prosecutors had brought before the court. The *Miami Herald* reported that "refugees broke out into singing and dancing on hearing news of the judge's ruling"; an exuberant refugee leader Vilsaint Michel shared, "even many soldiers are happy for us, rejoicing with us, because they knew it was illegal to keep us here."[40] The media declared not only Guantánamo closed, but the detention policies it enforced. "The ruling," rejoiced the *New York Times*, "…will close a painful chapter in America's immigration history."[41]

But Johnson's ruling was exceedingly narrow, securing only the release of the people in the camp named in the case. If Haitian refugees won the battle, they lost the war: Clinton lawyers cut a deal with the Haitian plaintiffs that the ruling would be vacated from case law, so it could not serve as precedent. They also won a separate case whose effect was to explicitly affirm the government's right to continue to detain people at GTMO without due process.[42] As Michael Ratner, one of the main lawyers on the case, wrote regretfully in 1998, "In the future… the United States will have *carte blanche* to treat or mistreat refugees at Guantánamo however it chooses."[43]

In the noisy celebration of the Haitians' release, the legal details and their implications were drowned out in public discourse. Public perception remained that GTMO was closed, including among advocates like Ronald Auboug, who worked closely on the case. During an event on Capitol Hill I organized in 2013 in which I invited Judge Johnson to reflect on the case, he remembered that even he believed that his ruling had resolved the problem, and did not fully anticipate the long-term implications of the settlement to vacate his ruling.[44] Even he was surprised by how tenaciously Guantánamo endured.

1996: Cuban Refugees

Thanks to the narrow rulings on GTMO, barely a year later, the tents were re-erected. In August 1994, when President Castro lifted an emigration ban, thousands of Cubans set to sea, many on makeshift rafts. These "rafters," or *balseros*, fled extreme food rationing, rampant power shortages, and the political repression of Cuba's post-Soviet "Special Period in Peacetime." Fearing domestic opposition to such a large influx of immigrants, President Clinton reversed US policy of automatically granting asylum to Cubans who left the island, and ordered approximately 32,000 Cubans sent to the "safe haven" of GTMO.

GTMO officials first told *balseros* they would never enter the US, but did not explain how long they would be held or where they would go. While some Miami-based Cuban leaders agreed not to protest *balseros'* detention at GTMO in exchange for administration promises of harsher sanctions against Cuba, other Cuban Americans staged nearly a year of public protests.[45] Under pressure from this powerful political constituency, the US government treated the *balseros* at GTMO much differently than they had Haitian refugees, including providing resources that helped them become much more publicly visible. For example, the administration constructed phone banks in the camps, through which *balseros* could be in regular touch with family and friends on the mainland, and also with reporters.[46]

Like in the Haitian case, high-profile celebrities used their status to show solidarity with the *balseros* and draw media attention to their plight. But while the Haitians' celebrity spokespeople were Americans with no direct connection to the refugees' history, such conduits to the larger American public were not particularly relevant for the *balseros*. Policy decisions were negotiated privately between the Clinton Administration and Cuban American leaders; conditions at the camps could only be alleviated through independent efforts by the exile community. The *balseros'* star advocates were Cuban-American heroes, seeking to mobilize financial and political support within Cuban-American communities. Within a few months of the *balseros'* arrival at GTMO, salsa star Willy Chirino visited; he created a foundation that delivered 20,000 tons of food to the camps.[47] Toward the end of the *balseros* first year, two major artists performed there: jazz trumpet player Arturo Sandoval and Gloria Estefan, accompanied by actor Andy Garcia on congas.[48]

After a period of languishing in dangerous conditions, *balseros* saw life in the camps improve. Mobilized by public campaigns, exiles organized to establish official ombudsmen who would liaise between *balseros*, the exile community, and the US government; sent doctors to screen for people who could be released due to medical needs; and opened a stream of supplies from clothes to art materials. Then, after eight and a half months, Clinton agreed to admit *balseros* in small batches.

The stay at GTMO was rationalized by community leaders. The line in Spanish-language media – and the quotes from *balseros* that were chosen to support them – was that GTMO was a necessary purgatory, even a crucible, to be endured in the process of passing from Cuba to the heaven of the US. In 1996, the last 124 refugees boarded a plane for Miami. Coverage of the event focused on the people, not the place; *balseros'* eyes looked forward, anticipating their new challenges in the US; they were not concerned with the future of the place they were leaving behind. "It's good to never look back," *El Nuevo Herald* quoted Margarita Uria Rodriguez, known as the "last balsera" since she had drawn the last number in the departure lottery. "The nightmare is over."[49]

With Uria Rodriguez's departure from the base, media attention in both the Spanish- and English-language press turned away from GTMO. Any attention to the rafter crisis was focused on *balseros'* new lives in the US. Only one prescient refugee journalist, Mario Pedro Graveran, observed in a little-circulated publication, "We must remember that the camps of Guantánamo are closing, but... Guantánamo Bay is a painful story that's not over yet."[50]

1999: Kosovar Refugees

Indeed, GTMO's next chapter began not three years later, across the world. In 1999, a refugee exodus began in the Balkans that dwarfed those from Haiti and Cuba. After ethnic Albanian insurgents in Kosovo rose up to assert control over the province they dominated demographically, the Serbian police and the Yugoslav army responded with a campaign of ethnic cleansing, to purge the majority ethnic Albanians from the territory, with brutality that drew intentional attention. In March, hundreds of thousands of displaced ethnic Albanians began pouring into Albania and Macedonia, as NATO began airstrikes on Serbian targets in Kosovo. Monitors on the ground estimated 4,000 people were entering Albania every hour.[51] Fearing this influx would ignite ethnic violence, the Macedonian government sent a desperate missive to NATO asking it to help resettle the refugees. NATO offered to organize an airlift and share the burden of resettlement. But whereas other NATO countries agreed to provide asylum to their portion of the refugees, the US proposed detaining them at Guantánamo. The refugee camp infrastructure – from facilities to protocols to personnel – was still standing, ready to be activated.

The proposal was public, communicated without any sense of shame or secrecy. Clinton officials were completely transparent about GTMO's state of exception and their desire to use it. They explained their choice of GTMO in the same terms as they had for Cubans and Haitians: that by sheltering the refugees outside of US soil and law, the US could provide them a safe haven without burdening American communities. They also claimed that guaranteeing these refugees easy and permanent political asylum would actually abet the ethnic cleansing campaign from which they were fleeing.

Those who remembered what GTMO's "safe haven" looked like mobilized immediately. Their criticisms focused largely on what GTMO felt like. The office of the United Nations High Commissioner for Refugees described GTMO as having the "flavor of a detention camp."[52] An op-ed in the *Washington Post* by two analysts from the Carnegie Endowment for International Peace, a policy think tank, argued Americans must understand that, "Although their basic physical needs could be met at Guantánamo, they will live in a camp under military control – with little or no access to family or other support organizations in the US. Such confinement (a polite word for detention) can only add to their incredible trauma."[53] In a letter to President Clinton, a group of American refugee organizations protested that "the inhospitable, isolated, prison-like environment is inappropriate and would exacerbate the trauma and suffering they [the refugees] have already experienced."[54] Even without direct experience of this, many refugees rejected the offer of a "purely voluntary" airlift on the grounds that it was much too far from home, preventing them from finding and reuniting with their families.

What gave GTMO its "flavor," what made it "prison-like," was not only its material conditions – barbed wire and military guard – but its legal ones. This environment was enabled, and exacerbated, by the legal black hole: it was a place where refugees had no protected rights, neither of asylum nor anything else. Far from a noble rescue, the Carnegie analysts noted, "a less praiseworthy motive may lie behind the decision to use Guantánamo. Refugees held there cannot apply for political asylum under U.S. law, as they could if they were brought to U.S. territory (including Guam)."[55] These and other critics were not pulling back the curtain on an unseen plot; they used essentially the same language Clinton officials did to describe what holding the refugees at GTMO meant. They just pointed out that holding people outside of US law – a move officials proposed as both practical and charitable – was in fact "unnecessary and inhumane."[56]

Within a week, the plan was abandoned. The discussion did not extend beyond limited policy circles, so did little to build larger public awareness of the legal black hole. But those who marshalled memory won the day; though they did not succeed in closing GTMO permanently, they did prevent its normalization. That is to say, they prevented it from becoming publicly accepted as a tool for managing immigration.

2002: "Enemy Combatants"

It took less than three years from the quiet defeat of Clinton's Kosovo plan for GTMO to reopen for indefinite detention. On January 11, 2002, the first "enemy combatants" were brought to Camp X-Ray, a prison originally constructed for Haitian refugees to imprison those who had broken camp laws. It soon became an international symbol of a new world order, in which human rights took a back seat to national security.

Public understanding of post-9/11 GTMO was refracted through the extraordinary verbal prism of Secretary of Defense Donald Rumsfeld. Barely a month after the September 11th attacks, Rumsfeld explained to the press how things were going to go: "There will be some things that people will see. There will be some things that people won't see. And life goes on."[57] Here Rumsfeld was transparent about his lack of transparency. But he did perform public accountability in regular press briefings. There his art was to spin obfuscations so dizzying that they worked by exhausting his listeners into submission. Rumsfeld's most famous comment came in 2002, justifying the US invasion of Iraq. In response to a reporter's challenge that there was no evidence that Saddam Hussein had weapons of mass destruction, Rumsfeld replied:

> Reports that say that something hasn't happened are always interesting to me, because as we know, there are known knowns; there are things we know we know. We also know there are known unknowns; that is to say we know there are some things we do not know. But there are also unknown unknowns – the ones we don't know we don't know. And if one looks throughout the history of our country and other free countries, it is the latter category that tend to be the difficult ones.[58]

Rumsfeld's ruthless evisceration of truth in this statement was so astounding that it inspired a mountain of books and articles; a film by acclaimed documentarian Errol Morris; and even an opera, which treated his rhetoric as lyric poetry.[59] His formulation is significant because it negates both the power of truth and the possibility of its denial. It erases both the crime and the cover-up, by avoiding one last category – what one psychoanalytic philosopher calls the "unknown knowns" – "the disavowed beliefs, suppositions and obscene practices we pretend not to know about, even though they form the background of our public values."[60]

The "known/unknown knowns" concepts and terminology were drawn from the language of corporate risk assessment, used since at least the late 1970s. But their use by Rumsfeld – to recast a military intervention as a defense when it was, in fact, an aggressive invasion the Bush Administration had its eye on before 9/11 – had much graver consequences for global politics, human life, and public trust. It established the idea that the US government could see a future reality the public couldn't – it had a kind of privileged access to future possibilities – and it would act on those possibilities in the public's interest. Regarding Guantánamo, a place the public couldn't see, this established the idea that the government would explain what was and wasn't there. If the present might be observed, or made known through any individual testimonies that might leak out, then the near future – the reality on which the government needed to act – was classified.

The reopening of Camp X-Ray in 2002 marked the beginning of GTMO's longest continuous use for extralegal detention. But even this period has seen false closings of sites and erasures of their memory that have enabled layers of secrecy and abuse. Camp X-Ray was active for less than four months. In this short time, though, thanks to the dramatic photographs circulated in the media of kneeling men in cages, the camp became the synecdoche for War on Terror GTMO in the popular imagination. In April, as the scope of renditions, and the prison population, exploded, a new facility was constructed, called Camp Delta. Where Camp X-Ray was hastily repurposed, Delta promised a rationalized approach to the War on Terror's new detention challenges.

On April 29, 2002, the military declared Camp X-Ray closed and turned what media attention was allowed to Camp Delta. Yet detainee testimony, confirmed by documents released by the Pentagon in 2016, has since revealed that Camp X-Ray remained secretly in use. Mohammed al Qahtani first entered the "interrogation booth" at Camp X-Ray in November of 2002 and was interrogated there with sleep deprivation and other forms of torture through at least January 2003.[61] Overall his abuse, which included waterboarding, was so egregious that the Pentagon decided not to prosecute him as a 9/11 attack conspirator.[62] Ahmed al Darbi arrived in GTMO nearly a year after Camp X-Ray was "closed," but recalled that guards threatened to take him there as punishment.

Camp X-Ray could remain open because detainees were denied the right to record their memories and make them public. It took two years for lawyers to win detainees the right to any legal representation, through which they could testify to what they had experienced, and over a decade after that for their testimony to be collected and shared to build public awareness and understanding. In March 2018, the Trump administration's Justice Department admitted that "Camp X-Ray operated as a detention camp for several months in 2002 and 2003" but insisted, "It has been vacant and unused since that time."[63]

In fact, Camp X-Ray was used, but as a representation of its former self, what could be called GTMO's first museum. Visiting journalists' tightly scripted tours of the detention centers included a trip to the abandoned Camp X-Ray, where dramaturgical models of cells had been constructed, demonstrating how Korans were provided and hung on cell walls to prevent them from falling on the floor, and showcasing clean beds and sheets. Journalist Carol Rosenberg's take was that the Camp X-Ray tours were designed "to illustrate it was no longer in use in a failed bid to persuade news organizations to no longer use the prison's most iconic photos of 20 men kneeling in a cage in orange jumpsuits, taken the day the prison opened."[64] Journalist Michelle Shephard agreed, describing how her tour began at Camp X-Ray, an already ancient-looking ruin, before proceeding to Camp Delta, presented as clean and efficient, to provide a stark contrast. "The point of the tours was clear: *That was then. This is now.*"[65] By the end of the Obama Administration, these tours were discontinued, and a key word in JTF's original motto, "transparent," was removed from its website.

Americans have seen GTMO through a kind of strobe light of historical consciousness – where starkly illuminated glimpses of horrific images alternated with total darkness – preventing them from witnessing a continuous story. This episodic forgetting has fueled GTMO's cycle of closings and reopenings, shaping a public memory of the place and its people that, in turn, has shaped a public policy that allows the legal black hole to evolve and thrive. The insistence on GTMO as exceptional, as opposed to integral, to American history among even those who virulently oppose the place makes them treat it not as a thorn deeply embedded in our side, but as a fly to be brushed off, which then lands again and again in a slightly different place. The highly visible celebrations of "closing Guantánamo," permitting people to turn to other issues after a job well done, have inadvertently created the conditions for it to stay open. Yet throughout the base's long life, diverse people have made significant attempts to sustain memories of GTMO and reckon with their implications. The next chapter will explore these efforts, on and off the base, online and in real life.

Notes

1 "Obama's Speech on Drone Policy," *New York Times*, May 23, 2013, http://www.nytimes.com/2013/05/24/us/politics/transcript-of-obamas-speech-on-drone-policy.html?pagewanted=9&_r=2&ref=world&

2 David Johnston and Charlie Savage, "Obama Reluctant to Look into Bush Programs," *New York Times*, January 11, 2009, https://www.nytimes.com/2009/01/12/us/politics/12inquire.html

3 Manfred Berg and Bernd Schäfer, *Historical Justice in International Perspective: How Societies Are Trying to Right the Wrongs of the Past* (Washington, DC: German Historical Institute, 2009).

4 "Obama's Speech on Drone Policy," *New York Times*, May 23, 2013, http://www.nytimes.com/2013/05/24/us/politics/transcript-of-obamas-speech-on-drone-policy.html?pagewanted=9&_r=2&ref=world&

5 Liz Ševčenko and Garry Pierre-Pierre, "History Is Repeating Itself at Guantánamo Bay," *The Grio*, July 1, 2013, https://thegrio.com/2013/07/01/history-is-repeating-itself-at-guantanamo-bay/

6 Jana K. Lipman, *Guantánamo: A Working-Class History Between Empire and Revolution* (Berkeley: University of California Press, 2009), 19–28; Jonathan M. Hansen, *Guantánamo: An American History* (New York: Hill and Wang, 2011), 112–35; Louis A. Perez, Jr., *The War of 1898: The United States and Cuba in History and Historiography* (Chapel Hill: The University of North Carolina Press, 1998).

7 Michael J. Strauss, *The Leasing of Guantánamo Bay* (Westport: Praeger, 2009), 193.

8 Strauss, *The Leasing of Guantánamo Bay*, 80–5.

9 Hansen, 277.

10 George Walls, interviewed by Tennessee Watson, 2012, transcript, Guantánamo Public Memory Project, https://gitmomemory.org/wp-content/uploads/2012/12/George-Walls.pdf

11 Brandt Goldstein, *Storming the Court: How a Band of Law Students Fought the President – and Won* (New York: Scribner, 2005); Michael Ratner, "How We Closed the Guantánamo HIV Camp: The Intersection of Politics and Litigation," *Harvard Human Rights Journal* 11 (1998): 187–220; Harold Hongju Koh and Michael J. Wishnie, "The Story of *Sale v. Haitian Centers Council*: Guantánamo and *Refoulement*," in *Human Rights Advocacy Stories*, eds. Deena R. Hurwitz and Margaret Satterthwaite with Doug Ford (New York: Thomson Reuters/Foundation Press, 2009), 385–432; Hansen, *Guantánamo: An American History*, 264–302.

12 Elizabeth Campisi, *Escape to Miami: An Oral History of the Cuban Rafter Crisis* (Oxford: Oxford University Press, 2016); Alfredo Fernandez and Susan Giersbach Rascón, *Adrift: The Cuban Raft People* (Houston: Arte Público Press, 1999).

13 Hansen, *Guantánamo: An American History*, 307. See also Carol Rosenberg, *Guantánamo Bay: The Pentagon's Alcatraz of the Caribbean*; Karen Greenberg, *The Least Worst Place: Guantánamo's First 100 Days* (Cary: Oxford University Press, Incorporated, 2009).

14 Hansen, *Guantánamo: An American History*, 233–64.

15 Lipman, *Guantánamo: A Working-Class History*.

16 Carol Rosenberg, "So Close to Home… Yet So Far", *Miami Herald*, November 17, 2002, https://www.miamiherald.com/news/nation-world/world/americas/guantanamo/article1928467.html

17 Carol Rosenberg, "Senate report confirms CIA had 'black site' at Guantánamo, hid it from Congress", *Miami Herald*, October 19, 2015 https://www.miamiherald.com/news/nation-world/world/americas/guantanamo/article4434603.html

18 Peter Finn and Anne E. Kornblut, "Guantánamo Bay: How the White House Lost the Fight to Close It," *Washington Post*, April 23, 2011, https://www.washingtonpost.com/world/guantanamo-bay-how-the-white-house-lost-the-fight-to-close-it/2011/04/14/AFtxR5XE_story.html; Jonathan Masters, "Closing Guantánamo?" Council on Foreign Relations, November 9, 2011, https://www.cfr.org/backgrounder/closing-guantanamo; David Wagner, "Obama's Failed Promise to Close Gitmo: A Timeline," *The Atlantic*, January 28, 2013, https://www.theatlantic.com/international/archive/2013/01/obama-closing-guantanamo-timeline/318980/; Charlie Savage, "Office Working to Close Guantánamo Is Shuttered," *New York Times*, January 28, 2013, https://www.nytimes.com/2013/01/29/us/politics/state-dept-closes-office-working-on-closing-guantanamo-prison.html?pagewanted=all

19 Anna Brown, Matthew Daloisio, Michael Foley, Patrick Stanley, and Matthew Vogel, eds., *Witness Against Torture: The Campaign to Shut Down Guantánamo* (New York: Yellow Bike Press, 2008); "The World Shouts 'Close Guantánamo,'" Amnesty International, January 16, 2008, https://www.amnesty.org/en/latest/news/2008/01/world-shouts-039close-guantc3a1namo039-20080116/; Sean Michaels,

"REM and Pearl Jam Campaign to Close Guantánamo Bay," *The Guardian*, October 23, 2009, https://www.theguardian.com/music/2009/oct/23/rem-pearl-jam-guantanamo-bay; David Jackson, "Groups Urge Obama to Close Guantánamo Bay Prison," *USA Today*, October 7, 2013, https://www.usatoday.com/story/theoval/2013/10/07/obama-guantanamo-bay-prison-cuba-aclu/2935385/; "12 Arrested In Anti-Guantánamo Protest At Federal Courthouse," *CBS New York*, April 22, 2013, https://newyork.cbslocal.com/2013/04/22/12-arrested-in-anti-guantanamo-protest-at-federal-courthouse/. For more on a 2014 "living exhibit" at the National Museum of American History in Washington, DC, see Megan Fincher, "Living Guantánamo Exhibit in D.C. Museum," *National Catholic Reporter*, January 17, 2014, https://www.ncronline.org/blogs/ncr-today/living-guantanamo-exhibit-dc-museum

20 Hansen, *Guantánamo: An American History*, 357.

21 Ibid., 349.

22 Giorgio Agamben, *State of Exception* (Chicago: The University of Chicago Press, 2005), 2.

23 Amy Kaplan, "Where Is Guantánamo?" *American Quarterly* 57, no. 3 (2005): 833.

24 See Mary A. Renda, *Taking Haiti: Military Occupation and the Culture of U.S. Imperialism, 1915-1940* (Chapel Hill: The University of North Carolina Press, 2001) and Kristin L. Hoganson, *Fighting for American Manhood: How Gender Politics Provoked the Spanish-American and Philippine-American Wars* (New Haven: Yale University Press, 1998).

25 Amy Kaplan, "Violent Belongings and the Question of Empire Today: Presidential Address to the American Studies Association, October 17, 2003," *American Quarterly* 56, no. 1 (2004): 1–18; Kaplan, "Where Is Guantánamo?" 833.

26 Jana Evans Braziel, "Haiti, Guantánamo, and the 'One Indispensable Nation': U.S. Imperialism, 'Apparent States,' and Postcolonial Problematics of Sovereignty," *Cultural Critique*, no. 64 (2006): 128. See also Lipman, *Guantánamo: A Working-Class History*, 5.

27 Hansen, 349–50.

28 Liz Ševčenko and Bix Gabriel, with Jonathan Hansen, Jana Lipman, Stephen Schwab, and Michael Strauss, "Project Blueprint," Guantánamo Public Memory Project (International Coalition of Sites of Conscience, September 2011), document held by Humanities Action Lab.

29 Ronald Aubourg, interviewed by Liz Ševčenko, 2012, transcript, Guantánamo Public Memory Project, http://gitmomemory.org/wp-content/uploads/2012/12/Ronald-aubourg.pdf

30 Carol Rosenberg, "Trump's Pentagon Wants to Spend Almost $500 Million on Guantánamo Construction," *Miami Herald*, August 21, 2017, http://www.miamiherald.com/news/nation-world/world/americas/guantanamo/article168273127.html

31 David Welna, "Trump Has Vowed to Fill Guantánamo with 'Some Bad Dudes' – But Who?" *NPR*, November 14, 2016, https://www.npr.org/sections/parallels/2016/11/14/502007304/trump-has-vowed-to-fill-guantanamo-with-some-bad-dudes-but-who

32 Deb Riechmann, "Trump Signs Order to Keep Guantánamo Military Prison Open," *AP News*, January 30, 2018, https://apnews.com/acdc3a7bf4bc4279b56b197cbddb314a/Trump-signs-order-to-keep-Guantanamo-military-prison-open

33 Hansen, *Guantánamo: An American History*, 357.

34 Paul Farmer, *AIDS and Accusation: Haiti and the Geography of Blame* (Berkeley: University of California Press, 2006), 181.

35 Elizabeth McAlister, *Rara! Vodou, Power, and Performance in Haiti and Its Diaspora* (Berkeley: University of California Press, 2002), 41–2; Braziel, "Haiti, Guantánamo, and the 'One Indispensable Nation,'"142–3.

36 Braziel, 144.

37 Harold Hongju Koh, "A False Choice on GuantánamoClosure," Just Security, November 2, 2015, https://www.justsecurity.org/27298/false-choice-guantanamo-closure/; Conor Friedersdorf, "Harold Koh's Latest Plan for Closing Gitmo," *The Atlantic*, May 15, 2013, https://www.theatlantic.com/politics/archive/2013/05/harold-kohs-latest-plan-for-closing-gitmo/275858/

38 Philip J. Hilts, "7 Haitians Held at GuantánamoUnconscious in a Hunger Strike," *New York Times*, February 15, 1993, http://www.nytimes.com/1993/02/15/world/7-haitians-held-at-guantanamo-unconscious-in-a-hunger-strike.html

39 Don E. Walicek and Jessica Adams, *Guantánamo and American Empire: The Humanities Respond* (Switzerland: Palgrave Macmillan, 2017), xxiii.

40 Andres Viglucci, "Judge Says 'Squalid' Camp at Guantánamo Must Close," *Miami Herald*, June 9, 1993.

41 Mary B. W. Tabor, "Judge Orders the Release of Haitians," *New York Times*, June 9, 1993, http://www.nytimes.com/1993/06/09/nyregion/judge-orders-the-release-of-haitians.html

42 Koh and Wishnie, "The Story of *Sale v. Haitian Centers Council*."

43 Ratner, "How We Closed the Guantánamo HIV Camp."

44 Judge Sterling Johnson, remarks made at "Voices of GTMO: Past and Present," Guantánamo Public Memory Project, June 23, 2014.

45 Elizabeth Campisi, *Escape to Miami: An Oral History of the Cuban Rafter Crisis* (Oxford: Oxford University Press, 2016), 49, 50.

46 Ibid.

47 Judy Cantor, "Willy Chirino Foundation as Diverse as the Singer's Music," *Billboard*, April 28, 2001, 28.

48 Campisi, *Escape to Miami*, 51–2.

49 Cynthia Corzo and Armando Correa, "Llegan a EU Los Últimos 124 Balseros," *El Nuevo Herald*, February 1, 1996. Original: "'Ya ni mirar para atrás es bueno,' dijo Margarita Uria Rodriguez, la ultima balsera en abandonar esta base. 'Terminó la pesadilla.'" Translation mine.

50 Mario Pedro Graveran, *Impacto: The Latin News*, January 1996. Translation mine.

51 "World: European Refugees Flee Kosovo Horror," *BBC News*, March 30, 1999, http://news.bbc.co.uk/2/hi/europe/307057.stm

52 Elizabeth Becker, "Crisis in the Balkans: Shelter; U.S. Plans Refugee Barracks in Albania and Drops Airlift," *New York Times*, April 9, 1999, http://www.nytimes.com/1999/04/09/world/crisis-balkans-shelter-us-plans-refugee-barracks-albania-drops-airlift.html

53 T. Alexander Aleinikoff and Kathleen Newl, "Let Them In," *Washington Post*, April 8, 1999, https://www.washingtonpost.com/archive/opinions/1999/04/08/let-them-in/3910924f-27c0-4c94-ae96-d85af57b258a/?utm_term=.e02c69a75d3d

54 Becker, "Crisis in the Balkans: Shelter."

55 Aleinikoff and Newl, "Let Them In."

56 Ibid.

57 Donald H. Rumsfeld, "DoD News Briefing," U.S. Department of Defense, October 12, 2001, https://avalon.law.yale.edu/sept11/dod_brief30.asp

58 Donald H. Rumsfeld, "DoD News Briefing," U.S. Department of Defense, February 12, 2002, https://archive.ph/20180320091111/http://archive.defense.gov/Transcripts/Transcript.aspx?TranscriptID=2636

59 David A. Graham, "Rumsfeld's Knowns and Unknowns: The Intellectual History of a Quip," *The Atlantic*, March 27, 2014, https://www.theatlantic.com/politics/archive/2014/03/rumsfelds-knowns-and-unknowns-the-intellectual-history-of-a-quip/359719/; Hart Seely, ed., *Pieces of Intelligence: The Existential Poetry of Donald H. Rumsfeld* (New York: Free Press, 2003); David C. Logan, "Known Knowns, Known Unknowns, Unknown Unknowns and the Propagation of Scientific

Enquiry," *Journal of Experimental Botany* 60, no. 3 (2009): 712–4; Errol Morris, dir., *The Unknown Known* (New York and Los Angeles: History Films, Moxie Pictures, and Participant Media, 2013); Bryant Kong, *The Poetry of Donald Rumsfeld and Other Fresh American Art Songs*, with Elender Wall, William Bolcom, Jerry Mueller, and John Duke (San Francisco: Stuffed Penguin Music, 2004), compact disc.

60 Slavoj Zizek, "The Empty Wheelbarrow," *The Guardian*, February 19, 2005, https://www.theguardian.com/comment/story/0,3604,1417982,00.html

61 "Interrogation Log, Detainee 063," in Al Qahtani v. Obama, Center for Constitutional Rights, November 23, 2002–January 11, 2003, https://ccrjustice. org/sites/default/files/assets/Al%20Qahtani%20Interrogation%20Log.pdf

62 Carol Rosenberg, "Pentagon Plans to Raze Camp X-Ray, Guantánamo Eyesore and Enduring Symbol of Torture," *Miami Herald*, March 6, 2018, https:// www.miamiherald.com/news/nation-world/world/americas/guantanamo/ article203645719.html

63 Ibid.

64 Ibid.

65 Michelle Shephard, *Guantánamo's Child: The Untold Story of Omar Khadr* (Mississauga, Ontario: Wiley, 2008), 186. Emphasis in the original.

6

REMEMBERING AND RECKONING WITH GTMO

This chapter explores several different attempts to publicly remember GTMO's history, from community Facebook pages to a congressional inquiry. It will examine why these attempts, while they gave voice to individual communities, could not create a national or global collective reckoning with GTMO and "who we are."

Saving Sites for Public Memory: Battles Over Historic Preservation at GTMO

Lawyers have become GTMO's historic preservationists. The legal cases of detainees have been the only means to save the site's physical fabric, critical in a place where no country's preservation laws clearly apply. In 2005, lawyers for Jamil El-Banna, Hani Saleh Rashid Abdullah, and a group of other detainees petitioned the Bush Administration for an order to "preserve and maintain all evidence, documents, and information regarding the torture, mistreatment, and abuse of detainees now at the Guantánamo Bay detention facility."[1]

The Department of Defense understood this to mean it shouldn't tear anything down, not that it was responsible for actually protecting the sprawling complex. In GTMO's Caribbean climate, structures were quickly consumed by vegetation; by 2014 Camp X-Ray was described as a "ghost prison overtaken by vines and scrub."[2] Preservation is also challenged, as it is anywhere, by needs for new development. As the prison population dwindles, and the needs of those who remain evolve with age and physical legacies of abuse, GTMO needs new facilities with new features. As of this writing, several critical parts of GTMO have been or are slated to be destroyed: Camp X-Ray;

DOI: 10.4324/9781003185826-9

Camp Iguana, where teenaged detainees were held, and later detainees cleared for release; and Camp 5, where hunger strikers were held and force-fed.

A further limitation of the preservation order is that, as part of a legal case, it centers around people, not places. The order does not recognize GTMO as a palimpsest, or take responsibility for saving the layers of history that the buildings contain from Haitians, Cubans, or anyone else who had previously been at GTMO. Their traces can only be saved through those of their successors. But the preservation order has played one critical role: it has forced the government to petition the court each time it seeks to destroy or gut a site, making the move public. Yet the government has tried to avoid even this degree of accountability, by submitting petitions in secret, or too late for the defense to contest them. For example, in September 2016, Obama administration lawyers notified the court of its plans to demolish part of Camp 5, a site where detainee hunger strikers were force-fed. But it did so secretly, under seal, before claiming the seal had been a mistake, and after destruction had already begun.

The most egregious secret destruction involved CIA "black sites," secret detention centers around the world in which the CIA, between 2002 and 2006, tortured detainees for information before bringing them to the "transparent" detention facilities at GTMO. Most of these sites were located in complicit third countries around the world, such as Romania, Poland, and Thailand.[3] But two were located at GTMO itself. Defense lawyers for Khalil Sheik Muhammad and 5 others accused of masterminding the 9/11 attacks were never allowed to know where their clients had been held, and the clients, having been abducted there while hooded, had no way of knowing. Despite not being able to name the sites, lawyers petitioned the judge in the case to preserve them, wherever they were, as critical evidence in the case. In July 2016, the judge shared that he had granted the government permission to decommission the one of the GTMO black sites. Lawyers began to puzzle through what exactly that meant for the site (ceding military authority over it? razing it to the ground?). All they managed to figure out was that although the site had not as of yet been fully destroyed, US agents had been given permission to remove "fixtures," which defense attorney Suzanne Lachelier interpreted as "contraptions or devices," with the potential to demonstrate the means of torture.

The main conflict in these preservation cases is over whether it is necessary to preserve the site itself, or only a detailed representation of it. The government has repeatedly argued that photographs, diagrams, and virtual tours are equivalent, for the purposes of justice, to the physical fabric. When notifying the court of its intention to demolish Camp Iguana in 2017, the government assured that three years earlier the FBI "conducted an operational site survey… to collect various types of data and recordings about the camp" which could be used to create a three-dimensional model of it. While the camp would be destroyed, "this data will be preserved."[4] In announcing its plans to tear down Camp X-Ray in March 2018, the Trump Justice Department explained that the FBI had created "an interactive, simulated, three-dimensional, digital virtual tour… that shows all areas of the camp where detainees were held, interrogated, or otherwise present."[5]

Lawyers in the black site case found themselves having to develop arguments that would prove that images of a site were not substitutes for the site itself. The government claimed the "facilities were completely documented," and that the documentation "could be used to create a fair and accurate representation of the facility."[6] But defense lawyers contested the idea that images – whether photographs or diagrams – could ever be objective representations, arguing that seeing the site from their perspective, the defense might have documented the site differently.[7] They also argued that because forensic technology was evolving, able to discover ever-more detailed knowledge contained in physical fabric, to destroy a site was to destroy future forensic findings. Finally, defense lawyers took a completely different tack: they argued that to destroy the black sites was to destroy the foundation of global conscience. It was precisely the site's affective qualities, not its objective ones, that were the government's obligation to preserve. Such emotional resonance could not be preserved through facsimiles, however accurate they may be. The place had a power to tell its own story that the government must preserve for future generations.

History Museums on and around the Base: US Military vs. Cuban Narratives

Meanwhile, the US military preserved a different heritage of GTMO: the Windward Point Lighthouse. Described by the *Guantánamo Gazette* as "a retainer of the history of the installation [GTMO] and its many changes over the years," the lighthouse was the icon of the base for its residents, adorning T-shirts and magnets, and serving as the frequent subject of photographs and artwork service members created to represent and remember their time at GTMO. Initially constructed in 1899, and, like the lease, permanently installed in 1904, the lighthouse was the lynchpin of US naval occupation of the Bay, enabling the movement of ships in and out, until 1955 when lights were moved to another structure.[8] At some point afterward, the lighthouse keepers' quarters were converted into a small museum. Its collection was created and supported by the base community, composed of, in the words of Heritage Committee Chairman Christopher Rice, "stuff people have found over the years on the beaches or when they are doing construction projects and find artifacts that have been buried."[9] Whereas the detainee lawyers focused on preserving the recent past, the naval community saved material that "kind of represents every era of what the base has [been] through," as Rice put it.[10] Designed to build community identity, not legal evidence, the museum welcomed field trips for base schools and servicemembers on leisure time. Most of the collection related to imperial conquest or base life, including an 18th-century gun used in battles against the British, dubbed "Old Droopy," for its bent nose; models of WWII battleships; photographs of base family life in the 1950s; and a "natural history" area, complete with a manatee bone, a dolphin vertebra, and a diorama of taxidermized land animals against a painted landscape.[11]

The museum also represented a naval perspective on GTMO's role as a detention facility for refugees. For years, the museum displayed several wooden boats that had borne Cuban *balseros* whom the Coast Guard then took to camps at GTMO; the boats adorned the front yard until they rotted in the sun and had to be dismantled. The museum also included other artifacts from "Operation Sea Signal," such as the life vests distributed to refugees during their interdiction, and artwork that refugees created while in the camps expressing their gratitude to their rescuers and their visions of freedom in the US. These artifacts are used to describe GTMO as a beacon of American freedom, to demonstrate the lengths to which foreigners would go to attain it, and to celebrate the heroism of the service members who rescued refugees from certain death at sea. As visitor Helene Lancaster commented: "all those boats - Proof that Hope floats!"[12]

By the time Afghani detainees began arriving at Camp X-Ray in 2002, the lighthouse was crumbling; by 2005, the museum had been closed for lack of anyone to run it. That year, a civilian contractor named Pete Becola arrived on the base to work as an interrogator for the Detainee Assessment Branch of the Joint Task Force (JTF) Intelligence Group. He was passionate about the base's history and volunteered to take over the museum. Within a year, he reopened it and became its volunteer curator and researcher, expanding its collection and revising its small exhibits. "I want to give people a better appreciation for what GTMO stands for," Becola explained, "because it's more than just a detention center."[13] Unlike his predecessors, Pete was not a Navy man. Working on the JTF side of GTMO, he became aware that many Navy personnel and their families had not seen and didn't know much about the base's detention facilities or activities. The JTF service people, in turn, had no place to learn about their branch's history on the base. Becola's Commander, RDML Harry Harris Jr., envisioned adding a display of "a detainee bed, 'comfort items,' various detainee uniforms, and a pictorial history of the JTF, beginning with Camp X-Ray."[14] The exhibit would make an inaccessible part of GTMO, and an inscrutable part of its story, more visible to the Navy community that could feel at once connected and alienated from it.

But the lighthouse was still in trouble. In 2010, it was placed on *Lighthouse Digest*'s "Doomsday List," slated for demolition.[15,16] After vigorous advocacy by service members, those in command decided to invest in restoring the lighthouse. All branches of the US military have offices to support historic preservation on military bases. But at GTMO, the Department of Defense instead turned to Islands Mechanical, the Florida-based contractor responsible for, among other things, detention construction on the base, including the 2007 contract to build a major new facility to hold migrants. The restoration was completed in 2015. An IMC spokesperson declared that "the preservation of the lighthouse ensures that it will remain a historic symbol and memorial for residents, base personnel and future visitors to GTMO."[17]

Just a few miles outside the base, but a world away, two other museums told a completely different history of GTMO. In Caimanera, the city closest to the base, GTMO was a significant part of residents' public memory. There, a visiting journalist observed, "Anyone will tell you that the Naval Station of Guantánamo Bay was established after annexing the Platt Amendment to the Cuban Constitution of 1901," something of which few Americans on the base were aware.[18] The Municipal Museum of Caimanera, opened in the early 1980s, described itself as dedicated to preserving "the history of the town closely linked to the struggles of the Cuban people against the Yankee military presence on our soil."[19]

In the city of Guantánamo, located over a dozen miles from GTMO, El Museo Provincial de Guantánamo has included exhibits on historic coins, the Soviet space program, and the history of the naval base.[20] This last focused on the experience of the thousands of Cubans who worked on the base from the early 20th century through the Revolution.[21] A central story was of Lino Rodriguez, who sought a job on the military base during World War II. When he attempted to jump on a launch boat out of turn, a US serviceman pushed him off, and he drowned. His death led to local protests and inquiries and signaled the Cuban community's uneasy relationship with the base. His story symbolized the long history of US abuses on the base. While base kids marveled at Old Droopy and the remains of boats used by refugees who risked their lives to leave Cuba, Cuban students learned about GTMO's history and its current significance through the lives of local base workers and their struggles against the base's instruments of US imperialism.

Visual Art and Public Memory Inside GTMO's Legal Black Hole

People held at GTMO have contributed to its spotty historical record, representing what they saw and felt during their detention through visual art. But this expressive form of evidence has become trapped in the same legal black hole as the people who created it, subject to intense repression and censorship. While most artmaking was a means of working through trauma, some artworks were consciously produced for an external public, to promote understanding of what took place at GTMO; others were given as gifts to lawyers, humanitarian aid workers, or military service people. The kind of artwork different detainees were able to produce was profoundly shaped by internal military control and external community support. And while some pieces have been preserved, a host of others are caught in legal battles over who owns the artwork, and who is permitted to see it.

Haitian refugees mainly used found materials to create images of their experience. Some used pieces of tent as a canvas; others painted rocks found on the ground. Some of the images were innocent seascapes, featuring sail-boats unburdened by hundreds of asylum seekers; others depicted GTMO's tent cities, surrounded by barbed wire and gun-toting guards; still others violent confrontations between refugees and the military. Artmaking was both facilitated and controlled by camp authorities. General George Walls, the first commander of the Haitian camps, remembers,

> to relieve the boredom and kind of keep their minds occupied, we provided them with art supplies and that was at their request... they were prolific artists. I mean there was art all over the place, just everywhere. Some of it was political and we allowed them to do that... as long as it wasn't overthrow the camp commandant and that kind of thing.[22]

Haitian refugee artwork was briefly promoted and supported by white progressive celebrities, as part of their championing of the Haitian refugee cause. Filmmaker Jonathan Demme organized an auction of Haitian art from GTMO to raise funds to help the refugees. The only public exhibit was held in a small gallery above a Haitian restaurant in Miami called Tap Tap. It included drawings by unaccompanied minors, depicting violence they experienced both in Haiti and at GTMO, displayed as part of the effort to close the camps.

Few works survived. When Haitians held at GTMO were repatriated back to Haiti, they were permitted to take only a very few belongings. As General Walls remembers, "when it came time for them to go back, we gave them a plastic garbage bag and they put all their things in them and we called them Haitian suitcases."[23] A few works were taken out of the camp by lawyers, translators, and other aid workers. Walls himself has a small collection of paintings, including a portrait of him. But for the most part, these individual items constituted neither fine art nor official legal or historical evidence, so they wound up in closets or file drawers. Almost none of the surviving works are legibly signed or can be attributed to the individual who created them.

Cuban refugees' artmaking experience was substantially different. The *balsero* population included a disproportionate population of trained artists, seeking greater freedom of expression outside of Cuba. In the early period of the camps, refugee artists used materials they could find or borrow from the military, such as ink from ballpoint pens, tent canvas, plywood, and house paint. But in response to their demands for more, soon both the military and a network of private supporters provided substantial materials, and the military set up a formal art program. *Balseros* created a rich array of expression, from furniture crafted from Meals Ready to Eat (MRE) cartons, to satirical comic strips, to formal paintings and sculpture.

In December of 1995, artists opened a gallery in a tent in one of the camps, with regular exhibitions of *balsero* work. JTF overseers organized closely monitored tours for residents of other camps, allowing the work to be viewed by many more thousands of people, and allowing a rare opportunity for *balseros* to move between camps. As anthropologist Betsy Campisi argues, the artwork was an important means for *balseros* to create and maintain a collective narrative of their experience, and a collective identity.[24]

The artwork was also an important means of introducing themselves and communicating their intentions to the first Americans they encountered, namely the military. A large amount of the work celebrated ideas of freedom, and the US as the land of freedom. The Navy organized a show of *balsero* work for Navy base personnel and their families, who did not work in the JTF camps, at the Navy Exchange Mall, and sponsored a competition among *balseros* for the best logo to represent them and "brand" the community, to be displayed at the base's Officer's Club. Campisi writes that "This indicated the extent to which the military recognized that the camps were a part of its history and wanted a memento of them as well."[25] Rafter artists even made interventions in the base landscape, creating lasting memorials of the *balsero* presence for the military community, to last long after the last rafter left. One large outdoor sculpture featured a listing boat supported by life preservers accompanied by a message laid in stones: "American friends: We the Cuban rafters want to thank you for rescuing us from the dangers of the sea." Today, several pieces of *balsero* art are displayed in the Guantánamo Lighthouse and Historical Center, forming a permanent part of the military memory of GTMO.

But *balsero* artists had their eye on the mainland American public. Unlike the Haitians, almost all Cuban refugees were ultimately admitted to the US. In theory, this should have facilitated their ability to preserve and disseminate their artwork, and to profit from it. Many *balseros* treated their work not just as something they did to while away the hours, but as intentional cultural production, clearly signed and with commercial value. Others who served as curators or gallery directors in the camps intended to become dealers in the US art market. But *balsero* artists' ownership of the work they created at GTMO often came under dispute. For instance, artists who had painted a series of murals to line the passageway that released *balseros* walked before boarding the plane to Miami were not allowed to take that work with them; the military claimed it as property of the US government.

The most heavily controlled and censored creative expression emerging from GTMO is that of the post 9/11 detainees. Around 2009, an art program was created as a reward for good behavior. Detainees were shackled to the floor by their feet, and were just as constrained in what they could paint. "We were not allowed to draw or paint anything in connection with 'camp security,'" remembers Djamel Ameziane, "or that sends a political or an ideological message."[26] Images were limited to still lives and landscapes; Ameziane recalled that instructors presented detainees with pictures printed from the internet or copied from art books to reproduce.[27] Many instead painted from their imaginations. An extraordinary number of artists chose to paint the sea, although none of them had seen it for more than a decade. Although they were on a bay, surrounded by water, they had no view of the ocean from their cells or yard. "It was hard not seeing the sea, despite its only being a few hundred feet away from us," Monsour Adayfi later wrote in an essay about his artmaking experience.[28] Detainees supplemented the limited supplies they were permitted with found materials, such as cardboard, MRE boxes; gravel, sand, and rock from the exercise yard T-shirts; and bottlecaps. Work included elaborate surrealist sculptures, such as a distorted clock representing time in indefinite detention, and model ships with exquisite detail of sails, ropes, and windows.

From at least 2010 to 2015, select works of detainee art were displayed at the prison book storage facility, where all JTF staff could see them. Artists' names were withheld, and no detainees were able to see the show. Journalists were invited to view it; several published articles featuring photographs of the still lives of fruit bowls and peaceful ocean sunsets, representing the erasure of detainees' real experiences that shaped public understanding of GTMO.

Artists' ownership of their work was precarious. A May 2015 base magazine explained, "When detainees finish their work, they have the option to request the original."[29] But possessing the original did not secure its safety. Just two years earlier, the military had raided the prison in response to the growing hunger strike, and confiscated both artwork and legal documents. The artwork, unprotected by any law or custom, was never returned.[30] Lawyers were not initially permitted to take any artwork off the base; art could only be released to the International Red Cross to be given directly to detainees' families.[31] But starting around 2015, the policy changed, and some detainees began passing their work on to their lawyers, whether to safeguard it, as gifts, or as intentional public statements.[32] As Yemeni Adbualmalik (Alrahabi) Abud explained, after almost 15 years of detention at GTMO, "What I want people to know when they look at my art is that we are humans, we have feelings and emotions, we love life, and we are not like they pictured us."[33] For Djamel Ameziane, on the other hand, "art work represented a form of expression during my prison time: expression of my feelings about the unclear future; things we were deprived of; things that I dreamed of. I wasn't trying to send any form of message through my artwork."[34]

The US government determined what vision of GTMO this artwork would provide to a larger public. Everything given to lawyers had to be inspected by military personnel and cleared for removal from the base. "Depictions of suffering are more or less categorically banned from release," reported Shelby Sullivan-Bennis of Reprieve US, an NGO representing detainees, in 2017.[35]

Even before it got to this point, many detainees had incentives to self-censor: those seeking to convince the Periodic Review Board, which had the power to clear them for release if they were deemed not a "significant threat," would have been eager to avoid creating images conveying anger or protest. "I can only speculate," said Aliya Hana Hussain of the Center for Constitutional Rights, "but beautiful and innocuous artwork of landscapes and flowers helped humanize our clients," and supported efforts to get some released.[36]

In October 2017, three professors at John Jay College of Criminal Justice opened a small show of detainee artwork loaned to them by lawyers. Artists understood the project as a way of building "active memory," reminding Americans that Guantánamo was not "history." Hussain said her clients hoped displaying their art would help ensure "the public does not forget about Guantánamo."[37] Sullivan-Bennis relayed that his client Khalid Qasim "doesn't want Americans to slide into a quiet comfort thinking that the degradation and cruelty ended with the entrance of Obama."[38]

The John Jay faculty displayed the exhibit in an upstairs hallway of the college's building, not visible from either the elevators or the floor's common seating area. Despite its limited public exposure, the exhibit garnered international media attention, which provoked a powerful reaction from the Pentagon. Claiming the issue was about ownership and profit – the exhibit website had provided an email visitors could contact if they were interested in purchasing any of the pieces – the Pentagon voiced concern over "where the money for the sales was going," and declared all Guantánamo detainee art "property of the U.S. government."[39]

The base commander blocked further artwork from being released "pending a policy review,"[40] underscoring how removed GTMO was from US law and custom; as journalist Carol Rosenberg pointed out, the US Bureau of Prisons allowed artwork to be shared and even exhibited outside prison facilities, though it was also subject to review by the warden.[41] Recognizing the impact of this restriction on public memory, The National Coalition Against Censorship called the artwork "documents of historical importance" and the restriction a "violation of the public's right to access this work and thus fully participate in the political conversation around Guantánamo."[42] Despite the New York exhibition, publicity, and protests, this political conversation was profoundly shaped by censorship.

Memory Communities Off the Base: Digital GTMO Diasporas on Facebook

GTMO has produced several diasporic communities: groups of people who shared an intense experience at this single place, scattered across the country and the world, and then sustained connection virtually, mainly on Facebook. While these communities were formed to support their members, not to educate an outside public, their Facebook pages stand as carefully curated digital exhibits that create and sustain collective memories of GTMO. The collectivity is siloed, however: the communities are completely isolated from each other, both geographically and on social media. Their narratives of GTMO almost never intersect.

Guatanamigos

"Gitmoites" or "Guantanamigos" are people who served or grew up on the base in military families, and who continue to identify with it. The Guantanamigo community is united across space and time: spread across the US and around the world, they feel connected to each other no matter when they served in Cuba. Gitmoites organize in-person events around particular common experiences: reunions of the base's WT Sampson High School, or the annual cruise for those who were evacuated during the Cuban Missile Crisis. But the community comes together as a whole on Facebook, which serves as a digital exhibit of GTMO as they wish to remember it, and as they wish it to be remembered by the rest of the world.

Gitmoites' collective memory maintains a few, remarkably strong and consistent tropes, striking for their consistency across time periods. Whether in the 1960s or the 1990s, Gitmoites remember the base as a Caribbean "Mayberry," an idyllic North American suburban community with the amenities of a tropical vacation resort. They recalled being safe from crime, leaving doors unlocked, and, especially as children, a year-round string of pool parties, barbecues, and outdoor movies. As historian Jonathan Hansen argues, this nostalgia is based on some material reality: for many, this *was* actually the best place they ever lived, since the base offered them access to a level of living they couldn't afford before or since. Even those who were children on the base during the Cuban Missile Crisis, who had the terrifying experience of being suddenly evacuated from their homes, retained the same attachment to GTMO. "Everything was so free down there," remembers Anita Lewis Isom. "I would give anything to go back."[43] Wherever else they had lived, as Gitmoite DL Gordon observed, many Gitmoites "have taken the base as a hometown"; their point of origin, the basis of their values and identity.[44] As Catherine Chapman expressed it, "Gtmo is home to me as if I, too, were born there and lived there my entire life. It is the one place in the world where I felt at home."[45]

Cuban- or GTMO-born children of Cuban staff, who also grew up on the base, nevertheless experienced it differently, and formed somewhat distinct memory communities. While all the children went to school together, the staff lived together in a trailer park, whereas military families lived in military housing. Some of the women worked as domestic workers for military families. Base-born children of Cuban parents did not have American citizenship, so had to apply to enter the US as immigrants. Their families would likely live out the rest of their lives on the base, whereas military families always eventually left GTMO. In school, then, Cuban- or base-born kids stayed together grade after grade, watching military kids pass through. Although the Cuban-American and base-born families we interviewed still maintained contact with each other, they do not appear or participate as strongly in Gitmo Facebook groups and reunions.

Another division developed in the memory communities from GTMO's later years, between sailors who served on the Navy base, which included those who oversaw the refugee camps, and those who served for the Joint Task Force in the post 9/11 detention centers. JTF postings to GTMO did not generally accommodate families, and, due to the intense stress of the job, JTF service members were rotated more frequently than their Navy counterparts. JTF people shared stories of gruelling and unforgiving workloads, in stark contrast to the endless memories of leisure that united Guantanamigos. One visited the GTMO community Facebook page and lashed out at its members, frustrated at what he felt was the false vision of GTMO the page perpetuated, insisting that the current abusive working conditions for JTF servicemen and women should be recognized, not buried by Navy nostalgia.

Gitmoites struggled with their relationship with GTMO as a detention center. Most grew up or served at GTMO before the first refugee camps were established, or worked on different parts of the base. This enabled their narrative of GTMO as "free" and "safe." When images of detainees in cages splashed across every front page after 9/11, many Gitmoites stationed at the base in earlier eras could not even picture where the prisons were. On the GTMO Facebook group, some were even confused as to whether the prisons were located on the windward or leeward side of the bay. Others asked the community for help figuring out where the prisons were located in relation to the landmarks they remembered, concerned about whether any of their favorite places had been destroyed to make way for the camps.[46]

GTMOites disagreed about the base's history as a detention center. When one posted his own timeline of the base on Facebook with a final entry reading "November, 1991 The base begins its use as a prison," he inspired confusion and corrections from his Guantanamigos. One questioned, "The 1991 prison? Is that accurate?" After another confirmed that a camp had been built for Haitian refugees then, and that Camp X-Ray was "born from that," the timeline author clarified that "the actual detention center was built after the 2001 attack on the World Trade Center."[47]

Refugees: Balseros and "Botpippl"

Balseros did not express a particular attachment to GTMO as a place: their common experience spanned Cuba, GTMO, and the US. Their identity – "rafters" – referred to the mode of transport between these places, and the site of their deepest trauma. *Balseros* main collective memory was of their harrowing journey by sea. Many saw friends and family drown, or eaten by sharks. Others suffered severe dehydration and other injuries. The journey ended with the sight of a superbly outfitted US Coast Guard ship, which rescued them from their leaking makeshift crafts and gave them water and life preservers. This ship, furthermore, represented the nation they had risked their lives to enter. Given this context, rafters interpreted their experience at Guantánamo in different ways, locating it differently in their immigration narratives.

For Sergio Lastres, aside from the terrible conditions, the fact was that "a place that keeps you against your will seems like a prison. I thought they were jailing us... We were locked in, we were kept in with all the barbed wire." The psychological effects of detention were compounded by its indefinite length. "When you're there, the feeling of uncertainty, not knowing what was going to happen to you, you become affected mentally and start thinking many things."[48] His friend Conrado Basulto, held there at the same time, described the experience differently, as an important and helpful stage in refugees' acculturation process. "I thought our detention was necessary," he reflected.

> A lot of us were leaving and entering a new country so they wanted to know what kind of people they were letting in. So, it was like a filter, a way to know who was entering the U.S. To me, personally, it was a good experience. I began to understand the American way of life, the demands of it, because they began to push that there, slowly, so you could be ready for the change.[49]

Despite their different interpretations, *balseros* formed a collective identity. Their need to form community and their own narratives of their experience was particularly strong, given that they were not fully accepted within any larger community. As anthropologist Betsy Campisi writes, after being championed by Miami Cuban exiles while detained at GTMO, once in Miami many faced resistance from older generations of exiles. Their emigration narratives also challenged the established and fiercely protected narratives of Miami Cubans in power.[50] In this context, Facebook provided a perfect tool for sustaining a unique *balsero* community.

Like the GTMOite Facebook group, the *balsero* group page offers a digital exhibit and archive of camp experiences, a place for *balseros* to curate their own history. Images on this page are particularly poignant, as *balseros* had almost no access to cameras on the base; photos were therefore shot by military or aid workers, who also took them to be developed (these were the days before digital photos), and then either returned to the camps with them, or sent them to *balseros* years later. In either case, the images of GTMO that appear on the Facebook page trace a long story of migration and memory that involve a network of people.

Much of the *balseros* Facebook page was dedicated to finding and reconnecting with people who had been together in the camps but were separated through the resettlement process. Many *Balseros* settled in South Florida, but resettlement programs scattered others across the country. Their missing person searches sometimes included military personnel they remembered being particularly kind – or who owed the *balsero* something, such as pictures they had taken and promised to send.

Unlike the Guantanamigos, *balseros* did not discuss public debates about the War on Terror, or connect the detention centers to the GTMO they knew. To the extent that the *balsero* memory was connected or used to interpret larger events, it was focused on US foreign policy toward Cuba. But for the most part, the memory community was inward looking, focused on using memory to connect people and heal trauma.

Haitian refugees' experiences were wildly different. Whereas Cubans were accepted as political refugees, the US government persistently maintained that Haitians, as a whole, were economic migrants, undeserving of political asylum, and returned the majority to Haiti. There they were either killed or were under threat of severe repercussions if they identified with the activist group of emigrants. For the few who made it to the US, there was little upside to maintaining any public or community memory of GTMO. Since the refugee crisis, Haitian and Haitian-American communities had been struggling against the widespread images, circulated in US media, of hundreds of black faces packed into the tiny skiffs that branded them "botpippl" (boat people), or straining against barbed wire in GTMO's overcrowded tent cities. These images reinforced the narrative of Haitians as a mass of impoverished and needy people, in contrast to the brave Cuban freedom-seekers, that structured the US government's inconsistent and racist immigration policy that excluded so many Haitians.[51] Compounding this was the persistent racist association of Haitians with HIV. While Haitian scholars, artists, writers, and musicians developed powerful counter-narratives of the diasporic journey and experience, most of those who made it to the US had every incentive to distance themselves as far as possible from any association with GTMO.[52] There was no Facebook group of Haitians held at GTMO; no associations; no reunions.

Reckoning: The Rise and Fall of the "Bush Truth Commission"

In March 2009, Tom Pickering, a former US ambassador to the United Nations, partnered with the retired Navy Vice Admiral Lee Gunn to organize a hearing before the US Senate Judiciary Committee, chaired by Senator Patrick Leahy (D-VT), on "Getting to the Truth through a Nonpartisan Commission of Inquiry" into post-9/11 counterterrorism practices – swiftly nicknamed the "Bush Truth Commission."[53] He had reason to believe the American public would support the idea: just a month before, a USA Today/Gallup poll found that two-thirds of respondents believed there should be an official inquiry into whether Bush Administration officials' counterterrorism practices violated the law.[54] Some voices, even within the military, called for criminal prosecutions. But by the time the conversation got to the Senate, it was strictly limited to a "middle-ground" process that would "get to the truth of what went on during the last several years in a way that invites cooperation." For Leahy, the key questions were as follows: "How did we get to a point where the US government tried to make Guantánamo Bay a law-free zone in order to try to deny accountability for our actions? How do we make sure it never happens again?"[55]

In this group's vision, the answer lay solely in the short years of the Bush Administration. Senator Russell Feingold (D-WI) echoed Leahy in declaring, "we must fully understand the mistakes of the past in order to learn from them, address them, and, of course, prevent them from recurring," but argued this should be done through "a detailed accounting of exactly what happened in the last 8 years and how the outgoing administration came to reject or ignore so many of the principles on which this Nation was founded."[56] There was no mention in the hearing of the word Cuba; the origins of GTMO's legal black hole; its application to Haitian refugees, Cuban *balseros*, or Kosovars; or anything else before 9/11. The commission's account of Guantánamo suggests that it was something conjured from the sea by the Bush Administration in 2002, disconnected from geography and history.

Some argued that the political transition from Bush to Obama precluded the need for an inquiry. As Senator Arlen Specter (R-PA) put it, "When this idea of the so-called truth commission first surfaced, I said it was unnecessary because you had a change in administration." Democracy already guaranteed transparency, he falsely claimed, so "You could walk in the front door, ask for directions to the relevant filing cabinet, go in and open the drawer, and find out anything you wanted to know."[57] Others agreed that all that was required was for the policies to change, a process they felt was safely underway. Even progressive voters, who were most likely to believe the Bush Administration had practiced torture, and most likely to oppose it, didn't see a truth commission as an urgent priority. When MoveOn.org members were asked their main goals for 2009, survey respondents listed "hold the Bush Administration accountable" seventh. Obama himself declared, "my general orientation is to say, let's get it right moving forward."[58] The proposal for an inquiry directed by Congress died on the vine. By October, it was little more than a thought exercise within policy circles.[59]

In the vacuum left by the implosion of the official inquiry, people with experiences of detention stepped in. Social media, having supported memory communities of Guantanamigos and *balseros*, here facilitated a new form of public reconciliation. In late 2009, Army Specialist Brandon Neely, a guard at GTMO, made headlines when he reached out to Ruhal Ahmed and Shafiq Rasul on Facebook. Ahmed and Rasul, residents of Tipton, England, two of those known as the "Tipton Three," were detained under Neely at GTMO and later (unsuccessfully) sued Donald Rumsfeld for damages from their treatment. Neely had already expressed horror at the abuse he had participated in and observed at the camp to various media; now he wanted to tell his former captives, according to BBC journalist Gavin Lee, "how he'd felt complicit in their detention, and acknowledge the wrong they were subjected to."[60] The BBC offered to organize a chance for the three to meet in person. As Ahmed and Rasul were British and also barred from the US, the reunion took place in England, broadcast to the world on television.

The BBC broadcast from London became one of the first experiments in what reconciliation could mean and look like in the context of counterterrorism. Three men lined up on a couch with an interviewer was a far cry from a state-sponsored truth commission or restorative justice process. But many of the same steps and stages took place. Shafiq Rasul told the BBC before the meeting, "There's a few people in my family who have said what do you want to meet someone like that for, the way he treated you, you stay away from him."[61] Neely faced his victims and apologized: "I am really sorry for you even getting caught up in the situation—the way you were treated when I was there. And I'm just as guilty as the people there, because I took part in a lot of the stuff that happened. Personally, I am really sorry. I wish I hadn't taken part in it, but I did, and I'm man enough to say I'm sorry for what happened."[62] When asked if Neely should be prosecuted, Ahmed replied, "He's realised what he did was wrong and he's living with it and suffering with it and as long as that he knows what he did was wrong. That's the main thing."[63]

The January 2010 BBC broadcast of the reunion was widely publicized across a variety of media, from the *New York Times* to military blogs, though only for a few days around the time it aired. The military officially and categorically denied Neely's claim that abuse was part of the culture and expectations on the base while he was there: spokesperson Cmdr. Leslie Hull-Ryde stressed it "is false and does not withstand scrutiny."[64] But Rasul affirmed Neely's truth telling and its power: "Basically, we had our story to tell when we got out, but when people like yourself come out and basically say the same things that we were saying—it helped people to believe that what we were saying was true. So I appreciate from the bottom of my heart what you've done."[65]

Overall, GTMO's memory communities bring to mind the parable of the blind men and the elephant: each could only access their own tiny section, which for them, represented the truth of the massive and complicated whole. There was no communication or exchange across these memory communities that could begin to piece together a common understanding of a larger story. To build a shared public memory of GTMO required bringing the pieces of its history and the communities that remembered them together, to explore how they connect and collide. Only then could there be a collective conversation about what happened there, why, and what should be done about it.

Notes

1 "Memorandum Opinion and Order," El-Banna v. Bush, Civil Action No. 04-1144 (RWR), and Abdullah v. Bush, Civil Action No. 05-23 (RWR), U.S. District Court for the District of Columbia, July 18, 2005, https://www.govinfo. gov/content/pkg/USCOURTS-dcd-1_04-cv-01144/pdf/USCOURTS-dcd-1_04-cv-01144-0.pdf
2 Damon Winter and Charlie Savage, "Camp X-Ray: A Ghost Prison," *New York Times*, August 31, 2014, "https://www.nytimes.com/interactive/2014/09/01/us/guantanamo-camp-x-ray-ghost-prison-photographs.html
3 Ryan Tate, "Nine CIA 'Black Sites' Where Detainees Were Tortured," *The Intercept*, December 9, 2014, https://theintercept.com/2014/12/09/map-of-cia-black-sites/; "Revealed: The Boom and Bust of the CIA's Secret Torture Sites," The Bureau of Investigative Journalism, October 15, 2014, https://www.thebureau-investigates.com/stories/2015-10-14/revealed-the-boom-and-bust-of-the-cias-secret-torture-sites; "ICRC Report on the Treatment of Fourteen 'High Value' Detainees in CIA Custody," International Committee of the Red Cross, February 2007, https://web.archive.org/web/20090419152929/http://www.nybooks.com/icrc-report.pdf
4 "Notice Regarding Camp Iguana."
5 Rosenberg, "Pentagon Plans to Raze Camp X-Ray."
6 "Notice Regarding Camp Four," Guantánamo Bay Detainee Litigation, U.S. District Court for the District of Columbia, January 30, 2018, https://www.documentcloud.org/documents/4363369-Notice-of-Camp-4-Demolition.html
7 Carol Rosenberg, "9/11 Defense Lawyers: Judge Let U.S. Secretly Destroy CIA 'Black Site' Evidence," *Miami Herald*, July 24 2016, https://www.miamiherald.com/news/nation-world/world/americas/guantanamo/article91617862.html
8 "Windward Point Lighthouse," Lighthouse Friends, http://lighthousefriends.com/light.asp?ID=1573
9 Kegan E. Kay, "193rd Battalion Donates to Lighthouse Museum," Guantánamo *Bay Gazette*, July 2, 2015, https://issuu.com/nsgtmo-gazette/docs/july_2_fbinternet
10 Ibid.
11 Guantánamo Bay Lighthouse and Historical Center, "New Exhibits in the Museum!" Facebook, May 16, 2015, https://www.facebook.com/Guantanamo BayLighthouseMuseum/photos/a.1443762745924443.1073741834.1413631048937613/1443762635924454/?type=3&theater
12 Guantánamo Bay Lighthouse and Historical Center, "Boat Removal 2014," Facebook, February 17, 2015, https://www.facebook.com/media/set/?vanity=GuantanamoBayLighthouseMuseum&set=a.1413762418924476&comment_id=1429860403981344
13 Lauren Coia, "How Well Do You Know GTMO history?" *Guantánamo Bay Gazette*, November 3, 2006, University of Florida Digital Collections, https://ufdc.ufl.edu/UF00098616/00058
14 Ibid.
15 "Windward Point Light, Guantánamo Bay, Cuba," The Lighthouse Directory, https://www.ibiblio.org/lighthouse/photos/Caribbean/WindwardPt/windward.htm

16 "Gitmo Lighthouse Gets Suffolk Help," *Suffolk News-Herald*, July 22, 2015, https://www.suffolknewsherald.com/2015/07/22/gitmo-lighthouse-gets-suffolk-help/

17 Tom Faunce, "Islands Mechanical Contractor Inc.," *US Builders Review*, February 29, 2016, https://www.usbuildersreview.com/case-studies/islands-mechanical-contractor-inc/

18 Yisell Rodriguez Milán, "Caimanera, El Pueblo Más Cercano a la Base Naval de Guantánamo," *OnCuba News*, August 22, 2013, https://oncubanews.com/tendencias/parajes/vivir-en-caimanera-el-pueblo-mas-cercano-a-la-base-naval-de-guantanamo/. Translation mine. Original text: "Cualquiera te explica que la estación naval de la Bahía de Guantánamo se estableció tras anexarse la Enmienda Platt a la Constitución cubana de 1901." https://oncubanews.com/tendencias/parajes/vivir-en-caimanera-el-pueblo-mas-cercano-a-la-base-naval-de-guantanamo/

19 "Museo Municipal de Caimanera 19 de Diciembre," Meet CUBA, https://conocecuba.com/museo-municipal-caimanera-19-de-diciembre. Translation mine. Original text: "El museo atesora la historia de la localidad estrechamente ligada a las luchas del pueblo cubano contra la presencia militar yanqui en nuestro suelo."

20 "Museo Provincial de Guantánamo," D-Cuba, January 5, 2015 https://d-cuba.com/museo-provincial-de-guantanamo

21 Jana K. Lipman, *Guantánamo: A Working-Class History Between Empire and Revolution* (Berkeley: University of California Press, 2009), 42 and 57.

22 George Walls, interviewed by Tennessee Watson, 2012, transcript, Guantánamo Public Memory Project, https://gitmomemory.org/wp-content/uploads/2012/12/George-Walls.pdf

23 Ibid.

24 Campisi, *Escape to Miami*.

25 Elizabeth Campisi, "Guantánamo: Trauma, Culture, and the Cuban Rafter Crisis of 1994-1996" (PhD Dissertation, University at Albany, State University of New York, 2008), 329.

26 "Art from Guantánamo," *Postprint Magazine*, October 2017, https://indd.adobe.com/view/567dd3ed-81fb-43b9-83c4-869107e21d52

27 Ibid.

28 Ibid.

29 Reba Benally, "Program Enriches Detainee Life," *The Wire: The Official Publication of Joint Task Force Guantánamo*, May 8, 2015, https://www.documentcloud.org/documents/4251220-May-8-2015-edition-of-the-prison-newsletter-the.html

30 Carol Rosenberg, "After Years of Letting Captives Own Their Artwork, Pentagon Calls It U.S. Property. And May Burn In." *Miami Herald*, November 16, 2017, http://www.miamiherald.com/news/nation-world/world/americas/guantanamo/article185088673.html

31 "Art from Guantánamo," *Postprint Magazine*.

32 Ibid.

33 Ibid.

34 Ibid.

35 Ibid.

36 Ibid.

37 Ibid.

38 Ibid.

39 Carol Rosenberg, "After Years of Letting Captives Own Their Artwork."

40 Ibid.

41 Ibid.

42 Carol Rosenberg, "U.S. Military May Archive Guantánamo Prison Art Rather Than Burn It," *Miami Herald*, November 28, 2017, http://www.miamiherald.com/news/nation-world/world/americas/guantanamo/article186891663.html

43 Anita Lewis Isom, interviewed by Alison Cornyn, 2011, transcript, Guantánamo Public Memory Project, https://gitmomemory.org/wp-content/uploads/2012/12/Anita-Lewis-Isom.pdf

44 DL Gordon, March 15, 2015, 10:36 a.m., comment on Alyssa Constad, "Hello everyone!" Facebook, March 13, 2015, https://www.facebook.com/groups/2239717910/posts/10152979850337911/?comment_id=10152984082197911. Comment on March 13, 2015 post.

45 Catherine Chapman, March 15, 2015, 10:34 a.m., comment on Alyssa Constad, "Hello everyone!" Facebook, March 13, 2015, https://www.facebook.com/groups/2239717910/posts/10152979850337911?comment_id=10152984075597911

46 Matt Maxson, "I was randomly looking on Google Maps today," Facebook, March 1, 2015, https://www.facebook.com/groups/2239717910/posts/10152945343277911

47 Comments within GTMO Public community Facebook page https://www.facebook.com/groups/2239717910

48 Sergio Lastres, interviewed by Dong Kyu Lee and Laken Garcia, 2012, transcript, Guantánamo Public Memory Project, http://gitmomemory.org/wp-content/uploads/2012/12/Sergio-Transcript.pdf

49 Conrado Basulto, interviewed by Noah DeBonis, 2012, transcript, Guantánamo Public Memory Project, http://gitmomemory.org/wp-content/uploads/2012/12/transcript.-Conrado-Basulto.pdf

50 Campisi, *Escape to Miami*.

51 Farmer, *AIDS and Accusation*; Braziel, "Haiti, Guantánamo, and the 'One Indispensable Nation'"; Alex Stepick, "Shading Objective Reality: Public Presentation on Haitian Boat People," *Human Organization* 48, no. 1 (1989): 91–4.

52 Braziel, "Haiti, Guantánamo, and the 'One Indispensable Nation.'"

53 Jeremy A. Rabkin and Frederick A. O. Schwarz, Jr., "A Bush 'Truth Commission': The Pros and Cons," *Los Angeles Times*, March 12, 2009, https://www.latimes.com/opinion/opinion-la/la-oew-schwarz-rabkin12-2009mar12-story.html

54 Jill Lawrence, "Bush Policies Still Divide," *USA Today*, February 11, 2009, https://usatoday30.usatoday.com/news/washington/2009-02-11-investigation-poll_N.htm

55 *Getting to the Truth through a Nonpartisan Commission of Inquiry: Hearing before the Committee on the Judiciary, U.S. Senate*, 111th Congress, 1st Session (March 4, 2009), Serial Number J–111–8, https://fas.org/irp/congress/2009_hr/truth.pdf

56 Ibid.

57 Ibid.

58 Lawrence, "Bush Policies Still Divide."

59 Center for Strategic and International Studies, "Approaches to Accounting for Post-9/11 Counterterrorism Policies and Actions: The Pros and Cons," October 8, 2009, https://www.csis.org/events/approaches-accounting-post-911-counterterrorism-policies-and-actions-pros-and-cons

60 Gavin Lee, "Guantánamo Guard Reunited with Ex-Inmates," *BBC News*, January 12, 2010, http://news.bbc.co.uk/2/hi/uk_news/magazine/8452937.stm

61 Ibid.

62 Patrick Trahey, "Gitmo Closure: Thanks to Facebook, Two Former Detainees Reunite with Their Guilty Guard," *In These Times*, February 26, 2010, http://inthesetimes.com/article/5580/gitmo_closure

63 Lee, "Guantánamo Guard Reunited with Ex-Inmates."

64 Jennifer Fenton, "Ex-Guantánamo Guard Tells of Violence Against Detainees," *CNN*, October 28, 2011, https://www.cnn.com/2011/10/28/world/meast/guantanamo-guard/index.html

65 Trahey, "Gitmo Closure."

7

MOBILIZING AN INTERNATIONAL MEMORY MOVEMENT FOR GTMO

Public memory of GTMO, as described in the previous chapter, was shaped by three distinct forces: a government with a deep commitment to denial, making official reckoning impossible and placing evidence of abuse at risk; strong memory communities that maintained important material and knowledge of GTMO, but were completely isolated from each other; and a wider public who knew virtually nothing about GTMO before 9/11, and often forgot it existed at all. This required an approach that would meet the particular challenges these characteristics posed. First, a civil society-driven effort that would not rely on US government action to remember, but combat the erasure of public memory that official denial can produce. Second, a space where distinct memory communities could come together to share experiences, identify connections and differences, and grapple with what they all added up to. And finally, perhaps most challenging, a means of enlisting people who knew and cared the least about GTMO's longer history – those inadvertently enabling denial – as active proponents of public memory. Sites of Conscience representatives brought their varied approaches to memory, dialogue, and action to the project. In the process, we developed a new form of participatory public memory that would launch a new coalition, focused on confronting American denial.

How to Remember Guantánamo: Debates among International Sites of Conscience and Other Stakeholders

The US government's refusal to officially confront Guantánamo became clear within a few months of Obama's inauguration. Members of the International Coalition of Sites of Conscience saw a moment of opportunity for civil society to step in, and an obligation to seize it. In January 2009, the President

DOI: 10.4324/9781003185826-10

announced his intention to close Guantánamo; in March, the "Bush Truth Commission" was shot down before it had the chance to stand up. In June, the Coalition staff and I convened a group of about 50 people with wildly different personal and professional experiences. All they had in common was a deep stake in how GTMO should be remembered.

Many were directors of Sites of Conscience who had built public memory of their own states' secret detention centers, including Patricia Valdez, still working on uncovering torture cells in the streets of Buenos Aires, and Darryl Petersen, charged with reimagining the Old Fort Prison in Johannesburg as a space to support public dialogue on justice and the new South African Constitution. The group also included young lawyers like Ben Wizner of the ACLU and Gita Gutierrez of the Center for Constitutional Rights, who had been traveling back and forth to GTMO fighting for the rights and release of men held there, and were eager to get their clients' stories told. They sat beside Pete Becola, the military contractor hired to interrogate what he called "'tainees," who in his spare time reopened the base museum to celebrate GTMO's military history, and scholars like Michael Strauss, who had scrutinized every aspect of the US lease with Cuba and was full of arcane knowledge on the origins of the legal black hole. The group also included people working through official processes to address historical harm, like Patricia MacBride, who had recently been named to Northern Ireland's Commission for Victims and Survivors, and Doudou Diene, who had served as the UN's Special Rapporteur on Contemporary Forms of Racism. At later meetings, the group involved others identified primarily as public historians or museum scholars, representing entities ranging from small university departments to the Smithsonian, with extensive experience developing archival collections, exhibits, and programs that helped their societies confront difficult and divisive histories. All shared either direct experience or deep concern with Guantánamo, although they had different takes about what happened in the past, and starkly different opinions about what should close or remain open at GTMO in the future.

We came together in Memphis. Although after September 11, 2001, I had decided we would convene our international coalition only outside the US, due to the hostile and invasive immigration process delegates would have at US airports, for a project about a history for which the US was uniquely responsible, I made an exception. We gathered at the National Civil Rights Museum, a Site of Conscience whose Executive Director, Beverly Robertson, had generously offered to host us. The Museum preserved the Lorraine Motel, on whose balcony Reverend Martin Luther King Jr. was shot in April of 1968. King, who famously argued "the problem of racism, the problem of economic exploitation, and the problem of war are all tied together," would have drawn direct connections between human rights struggles in Memphis and GTMO.[1] But in 2009, "Guantánamo" was a distant issue and unknown place to most of the National Civil Rights Museum's visitors.

The connections between racism and militarism King condemned, by contrast, were on full display in Memphis. One night, asleep in my room in the cheap chain hotel where all the delegates were staying, I was awoken by a call from an African Sites of Conscience director. She had just witnessed her colleague, from another African site, being dragged off to the local jail at the direction of the white night desk clerk, after the two of them, both considered Black in Memphis, had walked into the lobby late and loudly after enjoying Beale Street. Fortunately, the hotel was packed with civil rights lawyers, whom I roused to help me figure out where her colleague had been taken and how to get him out. After that experience, he elected to return home; the incident, and his absence, made a deep impact on the rest of the group and brought renewed urgency to our work.

After touring the museum's exhibits remembering Americans' struggles against the racist violence our colleague had just endured, the group spent days together debating why and how to remember Guantánamo. Debates began with the very premise of the project. Isn't it too soon for a "memory" project, when Guantánamo is not in the past? "The beds are still warm," protested one well-recognized preservation leader to me privately by phone, warning me that pursuing a memory project about Guantánamo would sully Sites of Conscience's reputation as a movement that addressed difficult histories while avoiding sensationalism and partisan politics. Lawyers for current detainees were deeply concerned that orienting the project around "memory" would enforce the false notion that GTMO's abuses were already "history." As Gita Gutierrez of the Center for Constitutional Rights warned, "there is a population that could look at a public memory project as celebrating the closure and it is over and we are done."[2] Other activists shared their fear that looking back could erase the people still languishing at GTMO from public consciousness at the moment when most attention to their unresolved conditions was needed.

Patricia Valdez of Memoria Abierta countered that memory could be mobilized precisely to remind people of those the state wanted its citizens to forget, at precisely the moment when their abuse was still happening but people were beginning to lose interest in it. "In Argentina, the Madres said that they made memory from the very beginning when they used the images to find the disappeared," she explained. "When they tried to create international awareness of the issue, this use of memory is memory action. It's not that you should wait until the problem is over to think about memory action."[3] Some historians stressed that although Guantánamo isn't something safely in the past, it has a history that's critical for confronting the present. "We need to look back much farther than the last eight years to understand how was this allowed to happen, which is related to the question of can this be replicated," legal historian Michael Strauss insisted. "What are the steps taken over time to make this possible?"[4]

What is the power of looking at Guantánamo as a place? Lawyers for detainees worried that focusing exclusively on GTMO obscured where and how human rights abuse occurred, given that the so-called War on Terror was being waged through an archipelago of prisons and "black sites" spread across the world. They argued the project should be called something like the "Torture Public Memory Project," since, for them, GTMO was not about place but represented more widespread abusive practices and the people suffering from them. Their job was to fight for people; their main weapon, which they had only recently won rights to, was *habeas corpus*, literally the recognition of those detained at Guantánamo as human beings with legal rights. Sites of Conscience directors, on the other hand, believed analyzing GTMO as a place could reveal the palimpsest of experiences there, how one use literally built upon the other. Only by looking at the layers of history on a single ground could we understand how deep its roots of abuse ran, and what it would take to eradicate them.

If we agreed to look back, then how far? To the beginning of the GTMO we recognize today – that is, its first use as a detention facility in the 1990s – or farther, to the foundations of what made that possible – the lease at the start of the 20th century? Lawyers again cautioned that by inviting people to wander the wilds of 19th-century American imperial history, we would draw them much too far away from the central issue, namely the men being detained and tortured there right now. Historians argued that it was actually the present that created the distraction. Focusing public attention solely on the people there right now suggested the problem could be solved simply by releasing them. But Guantánamo could only actually be closed by closing its legal black hole – releasing any one generation or category of detainees only left more room for others. To build a constituency for that definition of closure, more people needed to understand the original lease and its implications. People working for transitional justice in other countries attested to how even when addressing recent violence, more and more truth commissions, particularly in post-colonial contexts like Guantánamo's, were recognizing they needed to start by educating their citizenry about the deep historical roots of the violence. As Justice Albie Sachs, the driving force behind Constitution Hill in South Africa, declared at a follow-up discussion, "Guantánamo has been monopolized by the prison, but it has a much deeper past. The dream is for Guantánamo to become the symbol of reconciliation between South and North America, involving Americans themselves who are divided."[5]

The group also grappled with the question of how a collective examination of Guantánamo's past should be framed – as "public memory," official history, or something in between? Most importantly, what should count as truth, and what relationship should this truth have to accountability? The absence of official investigations imposed both burdens and opportunities for creating an alternative space to confront the past. Several participants objected strongly to using a framework of public memory, arguing that the term implies a national myth based on beliefs, without basis in scholarship, something the project should avoid at all costs. They argued that any history to be spread to a wider public must be grounded in verifiable evidence. This approach would focus on strong, grounded argumentation, not on raising questions or integrating multiple perspectives. Any interviews, such as oral histories, conducted outside of sanctioned legal processes would have to be clearly categorized as subjective perspectives. Lacking strong public consensus over the basics, GTMO's history could not afford to leave itself open even a crack to the barrage of public doubt and denial that would undoubtedly come at it.

Others sought an approach that would create a more dynamic, ongoing space for people to grapple with the changing meaning of what happened in the past. Such a project could make public as much information about as many different types of people involved in GTMO as possible, based on rigorous research. It might work closely with formal investigations to preserve evidence and gain official legitimacy for the truths it seeks to uncover. But unlike such investigations, the purpose of a memory project is not solely to bring select individuals to justice. Instead, it examines a longer time period and a broader range of experiences to uncover the deeper underlying causes of what happened and what is unfolding for the future. As Joe Margulies of Northwestern University Law School put it, "There are many facts out there, but the contested questions are the ones that are most meaningful."[6] A memory project could open a space between prosecution and impunity that involves a broader community in deeper questions of accountability over a longer period of time.

Ultimately, the group agreed on a shared set of principles for building a public memory of Guantánamo. It should involve a longer history of the site than its recent use in the "War on Terror"– from at least the US occupation in 1898, if not before. It should include multiple voices and perspectives such as recent and past detainees, military personnel, Cuban workers, and Third Country Nationals. And it must aim to restore the dignity of all as human beings with complex individual histories and backgrounds, while being grounded in rigorous scholarship. It should probe the past to raise questions about the present and the future – not only of the site but also of related policies and practices at sites around the world – and inspire open and ongoing public debate for societies everywhere about how to act on the lessons of GTMO. And, it should focus on reaching people off the physical site, without precluding the possibility of an on-site history museum at some point in the future.

Designing a Participatory Memory Process

Initially, the Project was organized so that a small group of experts would collect and curate media and materials on GTMO's history and present. During one of the final discussions, in which participants were asked to identify what they would contribute to the collective effort, Haidy Geismar, then a professor in Museum Studies at New York University, said she could invite her students to create a small exhibition, using materials the Project had collected thus far, to be displayed in windows overlooking Washington Square. Max Page, a professor who worked with the Public History program at the University of Massachusetts, mentioned he might be able to do something similar in Amherst.

This small exchange suddenly suggested an entirely new way of conceiving the Project's authorship and audience. Trying to find a museum willing to develop an exhibit on such a charged topic, and in a collaborative way with so many different institutions, would be exceedingly difficult. If it could happen at all, it would need to be done. on an extremely protracted timeline to allow for fundraising, vetting, and scheduling of space. Universities, on the other hand, were much freer in what they could "say," and could be much more experimental. Students in US public history and museum studies programs often made mini-exhibits in a single semester. Because they were produced quickly, and by non-experts, they were not held to the same standards and scrutiny as professional exhibits were. Museums sometimes even hosted such exhibits, but clearly framed them as non-expert work that did not represent the museum. If done on a national scale, a student-curated exhibit could build public memory in two ways at once: engage young people in learning about GTMO's history, and turn them into ambassadors responsible for raising awareness and opening dialogue around this history to a broader public.

The group took a gamble: instead of keeping the project in the hands of experts, we gave the most responsibility to some of the people who knew the least – US university students – inviting them to build their own understanding along with the rest of the world's. I began reaching out to other universities offering courses or programs that worked with students to produce interpretive public history projects. Elazar Barkan, who was just launching his Alliance for Historical Dialogue and Accountability at Columbia University, invited me to build the project from there. Project staff sought to recruit programs in different parts of the country, and in different types of institutions, to create a national student group that would represent a variety of political perspectives. By the end of that year, faculty from nine universities had come together, representing about 300 students. Faculty agreed to all simultaneously teach a course on GTMO's history and the challenges of interpreting it. They would also guide students in researching and curating one "chapter" of that history for a collective national traveling exhibit and website, and would then host the resulting exhibit somewhere in their city. In this way, the Project hoped to approach building Guantánamo's public memory as a process of ongoing dialogue, and create a corps of memory ambassadors in cities across the country who would inspire others to grapple with GTMO's history.

The first task was to create an overall frame through which individual contributions would cohere into a comprehensible whole. The frame needed to be both intellectual and physical, bringing the 300 curatorial voices into a common conversation, while allowing for independent interpretation. To create the intellectual frame, Project staff first invited participating faculty to share ideas for a common, overarching question all teams could pursue through their different chapters. What emerged was simply "Why Guantánamo?" This question encompassed why GTMO has played the role it has historically, and why we should remember or care about it today. Project staff assembled a team of historians, lawyers, and other experts to help structure how to investigate that question, and to review student work along the way. This group advised on how to divide GTMO's history into chapters – such as the creation of the lease; the Cold War; Haitian refugees; Cuban refugees; War on Terror – so that each local team would have a substantive story to dig into, and collectively the history of GTMO that emerged would hang together and cover the most important points. But apart from offering chapter headings and two to three sentences on what could be explored within them, local teams were invited to interpret their piece of the history as they saw fit.

Students: Confronting Ignorance and Denial

Most of the students were children when the 9/11 attacks happened, with little or no direct memory of the events and their immediate aftermath. They were a combination of undergraduate and graduate, coming from a wide variety of political perspectives. Some only stumbled into the project, without a specific desire to learn about GTMO; several professors ran the project through introductory or methodology courses students were required to take. From the beginning, the Project sought to work with them as both authors and audience, by structuring ways for them to acknowledge and reflect on their own assumptions and where these assumptions came from. An early writing assignment asked students to share what they knew or thought about GTMO coming into the project, to help them imagine themselves as visitors to the future exhibit. "I only knew it from the movie "Harold & Kumar Escape from Guantánamo Bay (2008)" admitted Teng Lee of Brown University.[7] His classmate Ria Mirchandani echoed, "When I initially started working on this project, I too was a blank slate, with little knowledge of Guantánamo and its multifarious problems."[8] Samantha Maley of Arizona State University recalled, "Crickets chirped loudly in my mind as I frantically tried to extract any information I had stored on Guantánamo in my mind. 'Isn't there a prison or something there?' This was the only fact I knew about the place."[9]

Some students realized their lack of knowledge stemmed from amnesia, not ignorance, prompting reflection on their own process of learning and forgetting. Marnie Macgregor of the University of Minnesota recalled that on her first day of class: "I sat there in my chair listening to the comment, 'I don't know much about Guantánamo,' follow nearly each of my peers' introductions, myself included."[10] But when she read a transcript of an interview with a post 9/11 detainee in class, she realized she had heard it on the radio in high school, and remembered it affecting her deeply at the time.

> Yet that information had not stuck. How is it that I had forgotten something that provoked such strong emotions in me? …It is as if a file was reserved within my mind labeled "Guantánamo" yet nothing lies within it. … What has struck me most while learning about Guantánamo is what I discovered on the first day of class – that this kind of forgotten memory was not unique.[11]

Students across the country connected with each other around the experience of forgetting Guantánamo. Megan Suster of the University of California at Riverside wrote Macgregor in Minneapolis, "You are right that this forgotten memory is not unique. I have had very similar experiences to yours."[12]

Reflecting on their own experiences with forgetting helped students focus their goals and strategies for helping a larger public remember. As Suster argued,

> Whether we push this information out of our memories due to basic lack of knowledge or willful ignorance, we must work to bring this information to the forefront and to inspire productive dialogue among those who see our [exhibit] panels.[13]

Macgregor also vowed that "Guantánamo must exit the informational blind spot it currently resides in and relocate to the forefront of the public mind," but was daunted by the task: "However, when I consider how this can be achieved I remember my own experience."[14] Suster encouraged,

> Perhaps some of the information on our panels will be stored as snippets in the Guantánamo files people keep in their minds, as you discuss… if this happens, I think we can call the exhibit a success. We have worked hard to absorb as much information about Guantánamo as we can, and now it is our task to share it with the public… hopefully we can create a memorable exhibit that people will think back on when they hear the word Guantánamo in the future.[15]

Amber Annis of the University of Minnesota agreed. "It is evident that we are involved in a project that surpasses the notion of merely knowledge sharing," she wrote, "but indeed are involved in a process of chipping away at historical amnesia, if such a thing is possible."[16]

While none of the students had direct experience with Guantánamo, a few came from communities directly impacted by the place and its policies. Students included a daughter of Haitian immigrants who had remained silent about their journey to the US; an Afghani-American struggling with the rise in Islamophobia and having been associated with "terrorists" at GTMO; and a student whose father had served in the JTF at GTMO. Their experiences also involved breaking silences: about their own family histories; about how their histories related to others'; and about why these histories were so hard to talk about. The project gave them the structure and excuse to "interview" their families and open new conversations.

Stakeholders: Struggles for Representation and Voice

GTMO's erasure from public consciousness was achieved by erasing the voices of the people who witnessed what happened there. To make students the sole voices of GTMO's history risked further erasing the truth of those witnesses. So each group of students was encouraged to collaborate with people who had experience at GTMO that related to the chapter of GTMO's history for which the group assumed responsibility: for instance, military dependents who grew up at GTMO during the Cold War; Haitians and Cubans held there in the 1990s; lawyers defending current detainees.

Most student teams assumed that to collaborate meant to conduct interviews, which they believed would allow witnesses to tell their own stories in their own words. Students across the country found people nearby them with stories to share and conducted over 100 interviews, which were integrated into the website and installation. Interviews allowed students to meet and learn first hand from their subjects, and allowed subjects' stories to be integrated into the collective narrative of GTMO shared with the public in the installation and website. However, the interviews, since students defined the questions and edited the answers, still allowed people without direct experience with GTMO to control its representation.

Project leaders were eager to explore other ways of granting witnesses curatorial authority, and encouraged student teams to imagine a wider variety of ways they could work with stakeholders to co-create their chapter of GTMO's history. Whatever form the collaboration took, the intention was to invite witnesses not only to share their own particular experience but also to interpret its wider implications; determine its place and role in building public memory of Guantánamo; and define what they wanted their experience to teach others. The forms of collaboration that emerged depended on the witnesses' visions for and investment in public memory.

Guantanamigos or Gitmoites

The group that felt most strongly about reaching a broader public were veterans who served at GTMO and their dependents, especially those who grew up on the base as children. These Guantanamigos, also referring to themselves as Gitmoites, were united in their dismay at how the world came to see GTMO after 9/11, sharing their feelings on Facebook. The fact that most Americans now associated GTMO with violence and crime – whether they imagined the perpetrators as terrorists or the military – was horrifying and hurtful. "'Gtmo' was not a word, an idea, or a place in ANY civilian mind until the prison was established," lamented Catherine Chapman. Particularly frustrating was the public's lack of historical consciousness: "Our concept of Gtmo goes back much further," she wrote.[17] Fellow Guantanamigo DL Gordon echoed, "the prison is simply a hiccup in the history of the base."[18] In the face of the vitriol the name of his old hometown suddenly inspired among strangers, Gitmoite Dave Alegre posted, "we are blessed to have experienced a place that most will never understand."[19] But that lack of understanding was exasperating: millions of people pontificating about and passing judgment on a place they had never been, so could know nothing about. Gitmoites had actually been there, yet no one was listening to them.

The University of West Florida (UWF) team was all ears. UWF is located in Pensacola, nicknamed the "cradle of naval aviation," home to a strong community of ex-military and the National Naval Aviation Museum. Patrick Moore, director of UWF's public history program, had taken students to GTMO in August 2001 to interview the remaining retired Cuban workers, and in the process had built relationships with Gitmoites past and present. UWF students worked with Gitmoites as sources of information, and as advisors on how to interpret it. Students attended a reunion of the Guantánamo Bay Association, and traveled on a cruise for residents evacuated during the Cuban missile crisis. They conducted dozens of interviews, and collected yearbooks, cookbooks, bus maps, and other artifacts. Finally, students conducted a focus group with Gitmoites to ask them what they wanted most to communicate to a larger public.

Gitmoites were generally enthusiastic about participating in the project, referring students and project staff to other Guantanamigos, donating artifacts, and reading and responding to student blog posts. They were highly motivated to shape the public memory of GTMO. Their collective memory of the base was an idealized vision of America, the foundation of their patriotism, proof that their nation was worthy of unqualified support: GTMO's America was not racist; it was not divided; it was peaceful and free of violence; it was made up of generous, good people who loved and supported each other; and it was all defended by a strong and highly respected military. That GTMO had become a symbol of America's moral failure, its fractured society, global racism, unbridled violence, and lawlessness, felt like a personal attack. By defending their GTMO, they could defend their America, and themselves.

Balseros

Students from New York University (NYU) were charged with working with *balseros* to develop the chapter on Cuban refugees held at GTMO. They were supported by students from the University of Miami, who conducted and edited video interviews of a small number of individuals. These *balseros* gave the students differing interpretations of GTMO, some seeing it as a prison, others as a stepping stone on the path toward freedom. Their stories were integrated side by side into the public installation.

The NYU students sought to engage a broader collective in identifying the big ideas and stories they felt were most important to communicate. Living far from the locus of the *balsero* diaspora, concentrated in South Florida, students experimented with facilitating conversations through Facebook, working with a member of the main *balsero* community page to invite members to participate in shaping the project, beginning with the big questions. In a second stage, students submitted a collection of possible images for inclusion in the exhibit, and invited page members to vote on which best communicated GTMO to non-*balseros,* and to write their own captions. The students' questions and suggestions did not inspire rancor, or debate; they just didn't inspire much response at all. Activity on the Facebook page remained focused on exchanges of individual memories between individual members. This might have been because the NYU students came from far outside the *balsero* community, including no Spanish speakers or Florida residents; or it could also have been that *balseros* on the Facebook page were less interested than Gitmoites in publicly interpreting the larger implications of their experience.

Haitian Refugees

Students from Brown University were aware that the subjects of the chapter they chose to focus on – Haitian refugees – had been particularly savagely silenced, and that this silencing had deeply shaped the refugees' experience and its long legacy. Recall that for Haitian immigrants and their descendants, there was little upside to maintaining any public or community memory of GTMO. But many of the people who fought for Haitians at GTMO in the 1990s as translators, social workers, or lawyers continued to work to address issues facing Haitian communities in the US. Although they had not been held at GTMO, they were concerned with how the people who had would be depicted, knowing how that depiction could affect how refugees, and other Haitians in the US, were treated.

With Project leaders' help, students identified a small group of Haitian community leaders who agreed to review exhibit materials, all based in New York. To combat the long history of erasure, the students sought to share as much authority as possible, without asking too much of already overburdened organizers. Through a series of phone calls, the group identified major themes and issues, chose images, and determined how to treat them. Primary among the concerns was how to combat the dominant imagery of "boat people" displayed in the media that therefore defined American consciousness of Haitian immigrants: images of ragged starving refugees crowded into tiny decrepit vessels.

Further, the majority of images featured people, including many children, who couldn't now be found. Finally, many people also didn't want to be identified, either collectively or individually, as having been at GTMO. While attending to these concerns, community leaders were also committed to making the Haitian chapter of GTMO's history more widely known, since it represented such an egregious example of racism driving immigration policy. They carefully chose a collection of images that would avoid reinforcing stereotypes, and suggested that subjects' faces be blurred to preserve their anonymity.

Post-9/11 Detainees

Students' experience was most mediated, most distant from, the people who were held at GTMO after 9/11. At the time the Project was being developed, a few organizations were conducting interviews with detainees who had been released, such as the ACLU and Witness to Guantánamo, dedicated to building a robust collection of filmed stories from the prison camps. These detainees were barred from entering the US, requiring funding for travel to meet with them, and their trauma was so severe that inexperienced students would not have been appropriate interviewers. Instead, the Project partnered with these organizations to share their interviews with students in the classroom, and feature the interviews on the Project's website and in the traveling exhibit. Students also worked directly with lawyers representing detainees, who shared the stories detainees told them, and described the parts of the detention centers to which they had access.

"An Exhibit in Dialogue with Itself": Fostering Multiple Perspectives and Policy Discussion

Prior to the Project, none of the GTMO memory communities had much contact with each other. For each group, their GTMO was *the* GTMO. While participants from each group were informed that their chapter was but one of 13, because they had spent months working with students solely on their own story, it was easy to forget, or perhaps hard to imagine, that their story would be placed alongside those of others in the completed exhibition. Similarly, each class of students, although they all read about multiple aspects of GTMO's history, was most deeply connected to "their" chapter, so began to see the base through the eyes of the witnesses with whom they partnered. In assembling the final project, all participants – students, stakeholders, and faculty – had to confront how widely their views on GTMO diverged, and how to talk about them with each other.

The Project tried to create space for students to embrace conflicting accounts in their sections, or to make a strong argument based on rigorous research that also owned up to its subjectivity. Each panel, curated by a different student team, had a different theme and time period, but also a different take. Each included a statement titled "Our point of view," in which the teams shared how their individual identities or community contexts shaped their interpretive approach. The result, as UMass Amherst's faculty project lead David Glassberg put it, is an exhibit that's "in dialogue with itself."[20]

"Fostering dialogue" was one of the Guantánamo Public Memory Project principles mandated by the original working group. To further this goal, the Project began by facilitating an internal, "practice" national dialogue among the approximately 500 participants in nine cities. In this way, participants could surface the main sources of conflict and confusion that would undoubtedly later come up with public audiences, and find ways of facilitating productive exchange around them. Student teams were required to periodically share what they learned about the slice of GTMO history they were focusing on, and the perspectives it was giving them on the whole, with their peers working on different slices in different parts of the country. They posted written reflections on their discoveries and the questions they raised for them on the Project blog at three points in the process, and commented on reflections from students at another school. People with direct experience at GTMO also participated in this virtual discussion. Finally, the Project set up video conferences between student teams. These mechanisms allowed participants to wrestle with their peers across the country on the central challenges of defining and building a public memory of Guantánamo.

Was the goal of the Project to create an objective account of Guantánamo's history? Jeremy Wells of Arizona State University, whose chapter focused on the development of the base during World War II, worried, "I am concerned about the exhibit's ability to maintain an objective tone within the collective narrative" and argued "we need to... strive to inform constructively through representing Guantánamo objectively and not allowing the present to dictate the direction or the voice of the exhibit."[21] Nick Sacco of IUPUI responded critically. "We as public historians are interpreters," he countered.

> The facts don't necessarily speak for themselves. Ultimately, while we should strive to be [as] objective as possible, we should also make sure to craft an interpretation that is honest; one that clearly states our goals and objectives and educates the public in a way that fosters discussion, allowing visitors to draw their own conclusions.[22]

But for Ria Mirchandani of Brown University, "There is a trade off between being well informed on the matter and being objective. To an extent I feel that the more I know, the less objective I become; but I am fine with this because it's better to hold justified biases than be ignorant."[23]

The question of how all the different chapters fit together – the political and ethical challenges of multiple perspectives – became a deep source of conflict, and the most generative source of dialogue, among all participants in the project. Was it the Project's purpose to explain, to create an "umbrella framework" that would make sense of the radically conflicting narratives, and the depth of the cruelty in some of them? Or was the goal to invite the public to find their own patterns in the patchwork presented to them?

The greatest source of conflict arose around how to interpret the Gitmoites' romantic memories of base life in the context of GTMO's history of abuse. Participants learning about base life and GTMO's longer history for the first time struggled to square these stories with each other, and with what meaning to draw from them together. "How can these two opposing viewpoints coexist?" wondered Kavita Singh of Indiana University-Purdue University Indianapolis.[24] Children who grew up in GTMO's naval station in the 1960s did not torture the men held in the Joint Task Force detention centers on the other side of the bay after 2002. But if Guantanamigos were not direct perpetrators of post-9/11 torture, what was the lesson, and legacy, of their memories? Hayley Whitehead of the University of North Carolina at Greensboro viewed Gitmoites as just regular people: "To me, it was like GTMO wasn't so different from the United States," she said, "people still gathered within a community."[25] Other students believed that while Gitmoites were not directly responsible for GTMO's abuses, it was important to explore how they were nonetheless part of a larger system that enabled them. Megan Kuensting of NYU urged her fellow project participants to place Gitmoites' stories in the context of American public memory of other events, such as the Vietnam War or civil rights struggles. She argued that GTMO military families should be understood as "part of a larger, ongoing strategy to maintain control in a region that is not geographically part of the US but that is uniquely tied to the US and its political interests by legal ambiguities and by our fears of Communism, terrorism, and immigration."[26] However stark the contrast in stories seemed, for some participants, they formed part of a single narrative of American military expansion.

Other students resisted the idea that GTMO's current status as a detention center was an inevitable outcome of its imperial history, and struggled with how to construct a chronological narrative. The Arizona State University team, which included students from military families or who had served in the military themselves, focused on the expansion of the base during WWII. From this vantage point, they struggled with the question of whether and how GTMO's current use and identity necessarily followed from its elaboration as a space to defend American interests. The group felt strongly that Americans should understand GTMO's history as one that could have gone another way: the base found itself at the center of a global conflict through a series of choices that might just as well have been made differently.

The next step was to invite a larger public into dialogue on such difficult issues. Project staff and advisors challenged local teams to identify an open-ended question, based in their chapter of GTMO's history, about which they honestly struggled as they learned about GTMO and discussed it with each other. The question formed the largest and most significant text in each section of the exhibit; large block letters were visible from far away, drew the visitor in, and served to introduce and frame the entire historical chapter.

While the questions were formulated by local teams, Project leadership set boundaries for what should be asked, to invite multiple perspectives without devolving into moral relativism. Certain questions would not be up for debate, such as whether torture occurred at Guantánamo, or whether torture is justified. Designed as a series of bold questions, viewed from a distance in its totality, the exhibit presented the history of Guantánamo as a set of ethical challenges that needed to be addressed collectively, within a common space, encircled by the lessons of the past.

Some questions were deceivingly simple, seeming to have easy answers, but turning out to be messy and confounding. Rutgers students began their study of GTMO's legal black hole by trying to trace its basic legal structure; in the process, they learned how deeply convoluted it was, if indeed it could be understood to have a "structure" at all. In the end, they put the question to the public, framing their chapter with: "What Laws Apply in a State of Exception?" Other questions were more open-ended. The story of Haitians at GTMO was shaped by battles over whether Haitians were "economic migrants," threats to public health, or persecuted people seeking asylum, and over what responsibility the US had to them while this was being worked out. The Brown students working with Haitian leaders extrapolated these historically specific debates into two enduring questions: "What is a refugee? What makes a refuge?" After listening to *balseros'* divergent interpretations of their experiences at GTMO and struggling with how to connect them, New York University students framed their chapter around the question: "Safe Haven or Prison Camp?"

While the questions framing the exhibit panels were meant to be wide and deep, to inspire reflection and conversation with no easy answers, teams were also charged with posing a narrower question on which audiences could vote via text message or on the Project website. This element of the exhibit, titled "Shape the Debate," was a way of capturing public opinion on key questions GTMO's history raised for current debates. Questions included: "Should the US government use GTMO for refugees in the future?" and "Is the US an empire today?" Responses to the questions – including respondents' comments – were displayed on a monitor in the exhibit, changing and evolving as the exhibit traveled, and as people in each new community weighed in.

In one case, the "Shape the Debate" question generated more discussion within a stakeholder community than with the outside public it was directed to. The UWF team decided to take their most difficult issue – what place or purpose Guantanamigos' memories served – and turn it over to the Project public through their Shape the Debate question: "Should the memories of past residents be part of the current dialogue on GTMO?" Fred Ward, one of the most avid Gitmoite history keepers with the longest family history on the base, posted the question on the GTMO Facebook page, and encouraged his community to vote. Over 40 members dutifully did, tipping the bar graph displayed to visitors in the exhibit resoundingly to "Yes." The question inspired over twice as many responses from Gitmoites on the Facebook page, catalyzing a conversation within the community about the base and its meaning. Comments ranged from reactions to the exhibit, to a long debate among two members about whether the US had earned its right to the base or whether it had "strongarmed" it from Cuba. But most related to whether and how the base should be closed, an issue at the heart of the public memory project, but far from the original "Shape the Debate" question.

Diverse stakeholders came together face-to-face, often for the first time in their lives, at public events accompanying the exhibit, starting with the launch in New York City in December 2012 and followed by dozens of others as the exhibit traveled around the country. Representatives from different memory communities, who up until that point had worked only with the team dedicated to "their" story, now shared the same stage, invited to exchange stories and explore how their radically different experiences fit together. At the Project's launch event, Jorge del Rio, a Cuban *balsero*, reflected on his experience side by side with Colonel Stephen Kinder, who oversaw the Haitian refugee camps and made significant improvements to them. Del Rio testified that while there may have been many parallels between the two refugee experiences at GTMO, the Cubans were treated far better, with far greater resources. This structural inequality persisted once those who were admitted to the US settled in Miami, entrenching conflict between the two communities. Del Rio's acknowledgment was a deeply significant gesture of truth-telling and reconciliation, creating a shared narrative around the ways the two communities were both connected and divided by their histories. For other participants, the shared stage forced their story into a frame they did not want it to be placed in. One Gitmoite who spoke at an event together with others relating experiences from the Cold War through the War on Terror protested that she felt blindsided and set up as a strawman. *Balsero* Sergio Lastres, who gave an interview to a University of Miami student, declined to participate in public events because he feared his story would be instrumentalized for a specific political agenda. Apologizing, he explained that after going to great lengths to escape Castro's Cuba, he was done with politics.

Making GTMO Matter to Local Communities: Connecting GTMO's History to Its Impact at Home

As the exhibit traveled around the country and the world, local hosts organized public dialogues around why remembering Guantánamo mattered for their local communities today. Exhibit hosts brought GTMO "home" to dozens of communities across the US, not only making this hidden site and its people visible, but demonstrating its local implications. As Tulane student Allison Caplan reflected, "it becomes clear that Gitmo, often thought of as a remote and isolated place, is really at the heart of what America is."[27] Arizona State University student Samantha Maley described that, "As each week has rolled by and I've steadily learned more about the area [GTMO], its people and its long complicated history, I have realized it isn't quite so different from where I live in Arizona," where local debates over the rights of "illegal immigrants" mirror national ones over "enemy combatants."[28] As Amber Annis of the University of Minnesota put it, "We will be asking residents of Minnesota to recognize that Guantánamo, as a symbol and set of ideas, essentially exists in their own backyard... We want to show that Guantánamo is everywhere, even in St. Paul, Minnesota."[29]

The content of the exhibit was the same wherever it traveled, displaying the same panels; yet it was refracted through the radically different contexts into which different hosts placed it. Spaces ranged from campus galleries, to public libraries, to community centers, to a congressional office building on Capitol Hill. Surrounding communities ranged from a predominantly African American urban neighborhood deeply impacted by incarceration, to a predominantly white suburban military community with many GTMO veterans. By inviting well-known local people to speak about the links between GTMO and other issues in the state, or by installing additional exhibits around the GTMO show that illustrated these comparisons, each local host framed the standard exhibit in different ways, highlighting and delving deeper into one story or issue to draw the most relevant connection to their local audiences.

Incarceration

In Indianapolis, Indiana, students learned their state housed a supermax prison with a segregated section for domestic terrorists so secret and prone to abuse it was nicknamed "Little Gitmo." Tracing the history of how this prison came to be in their state inspired dialogues around issues from whether and how to try and punish people accused of terrorism domestically, to conditions and practices of American correctional facilities. For other communities, GTMO was one part of America's outsized carceral state, as the country that led the world in incarcerating its own citizens. In states with high incarceration rates, local advocates understood GTMO as part of a larger American ethic and architecture of imprisonment. UC Riverside situated GTMO in California by hosting "Geographies of Detention: From Guantánamo to the Golden Gulag," the name scholar-activist Ruth Wilson Gilmore gave to California's massive prison system in a widely read book published a few years earlier.[30] They paired the Project exhibit with artwork created by people in California prisons. New Orleans hosts drew parallels between GTMO and Angola, the local prison that shaped the lives of so many of the city's residents. The Ashe Cultural Arts Center, a community and cultural center dedicated to serving and celebrating African American communities, organized a film screening of *Life Inside Angola;* Tulane hosted "Angola and Guantánamo: Art and Incarceration." Public events at the Phoenix Public Library compared GTMO's legal black hole to histories of Japanese internment in Arizona – some of which took place on American Indian reservations, another type of legally exceptional space.

The exhibit traveled internationally, to places where its history had much different resonance. In Istanbul, hosts centered their public events on a local effort to remember the Diyarbakir Prison, a facility used to detain political dissidents. The exhibit was hosted at Studio X, a space founded and politically protected by Columbia University's Graduate School of Architecture, Planning and Preservation as a space for "innovative forms of thinking" about urban issues facing Istanbul. While Project staff anticipated an east-meets-west discussion of GTMO as a symptom and a cause of rising Islamophobia and Islamic radicalism, Studio X and local partner universities were more concerned with using GTMO to focus attention on their own city's carceral landscapes and culture. Like Guantánamo, Diyarbakir Prison was slated to be closed, but the movement to make it happen had stalled. People were beginning to speak out about their experiences of abuse there; academics were beginning to record them.

The Istanbul team organized a series of public and internal workshops around the GTMO exhibit on how they could activate a Diyarbakir memory project to close the facility and bring justice to its victims, but more broadly, to open conversations about incarceration and control in Turkey. Hanging the exhibit in the center of the space, Studio X curators covered the walls with questions about crime and punishment, including: "when does a 'room' become a 'cell'?" "Is incarceration necessary?" "Do you know about alternatives to detention?" "Is imprisonment the only method of incarceration?" and "Should a prison be a space of deprivation or a source of punishment?"

Islamophobia

Around the country, Muslim communities continued to face severe Islamophobia, rooted in responses to 9/11, in everyday culture and national policy. A new generation of Muslim students grew up in a growing culture of mistrust and incidents of hate.[31] The portion of American adults with a favorable opinion of Islam dropped from 41% in 2005 to 30% in 2010, according to a Pew Research Center poll.[32] When the exhibit came to New Jersey, news had just broken that the New York Police Department had been illegally and secretly surveilling Muslims not only in New York City but in New Jersey. Project advisors from the Center for Constitutional Rights (CCR) were launching a lawsuit to stop the practice and hold the NYPD accountable. Rutgers University-New Brunswick students Jasmeet Bawa and Hajar Hasani organized a spoken word poetry event addressing Muslim student experiences and performing testimonies from Cuban, Haitian, and Muslim detainees. Project lead faculty Andy Urban invited Baher Azmy, one of the CCR lawyers working on the NYPD suit, to speak on its implications for New Jersey.[33] In the Twin Cities, the large Somali community was suffering under new restrictions on sending money to support their families in Somalia, based on suspicions the funds would support terrorist activities. The University of Minnesota team hosted a meeting of community leaders and then-Representative Keith Ellison, in which the group discussed how local Somali experiences, such as with surveillance, restrictions on remittances, and daily Islamophobic discrimination, were related and should be integrated into public engagement with the exhibit when it came to the Minnesota Historical Society.

Immigration

Because of GTMO's history as an extra-legal instrument for immigration control, detaining tens of thousands of Cuban and Haitian refugees in the 1990s, other communities used the project to explore immigration policy. In Providence, Rhode Island, Brown students organized exhibit tours with local high school students, most of whom were from Dominican immigrant families, and invited students to debate the questions with which they framed their chapter: "Who is a Refugee? What Makes a Refugee?" Making personal connections to GTMO was not always positive. As Brown student and program organizer Molly Kirker reflected, "the topic certainly hit a nerve. For at least one student, learning about refugees at Guantánamo led to a sense of helplessness; if the US government restricted immigration in the past and continues to restrict immigration in the present, is change even possible?"[34]

In Miami, home to huge Cuban and Haitian communities that are deeply divided from each other, including people who spent years detained at GTMO before being allowed to enter the US, the Project invited a range of institutions to organize programming for different audiences and spaces. The exhibit opened during the 20th anniversary of the Cuban *balsero* crisis and formed part of a city-wide commemoration. The *Miami Herald* launched a database of *balseros*; HistoryMiami and the Smithsonian organized a day when *balseros* were invited to come share oral histories and artifacts; Florida International

University organized a symposium. The Project wanted to bring Haitian voices into the events, so in addition to displaying the exhibit at the University of Miami, a private university protected by guarded gates, it was shown at the Little Haiti Cultural Complex (LHCC), a multi-media arts venue in the heart of Miami's largest Haitian neighborhood. There the exhibit was paired with a show by Pulitzer Prize-winning Haitian immigrant photographer Carl Juste, featuring his photographs of both Haitian and Cuban refugees at Guantánamo and on their traumatic sea voyages. By tracing the shared experience of Cubans and Haitians at GTMO – as well as the radical differences in how they and their asylum cases were treated – Juste, together with Project staff, hoped to create new possibilities for dialogue between these communities, and open debates over current immigration detention and asylum policies. But while the *balsero* events were well-attended, only a handful of people visited the combined exhibit at LHCC (a space that attracted huge crowds for dance and music performances), suggesting Haitian communities' conflicted feelings about GTMO and its place in public memory.

Military Service

Student teams located in communities with high military populations focused their programming on military life and service. In Pensacola, University of West Florida students worked with local Gitmoites to curate a companion exhibit of original artifacts from their experience at GTMO, staged together with the traveling exhibit at a state-run museum. University of South Carolina students set up a station at their campus exhibit through which (mainly student) visitors could write letters to service people on active duty and could meet and talk with veterans. "We hope visitors will take the opportunity to think about what military service means and has meant in the past," they wrote in their plans for the program, "and to create opportunities for visitors to engage with retired and active duty service members."[35]

Closing GTMO

After seeing the exhibit in St. Paul, Representative Keith Ellison, then the first Muslim member of the US Congress, invited the Project to Capitol Hill in June 2014. By then, the push to "close Guantánamo" had been reduced to incrementally transferring prisoners from the base to other countries or prisons in the US. In a week when congresspeople were readying to vote on the transfers, the Project hosted a day-long event for representatives to view the exhibit and meet key figures from GTMO's past: the judge who "closed" Guantánamo in 1993 to release hundreds of HIV-positive Haitian refugees indefinitely detained there, only to see it detain thousands of Cuban refugees a year later; a Cuban refugee held at GTMO who enlisted in the Navy and then served on the base as a nurse after 9/11, treating detainees, and the commander who received the first "enemy combatants." The event brought together over 150 people, including congresspeople and their legislative staff, for discussions of what it meant to "close Guantánamo" and the human costs of their decisions.

"I Can Do This!": Signs of Participatory Public Memory as Movement Building

Exhibits' effectiveness is most often judged by the number of people who visit, and the impact the exhibit has on them. About 550,000 people in 22 cities saw the exhibit; numbers-wise, this was considered a success. The Project surveyed these visitors – about 1,200 across about 20 cities – to measure what they took away. The first thing surveys sought to understand was what ideas about GTMO visitors brought to the exhibit, recognizing that different settings attracted different types. If the exhibit was displayed in a space where people would have to know about it or seek it out, such as a museum gallery, the exhibit primarily attracted people already interested in GTMO. In other places, the exhibit was installed in a public space, where people could encounter it unexpectedly: in New York City, it lined two city blocks where thousands of people passed each hour; in Phoenix, it appeared in the middle of the main public library. In those settings, people who did not come specifically to learn about GTMO, who may previously have known or thought nothing about it at all, were visually confronted with its history.

However they came to the exhibit, on walking in, over 40% of respondents reported, "I don't think a lot about GTMO." Those who did report having a strong feeling about GTMO coming into the exhibit were more likely to oppose it, though not overwhelmingly: while 30% came in believing GTMO should be returned to Cuba or used for something else, about 15% felt it should still be used to detain people suspected of terrorism. When asked how much they knew about GTMO before seeing the exhibit, the vast majority described themselves as knowing very little, rating their knowledge a 3 or lower on a scale of 1–6. Visitors professed things like "I really only knew about the stuff relating to 9/11," and nothing before; others knew even less, admitting, "I only knew the name, nothing about it." When asked what they learned, most respondents described surprise that GTMO has a history: the basic fact that "Guantánamo was used for other purposes before 9/11," but especially that it had held refugees.

With this new knowledge, the majority of people reported their feelings about GTMO shifted significantly, more than half saying by a magnitude of 4 or higher on a scale of 1–6. Many reported a new sense of urgency and disposition to act, saying things like, "I'm no longer indifferent. It opened my eyes to the tension and issues," and reporting the exhibit raised issues that were "relevant to me and/or my community." Judging solely by its impact on casual visitors, the Project achieved its main goals: it raised awareness and helped change people's minds.

But reports from the more than 300 students and stakeholders who participated in creating the project began to suggest unexpected, and more profound, potential outcomes. Many described a new sense of civic obligation – a desire to stay informed and engaged with social justice issues. And about 20% reported a new sense of civic capacity – a confidence that they were capable of making change around those issues. "This project doesn't advertise as 'join us, become a leader,' but it is," one student reported in an anonymous survey. "Public history, in some sense, is about leadership, even if your role is just to get a conversation going."[36] As Rutgers University-New Brunswick undergraduate Hajar Hasani put it, "As a student, there are actions that we can take to raise awareness and we do have the power to have an impact on an issue that may at first seem very distant. The Guantánamo Public Memory Project has been a great model for me in creating a sense of student empowerment."[37] When asked what lesson they derived from the experience, another said simply, "I can do this!" The sense of civic efficacy seemed to derive from the experience of creating a project around urgent civic issues, and then witnessing its impact on a larger public – in their community and around the world. In this way, the public memory project was giving them an experience of making change – one that was not a classroom exercise, but had real implications.

For those of us who planned the Project, as we observed the responses of the students and our communities, and assessed our own, we realized that the Project's significance lay not only in addressing the specific issues of GTMO, but also in the process we had created for engaging people in connecting memory, dialogue, and action. When taken together, the reactions of people who created the exhibit and the people who saw it; of people in one locality and across all 22; of people who lived this history and people coming to it for the first time; suggested new possibilities for how public memory could be activated for social change. Public memory could be participatory; it could break down the distinction between author and audience; it could reimagine who was a stakeholder by identifying shared stakes in the past; it could tap the power of local voices and perspectives while connecting them into a global chorus. This participatory public memory could use the modes and strategies of social movements to build a collective engagement with history, to mobilize people to address the legacies we live with. I and the faculty began to imagine how participatory public memory could be deployed to address other issues of shared concern whose public understanding, discourse, policy, and even activism suffered from a refusal to confront their historical roots.

Notes

1 Martin Luther King, Jr., "Where Do We Go From Here?," delivered at the 11th Annual Southern Christian Leadership Conference (SCLC) Convention, Atlanta, Georgia, August 16, 1967.

2 Gita Gutierrez, statement made during workshop at "Remembering Guantánamo: 1898-Present," University of Memphis, June 2009.

3 Patricia Valdez, statement made during workshop at "Remembering Guantánamo: 1898-Present," University of Memphis, June 2009.

4 Michael Strauss, statement made during workshop at "Remembering Guantánamo: 1898-Present," University of Memphis, June 2009.

5 Albie Sachs, statement made during workshop at "Remembering Guantánamo," Columbia University, April 28, 2011.

6 Joe Margulies, statement made during workshop at "Remembering Guantánamo: 1898-Present," University of Memphis, June 2009.

7 Teng Lee, December 13, 2012 (10:47 p.m.). Comment on Hayley Whitehead, "Growing up at Guantánamo," GuantánamoPublic Memory Project blog, October 24, 2012, http://blog.gitmomemory.org/2012/10/24/growing-up-at-guantanamo/

8 Ria Mirchandani, October 15, 2012 (2:12 a.m.). Comment on Jeremy Wells, "Maintaining Objectivity," Guantánamo Public Memory Project blog, October 4, 2012, http://blog.gitmomemory.org/2012/10/04/maintaining-objectivity/

9 Samantha Maley, "Arizona Immigration and GITMO," Guantánamo Public Memory Project blog, October 11, 2012, http://blog.gitmomemory.org/2012/10/11/arizona-immigration-and-gitmo/

10 Marnie Macgregor, "A Future Without a Past?" Guantánamo Public Memory Project blog, October 24, 2012, http://blog.gitmomemory.org/2012/10/24/a-future-without-a-past/

11 Ibid.

12 Megan Suster, November 14, 2012 (3:27 a.m.). Comment on Marnie Macgregor, "A Future Without a Past?" Guantánamo Public Memory Project blog, October 24, 2012, http://blog.gitmomemory.org/2012/10/24/a-future-without-a-past/

13 Ibid.

14 Macgregor, "A Future Without a Past?"

15 Suster, Comment on Macgregor, "A Future Without a Past?"

16 Amber Annis, "Ft. Snelling and Guantánamo: Corresponding Histories and Disparate Rememberings," GuantánamoPublic Memory Project blog, December 9, 2013, http://blog.gitmomemory.org/2013/12/09/ft-snelling-and-guantanamo-corresponding-histories-and-disparate-rememberings/

17 Catherine Chapman, March 15, 2015, 10:31 a.m., comment on Alyssa Constad, "Hello Everyone!" Facebook, March 13, 2015, https://www.facebook.com/groups/2239717910/posts/10152979850337911/?comment_id=10152984067952911

18 DL Gordon, March 15, 2015, 11:11 a.m., comment on Alyssa Constad, "Hello Everyone!" Facebook, March 13, 2015, https://www.facebook.com/groups/2239717910/posts/10152979850337911/?comment_id=10152984067952911

19 Dave Alegre, "I Smell a Rat!" Facebook, March 1, 2016, https://www.facebook.com/groups/2239717910/posts/10153772110902911

20 David Glassberg, remarks made during a private GPMP planning meeting at the Joint Annual Meeting of the Organization of American Historians and the National Council on Public History, April 18–22, 2012.

21 Jeremy Wells, "Maintaining Objectivity," Guantanamo Public Memory Project blog, October 4, 2012, https://blog.gitmomemory.org/2012/10/04/maintaining-objectivity/

22 Nick Sacco, October 7, 2012 (12:14 a.m.). Comment on Jeremy Wells, "Maintaining Objectivity," Guantanamo Public Memory Project blog, October 4, 2012, https://blog.gitmomemory.org/2012/10/04/maintaining-objectivity/

23 Ria Mirchandani, October 15, 2012 (2:12 a.m.). Comment on Jeremy Wells, "Maintaining Objectivity," Guantánamo Public Memory Project blog, October 4, 2012, http://blog.gitmomemory.org/2012/10/04/maintainingobjectivity/

24 Kavita Singh, "The Colorful Voices of Guantanamo," Guantanamo Public Memory Project blog, October 22, 2012, https://blog.gitmomemory.org/2012/10/22/the-colorful-voices-of-guantanamo/

25 Hayley Whitehead, "Growing up at Guantanamo," Guantanamo Public Memory Project blog, October 24, 2012, https://blog.gitmomemory.org/2012/10/24/growing-up-at-guantanamo/

26 Megan Kuensting, November 5, 2012 (8:15 p.m.). Comment on Hayley Whitehead, "Growing up at Guantánamo," Guantánamo Public Memory Project blog, October 24, 2012, http://blog.gitmomemory.org/2012/10/24/growing-up-at-guantanamo/

27 Allison Caplan, "GTMO in NOLA: New Website Showcases Tulane Students' Research on Gitmo," Guantánamo Public Memory Project blog, April 21, 2015, http://blog.gitmomemory.org/2015/04/21/gtmo-in-nola-new-website-showcases-tulane-students-research-on-gitmo/

28 Maley, "Arizona Immigration and GITMO."

29 Annis, "Ft. Snelling and Guantánamo."

30 Ruth Wilson Gilmore, *Golden Gulag: Prisons, Surplus, Crisis, and Opposition in Globalizing California* (Berkeley: University of California Press, 2007).

31 Vanessa Taylor, "Islamophobia Shaped the Lives of Muslim American Students After 9/11," *Teen Vogue*, September 9, 2021, https://www.teenvogue.com/story/islamophobia-911-muslim-students

32 "Public Remains Conflicted Over Islam," Pew Research Center, August 24, 2010, https://www.pewforum.org/2010/08/24/public-remains-conflicted-over-islam/

33 "Curating Guantánamo," Rutgers University-New Brunswick, March 28–29, 2013, https://gitmomemory.org/wp-content/uploads/2012/10/GTMO_Program-email.pdf

34 Molly Kerker, "A Reflection on Community Engagement in Providence, RI," Guantánamo Public Memory Project blog, April 15, 2015, http://blog.gitmomemory.org/2015/04/15/a-reflection-community-engagement-in-providence-ri/

35 "Dear Veteran: Operation Gratitude Letter Drive," Upcoming Events, Guantánamo Public Memory Project, November 11, 2015, http://gitmomemory.org/about/events/

36 Survey conducted by IUPUI, December 2012, held by Humanities Action Lab

37 Hajar Hasani, "Guantánamo and My Home," Guantánamo Public Memory Project blog, July 10, 2013, https://blog.gitmomemory.org/2013/07/10/why-participate-guantanamo-and-my-home/

PART III

States of Incarceration

April 16, 2016, was a day of reckoning in New York City. Hundreds of people swarmed the steps of City Hall to launch the #CLOSErikers campaign, which called for the permanent shutdown of the notorious Rikers Island jails. JustLeadershipUSA, then a new entity led by returning citizens – a term progressive reformers promoted to describe formerly incarcerated people – coordinated the participants from over 50 organizations representing generations of struggle for criminal justice reform. That evening, organizational leaders and much of the crowd joined students from 20 cities around the country to launch States of Incarceration: A National Dialogue of Local Histories (SOI), with an event on why and how to remember Rikers.

SOI brought together over 700 students with diverse experiences in the carceral state and others directly impacted in each participating city to create a collective exhibition on the roots of mass incarceration. In the year before the City Hall protest, #CLOSErikers members had worked with students at The New School on the New York City chapter of the exhibition, focusing on Rikers and its history, titled "Rikers Island, NY 11370: In Plain Sight." A month before, several #CLOSErikers members started collaborating with other criminal justice leaders as part of an independent commission formed by the Speaker of the City Council to make recommendations for the future of Rikers Island. One year later, the Commission announced its recommendation: close it down. The Mayor pledged to do so. But how?

#CLOSErikers members brought the power of public memory to public policy on Rikers' future. Throughout the Commission's deliberations,

DOI: 10.4324/9781003185826-11

they argued that closure of the jail should not mean closure on its past. This argument shaped the final report's vision for closing, which stated that

> Any redevelopment plan must recognize Rikers's unique history. For nearly a century, Rikers has been an open wound, placing thousands of New Yorkers, both detainees and corrections officers, in conditions that were substandard at best and inhumane at worst. We cannot undo this history. But we can acknowledge it and attempt to make some amends.[1]

This section will explore public memory in movements to end mass incarceration and imagine redress for its historical harm, in a specific moment – the mid-2010s – a turning point for attention to the issue among policymakers and progressive publics. It focuses on the experience of the thousands of people in 28 cities who created States of Incarceration and the Rikers Public Memory Project. SOI was the first initiative of the newly formed Humanities Action Lab, which grew out of the Guantánamo Public Memory Project. As the Guantánamo project unfolded, I and project faculty observed a methodology emerging – participatory public memory – that had great potential to mobilize people in similar ways around other issues. I invited the same faculty to work together in an ongoing way, forming the Humanities Action Lab.

Many of these faculty had been collaborating with criminal justice reform advocates through their work highlighting domestic connections to GTMO. We decided to harness the national participatory public memory structure we had created around Guantánamo to propel current movements against mass incarceration. But we soon learned that the methodology could not simply be reapplied in a new context. The historical denial that shapes and sustains mass incarceration is different from that shaping Guantánamo, requiring different participatory public memory strategies for confronting it. Whereas GTMO is a remote and restricted location, a place that few Americans have experienced directly, mass incarceration starkly shapes the daily landscape of a vast portion of the US Black and brown population, even as it is invisible to too many white people. The US carceral state is thus marked by a racially bifurcated public memory, with one citizenry raised with generational knowledge of racist state violence, and another largely blissfully ignorant of it. Within the Humanities Action Lab consortium, this bifurcation required attention to the different relationships different creators and audiences had to the subject, with different levels of awareness. In other words, it required interrogating who the presumed "public" was in "public memory."

8
PUBLIC MEMORY AND THE US CARCERAL STATE

"New York City doesn't have its very own Guantánamo [sic] Bay," wrote *Vice* reporter John Surico in 2014, "but Rikers Island comes pretty damn close." Presuming his readership wouldn't know what or where Rikers was, he went on to explain:

> Made up of ten different jails, the floating mass of a prison complex is where local criminals – mostly minorities – go to disappear into the purgatory of our criminal justice system. Stuck between the Bronx and Queens, Rikers has remained a symbol of American bureaucratic backwardness for decades to city and federal law enforcement agencies alike.[2]

Just as Barack Obama rode into office in 2009 on a "close Guantánamo" pledge, so in 2014, newly elected Mayor Bill de Blasio, who had campaigned on racial justice in policing and incarceration, was slammed with calls to reform the city's Gitmo-style "hellhole."[3] The US Attorney's office had completed an investigation that resulted in Rikers' "own version of a torture report" that detailed widespread violence resulting in serious injuries and deaths, and, in Surico's summary, "lots of really bad, unconstitutional shit."[4] While de Blasio immediately made statements and took steps to improve conditions, when nothing substantial had improved within a year, US Attorney Preet Bharara filed suit against the City of New York and called for a federal monitor to ensure "systematic, institution-wide reforms."[5]

Building on years of advocacy by BIPOC leaders, calls mounted to move beyond reform, and close Rikers. A new crop of progressive white allies appealed to those informed and outraged by abuses at GTMO but ignorant of the parallels in the US criminal justice system. In a 2015 *New York Times*

DOI: 10.4324/9781003185826-12

op-ed titled "Shut Down Rikers Island," Neil Barsky, who had recently founded the Marshall Project, a non-profit journalism organization focused on criminal justice, made his argument in terms he thought would best inspire his readers: "The complex is New York's Guantánamo Bay: a secluded island, beyond the gaze of watchdogs, where the Constitution is no guide."[6] In 2016, documentarian Marc Levin released *Rikers*, a film made in collaboration with journalist Bill Moyers, and when asked in an interview what he hoped viewers would take away from it, Levin replied, "Well, it's no longer out of sight, out of mind. You know, we don't have to think about Guantánamo. We don't have to think about Abu Ghraib," but solitary confinement practiced at Rikers, "it's a form of torture. And we've been doing it right here. And it's time to wake up." Echoing the language used around GTMO, Levin added, "And it's time to change who we are."[7]

That GTMO had become an immediately recognizable symbol of torture and lawlessness speaks to the incredible success of the "close Guantánamo" campaigns of the previous decade, including the Guantánamo Public Memory Project. But the use of this symbol to inspire outrage about Rikers highlights the astounding powers of denial that allowed those who remembered Guantánamo to forget the people and places in their own backyard. Communicators like Barsky and Levin seemed to be betting that for their audiences, a jail complex nestled in New York City, where over 10,000 of their fellow citizens were detained, visited, or worked each day, would become most legible as a moral concern when it was compared to a semi-secret prison in a remote part of Cuba.

This chapter explores the contours of historical denial about incarceration at this moment, and how it sustained the carceral state. It then looks at how criminal justice reform advocates saw the power of public memory to catalyze policy change and worked to build a shared historical consciousness around mass incarceration. This included building awareness about mass incarceration's recent history in the War on Drugs, showing it to be not a necessary response to crime, but a misguided set of policy decisions new enough to be reversed. But the strongest voices, of Black advocates with high public profiles, reframed mass incarceration in America's long history of racial control and violence, requiring a deeper and longer process of confronting white supremacy to dismantle the carceral state.

In this context, a diverse group of scholars and advocates came together to debate what a national public memory project on mass incarceration should look like, and how to design it as a social movement, launching States of Incarceration, which mobilized hundreds of students and others directly impacted by incarceration to confront the carceral state and its roots where they lived. Participants' racial identities and experiences in the carceral state shaped their relationships to the project, and the project struggled with questions around who was responsible for teaching whom; whether this knowledge exchange should focus on raising awareness among the uninformed, or mobilizing those who were all too familiar; and ultimately, about who were the most powerful agents of change.

Historical Denial in the Era of Mass Incarceration: How It Sustained the US Carceral State

By the 2010s, America's correctional apparatus had become so vast, so wide-reaching, that politicians, journalists, and scholars heralded a new historical era – "the age of mass incarceration" – that produced a distinct "incarceration generation," living in a new geography – "the carceral state."[8] These terms widened the focus from the prison system to a society that had been wholly transformed. By 2007, 1.7 million children had a parent in prison; by 2017, African Americans were incarcerated at six times the rate of whites.[9] Incarceration had become a primary tool for managing immigration: the number of people entering federal prisons for immigration offenses rose 145% from 1998 to 2011.[10] But "mass incarceration," refers not only to the staggering number of people who are imprisoned, but to the massive reach and impact of the correctional system as an instrument of racial control.

Mass incarceration remade the country's landscapes and communities. Whole urban neighborhoods were decimated by the disappearance of millions of residents and economic disinvestment in the shells they left behind, when inner cities and those who lived there were disproportionately criminalized and imprisoned. Rural communities were created out of whole cloth around new prisons. Between 1990 and 1999, a prison was opening somewhere in rural America every 15 days, whereas prior to 1980, only 36% of prisons in the US were located in rural communities and small towns.[11] The prison boom also created a new sector of the workforce and economy: as legal restrictions on prison labor lifted starting in 1979, dozens of states opened prisons to private companies – involved in everything from prison construction to goods and services as varied as tech support and T-shirts – with their own interests and influence. By 2005, 62,600 incarcerated Americans worked in correctional industries that sold goods to outside consumers.[12] This also shaped a new labor market outside prisons, as incarcerated people did and made more things workers on the outside once did, while outside workers made more things to serve incarcerated people. The impact of mass incarceration extended throughout the entire lifetimes of those it targeted, from massive school security and neighborhood police harassment pre-arrest to permanent loss of access to housing or employment after release.[13]

The spike in US incarceration was not only historically unprecedented, but it also had no international counterpart. Around the time States of Incarceration launched, the US had the largest total incarcerated population in the world, with 2.2 million people in prisons and jails, and the highest incarceration rate by a longshot: one and a half times greater than countries in second place (excluding tiny island nations), like Cuba and Russia.[14]

The carceral state governs through division and denial. For an enormous portion of Americans, vastly disproportionately Black and brown, prison experiences are part of the fabric of daily life and family history: part of a regular commute for a visiting family or corrections workers; the basis of stories of difficult pasts or imagined futures; a period of youth lost; the permanent legacy of living with a criminal record. Family and friends visiting people in prisons are subjected to some of the same surveillance and abuse as the people they are visiting, criminalized and dehumanized by association, subsumed into the citizenry of the carceral state. Meanwhile, too many Americans cannot locate the nearest prison or jail on a map, and do not recognize the other tendrils of mass incarceration that surround them. This denial is facilitated by a lack of official public acknowledgment of the massive scale, scope, and impact of mass incarceration.

How has this awareness apartheid been achieved in the US? In part, as in the case of Guantánamo, by keeping those incarcerated "out of sight, out of mind" of those who are not, physically removed from mainstream society. Collectively, they are erased from the official portraits of their communities, and of the country. Not only are incarcerated people excluded from the census of their home communities, but they are also not counted in poverty and unemployment statistics. This denial-accounting obscures the existence of millions of individuals, and creates a grossly inaccurate collective picture of what our country looks like and how well it's doing. The economic growth for which Clinton claimed credit, for instance, was aided by a crime bill that put millions behind bars and then dropped them from the books, artificially inflating the averages.[15]

The erasure continues after people are released from prison, for the rest of their lifetime through the regime of "invisible punishment" that is life with a criminal record. There is no "re-entry" into the society they left; instead, as advocate and legal scholar Michelle Alexander describes it, "They enter a separate society, a world hidden from public view, governed by a set of oppressive and discriminatory rules and laws that do not apply to everyone else."[16] By 2016, an estimated 6.11 million Americans could not vote because of a felony conviction.[17] Other collateral consequences include barriers to public housing, welfare assistance, school loans, vocational training, and living wage jobs.[18] Immigrants in detention are doubly invisible, not counted as part of the population to begin with. A 2015 study found that 86% lack legal representation and are often held indefinitely, through processes and in facilities that are not required to have any of the transparency or public access of criminal law.[19]

But the carceral state is also hidden by being *too* visible. It's not only that prisons and prisoners are invisible to those privileged enough to be divided from them; it's that prisons are so falsely seen and uncritically accepted. Unlike Guantánamo, which is understood as a bizarre anomaly by supporters and critics alike, as scholar-activist Angela Davis argues, "On the whole, people tend to take prisons for granted."

> It is difficult to imagine life without them. At the same time, there is reluctance to face the realities hidden within them, a fear of thinking about what happens inside them. Thus, the prison is present in our lives and, at the same time, it is absent from our lives.[20]

Denial of the scale, scope, and nature of mass incarceration is supported by a historical denial, a false narrative about the nature of American racism. Alexander argues that "our collective understanding of racism has been powerfully influenced by the shocking images of the Jim Crow era and the struggle for civil rights."[21] Here, "Nooses, racial slurs, and overt bigotry are widely condemned by people across the political spectrum; they are understood to be remnants of the past."[22] This has meant that "our understanding of racism is therefore shaped by the most extreme expressions of individual bigotry, not by the way in which it functions naturally, almost invisibly (and sometimes with genuinely benign intent) when it is embedded in the structure of a social system."[23] This public memory of racism, as residing in a dwindling number of individual "bad apples," or individual bad policies, has impeded recognition of the carceral state as a complex, integrated structure of racial control.

This historical denial was also supported by public histories of incarceration presented in prison museums, which invited those protected from criminalization to observe a sensationalized story of punishment in the past, full of colorful gangsters and stylized violence, emphasizing the distance between visitors and active prisons, and erasing the contemporary carceral state. As historian Seth Bruggeman observed in 2012, most prison museums avoided systemic analyses, such as "why people end up in jail in the first place and how that experience shapes our society."[24] Even more progressive museums, like Eastern State Penitentiary in Philadelphia, in the early 2010s still presented the prison's history in terms of evolving ideas of punishment, not as an instrument of racial control. As Eastern State staff explored how they might situate its 19th-century site in relation to current mass incarceration of Black and brown Americans, they were forced to contend with the fact that over 80% of its visitors identified as white, and most were "only moderately likely to think about criminal justice issues or connect the past with the present."[25] Staff began with a "big graph" that presented incarceration rates in sculptural form; and later developed a narrative exhibit designed to explain mass incarceration to visitors who hadn't necessarily come to learn about it.

Contesting Historical Denial in the Age of Mass Incarceration: Building a Public Memory to Dismantle the Carceral State

By 2015, teetering on the apex of the age of mass incarceration, the US was, very slightly, beginning to reduce its prison population.[26] A number of big-budget civil rights organizations and their funders sunk massive new energy and resources into criminal justice reform. In 2014, the Open Society Foundations awarded the American Civil Liberties Union $50 million to support its nationwide campaign to end mass incarceration. The next year, the MacArthur Foundation launched the Safety and Justice Challenge, "an initiative to tackle over-incarceration, one of America's greatest social problems," investing over $110 million in the program's first two years to support local communities' efforts to rethink and retool their justice systems.[27] Political discourse on mass incarceration had changed dramatically. A bi-partisan consensus emerged that the policies that created mass incarceration had failed, producing a stream of public statements unimaginable even five years before. That year, President Obama declared that "mass incarceration makes our country worse off, and we need to do something about it," and he became the first president to visit a correctional facility.[28] Speaker of the House Paul Ryan agreed that "criminal justice reform is probably the biggest [issue] we can make a difference on... there's a real way forward on that."[29] NYU's Brennan Center for Justice mobilized nearly every presidential candidate, Republican and Democrat (save then-candidate Trump), to make a statement for a collective volume titled *Solutions: American Leaders Speak Out On Criminal Justice*.[30] While the solutions proposed varied, the authors all agreed that mass incarceration was a problem.

Many advocates recognized the need to transform public understanding in order to make real change possible. The federally funded National Research Council (NRC) organized a blue-chip committee of 20 criminal justice experts to produce a report on the causes and consequences of the massive growth in America's prison population from the early 1970s through the 2010s. Historians such as Heather Ann Thompson and Khalil Gibran Muhammad, sociologists like Bruce Western, and corrections experts including Jeremy Travis and Jeffrey Beard comprised the study's authors. The report concluded "that the United States has gone far past the point where the numbers of people in prison can be justified by social benefits and has reached a level where these high rates of incarceration themselves constitute a source of injustice and social harm."[31] Travis, then President of John Jay College of Criminal Justice and chair of the NRC committee, argued reform was weak without a reframing through historical reckoning: "We can nibble around the edges, work with politicians to change sentencing laws, deepen our understanding of punitiveness in America, even adopt new crime prevention strategies," Travis argued,

> but a moral and historical imperative remains: We need to come to terms with the racial damage caused by the era of mass incarceration. We need to admit our government − acting in our name − has done great harm. We need to accept responsibility for that harm, and find ways to alleviate the consequences.[32]

The history for which Travis urged his colleagues and fellow citizens to accept responsibility was limited, however, to the recent era of the War on Drugs. In the NRC report on "causes and consequences," released in 2014, the majority-white committee of policy experts argued that while the "uniquely American combination of crime, race, and politics" that created the era may have had longer roots, the period was unique in its obsession with punitive criminal justice as a rhetorical and policy solution to myriad problems.[33] The study's major contribution was to decouple crime from punishment: it highlighted that while crime rates had risen in the 1960s, it was the disproportionate *response* to those rates that caused mass incarceration, starting with President Johnson's "War on Crime" of the mid to late 1960s and President Nixon's 1971 declaration of a "War on Drugs," and elaborating a policy, policing, and public relations apparatus that grew over the following administrations, including the profusion of "Three Strikes" laws in the 1990s.[34]

The study also sought to decouple race and criminality, noting how at every stage of criminal justice − from arrest to sentencing − Black Americans were targeted and penalized by the War on Drugs in harsher terms than white Americans. For example, while White and Black Americans reported similar rates of drug use, possession, and sales, Black Americans were arrested on drug charges at rates roughly three to six times as high as those of whites.[35] The report implied that the core issue was an obsession with punishment, not racial control, which was whipped up in just a few decades, making it feel feasible to reverse. Not unlike the approach of "close Guantánamo" advocates who hoped to undo the worst decade of GTMO's history without confronting its deeper roots, the NRC confined reckoning to the recent past. Many Black advocates, by contrast, were harnessing longer histories that rooted mass incarceration squarely in America's founding in anti-Black racism and violence as a means of labor control.

The fantastic popularity of Michele Alexander's *The New Jim Crow* helped ground public conversation in a history much longer than the War on Drugs. First published in 2010 and then popularized by the paperback release in 2012, it was a fantastic success. By 2014, 400,000 people had bought the book, and many others heard Alexander's arguments repeated across various media, from TV appearances to new national organizations it inspired, such as the Campaign to End the New Jim Crow, which grew out of a reading group.[36] The book played a role in policy change, cited by federal judge Shira Scheindlin in her decision declaring that the New York City Police Department's use of "stop and frisk," was racially biased and unconstitutional.[37] In the fall of 2015, a huge proportion of the nearly 700 students involved in the States of Incarceration project reported that the book introduced them to the phenomenon of mass incarceration. *The New Jim Crow* was just one part of a growing chorus of popular media calling attention to mass incarceration, and it built on the work of hundreds of other historians. But its tremendous popularity meant that many people first learned about mass incarceration in this historical context, as part of a long trajectory of racial control.

Other high-profile national public memory projects around this time also helped Americans understand mass incarceration as part of longer histories of structural racism. Ava DuVernay's 2016 documentary *13th* traced the 13th Amendment's perpetuation of slavery by permitting leasing imprisoned people as unpaid laborers, and the Amendment's legacy in mass incarceration. The film won and was nominated for dozens of awards, including an Academy Award nomination for best documentary, and was disseminated widely as a teaching tool. Released free of charge on Netflix soon after it debuted, it was screened in schools, churches, and homes across the world. Bryan Stevenson, a civil rights lawyer and founder of the Equal Justice Initiative (EJI), joined DuVernay in the crusade to combat historical denial. He started with the history of his own organization's fight for criminal justice, publishing *Just Mercy* in 2014, a book based on two decades of work providing legal representation to people who were wrongfully convicted, low income, or otherwise denied a fair trial.[38] Another major bestseller, the book was made into a movie in 2019. For Stevenson, confronting longer rooted historical racism, and in particular lynching, was a precondition for criminal justice reform. In April 2018, EJI opened a lynching memorial and didactic museum in Montgomery, Alabama, titled "From Slavery to Mass Incarceration," a manifestation of more than a decade of research by EJI into the history and legacy of racial injustice. EJI also built a "Community Remembrance" program as an ongoing part of its work, supporting local communities to research and reckon with their own histories of lynching and its legacies.[39] Voices like Stevenson and DuVernay resituated mass incarceration in a long tradition of racial control, as opposed to in a recent practice of punishment, using history to help Americans understand that the carceral state could only be dismantled by dismantling white supremacy, not just by reversing individual policies.

Other voices activated more recent memory to pursue accountability. In February of 2016, Ashley Williams, a 23-year-old activist from Charlotte, North Carolina interrupted a Hillary Clinton fundraiser to demand that Clinton "apologize to black people for mass incarceration."[40] Activists of the incarceration generation used the 2016 presidential campaign to force the Democratic Party to account for the consequences of the 1994 Violent Crime Control and Law Enforcement Act, a "tough on crime" bill which caused incarceration rates to grow by 60% during Bill Clinton's presidency.[41] While both Bill and Hillary publicly acknowledged the harm it caused, they worked hard to establish a historical narrative that placed responsibility for the bill on Black voters and leaders. Hillary Clinton told *BuzzFeed News* that "there was a great demand, not just from America writ large, but from the black community, to get tougher on crime."[42] While Al Sharpton acknowledged that "a lot of people forget a lot of us wanted something hard," they did not necessarily mean mass incarceration. "I mean," he added, "we've got to deal with this without feeding into where it went 'too far.'"[43]

But the incarceration generation understood that this historical narrative – that the bill was a "demand... from the black community" – was part of what scholars Elizabeth Hinton, Julilly Kohler-Hausmann, and Vesla Weaver called "a process of selectively hearing Black voices on the question of crime," used to support punitive crime policy.[44] A public memory focusing on the Clintons' agency was critical for focusing accountability. Protestors forced Hillary Clinton to answer for the Crime Bill for the entire remainder of her campaign, pushing their narrative of mass incarceration into mainstream discussion around the campaign.

Designing a Participatory Public Memory Project to Confront the Carceral State: States of Incarceration

As the faculty who had participated in the Guantánamo Public Memory Project explored the potential to bring its methodology to bear on other contemporary issues plagued by historical denial, mass incarceration stood out. When faculty consulted with local partner organizations about how to make GTMO relevant to their community, many urged local hosts to draw connections to domestic incarceration and criminal justice. In California, Cathy Gudis and Molly McGarry, faculty leads at the University of California at Riverside, worked with the California Institute of Photography to curate "Geographies of Detention: From Guantánamo to the Golden Gulag," pairing the GPMP exhibit with work and performances by artists focusing on mass incarceration in the US.[45] In Indiana, IUPUI students explored the post-9/11 rise in Muslim incarceration in their region, as Muslim Midwesterners became cast as the new "superpredators," targeted as suspected national security threats and detained in such numbers that prisons like Terre Haute in Indiana became known as "Guantánamo North."[46]

I invited Guantánamo faculty, together with a few others who had observed the project and wanted to get involved, to come together in an ongoing way as a new entity, later dubbed the Humanities Action Lab (HAL), and create a series of national participatory public memory projects comprising our local stories.[47] In 2014, I brought the group together to discuss what issues our coalition should address. The growing appetite for exploring mass incarceration historically through media like the *New Jim Crow* and *13th*, and EJI's work, combined with renewed local energy and activism around the carceral state, suggested a memory project on mass incarceration had the greatest potential for impact.

In January 2015, the newly formed HAL gathered about 50 people with a wide range of expertise to explore what role a public memory project could and should play in the public dialogue and social movements around mass incarceration. Coming together at The New School in New York City, which supported HAL's first home, participants brought agendas and investments in the project's possibilities that were as diverse as their expertise. They included young, Black, formerly incarcerated leaders starting new organizations with new strategies for confronting the carceral state, like Glenn Martin, who had just launched JustLeadershipUSA, and Marlon Peterson, who had months before founded the Precedential Group; both were looking to expand their work's public platforms. Also joining were white formerly incarcerated faculty at The New School, like photographer Graham McIndoe and former Missouri state senator Jeff Smith, working to share their stories of incarceration, which they had both recently published in books, in service of criminal justice reform.[48] Historians Elizabeth Hinton and Heather Ann Thompson, whose work was further articulating mass incarceration as a historical era, and a phenomenon at the center of post-war American history, came equally eager to bring their framing to audiences outside the academy.[49] More leading scholars later contributed, notably Khalil Gibran Muhammad, then Director of the Schomburg Center for Research in Black Culture, whose foundational book *The Condemnation of Blackness: Race, Crime, and the Making of Modern Urban America* traced the history of the criminalization of Black Americans in the first part of the 20th century, and who was committed to placing mass incarceration in a history of racism and racial control.[50] The first meeting also included policy experts like Marc Mauer, Director of the Sentencing Project, who had been laboring for criminal justice reform for so many decades, pushing quixotically against the powerful rise of mass incarceration, that he himself had become a witness to the history we were documenting – he recognized this unprecedented moment for shifting policy through public opinion, and the need to seize it.[51] Political scientist Marie Gottshalk, who had recently released a book on how the carceral state had become so tenacious, was also eager to leverage this work for lasting change, understanding, like Mauer, that data-driven policy campaigns required a paradigmatic shift in public understanding of the roots of the problem.[52] The largest group of participants, though, were the professors who had worked on the Guantánamo Public Memory Project, and other faculty who asked to join HAL later. Mostly public historians and museum studies scholars, whose main expertise was in questions of narrative, representation, and engagement, the majority knew next to nothing about mass incarceration or its history.

The group first discussed what a memory project could offer, if it could offer anything at all. The stars now seemed to be aligning to make substantive policy change around mass incarceration, with public awareness of the issue, energy among progressive activists, and commitment of elected officials, at an all-time high. It was critical to the founding group that a memory project should not be merely additive, but should contribute specific value to initiatives already underway, and support that work. To that end, the discussion began with the questions: Why should we remember the era of mass incarceration – what difference would it make? What should we remember about it? With whom – and for whom – should we remember? And how?

Why Remember?

For movement leaders in the group, it was all about timing. 2015 was a unique moment, one we had to seize. As Marc Mauer argued, "We're currently at a moment of criminal justice policy where reform is *actually* on the agenda... I think this project can build on those dynamics, those trends, hopefully extend that conversation nationally."[53] Scholars argued that this was a particularly promising moment not only for policy, but also for public dialogue. Historian Heather Ann Thompson reflected that as of recently,

> ...I think we can all be much braver in tackling this subject ... I have to say even four years ago talking about this, people tread very carefully, there weren't enough books written yet, there weren't enough articles. It was really hard to talk about this in a public forum.[54]

She and others noted that a new collective concern about mass incarceration afforded an opportunity to reframe it in the public imagination – and here public memory was critical. Historians in the group commented how mainstream discussion of *The New Jim Crow* and the 1994 Crime Bill suggested that a consciousness of the historical links between incarceration and structural racism could denaturalize mass incarceration and provide a new frame for voters and judges to make arguments about criminal justice. Advocates in the group echoed the "active memory" approach of Argentina's Memoria Abierta, arguing that a memory project could make abuses and the people experiencing them visible in the face of forces that work to hide them. Marlon Peterson, who would later develop a host of hugely popular public media to change narratives about mass incarceration, explained that for him, "the question is how do you get Americans to have a better understanding of an issue that affects so many Americans but at the same time is not really in their face day to day."[55] Advocates also argued that a public memory project should build a sense of shared responsibility for mass incarceration, even as it recognized how unshared the experience was.

What Should We Remember?

But what exactly should be publicly "remembered" about the past, to build a more informed discussion of ending mass incarceration in the present? What public memory would support what public policy? As with the discussion around how to remember Guantánamo, a key question was how far back the history should go. Historicizing mass incarceration by starting with slavery, emphasizing the continuous lineage of racial control and violence, focused attention on anti-Black racism as a central cause, and therefore a central target of reform. But stressing continuity risked eliding the distinctive period of the War on Drugs and asking why it brought such an outsized explosion of incarceration. The challenge would be to acknowledge and analyze the unique severity of recent decades while rooting the problem in the longer legacy of anti-Black racism, to build recognition that addressing mass incarceration would require deep work.

In addition to debating historical origin points, participants debated geographic ones. While the carceral state might have a shared American history, it was formed from distinct local lineages. The history popularized by Alexander and young memorializers of the 1994 crime bill was a generalized, national one, obscuring the ways the country arrived at a collective crisis from 50 state starting points. The 1994 bill covered only the 10% of the prison population the federal government controls. The vast majority of incarcerated people were affected instead by subsequent state and municipal legislation. The varying paths localities took – and the different populations that wound up impacted – were rooted in their own particular histories. Dismantling state policies requires understanding how each was constructed.

Further, while the slavery-to-mass-incarceration narrative gaining public attention was rooted in the specifics of African American experiences, in some local contexts, other groups – especially Latinx and Native Americans – were incarcerated at the highest rates. Incarceration of American Indians in the Upper Midwest and Latinos in the Southwest had different roots that could help explain how we got into the problem, and suggest specific strategies for solving it. For scholars and advocates rooted in these different experiences, a great potential of the project was to generate a popular consciousness of this diverse genealogy – and how different lines intersected.

Who Should Remember, and Be Remembered?

Finally, who should the project be created with, and for? Despite the growing national discussion of the failures of the criminal justice system, stigma around formerly incarcerated people and their families remained strong.

Many participants in the meeting shared concern for the silences perpetuated in affected communities and felt there was still a great need for spaces where people who had been incarcerated could, as one participant put it, "say it out loud." The project should provide an ongoing space for people whose lives had been adversely impacted by mass incarceration to come together and tell their stories as a shared experience and a critical piece of American history. As Glenn Martin later explained,

> For me, the "memory" that we refer to on this project is a synonym for direct personal experience. For people and communities impacted by mass incarceration, it's less about asking, "What happened?" and more about asking, "What happened to us?"[56]

This kind of story sharing could provide healing from trauma and build solidarity, supporting individuals while strengthening collective action. This theory of change did not depend on forcing an outside "public" to look at people and problems they had refused to see. But other participants worried about "preaching to the converted," arguing that the project must engage those who had thought little about the issue before. One museum director reported that in his experience with his museum visitors, "When it comes to this issue, the group that is the most challenging to reach out to… is the white middle class. If you start lecturing them they completely shut down."[57] Others worried that privileging this audience, and especially tailoring the project to avoid "shutting them down," would reproduce historic exclusions and erasures of voices of color that undergirded the crisis.

At the root of the debate about audience were different perspectives on who drives policy change. "Why is it important to communicate with the white middle class?" challenged one participant. "Because they are already the audience for museums? Or is it because they matter for the policy side?"[58] Focusing engagement on those least impacted by mass incarceration seemed premised on the assumption that those most impacted were not the drivers of change. A growing chorus of formerly incarcerated criminal justice reform leaders contested this assumption, organizing their work around the principle that "the people closest to the problem are also closest to the solution."[59] Ultimately, the working group developed a set of principles establishing that the project's first priority was to place the voices, expertise, and leadership of those "most directly affected from multiple perspectives" at the center, while also combating denial among those who believed themselves to be removed from the issue.[60]

The working group did not define whether anyone other than formerly incarcerated people comprised those "directly affected," or delineate the scope of multiple perspectives. Unlike during the Guantánamo Public Memory Project, the group did not insist on involving people from both sides of the power equation, such as corrections officers or administrators. In this case, participants argued that the voices of incarcerated people had been silenced for so long and distorted so severely that placing their stories side by side with those of guards would create a false equivalency. Participants' mistrust of corrections perspectives was particularly high in New York City, where the Correction Officers Benevolent Association (COBA) had been waging a PR campaign, including massive billboards, depicting COs as victims of violence by those they guarded. The mistrust was mutual: COBA President Norman Seabrook, known for his aggressive resistance to criminal justice reform (and later convicted of accepting bribes and sentenced to 58 months in prison), was invited to the working group meeting. He came to the building, but then refused to come inside.

How Should We Remember?

Here a vigorous debate arose about data versus storytelling. Participants had recently witnessed human stories of incarceration galvanizing new attention to the carceral state.[61] Many argued that the primary goal of the project should be to humanize incarcerated people, and therefore the project should focus on narratives of individual people's experiences. Mass incarceration is based on dehumanization of poor people of color as "superpredators" or "illegals," unindividuated groups with common characteristics that legitimize keeping them behind bars. A project to both reveal and heal that dehumanization must focus on restoring individuality and personhood in everyone. As cultural organizer Piper Anderson, who facilitated some of the discussions, later explained her view,

> Stories build empathy, but not so that we can humanize the incarcerated. People in prison are already human. Hearing a story is an opportunity for you, the listener, to show up more fully in your humanity.[62]

Others feared that focusing on individual stories would instead further obscure mass incarceration as a vast and complex system, sustaining the fiction that it can be dismantled one case at a time. Only by aggregating individual experiences in the form of large-scale data, they argued, could we demonstrate the scope and reach of the problem.

The Participants in Participatory Public Memory of Mass Incarceration: Navigating Race, Power, and Position

The working group hoped to lay the foundation for a collective confrontation of mass incarceration, involving people directly involved in the criminal justice system, people who had never thought about it before, and everyone in between. Gathering in a spacious lecture hall, directly impacted leaders, scholars of mass incarceration, and other stakeholders flowed in and out of breakout groups and large discussions, facilitated with all manner of stickers and wall charts to ensure every voice was heard. Together, they identified the overall principles of the project, and prioritized its narrative themes, emerging with a clear mandate to center the voices of those directly impacted through a history that centered anti-Black racism. But before the project even started, the process of framing it confirmed how participatory public memory is defined – and limited – by the perspectives and relative power of whoever is in the room.

Within the working group, it was the professors who were ultimately responsible for actually implementing the project, by steering their students to create the exhibit. Their universities were also the ones who were responsible for paying for it: each university contributed $5000 to a collective exhibit production fund. Faculty gathered in a smaller room to identify the piece of history each of their classes would focus on. When I opened the door to start this meeting, I looked out onto a conference table of white faces. I knew and had invited each of them, but until this moment, I hadn't admitted to myself how overwhelmingly white they were as a group. But since each of these progressive scholars had dedicated their lives to placing the stories of people who had been erased from or misrepresented in history back at its center, I believed that together we could surely apply the priorities we heard from Black advocates in the working group to the project's overall historical timeline.

Each professor wrote the topic they proposed to address on large cards, which we pinned up side by side: the complicity of pharmaceutical companies in the death penalty; immigration detention; changing ideas of rehabilitation. Squinting at a timeline of butcher block paper and scribbled marker stretched crookedly along the wall of the conference room, we saw that not one story explored anything related to slavery, convict leasing, or Jim Crow – missing the basic throughline of African American history. I know that all of the participating faculty genuinely believed this history to be central. But I can't deny the writing I literally saw on the wall: by asking a group of largely white faculty to each identify a history from their own locality or experience, one they felt confident in teaching to others, collectively, we created a timeline devoid of Black narratives.

The faculty group vowed not to move forward without bringing on additional professors representing a greater racial diversity in their own identities, that of their students, and the communities in which their universities were located. The University of Minnesota team, focusing on incarceration in Indian Country, was co-led by Ojibwe scholar Jean O'Brien, but she was one of the few non-white faculty. We also agreed that every faculty member would collaborate with an organization representing people who had been directly impacted by incarceration, whether incarcerated people, families, corrections officers, or others. Much as we tried to fill the gaps we could see, the table, to a certain extent, had been set, establishing contradictions between the project's vision and reality that we struggled with throughout the process. For example, there were no formerly incarcerated women advocates in the original group. Instead, one man played an outsized role: Glenn Martin, who had just founded JLUSA, was an incredibly charismatic leader and big-picture visionary with a fantastic talent for bringing intellectual clarity to our sometimes-muddled discussions, and inspiring participants around a common purpose. He also mobilized other directly impacted leaders to participate in the project in critical ways, and shaped the project throughout its development. Not until February 2018, more than three years after the working group meeting and two years after the project launch, where Martin was the featured speaker, did I learn from the *New York Times* that three women had accused him of sexually assaulting them while he was leading JLUSA.[63] On top of the risk of professional recrimination all women face for calling out powerful men in their field, women calling out Martin bore the burden of endangering the fragile public narrative repudiating mass incarceration and legitimizing the leadership of formerly incarcerated people. "I thought I was going to harm quote, unquote the movement," one of the women told the *Times*, explaining her hesitancy to go public with her story. Indeed, the 2018 article introduced Martin as an "ex-convict," a term Martin had spent his professional life advocating to eradicate, and one I would imagine these women would not support.[64] The 2015 working group did not include histories of sexual assault in its initial collective timeline of mass incarceration; but also didn't recognize the omission, the way it did with the absence of African American histories.

The working group experience highlighted the importance of moving far beyond ourselves, a small group of purported experts, to a more broadly participatory public memory. A few, or even a dozen, additional working group members would still not represent the multiplicity of historical experiences in the carceral state. We needed to organize this public history of mass incarceration more like a social movement, created by the widest cross-section of the incarceration generation we could manage, galvanizing engagement from many different agents of change. Starting in September 2015, over 600 students and scholars from 20 campuses in 17 states began collaborating with nearly 30 organizations led by or representing currently and formerly incarcerated people. Faculty at each campus taught courses, created from common curricular resources developed with scholar advisors, through which students collaborated with currently and formerly incarcerated people to research their local history. Each collaboration then created an exhibit chapter: a physical and digital exhibit module that, within parallel format and scale created by a central designer, could feature combinations of historic images, documentary video, and audio testimony unique to each local team.

The Humanities Action Lab's central team of designers would then compile the local chapters into a collective public history, framed by common questions and national interactives that invited people across localities to connect by sharing personal stories and "voting" on policy issues. The common exhibition would then travel to each of the communities that created it, with dialogues, actions, and additional local exhibits at each stop. Instead of trying to centrally curate a diversity of perspectives, in this way the project would generate an intersectional analysis organically, physically representing it through interlocking panels exploring different strands of race, gender, region, age, and myriad other vectors of experience. New communities were invited to add new chapters all along the way. The project thus hoped to foster an ongoing, participatory process of researching, reckoning, and identifying paths to redress.

The challenge was to create a space where people's different experiences could be respected and exchanged productively, even – and especially – when people did not fall neatly into categories of insider or outsider. Most participating students in the project's initial cohort self-identified as white. About 70% described themselves as not directly impacted by mass incarceration. Further, over half weren't even thinking about it: they came to the project through an introductory methodology course in public history, museum studies, or a related field, stumbling into the subject matter without having sought it out. Many students spent the first few weeks reflecting on their own denial. As Elsa Gunnarsdottir of Duke University noted,

> Safely bundled up in the comforts of the "Duke bubble," most of us will never think about the prison or the inmates that are being held within a 30-minute drive from campus. However, executed in the name of American citizens, the death penalty involves all of us, which again reinforces that we are more closely implicated in the prison system than we might think we are.[65]

Others discovered disturbing gaps in their understanding of the system and its structures. Yoselyn Paulino of the University of Miami admitted,

> On the first day of class, I had no idea what detention centers were. I loosely knew about immigration and deportation, yet never considered what stood between the two.[66]

Movements to resist the carceral state – including ones in which students like Paulino could have participated – were as invisible to many as the system itself. "Organizations that fight against anti-immigrant measures in Florida were equally as new to me as the anti-immigrant measures themselves," she observed.[67]

The project required all students to share written reflections with each other on the roots of their own view of the carceral state, or absence of one;

and on what stories, information, experiences, or encounters during the project helped them see it differently, or see it at all. In this way, the small group of 600 students in 20 cities provided a trial national audience for the project; reflecting on their own reactions shaped how they then tried to communicate with a larger public as exhibit authors. As Elizabeth Caroscio from The New School observed, "The majority of our class did not have a lot of previous knowledge on Rikers Island, and I have come to realize that this is a strength for us. We can take the aspects of the jail that we reacted to learning about the most in the semester and include it in our exhibit with the hopes that it will spark the same response out of our visitors."[68]

While the majority of students grappled with their own denial of mass incarceration, about a third came to class bringing lifelong familiarity with the system. As Amber Mitchell of IUPUI described it, while she herself had never been incarcerated, "the prison system has never been too far away, a ghastly shadow looming in the background of my every day life."[69] A New York City-based student echoed, "The prison system has always contributed to what you might call the background radiation of life in Harlem."[70] Other students were shaped by different carceral communities: for Garrett Weeden, growing up in Upstate New York, "If there was one thing that I thought of when it came to the criminal justice system it was jobs.... I know many families whose lives depend on the jails in the communities throughout the region."[71]

Some students highlighted how their life experiences gave these students a different relationship to classroom learning. As Meranda Roberts of the University of California Riverside (UCR) noted, growing up with incarcerated relatives and constant police harassment, "I find it hard to say that anything that I have learned this past week in my UCR seminar about the history of incarceration has surprised me."[72] But personal experience did not always ensure people "knew" the carceral state; its mechanisms could remain hidden even to those living in it. After reading about the school to prison pipeline, another UCR student wondered how "all of these facts remained largely invisible to me prior to this class, despite having relatives who were incarcerated, cousins who were wards of the state as a result."[73]

Those with lived experience brought different goals to the project. Some sought to understand their own history and family better. One Rutgers University-Newark student shared that

> Through this class I hope to revisit and remember the stories that my father told me as a child about his experience coming to the US. I hope to see them within the larger context of history, mass incarceration, and immigrant detention.[74]

One class of students incarcerated at Statesville Correctional Facility in Illinois, who participated through a prison education program at DePaul

University, articulated what they hoped to teach through the exhibit, within constraints of what was safe and permitted to express while incarcerated. In response to the prompt, "What do you want your legacy to be?" they responded with artwork and essays on their past lives and future visions, sharing larger lessons about incarceration they wanted to communicate to a wider public. Adolfo, a 39-year-old inside student who had been incarcerated since the age of 14, wrote, "...today I want my legacy to be educational. I want my life to be a testimony that will help save lives. I want my legacy to be a lesson."[75] Mike, another inside student, sought a legacy of making incarcerated people visible: "When I came to jail I saw more people being move through the system unseen... I still seen the people, unseen people that can't fight for themselves."[76]

Except for those who were incarcerated, students who felt personally impacted by incarceration were not organized into a separate group of "people with direct experience." They sat side by side with, and had to collaborate with, classmates who had grown up with the privilege of being able to deny the carceral state that surrounded them, and who spent considerable class time grappling with their denial. After a few discussions with her classmates, Amber Mitchell of IUPUI wrote, "What I have found to be most surprising about the course thus far has not been from our readings but my classmates' surprise to the state of the prison system in the United States."[77] This surprise could be productive for the project, as Mitchell reflected:

> My classmates, I realize, represent the public that we are trying to reach through this exhibition. In the short amount of time that we have been studying this topic, these students have voiced deep changes and developments within themselves that bring these issues to life for them. That's what makes this project so imperative: there are too many people who are unaware of just how damaging mass incarceration has been to generations of people, especially those in black and brown communities. People who come from backgrounds like mine, who have been experiencing this world for so long, sometimes forget that others can be blind to it.[78]

But students like Mitchell bore the unsolicited burden of educating their classmates, obliged to join them in a group project implicitly geared toward enlightening equally uninformed audiences, implying such audiences were the only key to change. Over the course of the project, Mitchell had "come to realize just how exhausting it is to try to explain why prison reform is important to people who have never been impacted by the prison industrial complex."[79]

In some participating universities, such as at Rutgers University-Newark or University of California-Riverside, students who described being personally impacted did share a classroom with others who identified similarly, and could exchange ideas and experiences. Discussions in classrooms with high proportions of directly impacted students, and the collective analysis of their historical experience, demonstrated the potential of opening greater space to explore, "what happened to us," and identify different audiences and goals for change. HAL central leadership piloted new partnerships with historically Black colleges and universities (HBCUs), starting with Winston-Salem State University and Johnson C. Smith University, both in North Carolina. This part of the project was guided by HAL staff member Dr. Shana Russell, herself an HBCU graduate. In this way the project hoped to learn how to provide a more supportive experience for directly impacted curators, and speak to audiences who were also closer to the issues, engaging them as primary agents of change.

Students' stated goals for participating in the project had less to do with discovering something they'd never seen and revealing it to others who were unaware of it, and more to do with gaining tools to support and mobilize directly impacted communities. "My older brother is in and out of jail," wrote one student. "I look forward to discovering the reason people who look like me are in and out of prison. Maybe this will allow me to better help my brother along the way."[80] Another student hoped history would provide new perspectives on frequent police encounters: "I will try to understand the root to incarceration. I want to understand why it is that blacks are more often targeted, stereotyped, and profiled than another race. This experience will heighten and expand my thoughts and feelings as it pertains to law enforcement."[81] One student anticipated that their experiences would "give me some sort of stance or position to take in the project," suggesting that having a real stake in an issue allowed curators to make a clearer and stronger interpretive argument.[82]

Each participating faculty member committed to exploring their local history – and curating it for a national public – through a collaboration between students and people directly affected by mass incarceration. Local faculty were left to design how to collaborate, and with whom. The collaboration between different types of people would be facilitated through organizations that represented them: for instance, between a university and a reentry organization. The project hub provided stipends to support the time and other costs of non-student participants. Partners were encouraged to design a collaboration that would allow all participants to provide both testimony and analysis, so that, for instance, formerly incarcerated people were not only sharing their personal history but articulating its implications. Amy Halliday, Chel Rose, and Julie Peterson of the University of Massachusetts Amherst wrote of their team's

> early recognition that expertise lies in lived experience: incarcerated and formerly incarcerated women, their families, and those fighting in

and for communities affected by incarceration are those best placed to ask the best questions, to mine the details, to track the way policy and politics plays out in real lives. These individuals, whose lives are directly impacted on a daily basis by the carceral state, are the voices society should look to in order to engage and interrogate historical and contemporary narratives of incarceration.[83]

The overall goals of the collaborations were to build empathy for the experience of incarceration and allow people with different positions in the carceral state to decide together what story to tell about it and how. As DePaul student Austin Kiesewetter reflected,

The criminal justice system and prisons specifically, by design, dissolve the bonds between people that allow for the creation of a coherent public memory. The lesson is this, perhaps: if we, as scholars and critics of the United States prison system, want to be the catalysts for a national dialogue on this issue, we need to work to reestablish the human bonds that prisons inherently dismantle.[84]

Students without incarcerated friends and family members identified their encounters with currently and formerly incarcerated people as the single most powerful influence on their understanding and perspective, the main catalyst for their "aha" moments.

The impact of the encounters on students depended entirely on how they were structured. This was particularly true of visits to prisons. Many criminal justice reform advocates with whom university faculty partnered felt strongly that students should see a prison for themselves if they were going to teach other people about incarceration. Even if the visits were only to demonstrate how correctional facilities represent incarceration on their official tours, these advocates argued they would still have tremendous pedagogical value. As Emma Marston of IUPUI noted,

When I started this project, I knew very little about the carceral system, and in general I was pretty far removed from both prisons and mental health care. Since then, I've learned a lot through books and articles, news media, professionals, activists, and other sources. However, being physically inside a prison and experiencing that space was very different from reading about it, and I feel that my visit to New Castle [Correctional Facility] was crucial to my understanding.[85]

But many students felt prison visits deepened divisions and further dehumanized incarcerated people. After his tour of death row at the Louisiana State Penitentiary, Daniel McCoy of the University of New Orleans complained that "For visitors to gawk at those sitting on death row trapped in their cages awaiting their collective fate handed down from the State is both dehumanizing and numbing for both parties involved."[86] For some, concern about voyeurism and "trauma porn" suggested the exploitative potential of individual stories, and made them question whether and how to tell them. Scott Olsen from Arizona State University wrote, "we should not place the individuals who have been unjustly imprisoned at the center of our project's focus, in order to avoid making their personal tragedy into a spectacle."[87]

Visitation programs organized by advocacy organizations framed a very different interaction than tours organized by facility authorities, based more on building relationships with individual incarcerated people than observing the facility's population from a distance. Grassroots Leadership, a Texas organization advocating for people in immigrant detention, organized University of Texas students to visit women detained at the T. Don Hutto Residential Center. "It was incredibly important for me to see Hutto and connect with a woman who is detained there," wrote Anju Palta.

> To experience a human connection and give reality to the commodification and resulting effects of dehumanization of the immigration system, I believe, is one of the most important means of combating detention.[88]

Some students found unexpected connections between their own experience and the experiences of those purportedly from the other side of the divide. University of Miami students conducted several visits with individual people detained at the Krome Detention Center, organized by their partner organization, Friends of Miami-Dade Detainees. As one University of Miami student reflected at the end of the project,

> The most meaningful aspect of this experience was meeting a man named Tariku from Ethiopia and hearing his story. Tariku and I had so much in common due to the fact we spoke the same language and were part of the same ethnic group being oppressed in Ethiopia... As a first generation immigrant myself, I never understood the extent of systematic oppression of immigrants in America.[89]

In other cases, formerly incarcerated people were the ones to enter students' space, when they came to a classroom to share their personal experiences. These encounters led students who had felt no connection to the criminal justice system previously to argue vigorously for a public memory strategy based on personal interaction. As one Duke University student wrote,

> showing the personal side of incarceration is crucial as we begin to think about how we want to create a national dialogue. Showing the faces

and voices of incarceration can engage the public on an emotional and personal level and portray the current injustices within the justice system in more depth.[90]

When Darrell Cannon visited DePaul University's class and shared his experience of torture by the Chicago Police and the campaign to publicly reckon with that history of abuse, student Austin Kiesewetter reflected,

> What incited my interest in carceral issues was not a shocking statistic, but instead a flesh-and-blood person – Darrell Cannon... We need to put real faces, like Darrell Cannon, behind the inscrutable numbers, and force a reckoning with the human cost of racist mass incarceration. If the whole of the American public looked him in the eyes, would the current prison system last another day?[91]

Personal engagement had the greatest transformative impact when it was most equitable; when it centered on exchange, not display, as the prison tours did. Professors Julia Foulkes and Radhika Subramaniam at The New School in New York City invited six members of the Fortune Society, an organization supporting returning citizens, to join the class several times over the course of the semester and consult on a local history of the Rikers Island jails. Student Elizabeth Caroscio noted, "The biggest takeaway that I got was that education is a two way street between those involved in the system and those who are not; if these two groups of people work together, then the system will be improved."[92] Benjamin Weber of the University of New Orleans (UNO) organized a unique collaboration between his students and men currently incarcerated at Angola. Inspired by the work of artist and activist Mark Strandquist, who consulted with the team, UNO students wrote men incarcerated in Angola to ask if they would like the student on the outside to commemorate someone who had passed away while the person was in prison. If so, the incarcerated person should write the story of their loved one, and describe the act of commemoration they wanted the student to perform, and where. Students recited prayers at a gravesite; danced with "outside" family at a family home; and placed flowers and a bingo marker on top of a waterfall in a public park. The stories and acts revealed and enacted a web of connections: one man's loved one had graduated from UNO; another student was asked to meet and visit with the family of the incarcerated man, when she could not meet the man herself. For student Hannah Galloway, when she fulfilled Gerald Davis's request to release multi-colored balloons over a special street corner to remember his late girlfriend, the healing was mutual: "The project had a positive effect on both of us. It means a lot to him to know someone who he has never met cares about him and wants to see him be successful and it means a lot to me to know someone is willing to teach me."[93]

In addition to educating and building empathy for people who had been incarcerated among the uninformed, the overall goal of the collaborations was for people with different positions in the carceral state to decide together what story to tell about it and how. Collaborations between returning citizens and students faced no physical or administrative obstacles – members of the Fortune Society could huddle with New School students in their classrooms to map out an exhibit panel. But facilitating equitable and open co-creation between people inside and outside correctional facilities was extremely difficult. Despite a large number and variety of prison education programs across the country at the time, many universities had no relationship with a correctional facility. Those that did very often had only one faculty teaching inside, often on subjects unrelated to criminal justice or history, such as GED prep or accounting. Establishing new programs and relationships with correctional facilities was a multi-year undertaking for which faculty participating in the project did not have the capacity. For those who did teach history within correctional facilities, a *public* history project, in which incarcerated students' work would be exhibited nationally, challenged established approaches to teaching both inside and outside of prisons.

In Illinois, Statesville students were constrained in the form of expression that could be publicly exhibited. The initial idea was for all students to decide how to tell the history of incarceration in Illinois. But for men who were under correctional control, some up for parole, there was concern that any criticism of mass incarceration could jeopardize their good standing. DePaul University faculty were also concerned that such a discussion could jeopardize the university's relationship with Statesville, and their ability to continue the program. The solution was to pose the common question to all students "What do you want your legacy to be," and invite each to respond through their own modes and media. Where inside students created artwork and written reflections, outside students explored different moments in Chicago's and Illinois' history of incarceration – both the construction of the carceral state and the struggle against it – whose legacies were felt today. Both types of student work were displayed side by side in the final exhibit.

While States of Incarceration's interpretation was shaped by people with a diverse combination of life experiences and perspectives, the way it designed collaboration between people privileged one group. The project was structured around the assumption that students, as a category, were all privileged and protected and needed mass incarceration to be made visible to them; they would be educated through collaborations with people outside the classroom, coming from criminal justice organizations. After reading students' reflections and consulting with community partners, I realized that during the initial research and interpretation phase, those with direct experience – both students and people outside universities – became more educators than co-creators. In addition to being exhausting for many of those in that position, this emphasis on educating those insulated from incarceration risked reinforcing the idea that the main path to change lay in raising awareness among unaffected audiences, as opposed to supporting the leadership of those directly impacted.

In New York City, however, the States of Incarceration process gave rise to a new, ongoing public memory project that was squarely rooted in and created for impacted communities: The Rikers Public Memory Project. Calling the project a "Community Truth and Healing Process,"[94] organizers sought to activate memory of the Rikers Island jails to identify their historical harm, and support those impacted by Rikers as leaders of campaigns for redress and revisioning. In this way, they integrated truth telling, reckoning, and reparations that explicitly linked public memory to public policy around criminal justice.

Notes

1 Independent Commission on New York City Criminal Justice and Incarceration Reform, *A More Just New York City: Independent Commission on New York City Criminal Justice and Incarceration Reform*, April 2017, https://static1.squarespace.com/static/5b6de4731aef1de914f43628/t/5b96c6f81ae6cf5e9c5f186d/1536607993842/Lippman%2BCommission%2BReport%2BFINAL%2BSingles.pdf

2 John Surico, "The Feds Are Suing New York City Because Rikers Island Is a Hellhole," *Vice*, December 18, 2014, https://www.vice.com/en_us/article/exmwae/the-feds-are-suing-new-york-city-because-rikers-island-is-a-gitmo-style-hellhole-1218

3 Ibid.

4 Ibid.

5 Ibid.

6 Neil Barsky, "Shut Down Rikers Island," *New York Times*, July 17, 2015, https://www.nytimes.com/2015/07/19/opinion/shut-down-rikers-island.html?campaignId=7JFJX

7 "Shut Down Rikers: Meet Akeem Browder, Who Is Fighting to Close Jail That Took His Brother's Life," *Democracy NOW!*, November 2, 2016, https://www.democracynow.org/2016/11/2/shut_down_rikers_meet_akeem_browder

8 Jake Miller, "Hillary Clinton: Time to 'end the era of mass incarceration,'" *CBS News*, April 29, 2015, https://www.cbsnews.com/news/hillary-clinton-baltimore-riots-to-end-the-era-of-mass-incarceration/; Ta-Nehisi Coates, "The Black Family in the Age of Mass Incarceration," *The Atlantic*, October 2015, https://www.theatlantic.com/magazine/archive/2015/10/the-black-family-in-the-age-of-mass-incarceration/403246/. The June 2015 issue of the *Journal of American History* featured the theme of "Historians and the Carceral State," and included 14 articles by historians of mass incarceration.

9 Steve Christian, "Children of Incarcerated Parents," National Conference of State Legislatures, March 2009, https://www.ncsl.org/documents/cyf/childrenofincarceratedparents.pdf; John Gramlich, "The Gap Between the Number of Blacks and Whites in Prison is Shrinking," Pew Research Center, April 30, 2019, https://www.pewresearch.org/fact-tank/2019/04/30/shrinking-gap-between-number-of-Blacks-and-whites-in-prison/

10 "Warehoused and Forgotten: Immigrants Trapped in Our Shadow Private Prison System," American Civil Liberties Union, June 2014, https://www.aclu.org/sites/default/files/assets/060614-aclu-car-reportonline.pdf

11 Tracy Huling, "Building a Prison Economy in Rural America," in *Invisible Punishment: The Collateral Consequences of Mass Imprisonment*, eds. Marc Mauer and Meda Chesney-Lind (New York: The New Press, 2002), 197–213.

12 Sarah Shemkus, "Beyond Cheap Labor: Can Prison Work Programs Benefit Inmates?" *The Guardian*, December 9, 2015, https://www.theguardian.com/ sustainable-business/2015/dec/09/prison-work-program-ohsa-whole-foods-inmate-labor-incarceration. This number, or at least the data supporting it, seems to have held steady over the following years. By 2020, about 63,000 incarcerated individuals produced goods for external sale. Hannah Dreier, "'A Recipe for Disaster': American Prison Factories Becoming Incubators for Coronavirus," *Washington Post*, April 21, 2020, https://www.washingtonpost.com/national/ a-recipe-for-disaster-american-prison-factories-becoming-incubators-for-coronavirus/2020/04/21/071062d2-83f3-11ea-ae26-989cfce1c7c7_story.html

13 For a succinct overview of the transformative impact of mass incarceration on so many aspects of American life summarized in this paragraph, see Heather Ann Thompson, "Why Mass Incarceration Matters: Rethinking Crisis, Decline, and Transformation in Postwar American History." *The Journal of American History* (Bloomington, Ind.) 97, no. 3 (2010): 703–34.

14 Roy Walmsley, "World Prison Population List (10th edition)," International Centre for Prison Studies, https://www.prisonstudies.org/sites/default/files/ resources/downloads/wppl_10.pdf; Michelle Ye Hee Lee, "Yes, U.S. Locks Up People at a Higher Rate than Any Other Country," Washington Post, July 7, 2015, https://www.washingtonpost.com/news/fact-checker/wp/2015/07/07/yes-u-s-locks-people-up-at-a-higher-rate-than-any-other-country/. "The United States had the highest prison population rate in the world, 716 per 100,000 of the national population, followed by St Kitts & Nevis (714), Seychelles (709), US, Virgin Is. (539), Barbados (521), Cuba (510), Rwanda (492), Anguilla – UK (487), Belize (476), Russian Federation (475), British Virgin Is. (460), and Sint Maarten– Netherlands (458)."

15 Bruce Western, *Punishment and Inequality in America* (New York: Russell Sage, 2006); Becky Pettit, *Invisible Men: Mass Incarceration and the Myth of Black Progress* (New York: Russell Sage Foundation, 2012); Michelle Alexander, *The New Jim Crow: Mass Incarceration in the Age of Colorblindness* (New York: The New Press, 2010), 228.

16 Alexander, *The New Jim Crow*, 186.

17 Chris Uggen, Ryan Larson, Sarah Shannon, and Arleth Pulido-Nava, "Locked Out 2020: Estimates of People Denied Voting Rights Due to a Felony Conviction," The Sentencing Project, October 30, 2020, https://www.sentencingproject.org/ publications/locked-out-2020-estimates-of-people-denied-voting-rights-due-to-a-felony-conviction/

18 Marc Mauer and Meda Chesney-Lind, "Invisible Punishment: The Collateral Consequences of Mass Imprisonment," January 1, 2002, https://www.sentencingproject. org/publications/invisible-punishment-the-collateral-consequences-of-mass-imprisonment/

19 Ingrid V. Eagly and Steven Shafer, "A National Study of Access to Counsel in Immigration Court," *University of Pennsylvania Law Review* 164, no. 1 (December 2015): 2.

20 Angela Y. Davis, *Are Prisons Obsolete?* (New York: Seven Stories Press, 2003), 15.

21 Alexander, *The New Jim Crow*, 183.

22 Ibid., 222.

23 Ibid., 183.

24 Seth C. Bruggeman, "Reforming the Carceral Past: Eastern State Penitentiary and the Challenge of the Twenty-First-Century Prison Museum" *Radical History Review* 2012, Issue 113 (Spring 2012), 171.

25 Ibid., 173.
26 E. Ann Carson, "Prisoners in 2016," Bureau of Justice Statistics, U.S. Department of Justice, January 2018, https://bjs.ojp.gov/content/pub/pdf/p16.pdf
27 "ACLU Awarded $50 Million by Open Society Foundations to End Mass Incarceration," ACLU, November 7, 2014, https://www.aclu.org/press-releases/aclu-awarded-50-million-open-society-foundations-end-mass-incarceration; "Safety and Justice Challenge Evaluation Report," MacArthur Foundation, May 22, 2019, https://www.macfound.org/press/evaluation/safety-and-justice-challenge-evaluation-report
28 Barack Obama, "Remarks by the President at the NAACP Conference," July 14, 2015, https://obamawhitehouse.archives.gov/the-press-office/2015/07/14/remarks-president-naacp-conference
29 Jake Sherman, "Paul Ryan Dreams of a Kinder, More Substantive GOP," Politico, January 10, 2016, https://www.politico.com/story/2016/01/paul-ryan-gop-2016-house-republicans-217547#ixzz3z7GKxPhu
30 Inimai Chettiar and Michael Waldman, eds. "Solutions: American Leaders Speak Out on Criminal Justice," Brennan Center for Justice. April 27, 2015, https://www.brennancenter.org/sites/default/files/publications/Solutions_American_Leaders_Speak_Out.pdf
31 "The Growth of Incarceration in the United States: Exploring Causes and Consequences," Overview, National Research Council, https://www.nap.edu/catalog/18613/the-growth-of-incarceration-in-the-united-states-exploring-causes#overview
32 Chettiar and Waldman, "Solutions."
33 Jeremy Travis, Bruce Western, and Steve Redburn, eds., *The Growth of Incarceration in the United States: Exploring Causes and Consequences* (Washington, DC: The National Academies Press, 2014), 104.
34 Ben Schreckinger and Annie Karni, "Hillary's Criminal Justice Plan: Reverse Bill's Policies," Politico, April 29, 2015, https://www.politico.com/story/2015/04/hillary-clintons-criminal-justice-plan-reverse-bills-policies-117488
35 Alana Rosenberg, Allison K. Groves, and Kim M. Blankenship, "Comparing Black and White Drug Offenders: Implications for Racial Disparities in Criminal Justice and Reentry Policy and Programming," *Journal of Drug Issues* 47, no. 1 (2017): 132–42; "Decades of Disparity: Drug Arrests and Race in the United States," Human Rights Watch, March 2, 2009, https://www.hrw.org/report/2009/03/02/decades-disparity/drug-arrests-and-race-united-states; "Report to the United Nations on Racial Disparities in the U.S. Criminal Justice System," The Sentencing Project, April 19, 2018, https://www.sentencingproject.org/publications/un-report-on-racial-disparities/
36 "The New Jim Crow: Mass Incarceration in the Age of Colorblindness: A Case Study on the Role of Books in Leveraging Social Change," November 2014, The New Press, https://mediaimpactfunders.org/wp-content/uploads/2014/12/The-New-Press-NJC-Case-Study-Nov20141.pdf
37 "Opinion and Order," Floyd, et al. v. City of New York, et al., Civil Action No. 1:08-cv-01034-SAS-HBP, U.S. District Court for the Southern District of New York, August 12, 2013, http://s3.documentcloud.org/documents/750446/stop-and-frisk-memoranda.pdf; "Floyd, et al. v. City of New York, et al.," Center for Constitutional Rights, https://ccrjustice.org/home/what-we-do/our-cases/floyd-et-al-v-city-new-york-et-al. "Stop and frisk" is a policing practice of temporarily detaining and searching a civilian for contraband items that the New York City Police Department used disproportionately on BIPOC residents, driving racial disparities in arrests and jail populations. The Fourth Amendment requires that the police must have a reasonable suspicion that a crime has been, is being, or will be committed by the suspect.

38 Bryan Stevenson, *Just Mercy: A Story of Justice and Redemption* (New York: Spiegel & Grau, 2014).

39 EJI began commemorating racial terror lynchings in 2015 by collaborating with communities to collect soil at lynching sites. EJI's website explains, "We believe that understanding the era of racial terror is critical if we are to confront its legacies in the challenges that we currently face from mass incarceration." "The Legacy Museum: From Enslavement to Mass Incarceration," Equal Justice Initiative, https://museumandmemorial.eji.org/museum; "Community Remembrance Project," Equal Justice Initiative, https://eji.org/projects/community-remembrance-project/

40 Anne Gearan and Abby Phillip, "Clinton Regrets 1996 Remark on 'Super-Predators' after Encounter with Activist," *Washington Post*, February 25, 2016, https://www.washingtonpost.com/news/post-politics/wp/2016/02/25/clinton-heckled-by-black-lives-matter-activist/

41 Ben Schreckinger and Annie Karni, "Hillary's Criminal Justice Plan: Reverse Bill's Policies," Politico, April 29, 2015, https://www.politico.com/story/2015/04/hillary-clintons-criminal-justice-plan-reverse-bills-policies-117488

42 Katherine Miller, "Clinton: America, Including the Black Community, Wanted Tough-On-Crime Policies in the '90s," *BuzzFeed News*, October 11, 2015, https://www.buzzfeednews.com/article/katherinemiller/clinton-america-including-the-black-community-wanted-tough-o

43 "Hillary Clinton Interview with Al Sharpton of MSNBC's 'Politics Nation,'" October 4, 2015, The American Presidency Project, https://www.presidency.ucsb.edu/documents/interview-with-al-sharpton-msnbcs-politics-nation

44 Elizabeth Hinton, Julilly Kohler-Hausmann, and Vesla M. Weaver, "Did Blacks Really Endorse the 1994 Crime Bill?" April 13, 2016, https://www.nytimes.com/2016/04/13/opinion/did-blacks-really-endorse-the-1994-crime-bill.html

45 The exhibition title referenced the recent, highly publicized study of California's driving role in the development of the US carceral state: Ruth Wilson Gilmore, *Golden Gulag: Prisons, Surplus, Crisis, and Opposition in Globalizing California* (Berkeley: University of California Press, 2007).

46 Nausheen Husain, "'Guantánamo North' Prison Units in the Midwest Are Under Fire for Their Harsh Conditions. After 10 Years, One Man Is Still Fighting His Case." *Herald & Review*, December 7, 2019, https://herald-review.com/news/state-and-regional/guantanamo-north-prison-units-in-the-midwest-are-under-fire/article_183e300f-ba14-5859-86d0-04615304f36f.html

47 Thanks to Laura Aurrichio, then a Dean at the New School for Public Engagement (which was incubating the idea) and a big *2001: A Space Odyssey* fan, for choosing a name with the acronym HAL.

48 Susan Stellin and Graham MacIndoe, *Chancers: Addiction, Prison, Recovery, Love: One Couple's Memoir* (New York: Ballantine Books, 2016); Jeff Smith, *Mr. Smith Goes to Prison: What My Year Behind Bars Taught Me About America's Prison Crisis* (New York: St. Martin's Press, 2015).

49 Elizabeth Hinton, *From the War on Poverty to the War on Crime: The Making of Mass Incarceration in America* (Cambridge, MA: Harvard University Press, 2016); Thompson, "Why Mass Incarceration Matters"; Heather Ann Thompson, *Blood in the Water: The Attica Uprising of 1971 and Its Legacy* (New York: Pantheon Books, 2016).

50 Khalil Gibran Muhammad, *The Condemnation of Blackness: Race, Crime, and the Making of Modern Urban America* (Cambridge: Harvard University Press, 2011).

51 Sabrina Jones and Marc Mauer, *Race to Incarcerate: A Graphic Retelling* (New York: The New Press, 2013).

52 Marie Gottschalk, *Caught: The Prison State and the Lockdown of American Politics* (Princeton: Princeton University Press, 2015). Other scholars participating and

their main works recently released or in process at that time included: Douglas A. Blackmon, *Slavery By Another Name: The Re-Enslavement of Black Americans from the Civil War to World War II* (New York: Anchor Books, 2009); A. Naomi Paik, *Rightlessness: Testimony and Redress in U.S. Prison Camps since World War II* (Chapel Hill: University of North Carolina Press, 2016); and Juliet Stumpf, "Doing Time: Crimmigration Law and the Perils of Haste," *UCLA Law Review* 58, no. 1705 (2011).

53 Statement made at Humanities Action Lab Global Dialogues on Incarceration Working Group Convening January 5–7, 2015, The New School, New York City.

54 Statement made at Humanities Action Lab Global Dialogues on Incarceration Working Group Convening January 5–7, 2015, The New School, New York City. Additional works that received significant attention in that moment, contributing to both scholarly and broader public discussion of mass incarceration, included: Ruth Wilson Gilmore, *Golden Gulag: Prisons, Surplus, Crisis, and Opposition in Globalizing California* (Berkeley: University of California Press, 2007), Piper Kerman, *Orange Is the New Black: My Year in a Women's Prison* (New York: Spiegel & Grau, 2010); Naomi Murakawa, *The First Civil Right: How Liberals Built Prison America* (New York: Oxford University Press, 2014); and Amy E. Lerman and Vesla M. Weaver, *Arresting Citizenship: The Democratic Consequences of American Crime Control* (Chicago: The University of Chicago Press, 2014).

55 Statement made at Humanities Action Lab Global Dialogues on Incarceration Working Group Convening January 5–7, 2015, The New School, New York City. Peterson later launched the Decarcerated podcast and published a memoir, *Bird Uncaged: An Abolitionist's Freedom Song* (New York: Bold Type Books, 2021).

56 Glenn Martin, keynote address at "States of Incarceration in the Age of Trump," Humanities Action Lab International Working Group Convening (October 18–-21, 2017), Rutgers University-Newark, October 19, 2017, text held by Humanities Action Lab.

57 Statement made at Humanities Action Lab Global Dialogues on Incarceration Working Group Convening January 5–7, 2015, The New School, New York City.

58 Statement made at Humanities Action Lab Global Dialogues on Incarceration Working Group Convening January 5–7, 2015, The New School, New York City.

59 "Ways to Support," JustLeadershipUSA, https://jlusa.org/ways-to-support/

60 Report from Humanities Action Lab Global Dialogues on Incarceration Working Group Convening January 5–7, 2015, The New School, New York City, held by Humanities Action Lab.

61 Bryan Stevenson's 2014 book *Just Mercy* reopened critical discussion of the death penalty (Bryan Stevenson, *Just Mercy: A Story of Justice and Redemption* (New York: Spiegel & Grau, 2014)). *New Yorker* journalist Jennifer Gonnerman's 2014 article on Kalief Browder inspired national liberal critique of juvenile detention (Jennifer Gonnerman, "Before the Law," *The New Yorker*, September 29, 2014, https://www.newyorker.com/magazine/2014/10/06/before-the-law). Building on the long history of prison writing, a host of other projects, including the photography exhibit *Prison Obscura*, the podcast *Ear Hustle*, and art fellowships funded by the Rauschenberg Foundation and the Art for Justice Fund, emerged to make space for currently and formerly incarcerated people to narrate their own experiences more directly.

62 Piper Anderson, "Can Stories Create Justice?" *TED Talk*, November 2016 https://www.youtube.com/watch?v=R3yzmTWA3Bw

63 Nikita Stewart, "A Report of Sexual Misconduct, a $25,000 Payment and an Activist's Abrupt Exit," *New York Times*, February 2, 2018, https://www.nytimes.com/2018/02/02/nyregion/glenn-martin-rikers-advocate-report-of-sexual-misconduct.html

64 Ibid.

65 Elsa Gunnarsdottir, "Approximating the Prison System" States of Incarceration, Fall 2015, student reflection held by Humanities Action Lab.

66 Yoselyn Paulino, "Crimmigration and Immigrant Detention in South Florida," States of Incarceration, Fall 2015, student reflection held by Humanities Action Lab.

67 Ibid.

68 Elizabeth Caroscio, "Education as a Two Way Street," States of Incarceration, Fall 2015, student reflection held by Humanities Action Lab.

69 Amber Mitchell, "Mass Incarceration: Coming to Terms with the Personal," States of Incarceration, Fall 2015, student reflection held by Humanities Action Lab.

70 "No Haven in a Heartless World," States of Incarceration, Fall 2015, student reflection held by Humanities Action Lab. Student gave permission to use quote but asked for their name to be withheld.

71 Garrett Weeden, "The People the Law Forgot – Immigrant Detention," States of Incarceration, Fall 2015, student reflection held by Humanities Action Lab.

72 Meranda Roberts, "Recognizing Your Place in The Global Dialogue of Incarceration," States of Incarceration, Fall 2015, student reflection held by Humanities Action Lab.

73 "An Intimate and Pervasive System," States of Incarceration, Fall 2015, student reflection held by Humanities Action Lab.

74 "Records, Categories, and Papertrails: A Reflection on the Language of Immigrant Detention," States of Incarceration, Fall 2015, student reflection held by Humanities Action Lab.

75 DePaul University students Meredith Bennett-Swanson, Raquel Boton, Megan Marie Deppen, Aliya C. Flanagan, Alexandra C. Garcia, Roxanna Haveman, Amy L. Hildebrand, Austin Kiesewetter, Joseph Magnelli, Jacquelyn Beasley Ross, Meghan Elizabeth Salvon, Carly C. Schanock, Mollie Elisabeth Thiriot, Jill M. Walker, Scott Zwierzchowski, and faculty lead Amy Tyson, "Illinois: Legacies and Voices," States of Incarceration, https://statesofincarceration.org/states/illinois-legacies-and-voices

76 Ibid.

77 Mitchell, "Mass Incarceration: Coming to Terms with the Personal."

78 Ibid.

79 Amber Mitchell, "Reflecting and Moving Ahead," States of Incarceration, Fall 2015, student reflection held by Humanities Action Lab.

80 Anonymous student response, surveyed by the States of Incarceration project team, 2018, survey held by Humanities Action Lab.

81 Anonymous student response, surveyed by the States of Incarceration project team, 2018, survey held by Humanities Action Lab.

82 Anonymous student response, surveyed by the States of Incarceration project team, 2018, survey held by Humanities Action Lab.

83 Amy Halliday, Chel Rose (formerly Chelsea Miller), and Julie Peterson, "'What Are Women's Prisons for?' Gendered States of Incarceration and History as an Agent for Social Change," *Museums & Social Issues* 12, no. 1 (2017): 60.

84 Austin Kiesewetter, "Facing the Human Cost of Mass Incarceration," States of Incarceration, Fall 2015, student reflection held by Humanities Action Lab.

85 Emma Marston, "Reflections on Incarceration and Mental Illness," States of Incarceration, Fall 2015, student reflection held by Humanities Action Lab.

86 Daniel McCoy, "The Specter of Execution at Angola," States of Incarceration, Fall 2015, student reflection held by Humanities Action Lab.

87 Scott Olsen, "Immigrant Detention in Arizona," States of Incarceration, Fall 2015, student reflection held by Humanities Action Lab.

88 Anju Palta, "Detention Centers – Sites of Capital Extraction," States of Incarceration, Fall 2015, student reflection held by Humanities Action Lab.

89 "Final Reflection," States of Incarceration, Fall 2015, student reflection held by Humanities Action Lab. Student gave permission to use quote but asked for their name to be withheld.

90 "Is Our Justice System Blind?," States of Incarceration, Fall 2015, student reflection held by Humanities Action Lab.

91 Kiesewetter, "Facing the Human Cost of Mass Incarceration."

92 Caroscio, "Education as a Two Way Street."

93 Hannah Galloway, "Stories from Prisons, Honoring Loved Ones," *Museums & Social Issues* 12, no. 1 (2017): 48.

94 "About Us," Rikers Public Memory Project, https://rikersmemoryproject.org/

9

REMEMBERING RIKERS

Participatory Public Memory for Public Policy

States of Incarceration's national initiative to reckon with mass incarceration launched in New York City, where the city's largest local jail complex – Rikers Island – had been recently recognized as "an international symbol of despair and damage," the capital of the carceral state, a synecdoche for the abuses and excesses of the US criminal justice system. The exhibition opened on the day in 2016 that hundreds of people, representing a coalition of over 50 organizations coordinated by JustLeadershipUSA, launched the #CLOSErikers campaign. After blanketing the steps of New York's City Hall, calling on the Mayor to permanently shutter the jails, participants moved uptown to The New School to open the States of Incarceration exhibit with an event on "Remembering Rikers." They joined the students, faculty, and advocates from across the country who had explored the histories of Angola's plantation, Dakota detention camps at Fort Snelling, and the path from Ellis Island to the Esmor immigrant detention center in New Jersey. As the national group prepared to organize events and actions in their own localities, they came to learn from the #CLOSErikers campaign's extraordinary success activating participatory public memory to change criminal justice policy.

Rikers Island is an unparalleled site of collective trauma for New Yorkers. For over a century, the lives of hundreds of thousands of the city's residents – whether they were detained there, worked there, visited, or lived every day under the shadow of its threat – were fundamentally shaped by the place. There may be no other site in New York with an experience of violence and pain so widely shared – yet shared so unequally. For most of its history, the jail was as invisible to some as it was omnipresent to others. But in the 2010s, a new generation of formerly incarcerated leaders forced public discussion of mass incarceration, in both their own communities and in elite policy circles,

DOI: 10.4324/9781003185826-13

to create a different visibility and context for Rikers. By 2016, a series of new exposés on abuse at Rikers, buoyed by new attention to mass incarceration, brought Rikers into mainstream media and policy discussions far beyond New York City.

The story of denial and dialogue around Rikers is significant not only because the jails have become a national symbol of America's perverted criminal justice system. It also provides a particularly strong example of the potential for policy change when all three elements of participatory public memory – reconnecting, reminding, and redress – are effectively combined.

Rikers On and Off the Map: Hidden Histories and Hauntings

New York City is a scattering of islands. Only one of its boroughs, the Bronx, is located on a landmass. Manhattan Island occupies the center, flanked by Roosevelt Island; Brooklyn and Queens sit on Long Island; Staten Island lies to the southwest. The waters between are dotted with others – Liberty Island, Ellis Island, Governors Island – open for leisure and learning. Over 11 million New Yorkers and 70 million tourists criss-cross these islands each year on subways, busses, ferries, and even a gondola.

One island, though it sits right in the middle of New York's waterways, stands apart: Rikers. Officially part of the Bronx, it is less than 300 feet from the shore of Queens.[1] Rikers is not remote; it's just removed. Accessible by a single bridge, from Queens, known as the "Bridge of Pain," it is served by a single bus line, the Q100.

In the 50 years from the day the "Bridge of Pain" was opened in 1966, to the launch of the #CLOSErikers campaign in 2016, millions of New Yorkers were incarcerated at Rikers, while hundreds of thousands of others visited or worked there.[2] At its height in the early 1990s, the number of people on Rikers on any given day might have exceeded 30,000: over 20,000 incarcerated people, and more than 10,000 corrections officers, lawyers, service providers, and visiting family members.[3] "It is in many ways a small city," a 2017 report described, "complete with a power plant, hospital, bakery, and other services."[4]

The vast majority of people incarcerated at Rikers are not convicted of a crime. Instead, they are awaiting a trial to determine their guilt or innocence. They are theoretically free to leave the island, provided they can pay their bail. But because most cannot, they wind up incarcerated for months or years waiting for their court date. Even for those with someone who can pay their bail, the process of scheduling time off work or finding childcare to spend a day traveling to the bailbondsman and to Rikers could take weeks.

The map of Rikers' impact thus extends far beyond the island. Rikers represents a carceral city within New York, whose territory includes a web of neighborhoods such as the South Bronx, Brownsville, and East and Central Harlem, neighborhoods with predominantly Black and Latinx low-income earners, from which a vast majority of the jail's population is drawn.[5] This carceral city is dominated by policing and jail as its strongest civic structure, with weak investment in other public institutions like education or public health. Some blocks had vast proportions of their residents incarcerated, as Laura Kurgan and Eric Cadora visualized in their 2006 project, "Million Dollar Blocks," referencing the astronomical cost of incarcerating residents from some streets.[6] In 2015, nearly 120,000 of New York City's Black men between the ages of 25 and 54 were "missing," due largely to incarceration, but also to early death.[7] When huge numbers of people are removed from a neighborhood, breaking up families and social networks, the entire community's social fabric is torn. When huge numbers of workers are removed, there are ripple effects of their lost wages for families, local businesses, and other economic infrastructure.[8]

Those left behind do plenty of time at Rikers too. Visiting can take an entire day. The journey alone can take hours. Upon arrival, visitors are criminalized by association, subject to dehumanization and hostility like the people inside. Visitors are subject to humiliating security checks, strip searches, and verbal harassment. Davon Woodley, incarcerated at Rikers in 2013, remembers that his mother told him "They (jail officials) treat me like I'm in here with you."[9] Anna, whose son served six years at Rikers awaiting trial, remembers the violence she saw every week during her visits: "I saw people beating each other up. I saw people attacking other people. I saw blood in there. I saw violence. I saw abuse. I was violated too. My daughter was violated when we went there with strip searches and stuff like that, with abusive talk. It was just so shocking."[10] Rikers' carceral city, then, contained entire communities: incarcerated people, their families, friends, and neighbors.

The mechanisms for silencing and erasure are built into Rikers' foundations. As historian Shana Russell observes, Rikers did not begin with the best of intentions and then devolve into its current state. Its roots are rotten. The Island was literally constructed by, and for, incarcerated people. Of its current 440 acres, only about 20% – 87 acres – is natural. After acquiring the land in 1884, the New York City Department of Public Charities and Correction conscripted people incarcerated on nearby Blackwell's Island to begin expanding the island into a facility for incarceration. Blackwell's housed all categories of the city's undesirables: mental health asylums, poor houses, and penitentiaries were crowded together in the same space. To a new generation of reformers, Jarrod Shanahan and Jack Norton explain, Rikers represented a way to relieve overcrowding and draw what the *New York Times* celebrated as "'a distinct line of demarcation by territorial restriction between institutions for the relief of the distressed,' who would remain on Blackwell's Island, 'and those for punishment of the guilty.'"[11] After decades of construction by several generations of incarcerated people, the penitentiary on Rikers Island opened in 1935, heralded as a major reform of the deplorable conditions on Blackwell's. Blackwell's would later be renamed Welfare Island (it is now known as Roosevelt Island), while Rikers would become, as a City commission later described it, a "de facto penal colony."[12]

Rikers' roots were rotten in a second sense: the Island is constructed of garbage, landfill from the waste of the rest of the City's growth and progress, including soil excavated for the construction of the subway system (which would later exclude the island from its maps).[13] As Shanahan and Norton recount, "The Department of Sanitation continued to enlarge the island with the burnt remains of street sweepings and garbage, until Robert Moses demanded that the practice be halted in anticipation of the 1939 World's Fair. So that the island would look bucolic from the nearby fairgrounds in Flushing, Works Progress Administration crews leveled off and landscaped the trash that covered the island in 1939."[14] Rikers is haunted by its toxic origins. The decomposing garbage that forms its ground emits methane, a gas both poisonous and flammable; parts of the island spontaneously catch fire on a regular basis. In 2011, seven corrections officers filed suit against the city, after being diagnosed with cancer they believed was caused by prolonged exposure to the toxic landfill.[15]

Rikers Island's history is entwined with histories of racial control. Its Lenape identity was erased by colonization: while the Lenape name for other islands is known, the one for Rikers remains obscured.[16] The island's first colonial name derived from Abraham Rycken, a Dutch settler who secured title to the island from New Netherland director-general Peter Stuyvesant in 1664. The Ryckens claimed ownership of enslaved people for generations, building up wealth and eventually Anglicizing their name to Riker. But it was Abraham's descendant Richard Riker, born in 1773, who became the symbol of the family's history of controlling Black labor, specifically through the criminal justice system. Richard Riker served as the City's recorder in the 1820s and 30s, which meant he oversaw the main criminal court in New York City. He was responsible for, among other things, enforcing the Fugitive Slave Act, returning enslaved people who had escaped from the South back into slavery, even though slavery was abolished in New York State in 1827. Riker was decried by abolitionists for using the Act to justify the "Kidnapping Club," a ring of white officials – from police to lawyers to judges – who sent Black New Yorkers – whether free or enslaved – into southern slavery without granting them proper hearings.[17]

Decades later, a new generation of young Black New Yorkers was brought to Rikers Island, often forcibly, for their labor. During the Civil War, the Island was used as a training ground for Union soldiers. To fill the newly approved Black regiments, recruiters kidnapped or drugged young men and brought them to the Island,[18] where they were segregated in deplorable living conditions and paid a fraction of what white soldiers were paid.[19] Some Black New Yorkers lived through two generations of kidnapping: as a child, Henry Highland Garnet had witnessed his sister snatched for Richard Riker's "court"; as an adult, he saw Black children abducted by Union Army recruiters. Garnet created an early historical record of Black voices on Rikers, visiting the Island and taking statements from recruits who had been swindled by bounty hunters, in order to advocate for them.[20]

Later generations of voices from Rikers transformed the cultural landscape of America. Rikers was instrumental in the birth of hip hop; many of its later artists were detained there, including Slick Rick, Tupac Shakur, Ol' Dirty Bastard, and Lil Wayne, who in addition to his music, published an account of his time at Rikers, in the tradition of prison memoirs.[21] Artists who had no personal experience at Rikers also spoke to its impact and shared experience through their music, performance, and writing, whether to support affected communities, to raise awareness beyond them, or for personal promotion. In 1987, when the population of Rikers was nearing its highest, D.J. Polo and Kool G. Rapp released the single "Rikers Island." In 1990, reggae artist Cocoa Tea, who lived in Jamaica, released his own "Rikers Island," as the title track for his album, speaking to Black immigrant youth experience there.[22] In 1988, Public Enemy performed at Rikers, the first rap group to do so. The media coverage focused more on Public Enemy than on Rikers, but the performance cemented the place of Rikers in the Hip Hop Nation.[23] Despite this cultural production, the most widely circulated representations of Rikers were in comics and television shows, depicting a frightening fortress for detaining brutal criminals. As historian Shana Russell observes, "The role played by Rikers in our cultural history shapes what the rest of the world 'knows' about the island and all but erases the existence of the millions of people who have entered its doors."[24]

The denial of Rikers was so complete as to be disorienting: the island was literally wiped off the map. New School students working on a history of Rikers for States of Incarceration were stunned to learn that over the course of the City's history, Rikers continually appeared and disappeared on subway maps.[25] Rikers officially opened as a jail in 1935. It appeared on the 1939 subway map. In 1964 and 1972, however, the island was not only not labeled, but the landform was erased from the map altogether. It appeared in 1968, but not 2007, and though it reappeared on new maps for distribution to riders printed in 2015, on the maps posted inside subway cars, which were printed smaller, Rikers remained a blank shape. As students Estefanía Acosta and Laura Sanchez conducted their research in the fall, they noted that "Rikers Island is labeled on station maps but not inside trains, on digital versions but not in digital kiosks."[26] That year Rikers was therefore simultaneously there and not there.

The erasure of the Island from the consciousness of unaffected parts of the City was so complete that even those with some connection to it had no sense of where it was. As Emily Patka reflected after looking at a map on which Rikers was marked,

> It struck me how physically close Riker's [sic] Island is to NYC main-
> land. I suppose it makes sense, but for someone who has spent a lot of
> time working on and thinking about issues of incarceration, has loved
> ones currently in prison (and who have been on Riker's [sic]), and has
> worked in prisons, I was surprised, and a little embarrassed, that I had
> never actually looked up Riker's [sic] on a map before. It floated in my
> mind [as] somewhere around the city but I truly had no idea where.[27]

Even people who had been held there found their own presence erased. Graham MacIndoe, the professor of photography at The New School who created portraits of participants in States of Incarceration for the exhibit, encountered a massive hole in the official record of his incarceration experience. MacIndoe, originally from Scotland and in New York with a green card, spent four months on Rikers Island for drug possession in 2010, but was then transferred from Rikers into ICE detention, which he describes as far more harrowing.[28] In 2015, to protect himself from immigration detention, MacIndoe decided to apply for US citizenship, for which he needed proof of his time at Rikers, but securing a record of his own experience proved astoundingly difficult. He told me that when he finally got a copy of the papers, he saw that they grossly misstated how long he had been there, erasing thousands of hours of pain and trauma he had experienced. The public historical record for posterity was false; the reality lived only in his memory.

In the 2010s, reformers thrust Rikers into the view of those who had denied it for decades. In August 2014, Manhattan US Attorney Preet Bharara, together with US Attorney General Eric Holder, released a damning report of a "culture of violence" on Rikers Island, which found a "pattern and practice of excessive force" from 2011 to 2013 that violated the constitutional rights of adolescents there.[29] The report's findings of abuse were not news to the many New Yorkers who had witnessed or endured them; but they constituted an important and unprecedented official acknowledgment. And to those who lived outside Rikers' territory of impact, they were shocking.

But one month later, it was Kalief Browder who opened millions of eyes around the country to Rikers, and the carceral state of which it was the capital, by telling his story to Jennifer Gonnerman of the *New Yorker*, in a piece published in September.[30] Browder was held at Rikers for three years, beginning when he was 16 years old, because he was accused, but never convicted, of stealing a backpack. Browder maintained his innocence throughout. His case was ultimately dismissed, but not before he suffered severe violence and trauma, including nearly two years in solitary confinement and abuse by corrections officers and others incarcerated at Rikers. Almost immediately, Browder's story began having a major impact on discussions of criminal justice issues among media and policy elites. Jay-Z reported putting down the *New Yorker* and picking up the phone to find Browder, ultimately making a documentary of Browder's experience.[31] Republican presidential hopeful Rand Paul told Browder's story at the Conservative Political Action Conference (CPAC) to argue for criminal justice reform.[32]

But Browder, now home with his family, was still suffering from major mental illness related to his trauma. On June 6, 2015, he killed himself. Together with the New York communities for whom he had become a symbol, *New Yorker* readers across the nation felt his loss, and were confronted with the debilitating and destructive legacies of imprisonment for incarcerated people – especially children – long after their release. Browder's suicide prompted even greater coverage of Rikers in liberal media outlets, making it a familiar name to huge numbers of Americans who had never seen a jail or prison, and catalyzing further policy change. A few weeks after Browder's suicide, The Marshall Project, a non-profit news organization founded the year before to bring attention to criminal justice issues, partnered with *New York* magazine to publish a major multi-media portrait of Rikers, featuring interviews with over a dozen people who were held and who worked there. In the Fall of 2016, Bill Moyers released a documentary on Rikers that aired on PBS and was screened around the country. The same year, Jay-Z announced he would be producing a six-part mini-series on Browder's Rikers experience; released in 2017, it won a Peabody Award. Mayor Bill de Blasio, who had recently announced an initiative to speed up the cases of hundreds of defendants held at Rikers, said after Browder's death that "Kalief's story helped inspire our [reform] efforts," including the mayor's plan to move Rikers detainees under the age of 18 to a dedicated youth facility in the Bronx.[33] President Obama led with Browder's story when explaining his decision to ban solitary confinement of juveniles in federal prisons.[34]

Gonnerman, the *New Yorker* reporter who broke Browder's story, remembered that Browder "wanted the public to know what he had gone through, so that nobody else would have to endure the same ordeals."[35] But who was this "public," and how were they uniquely equipped to ensure that the abuses of Rikers would end? The audiences for the *New Yorker*, *New York* magazine, and many of the other outlets exposing Rikers were not dominated by people with direct experience. Neither were the ranks of authors and editors. Policymakers often credited these professional mediators for the sea change in awareness, like the 2017 city-commissioned report that celebrated how: "Intrepid reporters from *The New York Times*, Associated Press, *New Yorker*, *Village Voice*, Marshall Project and other outlets have highlighted the routine mistreatment of people held at Rikers." These were "assisted by a variety of advocacy groups and numerous defense agencies that have worked assiduously," unnamed in this supporting role; directly impacted advocates were not

credited at all.[36] The spotlight on mainstream journalists reflected reformers' assumptions that those with a shared memory and deep knowledge of
Rikers were not the primary leaders and "public" driving change. Directly
impacted people's narratives were recognized for their power when mediated by a professional journalist for an uninformed public, but the people themselves were not yet widely acknowledged as a powerful political
constituency.

The Campaign to Close Rikers: Marshalling Memory to Shift the Policy Imagination

That's not to say that the sudden attention from people newly appalled by the
abuses of Rikers was unwelcome to directly impacted leaders. A few weeks
after Browder's suicide, New York City agreed to settle a federal lawsuit
over the abuses at Rikers, imposing a federal monitor and new policies on
corrections officers' use of force.[37] But *New Yorker* readers had short attention
spans; once they witnessed a win, those who knew Rikers only through
reading might assume the issue was resolved, and move on to other causes.
Meanwhile, those still on Rikers, or with loved ones still there, knew well
that the jails remained open, detaining nearly 10,000 people each day, including young boys like Browder.[38]

. In this moment, although awareness of abuses at Rikers and calls for reform
were growing, closing the jails altogether was still a radical idea, outside
mainstream discussion. For many longtime policymakers, the mayor, and the
media, "closing Rikers" was a thought exercise, a leap of imagination that
might encourage new thinking but was logistically impractical and politically
impossible. White liberal policy makers had been trying to make it happen for
decades, starting with Herb Sturz, deputy mayor for criminal justice in the
Koch administration. In the late 1970s, Sturz sought to sell Rikers to New
York State, advocating for "the idea of putting accused persons right near
the courthouse, closer to their families" through borough-based jails. "It just
seemed to me a rational and decent thing to do for the administration of justice," he told *The Village Voice*.[39] But by 1981, the New York City correction
commissioner Benjamin Ward declared the plan "dead and buried."[40] 20 years
later, a new correction commissioner, Martin Horn, took another run at closing Rikers and failed decisively. "I was buzz-sawed," he later told the *New
York Times*, remembering the avalanche of resistance he encountered from
community groups opposed to replacement jails being built in their neighborhoods. So when he learned, not a decade after his own defeat, that advocates
were calling once more to close Rikers, he acknowledged that "It can be done
physically, it can be done programmatically, it's good policy," but warned,
"I don't think it's any more politically feasible today than it was then."[41] Mayor
de Blasio agreed, calling the idea a "noble concept," but, as the *New York Times*

characterized it, something he considered "a fanciful proposal somewhere on the spectrum between a hassle-free subway ride and world peace."[42]

Policy makers wrote off closing Rikers as politically unfeasible because they only attended to certain political constituencies: a closed universe of white liberal policymakers, the Corrections Officers' Union, and conservative neighborhood organizations. Directly impacted leaders, representing a huge constituency for closing Rikers, refused the "reality" that only reform was politically possible. In April 2016, two months after de Blasio called closing. Rikers impractical, JustLeadershipUSA (JLUSA) launched its #CLOSErikers campaign. Founded by Glenn Martin, himself once incarcerated at Rikers, just two years earlier, JLUSA rallied dozens of other organizations to the campaign with the mantra, "those closest to the problem are closest to the solution." Unlike the failed attempts of the previous decades, this drive to close Rikers would succeed by centering those who had been there.[43]

The campaign marshalled public memory at every stage, as a critical strategy for changing public policy. At the opening event for the States of Incarceration exhibit, "Remembering Rikers," leaders framed the #CLOSErikers campaign's memory strategy: memory as reminding. Venida Browder, mother of Kalief Browder, who was the featured speaker, explained, "Every time I tell his story, I hope that eventually someone will listen and do something. I'm stuck with a lifetime sentence of grief and pain. By me retelling my story, his story, I'm hoping that it will save another child. It's never going to end, until it's time for me to go."[44] Six months later, Venida Browder died of a heart attack. Her son Deion Browder later wrote, "The stress of fighting for justice and the pain over her son's death literally broke my mother's heart." Deion carried on his mother's commemorative advocacy for criminal justice reform with the plea, "My mom died trying to preserve the legacy of her son. Keeping kids out of solitary will preserve hers."[45]

Before hearing Browder, the audience had visited the exhibit on Rikers created by students from The New School (TNS) and members of the Fortune Society, the reentry organization with high percentages of formerly incarcerated leadership where Glenn Martin served as Vice President before founding JLUSA. Students and Fortune members decided to focus on Rikers' visibility and invisibility, titling their chapter "In Plain Sight: How Do You See Rikers Island?" Elements included excerpts of audio testimony from Fortune members, a brief history with historic images, scans of artifacts donated by Fortune members, like commissary receipts, a playlist of music created on or inspired by Rikers, and a data visualization of traffic across the "Bridge of Pain."

In addition to the exhibit, the team created a participatory memory campaign to support the #CLOSErikers campaign. After learning of Rikers' erasure from subway car maps, students Laura Sánchez, Estefanía Acosta de la Peña, and Misha Volf created stickers printed with a big red arrow and the words "Rikers is Here" for New Yorkers to stick on the blank blob on the maps in trains, to make the island visible to other passengers. They began distributing the stickers to whoever would take them, at rallies, around campus, and among friends; they also created a downloadable file with instructions on how to print your own. Anyone who placed a sticker on the map was asked to snap a photo of it and post it on Twitter and Instagram with the hashtag #seerikers. "The sticker invites a simple gesture, and yet to put it on the map is to make an explicit political action," the students wrote. "With the adhesive artifact in hand, the passenger must publicly acknowledge and address the erasure."[46] The campaign was short-lived, but garnered several media articles. As I rode the subway in the Spring of 2016, I was pleased to see stickered maps in my train car.

Meanwhile, public memory was forming the foundation of a new public policy initiative on Rikers: the Independent Commission on New York City Criminal Justice and Incarceration Reform, popularly known as the Lippman Commission, after former chief judge Jonathan Lippman, its chair. A month before the launch of #CLOSErikers and States of Incarceration, the Speaker of New York's City Council appointed a commission to research the viability of closing Rikers and make recommendations for reforming New York City's criminal justice system. Over the course of the next year, the Lippman Commission became a public memory project in itself, of a sort: through individual interviews and community conversations in each of the five boroughs, it collected memories of Rikers, analyzed the material impact and legacy of the experiences described, and used them to identify remedies. Glenn Martin, leaders from Fortune Society, and others who had been involved in States of Incarceration served on the Commission's committees.

As the Commission considered options for Rikers' future, JLUSA and the Katal Center for Equity, Health, and Justice proposed a "community restorative justice approach" that included both physical reminders of past harm and material redress for it. The proposal included a physical memorial, "a permanent marker of the historic harms of Rikers and the City's commitment to memory and truth" as Martin later described it, and a symbolic reburial site for those who died on Rikers, "to recognize the role of Rikers in the loss of life." The proposal also suggested leveraging the value of the land and using revenue to invest in ongoing restorative justice work, and investing in job creation for communities historically hardest hit by Rikers.[47] This integrated vision of memory and redress engaged every New Yorker in accountability for incarceration's harm – a far cry from the long tradition of prison museums that sensationalized colorful criminals to reaffirm the need for prisons.

Just one year after the launch of the #CLOSErikers campaign and States of Incarceration, the Lippman Commission released its report, recommending that Rikers be closed. The Commission recognized the central role of memory in public policy: its road map for closing made remembering a key component of criminal justice reform and redress, asserting that future policy must be designed to remedy the past. "We believe," the report stated, "that a twenty-first century justice system must acknowledge the multiple harms that incarceration, and Rikers Island in particular, has caused hundreds of thousands of New Yorkers, their families, and their communities."[48]

The Commission recommended these harms be acknowledged through both reinvestment in historically impacted communities, and by

> establishing a memorial and/or museum that would honor the people whose lives were changed forever by their time on the Island – both those held and those who worked there. The goal would be to educate future generations about the history of the Island and spark a conversation about the administration of justice.[49]

Painting a portrait of a future Rikers museum and memorial, in addition to being a sincere policy prescription, was a critical rhetorical device to make Rikers "history," to frame the jails as a thing of the past. In this way, the push for a museum was an integral part of the push for closing.

Seeing the tides turning, as the report was released Mayor de Blasio quickly declared he would close Rikers. Echoing the new progressive policy language ricocheting across the country, he stated that "Mass incarceration can be ended. … It didn't begin here in New York City, but it will end here in New York City." [50] But unlike Obama when he made his declaration to close Guantánamo, de Blasio made it clear closing would be a long and arduous process, setting a target of ten years. While for #CLOSErikers organizers, the Mayor's declaration was a major victory, it did not mark the end of the campaign; it was only the beginning of its next phase. The declaration was only a statement of intention, with a timeline that stretched beyond the mayor's term. Rikers would not be closed, and its abuses would not end, without a clear policy vision and sustained pressure to implement it. This next phase of the campaign to close Rikers would require a parallel memory strategy.

Departing from the Commission's narrow focus on a "memorial and/or museum," in the next phase of the campaign to close Rikers, leaders harnessed all three of the memory strategies used by Sites of Conscience: *reconnecting* a distant past with the present; *reminding* people of those still suffering; and *redress*, demonstrating the ongoing legacies of this past and the need to repair them.

Closing Rikers and Slavery: Reconnecting Past and Present Through Historical Haunting

The Commission called on New Yorkers to confront a relatively recent history of late 20th-century over-incarceration, demonstrating specific, causal linkages to the decimation of Black and brown neighborhoods traceable with demographic and economic data. But while the data was indisputable, the War on Drugs still had many defenders. So the campaign turned to a history more widely repudiated – slavery – and worked to demonstrate the roots of Rikers there, joining the growing national call for reckoning with the country's foundations in racial violence. This narrative did not make data-based causal linkages, but instead traced a haunting – patterns of racial control repeating themselves in ways that were not coincidental, but due to a continuation of abuse across generations – that challenged academically defined history and social science. Like at the Slave House in Senegal, the campaign's summoning of spirits surfaced the tension around how to remember for redress.

In January 2015, Eric Foner, a venerated historian of American slavery and Reconstruction, published *Gateway to Freedom: The Hidden History of the Underground Railroad*, which included an account of Richard Riker and the "Kidnapping Club." His book soon became a *New York Times* bestseller. Foner was far from the first to publish on the Kidnapping Club; but on the heels of *The New Jim Crow*, the movements to eradicate racist monuments and statues in the American landscape, and to close Rikers Island, the book and the publicity around it sparked new discussion of a local lineage from slavery to mass incarceration in New York. A reporter recounted that Jacob Morris, director of the Harlem Historical Society, "read *Gateway to Freedom* last spring [2015], right as a new series of prisoner abuse scandals on Rikers Island was seizing national headlines," finding that "accounts of life at the contemporary jail were eerily harmonious with Foner's descriptions of the pre-Civil War justice system."[51] Morris started a petition to rename Rikers Island, to reject what he saw as its "disgraceful" lineage.

What was the historical relationship between Richard Riker, the Kidnapping Club, slavery, and the Rikers Island Jail complex? For historian Eric Foner, the sources didn't support one. In response to Morris' renaming proposal, Foner cautioned, "As I understand it, the island is named not for the infamous Richard Riker but for a distant ancestor, which makes the situation much more murky."[52] The specific historical connection between Rikers and slavery was far thinner than it was at, say, the Louisiana State Penitentiary, known as Angola, an actual plantation that was converted to a prison farm, its land continuously the site of African American forced labor. But Leslie Harris, a historian who published on the Kidnapping Club a decade before Foner, countered that even if the "Riker" in Rikers Island was not the slave catcher, the connection between slavery and the jail remained through ideas and practices: Richard Riker "is one of the rare cases where the history of the person and the legacy of his beliefs align very well."[53]

In any case, debates over forensic historical connections were drowned out by the ghosts of the past: once the door was opened between 19th-century slavery and 21st-century Rikers Island, it released spirits that could not be exorcised. As African American literature scholar Anna Mae Duane put it, "The history of Rikers Island carries the suppressed memories of a system that moved seamlessly from slavery to abduction and forced conscription, to incarceration in the service of profit."[54] For Venida Browder, Richard Riker was alive, while her son was not. "I understand that Rikers was named for a slave owner," she said at the opening of the States of Incarceration exhibit. "What if it was his son at Rikers? What kind of decisions would he make? He is making decisions for our kids."[55]

The specter of Richard Riker became a force in the #CLOSErikers campaign, with JLUSA tweeting:

> Did you know that Rikers Island is named after the family of a slave catcher? … He routinely allowed slave catchers to kidnap free Blacks and sell them to the Confederate south. Today, 89% of the people caged at Rikers Island, named for Richard Riker's family, are Black and Latino.[56]

The text, accompanied by an image of Riker with Mayor de Blasio's face in the background, was circulated on social media and at events, including a modified version on T-shirts campaign members wore during actions.

Debates over whether to rename Rikers mirrored similar contests over markers of white supremacy around the country. 2017 was a year of virulent, and violent, contests over the hauntings of white supremacy in American urban landscapes, and an insistence on confronting how ghosts empower the living. These were mainly focused on dismantling celebrations of slavery in the American South, removing statues of Robert E. Lee and other Confederate generals from public spaces, or renaming streets and buildings named after them in New Orleans, Richmond, Baltimore, and dozens of other cities. But in August of 2017, in the wake of the violence in Charlottesville, VA, Mayor de Blasio announced that he would be forming a Commission to review all "symbols of hate" on New York City property, meaning contested art, monuments, and markers. Days later, #CLOSErikers organized a protest in front of the sign at the entrance to the jail, labeling Rikers a Confederate monument. Organizers harnessed history to form another argument for the jail's closure: it should be removed as a "symbol of hate," just like a statue of Robert E. Lee. Activists held signs that read "Confederate monument" and "Torture," while others wore chains around their waists.[57] The protest did not involve a huge number of people; it was blisteringly hot and held on-site at Rikers, requiring an hours-long journey for most people. But the recording of it was circulated widely through #CLOSErikers social media, setting an important frame for campaign members and supporters.[58] Ivelisse Gilestra later reflected, during the oral history she shared about her experience at Rikers, "We are seekers of truth, and this is what we do with really exposing what Rikers is, which is, the ramifications of the institution of slavery. That is what Rikers is, and it needs to be said just like that."[59]

The story of Rikers as a slave catcher – particularly linking Kalief Browder to the Kidnapping Club, which preyed on children – echoed the popular discussion around the genealogy of slavery to mass incarceration sparked by *The New Jim Crow* and other efforts. Further, it raised Rikers out of its local specificity and allowed the jail to be understood in the national context of the African American historical roots of mass incarceration. Finally, by leaning into an American history that was much more widely condemned than was mass incarceration, it connected to other movements for redress and reparations that had won successes.

Closing Rikers and Lived Experience: Memory as Reminding and Redress

The ghost of Richard Riker rode alongside hundreds of living people who began sharing their own histories at Rikers Island. In June 2016, a few months after the launch of the #CLOSErikers campaign and States of Incarceration, community arts practitioner, writer, and educator Piper Anderson, who had been a key organizing and facilitating partner on States of Incarceration, hosted one of her first "Mass Story Labs," focusing on people incarcerated at Rikers Island and their families. Mass Story Labs were designed around concentric circles of participants, centering those with direct experience, using memory and storytelling to inform policy and inspire participation in shaping it. Anderson's vision was that "the stories of people directly impacted by mass incarceration become the lens through which communities imagine a world beyond prisons."[60] This approach to memory was focused on healing and transformation by and for the individuals who had been harmed, and was explicitly designed to support the movement to close Rikers. When Mayor de Blasio announced his intention to close Rikers and the Lippman Commission recommended creating a "memorial/museum," I reached out to Anderson to explore the potential of building a Rikers Public Memory Project. We formed a three-way partnership between Anderson's organization Create Forward, JLUSA, and the Humanities Action Lab, where Shana Russell, the historian who had overseen the second phase of States of Incarceration, managed the project and began digging into archives to release Rikers' early history.

Sarita Daftary, then with JLUSA, organized the participation of #CLOSErikers campaign members and ensured the project remained accountable to the goals and needs of the campaign.[61] Daftary was grounded in a memory-based approach to movement building, having previously led an oral history project around East New York, near where she lived, to support local organizing in that neighborhood. Working with reentry organizations and the public library system, who hosted "collection days" with formerly incarcerated people already gathering at their spaces, Russell built an infrastructure of volunteers and oral history trainings and began collecting oral histories of people who had been incarcerated at Rikers over multiple generations. The interviews were conducted through a trauma-informed approach, including after-care for both the interviewee and the interviewer. Project Manager Regina Campbell later realized after-care was needed even for the transcribers of the stories.

While from a public history standpoint, the project's main work was quite conventional – creating an oral history archive to be accessioned by the New York Public Library – its intentions and uses were not. Project organizers subtitled it a "Community Truth and Healing Process," by and for those who had been incarcerated at Rikers and their families. From its inception, the project's explicit mission was to support the campaign to close Rikers and transform criminal justice in the City. To that end, JLUSA linked the project to its #buildCOMMUNITIES initiative, which organized discussions in impacted communities across the city to define key priorities for reinvestment to address the historical harm Rikers caused. One of the questions participants were asked was, how do you want Rikers to be remembered? Overwhelmingly, participants called for memory through redress: understanding Rikers' historical harm in order to direct investments of city money to services and institutions that would remedy that harm and transform their communities.

The Rikers Public Memory Project's mission, audience, and theory of change shaped whose voices it comprised. Other public media portraying Rikers had, like the Guantánamo Public Memory Project did for GTMO, worked to provide a 360-degree portrait of Rikers to raise awareness among uninformed audiences, featuring corrections officers, nurses, teachers, or the many others who made up the jails' ecosystem.[62] The Rikers Public Memory Project was created for those who had been incarcerated there, and the families who were criminalized and suffered trauma along with them. As Project Manager Regina Campbell later explained, "We were particularly responsible about resisting any popular notions of having a balanced story. We wanted to maintain that accountability to the narrators."[63] A "many sides" approach risked creating false parallels, crowding and curtailing the voices of those who had been disappeared, silenced, and abused for so many generations. It was precisely this violent silencing that supported the structure of disappearing people to a penal colony in the first place. Focusing on their stories and agency now supported a vision and movement driven by their experience and perspective. So while organizers might acknowledge that the dehumanizing system negatively impacts those who enforce it as well, the voices of those who had been disappeared, silenced, and abused for so many generations must be given full space, not muffled in an attempt to represent multiple perspectives that ignored the gross power imbalance that structured them. By the end of 2020, the project had collected over 100 oral histories.

The #CLOSErikers campaign's memory strategy involved *reminding* New Yorkers of the tens of thousands of their fellow residents still being abused or bearing the scars of abuse from Rikers; *reconnecting* the structures supporting this violence to the long trajectory of racial control on the island and in the country as a whole; and *redressing* the legacies and continued repetition of these historical harms. This strategy integrated two forms of historical truth. First, history as haunting: calling out the ghosts of the slave past whose powerful presence continuously menaced the present, even if the material connections were disjointed. Second, memory as evidence: highlighting direct testimony from those who experienced Rikers which, in addition to serving as a healing process for those who shared their stories, and humanizing those incarcerated there for those who listened, also provided the only body of evidence for the myriad undocumented or suppressed abuses of the jails, from the specific methods and instances of violence by corrections officers, to ways visitors were harassed, to accurate information about the actual amount of time someone was incarcerated. Together, these approaches mobilized memory for redress, providing the data and framing the need for reinvestment in neighborhoods decimated by Rikers.

The result was significant strides in memory for public policy and public policy of memory. With its memory strategies, the campaign won significant criminal justice policy change. Additionally, the Lippman Commission's instructions for Rikers' closure included the creation of a memorial or museum. Adhering instead to a vision driven by directly impacted communities, the campaign launched a dynamic process of remembering for redress, rather than raising funds for a representation of the past, reckoning with Rikers' history by advocating for reinvestment in the communities it harmed.

Notes

1 Maurice Chammah, Simone Weichselbaum, Nick Tabor, Eli Hager, Dana Goldstein, Alysia Santo, Christie Thompson, and Beth Schwartzapfel, "Inside Rikers Island, Through the Eyes of the People Who Live and Work There," *New York Magazine* (in collaboration with The Marshall Project), June 28, 2015, http://nymag.com/daily/intelligencer/2015/06/inside-rikers-island-interviews.html

2 "What Is Rikers Island?" *New York Times*, December 15, 2014, https://www.nytimes.com/2014/12/16/nyregion/what-is-happening-at-rikers-island.html. This article states that 77,000 people cycle in and out of Rikers each year.

3 Craig Wolff, "Crowding of Rikers Inmates Is Ordered Eased," November 9, 1990, https://timesmachine.nytimes.com/timesmachine/1990/11/09/622090.html?pageNumber=38

4 Independent Commission, *A More Just New York City*, 27.

5 Ibid, 39.

6 "Million Dollar Blocks," Center for Spatial Research, Columbia University, https://c4sr.columbia.edu/projects/million-dollar-blocks

7 Justin Wolfers, David Leonhardt, and Kevin Quealy, "1.5 Million Missing Black Men," *New York Times*, April 20, 2015, https://www.nytimes.com/interactive/2015/04/20/upshot/missing-black-men.html

8 Ibid.

9 Davon Woodley, interviewed by Darlene Jackson, October 17, 2018, transcript, Rikers Public Memory Project.

10 Anna, interviewed by Tamika Graham, May 13, 2020, transcript, Local Voice Network Community Zoom Conversation, Rikers Public Memory Project. Anna's last name has been withheld to protect her privacy.

11 Jarrod Shanahan and Jack Norton, "A Jail to End All Jails," *Urban Omnibus*, December 6, 2017, https://urbanomnibus.net/2017/12/jail-end-jails/?printpage=true

12 Independent Commission, *A More Just New York City, 3.*

13 Shanahan and Norton, "A Jail to End All Jails."

14 Ibid.

15 Mark Wilson, "Rikers Island Guards File Suit Alleging Cancer-Causing Toxin Exposure," *Prison Legal News*, February 15, 2012, https://www.prisonlegalnews.org/news/2012/feb/15/rikers-island-guards-file-suit-alleging-cancer-causing-toxin-exposure/

16 The names of Tenkenas (Ward's Island) and Minnahanonk (Roosevelt Island) were published by William Wallace Tooker in *Indian Place-Names on Long Island and Islands Adjacent* (G.P. Putnam's son, 1911), but he did not include Rikers. Thank you to Kerry Hardy for his research into this and several other sources.

17 Eric Foner, *Gateway to Freedom: The Hidden History of the Underground Railroad* (New York: W. W. Norton & Company, 2015). See also Jonathan Daniel Wells, *The Kidnapping Club: Wall Street, Slavery, and Resistance on the Eve of the Civil War* (New York: Bold Type Books, 2020).

18 Anna Mae Duane, "The Shame of Rikers," *Slate*, July 13, 2017, http://www.slate.com/articles/news_and_politics/history/2017/07/rikers_island_is_the_northern_equivalent_of_confederate_monuments_but_worse.html?via=gdpr-consent

19 *Report of the Committee on Volunteering*, Union League Club, October 13, 1864, https://archive.org/details/reportofcommitte00unio/page/n3/mode/2up

20 Duane, "The Shame of Rikers"; *Report of the Committee on Volunteering*, Union League Club.

21 Lil Wayne, *Gone 'Til November: A Journal of Rikers Island* (New York: PLUME, 2016).

22 D. J. Polo and Kool G. Rapp, "Rikers Island," Cold Chillin' Records, Inc., 1987, vinyl, https://www.discogs.com/release/3610488-DJ-Polo-Kool-G-Rap-Rikers-Island; Cocoa Tea, "Rikers Island," track 6 on *Rikers Island*, Greensleeves Records, 1990, compact disc, https://www.discogs.com/release/1519222-Cocoa-Tea-Rikers-Island

23 Amy Linden, "Public Enemy at Rikers: An Oral History," Red Bull Music Academy, April 29, 2013, https://daily.redbullmusicacademy.com/2013/04/public-enemy-at-rikers-oral-history

24 Rikers Public Memory Project, "History of Rikers: The First 50 Years," accessed February 2021 https://rikersmemoryproject.org/

25 Michelle Young, "Fun Maps: Rikers Island Keeps Disappearing and Reappearing (on MTA Maps)," *Untapped New York*, https://untappedcities.com/2013/08/30/fun-maps-rikers-island-keeps-disappearing-reappearing-mta-maps/

26 "Put Rikers on the Map!" #SeeRikers, https://seerikersorg.wordpress.com/

27 Emily Patka, "Riker's Island, the Physical Place," States of Incarceration, Fall 2015, student reflection held by Humanities Action Lab.

28 Susan Stellin and Graham MacIndoe, *Chancers: Addiction, Prison, Recovery, Love: One Couple's Memoir* (New York: Ballantine Books, 2016).

29 U.S. Attorney's Office, Southern District of New York, "Manhattan U.S. Attorney Finds Pattern and Practice Of Excessive Force and Violence at NYC Jails on Rikers Island that Violates the Constitutional Rights of Adolescent Male Inmates," press release, August 4, 2014, https://www.justice.gov/usao-sdny/pr/manhattan-us-attorney-finds-pattern-and-practice-excessive-force-and-violence-nyc-jails

30 Jennifer Gonnerman, "Before the Law," *The New Yorker*, September 29, 2014, https://www.newyorker.com/magazine/2014/10/06/before-the-law

31 Camille Augustin, "Jay Z Shares the Story of the Day He Met Kalief Browder," *Vibe*, October 6, 2016, https://www.vibe.com/music/music-news/jay-z-kalief-browder-spike-tv-457680/

32 Anthony Terrell, "Man Cited by Rand Paul in Press for Criminal Justice Reform Dies," MSNBC, June 8, 2015, https://www.msnbc.com/msnbc/man-cited-rand-paul-press-criminal-justice-reform-dies-msna613126

33 James C. McKinley, Jr., "Calls Mount for Changes to Speed Criminal Cases to Trial," *New York Times*, June 17, 2015, https://www.nytimes.com/2015/06/18/nyregion/calls-mount-for-changes-to-speed-criminal-cases-to-trial.html; Benjamin Weiser, "Kalief Browder's Suicide Brought Changes to Rikers. Now It Has Led to a $3 Million Settlement." *New York Times*, January 24, 2019, https://www.nytimes.com/2019/01/24/nyregion/kalief-browder-settlement-lawsuit.html

34 Barack Obama, "Why We Must Rethink Solitary Confinement," *Washington Post*, January 25, 2016, https://www.washingtonpost.com/opinions/barack-obama-why-we-must-rethink-solitary-confinement/2016/01/25/29a361f2-c384-11e5-8965-0607e0e265ce_story.html?tid=a_inl

35 Jennifer Gonnerman, "Kalief Browder, 1993-2015," *The New Yorker*, June 7, 2015, https://www.newyorker.com/news/news-desk/kalief-browder-1993-2015

36 Independent Commission, *A More Just New York City*, 25.

37 Benjamin Weiser, "New York City Settles Suit Over Abuses at Rikers Island," *New York Times*, June 22, 2015, https://www.nytimes.com/2015/06/23/nyregion/new-york-city-settles-suit-over-abuses-at-rikers-island.html

38 The City of New York Board of Correction, "Violence Indicators Report," March 17, 2015, http://www.nyc.gov/html/boc/downloads/pdf/reports/Violence_20150317.pdf

39 JB Nicholas, "A History of Hell: How Rikers Island Became a Modern Municipal Abomination," *The Village Voice*, April 11, 2017, https://www.villagevoice.com/2017/04/11/a-history-of-hell-how-rikers-island-became-a-modern-municipal-abomination/

40 Ibid.

41 Michael Schwirtz and Michael Winerip, "Close Rikers Island? It Will Take Years, Billions and Political Capital," *New York Times*, March 2, 2016, https://www.nytimes.com/2016/03/03/nyregion/closing-rikers-island-despite-rhetoric-intractable-obstacles-remain.html?_r=0

42 J. David Goodman, "De Blasio Says Idea of Closing Rikers Jail Complex Is Unrealistic," *New York Times*, February 16, 2016, https://www.nytimes.com/2016/02/17/nyregion/de-blasio-says-idea-of-closing-rikers-jail-complex-is-unrealistic.html

43 For written accounts of the campaign's development and strategy, see Janos Marton, "#CLOSErikers: The Campaign to Transform New York City's Criminal Justice System," *The Fordham Urban Law Journal* 45, no. 2 (2018): 499; Katal Center for Health, Equity, and Justice, "Reflections and Lessons from the First Two Phases of the #CLOSErikers Campaign: August 2015–August 2017," January 2018, https://d3n8a8pro7vhmx.cloudfront.net/katal/pages/1742/attachments/original/1546756046/Katal_CLOSErikers_Campaign_Report_PRINT_-_final.pdf?1546756046

44 Venida Browder, statement made at "National Exhibition Launch: Remembering Rikers Island," States of Incarceration, April 14, 2016, The New School, New York City, https://statesofincarceration.org/event/national-exhibition-launch-remembering-rikers-island

45 Deion Browder, "My Mom Died Trying to Preserve the Legacy of her Son. Keeping Kids Out of Solitary Will Preserve Hers," *USA Today*, April 23, 2019, https://www.usatoday.com/story/opinion/policing/spotlight/2019/04/23/kalief-browder-suicide-solitary-confinement-venida-browder-policing-the-usa/3540366002/

46 "About the Sticker," #SeeRikers, https://seerikersorg.wordpress.com/put-rikers-on-the-map/about/

47 JLUSA and Katal Center for Equity, Health, and Justice, "Addressing the Harm Caused by Rikers through Community Restorative Justice," memo submitted to the Independent Commission on New York City Criminal Justice and Incarceration Reform, February 2017, shared with author, held by Humanities Action Lab.

48 Independent Commission, *A More Just New York City*, 2.

49 Ibid, 19.

50 Gloria Pazmino and Colby Hamilton, "Rikers Plan Marks a Shift for New York City, and Its Mayor," *Politico*, April 3, 2017, https://www.politico.com/states/new-york/city-hall/story/2017/04/de-blasios-long-thaw-on-closing-rikers-110928

51 Will D. Novi, "Re-Naming Rikers," *Pacific Standard*, May 18, 2016, https://psmag.com/news/re-naming-rikers

52 Ibid.

53 Ibid.

54 Duane, "The Shame of Rikers."

55 Browder, statement made at "National Exhibition Launch: Remembering Rikers Island."

56 #CLOSErikers, Twitter post, September 23, 2017, 10:00 a.m., https://twitter.com/CLOSErikers/status/911591209063391237

57 Jennifer Bain and Sara Dorn, "Protestors Want Rikers Closed for Its Name Tie to Slave-Catcher," *New York Post*, August 26, 2017, https://nypost.com/2017/08/26/protesters-want-rikers-closed-for-its-name-tie-to-slave-catcher/

58 Marton, "#CLOSErikers: The Campaign to Transform New York City's Criminal Justice System," 546.

59 Rikers Public Memory Project, "One Voice Closing Rikers," https://youtu.be/YLZFXHDokgs

60 See http://www.massstorylab.com/

61 Daftary and campaign colleagues later co-founded their own organization, Freedom Agenda: https://fa.urbanjustice.org/

62 "This Is Rikers: From the People Who Live and Work There," The Marshall Project (in collaboration with *New York Magazine*), June 28, 2015, https://www.themarshallproject.org/2015/06/28/this-is-rikers

63 Regina Campbell, "COVID in Confinement: Archiving the Pandemic in Prisons and Jails," presentation at Abolitionist Storywork: Weaving Collective Narratives of Freedom," The Laundromat Project, September 24, 2021, https://youtu.be/A40gVKC6AY8

10

LOCAL STORIES, NATIONAL GENEALOGY

Memory Movements against Mass Incarceration

The Rikers chapter was one of 20 local initiatives working together on States of Incarceration, each mobilizing memory to confront the roots and legacies of mass incarceration from their own perspective. The growing popular discussion around the roots of mass incarceration was based in a broad national story centering on the legacies of American slavery for the criminalization and imprisonment of Black men.[1] That "big picture" story was critical for reframing public understanding of incarceration as a method of racial control as opposed to a response to an increase in crime. But it elided a host of alternative genealogies grounded in intersecting historical experiences, such as of Black women, immigrant families, or Native youth.

The founding working group of States of Incarceration saw an opportunity to build on the new popular interest in seeing mass incarceration historically, and to introduce new strands to the story. Instead of deciding ourselves what those new strands would be, the project posed a common question – how did the US become the world's leader in incarceration, and how does that history continue to impact different communities today? – and invited each local team to answer it from the perspective of their own local history and experience. Relying on a small centralized circle of "experts" to identify and pull together a comprehensive list of histories was the traditional strategy for developing exhibits and other historical interpretive projects. But as the working group experienced in its founding meeting, described in Chapter 8, even if this circle of experts were diverse and carefully curated, its vision risked being limited by the imaginations and experiences of its members. Further, as participating faculty and I had witnessed in the Guantánamo Public Memory Project, taking a community organizing approach to public memory – inviting people from multiple communities to step up as leaders of their own local histories – could

DOI: 10.4324/9781003185826-14

activate public history for social movements. Leaving it up to the local partners did risk that no one would choose to talk about certain historical experiences, so silences would be replicated and reinforced. But the project would continue to invite new communities to add their "answers" to this common question, enabling new historical strands to be woven in over time. The hope was that by working in coalition, grounded in and connecting local communities, we would be able to continually expand representation in the project's narrative and participation.

Individually and as a class, students were asked to reflect on their own relationship to the issues and people they were studying, and how that shaped the stories they shared in the exhibit. Each chapter was framed by a brief collective statement titled "Our Point of View," in which the student team described who they were and what they were trying to communicate. Some teams used the statement to establish that they had personal experience with mass incarceration, describing themselves as including "many people directly affected by racial profiling, detention, and incarceration."[2] Others made clear they had none, introducing themselves as "graduate students... who have never experienced detention or international migration."[3] Still others asserted the ways they felt nevertheless connected to the subject, writing, "As undergraduate students at an elite southern university, we feel both separated from and implicated in the prison industrial complex."[4] Some drew their perspective and sense of responsibility from where they were located: "As graduate students in Arizona, the site of controversial immigration legislation and home to 8% of all immigrant detention beds in the United States"; others from how they felt: "We are troubled that while conditions have changed, historic racial patterns persist."[5] Featuring these statements next to the exhibit narratives showed visitors that the official-looking panels were created by people without the expertise visitors normally associate with such an exhibit. It also invited visitors into the subjectivity of historical interpretation, ideally prompting them to reflect on how their own backgrounds shaped their understanding of mass incarceration.

Digging for Local Roots and Letting Intersectionality Grow Organically

Louisiana and Legacies of Slavery

Even if they had read books like *The New Jim Crow*, until students visited local sites of incarceration, broad national arguments about the direct lineage from slavery to mass incarceration could remain abstract. Confronting local places, and excavating the material layers of use and abuse visible there, could bring the history home.

Ryan Bourgeois, a student at the University of New Orleans, thought he knew Louisiana. "I promote the wonders of my state to anyone who cares to listen. From festivals and Mardi Gras to LSU tailgates and crawfish boils, I am extremely proud to have been raised in this unique state."[6] He also thought he knew something about Angola, a prison made infamous through films, songs, and news media. His tour of the Louisiana State Penitentiary, as Angola is officially called – a sprawling territory the size of Manhattan, 18,000 acres of farm and prisons – reintroduced him to his home and its history. "To say Angola is huge is a vast understatement," he wrote after the tour, organized for the team of students responsible for curating the Louisiana chapter of States of Incarceration. "The size of the facility is simply overwhelming."[7] Angola was the largest prison complex in the US. At the time Bourgeois toured it in 2015, Louisiana had the country's highest incarceration rate, which meant more of its people were incarcerated than in any other place on earth.[8] Beyond Angola's size, it was what Bourgeois saw there that surprised him:

> In some areas, fields of various agricultural goods are all that can be seen in any direction… In connecting the past and present at Angola, it is of my opinion that the best way to do so is by looking at the land. … The land tells the story, just look at it.[9]

Driving by the sugar cane, Bourgeois and his classmates were confronted by America's long history of using prisons as a means of racial control of labor. Louisiana's largest prison complex – also the largest prison complex in the US – Angola contained a continuous history of slavery, convict leasing, and mass incarceration, on the same literal ground. Before the Civil War, the 8,000-acre territory was the Angola Plantation, named for the area in Africa its owner believed the enslaved people working its land to be from. Soon after Emancipation, the plantation was converted to one of the nation's first private prisons, leased to a Confederate Major, Samuel James. Before new prison buildings were constructed, Angola's first incarcerated people were housed in the plantation's slave quarters. This slave past clung to its name: the prison has always been better known as "Angola," embedding the memory of the slave trade and slave labor in the experience of every subsequent generation held there.

A new system of criminal justice emerged during Reconstruction to support a new system of labor after the end of slavery. Incarcerated people were "leased" to private businesses, sometimes to work the same fields that had been tended by enslaved people, with neither wages nor any protection from abuse. Men incarcerated at Angola worked sugar cane fields and built levees. To ensure the supply of labor, a host of new criminal laws targeted African Americans for minor infractions such as vagrancy and petty larceny, filling penitentiaries with Black "convicts" ready for leasing.

With no oversight or accountability, private businesses, farmers, and large corporations held tens of thousands of African Americans in forced servitude until the eve of World War II – a system of labor exploitation that the journalist Douglas Blackmon has called "slavery by another name."[10] Even after convict leasing legally ended and the state took over correctional facilities like Angola, as legal scholar Andrea C. Armstrong put it, "profit – and not rehabilitation, retribution, or deterrence – became the guiding penological goal of Louisiana State Penitentiary."[11]

The same was still true a century later. The prison's policy required all men incarcerated there to work the fields for at least the first 90 days, after which they could theoretically choose another work assignment. But openings were too few, and the prison's demand for field labor was too high, so many found themselves back picking cotton.[12] With African Americans incarcerated in Louisiana at twice the rate of whites as of 2010, the men picking cotton on the students' visit were overwhelmingly Black.[13] UNO student Hannah Galloway reflected, "Cotton, to me, is the first thing that comes to mind when I think of slave labor. It was surreal to see acres and acres of cotton at Angola, knowing thousands of men worked the fields for free. So much has remained the same since slavery's ugly past."[14] Indeed, the warden in charge at the time Hannah and Ryan toured Angola, Burl Cain, hailed as a progressive reformer, himself described Angola as "like a big plantation in days gone by."[15] A few years after the students' tour, men incarcerated at Angola organized a strike. "Guys are getting fed up and a lot of guys are just not going [to work]," said an organizer and member of Decarcerate Louisiana who gave only his first name, Ron, to a reporter. "They don't want to work for free [because it's] modern-day slavery."[16]

Led by a visiting scholar named Benjamin Weber, the UNO team decided to help the rest of the country see this local place as both unique in its extremeness but also as a microcosm of a national history of racial control in the service of capital. Using long-buried archival photographs that Weber had only recently digitized of life and labor at Angola from the 1930s, students created a series of short videos titled "Windows on Angola," focusing on the relationship between mass incarceration and labor at Louisiana State Penitentiary.

Incarceration in Indian Country

Students in the Upper Midwest found different legacies in their land. The University of Minnesota (UMN) team's exploration was led by the words of Native activist Stormy Ogden: "For American Indians, incarceration is an extension of the history and violent mechanisms of colonization."[17]

Stormy Ogden is a recognized member of the Tule River Yokuts, Kashaya Pomo, and Lake County Pomo Nations. But when she was incarcerated at the California Rehabilitation Center in Norco, the identification card outside her room listed her ethnicity as "other." She began a campaign to be recognized. "Every morning as I left for my job assignment, I would cross out Other and write AI (American Indian). Then each afternoon when I returned for count there would be a new card with Other written on it."[18] The "other" card not only erased Ogden's identity as an incarcerated woman, but a whole branch of the history of incarceration. "Europeans locked up Native people in military forts, missions, reservations, boarding schools," she explained, "and today, increasingly, in state and federal prisons."[19]

Where many of the other teams were led by white faculty, Minnesota's was coordinated by Jean O'Brien, of White Earth Band of Ojibwe ancestry, with her longtime collaborator, American historian Kevin Murphy. O'Brien had just published *Why You Can't Teach United States History Without Indians,* and she was determined to center settler colonialism in the project's history of US incarceration.[20] As O'Brien's student, Lakota historian Amber Annis explained, "it is colonial terror and violence of American Indians and their land that created the systems of surveillance and confinement in the United States."[21]

Annis was a student contributor to the Guantánamo Public Memory Project from the University of Minnesota in 2012. By the time States of Incarceration was being developed in 2015, she was a recognized American Indian Studies scholar. Having witnessed the potential of participatory public memory during the Guantánamo project, she eagerly served as a historical advisor for States of Incarceration. Frustrated by the ways, as she later wrote, "American Indian history and Native voices tend to be either erased or relegated to the 'and others' portion of the graphs, tables, PowerPoints, or other informational tools that are meant to show the disparities within the criminal justice system," Annis, like O'Brien, hoped to make this project different.[22]

When University of Minnesota students analyzed incarceration rates in their state, they discovered that the group with the highest rate of incarceration was not African Americans or Latinos, but American Indians. Josh Olson, who grew up north of Minneapolis, was stunned. "Native Americans are incarcerated at a rate THIRTY-EIGHT percent higher than the national average. That is a staggering statistic and is incredibly disturbing to me," he wrote. "How could I have been previously unaware of this, and why is this problem not well known?"[23] Olson was hardly the only one in the dark. "I have lived in Minnesota my whole life and was unaware of this disparity," one of his classmates also admitted, recognizing the important lessons in starting local: "although on a national scale this issue mainly affects African Americans, that does not reflect each individual state."[24] The Minnesota team framed their project around a question drawing attention to mass incarceration's other origins: "How has settler colonialism shaped the carceral state?"

In the years preceding work on States of Incarceration, Native peoples were actively contesting the interpretation of Native incarceration in the public history of the state.[25] Their protests coalesced around the interpretation of Fort Snelling, where about 1,700 Dakota people were placed in concentration camps from 1862 to 1863 after being forcibly moved over 100 miles, as part of a project to exile Dakota people from Minnesota after the US-Dakota War. Hundreds died of disease during the brutal winter; 38 were hanged after their detention, in the largest mass execution in US history.[26] The violence left a lasting legacy of trauma in popular Dakota memory. The UMN team decided to ground their local history in this site, as it provided a critical window on the national history of imprisonment in Indian Country, and its denial.

The state-funded Minnesota Historical Society operated Historic Fort Snelling. A field trip there was a key feature of Twin City kids' school experience, one many of the UMN students remembered. Tours featured reenactments of military exercises from the 1820s, complete with costumed interpreters and giant firearms. At the time UMN students were in elementary school, tours did not include interpretation of the Dakota Wars. Around 2008, MHS installed four interpretive panels outside the Fort that discussed the internment, as well as six more in an area of the Fort that told the story of the Indian Agency there.

Although muted in its public interpretation, the violent history of the Fort lived strong in public memory among Dakota people. Jim Anderson, then historian and cultural chair of the Mendota Mdewakanton Dakota Community, described the Fort as "both the place of our genesis and our genocide," a phrase that was adopted and repeated by other Dakota activists protesting the site.[27] Dakota and Upper Sioux Community members Dallas Ross and Carrie Schommer, while sharing their oral histories with MHS, tried to explain how the Fort's history lived on. "The memories of the Dakota come generation [after] generation [after] generation so that we don't forget," said Ross.[28] Schommer articulated why so many Dakota did not want to visit Fort Snelling: "We know a lot of our people lost their lives or suffered there, and when you go there you feel all of the things that have happened there."[29] Specifically, the site figured in Dakota public memory of criminal justice and incarceration. As Dr. Clifford Canku, of the Sisseton Wahpeton community of Dakota, remembered of the "non-combatants" who were rounded up and held at Fort Snelling, "They were implicated for being Dakota. Just being Dakota means that you were guilty before any consideration of being innocent."[30]

Dakota activists staged protests over the stories the Fort told Minnesotans, and how the site was used by the state, including organizing a massive Wagon Train along the road to the state park entrance, and calling to Take Down the Fort.[31] In 2011, Historic Fort Snelling became a member of the International Coalition of Sites of Conscience, pledging to offer "more complexity, more sides to the story" and working with Dakota leaders on a "big shift" to foreground the Dakota history and create new memorial spaces.[32] In the fall of 2012, UMN students in the Guantánamo Public Memory Project displayed digital exhibits they created on the Dakota history of Fort Snelling and the suppression of its memory beside the exhibition on GTMO, as an example of the legal back hole's local relevance. But States of Incarceration offered the

Minnesota team an opportunity to situate Fort Snelling in a national history of incarceration. And starting from Fort Snelling, the Minnesota team could resituate mass incarceration as a legacy of Indigenous people's displacement and removal from their land.

As local teams each developed their chapters, they exchanged reflections on their learning with each other; the Minnesota team's work was particularly eye-opening for students in other regions. As one East Coast student wrote in response to a Minnesota student's post about their work, "While we studied the source of African American imprisonment, we never really looked at why Native Americans have equal if not greater rates of incarceration."[33] An Arizona State University participant reflected,

> Personally I had no idea that the proportion of Native Americans incarcerated was that high in Minnesota. But there is the key to this discussion. No one knows what is going on in other areas of the country.[34]

But as ASU students would discover in their own project, whereas the non-incarcerated public in New Orleans had direct access to Angola, and those in Minnesota could study statistics – in other words, people had only to take the time to look in order to learn – teams confronting immigration detention found a blank map and a brick wall.

Immigration Detention in the Borderlands

Professor Sarah Lopez of the University of Texas-Austin came to the project knowing that her vast state was riddled with immigrant detention centers, more than any other in the country; this, she thought, made it an ideal site from which to explore immigration detention as a national phenomenon. She had decided to bring together her architecture students with people who had been detained to explore the role of spaces and structures in their experience, asking: "How does architecture shape punishment?"

Lopez figured the first thing she needed was a comprehensive list of immigration detention centers in the state, and started looking for one. It didn't exist.[35] As a public agency, ICE had to provide a list of all its centers. Advocacy organizations like Detention Watch Network got that information to the public by translating ICE spreadsheets into a national map. But detention centers operated by private companies through contracts – some in separate facilities, others nestled in existing prisons and jails – were not required to report their existence. Lopez then tried to get plans/designs of detention centers, to understand their varying forms and shapes. She was denied. She filed a FOIA request. But, she discovered, FOIA only applied to public agencies. The huge number of detention centers under private contracts were under no obligation to disclose anything to anyone. Finally, she requested permission to tour a facility; but this too was denied. Lopez came to realize the depth of suppression of information and evidence about immigrant detention: that across the state, and across the country, there was an entire landscape of buildings, sites, and stories erased from the map.

If the physical facilities were obscured, so were the legislative mechanisms that create them, like the American Legislative Exchange Council (ALEC), a group of corporations, including those that profit from detention, that quietly works with policymakers to draft legislation around immigration detention.[36] Even Ava DuVernay admitted that while developing her documentary *13th*, which rooted mass incarceration in a genealogy of anti-Black racism, "I was so shaken up about discovering ALEC that I delved into that research for a good six months so that I could learn it fully enough to share it in the documentary.[37] One of Lopez's students lamented, "I hadn't been aware of what ICE and border patrol did when confronted with families and minors – I honestly just didn't think about it!"[38]

Mass incarceration and immigrant detention are intertwined in the present, but rooted in different places and policies. Where UNO students traced Black mass incarceration to plantations and prison farms, the four teams whose local experiences were dominated by immigration – the Texans were joined by teams from New Jersey, Florida, and Arizona – started their exhibit chapters from Ellis Island, in New York harbor and Angel Island, in San Francisco Bay. Popularly celebrated as gateways to the American Dream, these processing centers implemented race-based immigration laws like the Chinese Exclusion Act and the Immigration Act of 1924, which restricted immigration from Southern and Eastern Europe, imprisoning immigrants from excluded categories. By the post-World War II era, reformers were decrying detention at New York's "island prison," and the Immigration and Naturalization Service announced it was moving away from the policy of immigrant detention.[39] Angel Island stopped processing immigrants in 1940; Ellis Island in 1954. But in the 1980s, immigration policy and politics witnessed a "militarization" and criminalization, spurred by the growing War on Drugs.[40] This set the stage for immigration to be managed through detention even more widely than in the past, integrating it into the growing carceral state.

Rates of immigration detention skyrocketed in tandem with criminal incarceration. Between 1995 and 2011, the average daily population of noncitizens detained by ICE increased nearly fivefold, from 7,475 to 33,330. (In 1995, the annual total number of ICE detainees was 85,730. In 2011, it was 429,247.)[41] Immigrants were detained in the same facilities as "criminal" detainees, in separate sections of existing jails and prisons, as well as in new, purpose-built immigration detention centers. The detention building boom was fueled in part by a "bed quota" imposed by Congress in 2009, mandating that ICE fill 34,000 beds every day with immigrant detainees, incentivizing the agency to seek out immigrants to lock up.[42] Private prisons contracted by ICE were (and continue to be) similarly paid by the bed.[43] But while the citizen and immigrant prison booms intertwined, the systems were significantly different. The incarceration of citizens is subject to all kinds of scrutiny, transparency, and accountability through the criminal justice system; but the detention of immigrants, who have no rights of citizens and are categorized as being under "administrative" detention, is closed to the public view. In other words, where mass incarceration thrives on a largely self-imposed public denial, immigration detention is almost impossible to see.[44]

In Texas, professor Sarah Lopez turned to Bob Libal, director of Grassroots Leadership, an advocacy organization against immigration detention and mass incarceration. Libal connected her to people at Casa Marianella, a shelter housing people who had recently been detained. Lopez had originally imagined working with Casa Marianella residents to create an experiential portrait of individual sites of incarceration to complement the state-wide data her students would collect. But she now realized she'd also have to rely on residents for basic information about the shape and location of detention centers.

Casa Marianella residents diagrammed the extraordinary journeys they had taken, usually through at least seven different countries, using all manner of transportation, from busses to rowboats; and then drew the tiny spaces in which they were detained at the end. One resident named Miguel mapped how movement, as well as confinement, was used as an instrument of control, depicting how he was constantly moved from pod to pod within the detention center, to disrupt any possibility of organization or solidarity among detained people.

In interviews accompanying their drawings, Casa Marianella residents communicated that immigrant detention was in fact incarceration, but lacked any of the due processes of the criminal justice system. As Elvis, a Cameroonian asylum seeker, explained, "It [the detention center] is a jail. I am not a criminal, I did not commit a crime, and I was treated like that."[45] Others emphasized the conditions that thrived in environments unfettered by transparency and accountability. Ahmed described being thrown into solitary confinement without understanding why, and other arbitrary abuse by authorities. "The people working the detention, the people, they abusing the people like an animal. You understand? They cut our power, you cannot ask for something…If you ask it, they can be mad."[46]

Meanwhile, students worked to collect as much data as they could from other sources to build a basic map of detention centers in Texas over space and time, building on the mapping work of advocacy groups like Grassroots Leadership and the Detention Watch Network. Student Josephine Hill described "collecting Immigration and Custom Enforcement (ICE) contract documents, cold-calling detention centers, combing through local newspaper archives and ICE maintenance audits, and zooming in as close as possible on Google street view."[47] Students also sought to map the extent of privatization of immigrant detention in the state, by marking which centers were run by ICE and which by contractors. But they found that facilities were constantly changing hands, making it impossible to pinpoint. If the forensic evidence was blurred, the larger lesson was clear: As Hill noted, "We quickly learned that the landscape of detention is elusive and ever evolving."[48]

Students also visited women at the T. Don Hutto Detention Center in Taylor, Texas through a program organized by Grassroots Leadership. In October 2015, one month into the team's work, at least 27 women at Hutto began a hunger strike protesting their conditions. At the time of the strike, the Center was operated by the Corrections Corporation of America (CCA), one of the two largest private prison contractors. Perhaps, as a result, ICE could deny the existence of the strike and the conditions that led to it, stating, "ICE takes the health, safety, and welfare of those in our care very seriously and we continue to monitor the situation. Currently, no one at the T. Don Hutto Detention Center was identified as being on a hunger strike or refusing to eat."[49]

The women combatted ICE's denial by writing letters protesting conditions and the criminalization of their immigration processing. "I don't know why [I am being detained] because I have never committed a crime in this country, I haven't killed, robbed, I don't deserve this suffering," wrote one.[50] After visiting women in Hutto, the UT students amplified the protestors' message by featuring their letters in the physical exhibit and on the project website, together with a visualization of how protest leaders were dispersed to three other detention centers to break up the hunger strike.

By the end of the semester, the team could report: "Texas has 26 detention centers, 5 prisons, and 2 county jails used to detain migrants in connection with immigration proceedings or immigration related crimes."[51] This simple statement, the introductory sentence to the team's chapter of the exhibit, was the result of an extraordinary battle to make the basic contours of immigration detention publicly visible. After the exhibit opened, when visitors were asked, "What is one new thing you learned from States of Incarceration?" respondents most frequently cited immigration detention. "I only knew about the mass incarceration of Black Americans," explained one. Many reported they didn't realize that immigrants were imprisoned as their cases were decided, or that immigrants were often literally detained within existing prisons and jails.[52]

Criminalization of Youth in California

Posing a common question and inviting localities to answer it, each from their own perspective, surfaced the interconnected experiences of African Americans, Native Americans, and immigrants. The translocal coalition also connected stories from other vectors of identity and experience. When professors Cathy Gudis and Molly McGarry at the University of California at Riverside asked their students how they would identify the roots of mass incarceration in their own state, students began with their own experiences in school. As students Mayela Caro and Marissa Friedman later wrote, "Many students recounted 'toeing the line' during random searches with dogs sniffing them for drugs, forced to stand at attention for hours despite no evidence being found."[53]

After sharing these stories, the student team decided to explore how youth – as a group of people and an identity – had been criminalized over time, and how this history shaped the larger history of the carceral state. Titling their chapter "In Detention: The War on Youth," they explored schools as carceral institutions. As Caro and Friedman later explained,

> the exhibition sought to illustrate that the ongoing criminalization of marginalized youth in California has deep historical roots, which extends the logic and function of incarceration far beyond the confines of the prison cell, to the sidewalks, neighborhoods, and classrooms of youth of color.[54]

Students worked with Manuel Criollo, Director of Organizing for The Labor/ Community Strategy Center in Los Angeles, who was himself grappling with the fact that the Los Angeles School Police Department (LASPD) had become the largest dedicated police department in the country. "We didn't literally see a school to jail, school to prison track," he told Caro and her professor Cathy Gudis,

> ... the punishment culture that existed in the schools, seemed to us that it was more sort of a conditioning to prep you for that kind of reality, rather than that you were literally ... going to the system.[55]

Criollo sought to re-center race in public discussion of the carceral state, arguing that while recent analysis of the "prison industrial complex," exposed its economic foundation, "There's a more inherent racist basis to the system [and] we felt like we wanted to contribute to that conversation.[56]

Looking around their locality for the roots of their own experience, students could find some of the country's earliest experiments in racialized institutional control of youth, as well as their more recent legacies. The students' town, Riverside, was home to the Sherman Indian Boarding School, founded in 1902, one of a tiny handful of such schools then preserved as a museum. Indian Boarding Schools opened across the country around the turn of the century to remove Native children from their families and communities and assimilate and discipline them, causing deep community trauma with lasting legacies for Native language and culture. Nearby was the Whittier State School, one of the first correctional facilities constructed in California, an institution for boys that detained disproportionate numbers of Mexican Americans and African Americans, and used solitary confinement. Students discovered that in 2011–2012, when many of them were in school, Black and Latino students received 93% of all LASPD tickets and arrests.[57]

Students also looked to the urban spaces surrounding schools, and how they were similarly controlled and criminalized. They discovered that California was the first state to introduce and elaborate civil gang injunctions in the 1980s, measures that prohibit gang members from certain spaces and places in the city. As Caro and Friedman learned, these injunctions "prompt heavy policing of youth clothing, behavior, and appearance in ordinary public spaces... and communities inhabited primarily by people of color."[58] Studying the history of gang injunctions helped students understand the changes they saw in the neighborhoods around them, and the ways criminal justice policy shaped their city. Student Sonia Mehrmand later presented what she learned about one neighborhood:

> Echo Park is a predominantly Latino community in Los Angeles whose demographics are shifting as gentrification displaces long-time residents. Civil gang injunctions... have been employed here and elsewhere in Southern California as tools to push long-time residents out of the community, under the pretense of maintaining "safety."[59]

Finally, students came back to where they started, in their own education system. The team framed their local chapter of the exhibit with an image of heavily fortified metal cell-like structures, lined with surveillance equipment, surrounded by barbed wire. The image was not of a prison, but of Silverado High School, a school in Victorville, another city in the students' local area, known as the "Inland Empire." The image of the prison-like school, together with the testimony from detained Native American and Latino students from generations past, powerfully communicated the "school-to-prison pipeline" for individual youth and across generations. Understanding the long history of racialized control of youth was critical for helping students make sense of their own past experiences, and of the events that were unfolding around them. "To begin to untangle the crises of the present," Caro and Feidman wrote, "we must make public these histories of incarceration, surveillance, and criminalization."[60]

Women's Incarceration in Massachusetts

At the time UMass Amherst students began exploring incarceration in their state, women were the fastest-growing segment of the prison population, their rate of imprisonment growing twice as fast as men's since 1980.[61] Massachusetts provided a unique window onto gender in the carceral state. While it ranked dead last in the nation in rates of women's incarceration, for over a century, it had been on the cutting edge of women's prison reform[62]. Students learned that their state was home to one of the oldest continuously used women's prisons in the country, as well as one of the nation's newest: the Framingham Reformatory Prison for Women was founded in 1877 as an early attempt to define how women's incarceration should be distinct from men's; the Western Massachusetts Regional Women's Correctional Center in Chicopee was built in 2007 and had just expanded in 2014.

Students traced changing ideas around gender and corrections, connecting their historical research with what they learned from project partners like the Statewide Harm Reduction Coalition (SHaRC). After Massachusetts allocated $27 million for a "gender-responsive" women's jail, SHaRC spent years organizing against construction and for investment in alternatives to incarceration. SHaRC and other groups' definition of being "gender responsive" was instead to reframe mass incarceration to demonstrate how women's incarceration – specifically, incarceration of pregnant women and mothers – had different ripple effects than incarceration of men and fathers. Incarcerating mothers at such high rates placed millions of children into foster care, destroying families and creating a whole generation marked by trauma, shaping future communities. Activists also foregrounded one key issue specific to women's prisons, around which they were mobilizing at that moment: shackling of incarcerated pregnant women during childbirth. While they had successfully pushed the governor to sign an anti-shackling bill in 2014, enforcement was weak, and the practice continued. Guided by this mandate, students framed their chapter with the question: "What Are Women's Prisons For?" exploring both historic and contemporary attempts at "gender responsive" reform, leading with a SHaRC member's statement that: "A cage is a cage is a cage. We want strategies that let people out of cages, not ones that are for building nicer or better cages."[63] Students Amy Halliday, Chel Rose, and Julie Petersen later described the project as "a deliberate provocation, intended to alert viewers to the many interwoven agendas at play in the incarceration of women."[64]

Incarcerating Mental Illness in Indiana

Professor Modupe Labode's museum studies program at Indiana University-Purdue University Indianapolis (IUPUI) had been sending students to the Indiana Medical History Museum in Indianapolis for years. The museum is housed in the historic pathology building that served the state's oldest and largest psychiatric facility: Central State Hospital. Students learned about conservation techniques and the history of science through the original anatomical museum, where slices of patients' brains were preserved in jars, and through a historic dissecting room and other laboratories. But the Museum was also one of the few historic sites in the country dedicated to interpreting, among other things, "mental health care past and present." This year, Labode sent her students to explore a different story contained in the old building: the connections between mental health and mass incarceration.

Starting in the 1960s, large, overcrowded psychiatric hospitals around the country began closing their doors, with the hope that the discharged patients would find mental health care within their communities. The number of residents at Central State Hospital steadily decreased, but the hospital did not close until 1994. While the closings were in part in response to advocacy for more humane and comprehensive treatment for people with mental illness, with inadequate investment in alternatives, people were released without a support system. A person with mental illness on the street often fell under the purview of law enforcement, which placed people with treatment needs in institutions ill-equipped to care for them: jails and prisons. Whether and where there's a causal relationship between mass incarceration and the close of mental hospitals is a subject of debate, but the end results were stark and staggering.[65] From 1955 to 2012, the number of people in mental institutions plummeted by nearly 94%, while incarceration rates skyrocketed.[66] The number of people with mental illness in correctional institutions in 2012 was ten times higher than the number in psychiatric hospitals;[67] in 2015, 40% of those incarcerated in prisons suffered from mental illness.[68] A few years before students began exploring what happened to the people released from Central State Hospital, the ACLU sued the state of Indiana for overusing solitary confinement for incarcerated people with mental illness; a federal judge declared such people received "cruel and unusual punishment," while another charged the state with being "deliberately indifferent."[69] As the students were delving into the long history of mental illness and incarceration in their state, advocates were working on a settlement, to include more mental health care.[70] Professor Labode's team asked: "Why are prisons the nation's mental hospitals?"

"So many people have either experienced mental illness or are close to someone with a mental illness," noted student Emma Marston, "and our contribution to this exhibit will be a great opportunity to spark conversations about these issues."[71] Marston remembered growing up near the Elgin Mental Health Center in Elgin, Illinois, opened in 1872 as the Northern Illinois Hospital and Asylum for the Insane, an imposing institution that generated a constant stream of anxieties and myths about ghosts and dangerous madmen. Labode arranged for members of the Indianapolis branch of the National Alliance for Mental Illness to collaborate with her students on how to educate exhibit visitors about mental illness and incarceration, focusing on destigmatizing and decriminalizing them, a mission to which students had become passionately committed. Student Vickie Stone reported that during one early class discussion,

> someone shouted one phrase that reverberated the sentiments of the entire team: "THIS IS IMPORTANT! THIS IS A RESPONSIBILITY!!"... We have been invested in producing a meaningful narrative about the serious and complicated intersectionality of mass incarceration and mental health.[72]

Dialogue and Dissonance: How Local Narratives Connected and Collided

In addition to opening up the exhibit to diverse roots of mass incarceration, the decentralized approach allowed for different takes on the subject, shaped by each team's politics, the approaches of their faculty, the pedagogical and political histories of their institutions, and the students' own experience. In their "Our Point of View" statement, students from Winston Salem State University, a historically Black university with a diverse population of Black students, framed mass incarceration in deeply structural terms. "Most of us are all too familiar with the United States' history of oppression and state violence targeting Black people," they wrote.

> For this project, we examined the long history of Black resistance to regimes of incarceration in North Carolina, beginning with enslavement and Maroon Societies and culminating with the state's attempt to repress the Black Lives Matter movement.[73]

They situated their analysis in an intellectual tradition and internationalist vision that was absent from the rest of the exhibition, citing "Black feminist research methodology to honor the Black Radical Tradition and the interdependence of liberation movements everywhere."[74]

By contrast, students at another historically Black university, Johnson C. Smith University (JCSU), focused on personal responsibility over institutional structures. Inspired by their collaboration with The Village, an independent living facility right by the JCSU campus for young men over 18 who recently aged out of foster care, students focused on the pipeline between foster care and prison. Concerned by statistics they cited that 20% of the national foster care population is Black, and that one in four of those who age out of foster care become involved with the criminal justice system within two years, students echoed the Village's assessment that "Unhealed trauma creates huge barriers for foster care youth because many have never learned to exercise good judgment, or to develop a healthy sense of self-worth. At the age of 18 they simply exit the system, most find it very difficult to live on their own, and many turn to criminal behaviors like selling drugs or prostitution to pay for living expenses."[75] As the SOI university-community collaborative partnership structure encouraged them to do, students relied on the expertise of their partner for the solution: "According to The Village director, April," students stated in their panel, "these young men need to be taught important social skills like dating behavior and how to show respect for yourself and the people around you... life-skills without the streets, homelessness, drugs, and incarceration so that there is no excuse not to achieve their goals."[76]

In the main exhibit, local teams "spoke" sequentially, through separate panels arranged side by side in a sort of patchwork quilt. But one element – "How Close Are You to Incarceration?" a participatory installation that traveled to each city – gave space for a messier, collective conversation. "How Close Are You to Incarceration?" consisted of five panels, each describing a different relationship to incarceration, located on a spectrum from "I've Been Arrested or Incarcerated/I've Worked with Law Enforcement or Corrections" to "I've Broken the Law and Not Been Caught." Visitors were invited to write their experience on a paper tag and stick it up on the panel that best described their relationship to incarceration, using a sticker printed with the initials of their state. Whereas less than a third of student curators identified themselves as directly impacted by incarceration, a majority of audience contributors to the installation did. From a distance, visitors in each locality saw the section headed "I've Been Arrested or Incarcerated" blanketed with fluttering white tags, each representing an individual experience, together representing a collective phenomenon. At the end of each installation, the tags were removed to make way for new stories from the next state, but the stickers bearing the name of the state remained, leaving a legacy of dots connecting experiences across the country. This element not only invited visitors to "place themselves" in the story and opened space for visitors to anonymously share and reflect on their own personal histories with incarceration, but it helped demonstrate mass incarceration as a collective experience, however unequally shared.

Local Actions and Impact

Criminal justice policy in the US is a local affair: it's shaped most significantly at the state level. One exhibit, featuring 20 local histories, moved from state to state across the country; but in each new location, it refracted an entirely new context. Each community organized new voices, new spaces to hear them, at new political moments – all shaping different urgent policy questions at stake.

The exhibit traveled in both space and time, across a rapidly changing political landscape. Often, local hosts had issues thrust upon them, as unexpected events shaped the conversation and demanded a response. In Greensboro, North Carolina, Piper Anderson worked with students at UNCG to organize a Mass Story Lab at the International Civil Rights Museum, complementing other policy discussions about the long-term impacts of incarceration on workers and families. But on the exhibit's opening day, President Trump was elected; shortly after, the North Carolina Ku Klux Klan announced plans for a rally to celebrate his victory. The story circles became healing circles, with discussions of how the historical structures of racial violence and control explored in the exhibit could help make sense of what was happening; the policy discussions on employment law were redirected to preventing immediate violence.

A few months later, in Miami, local hosts planned a story exchange on intersecting experiences of mass incarceration and immigration detention. That morning, in response to one of Trump's cryptic tweets, a rumor spread that the Immigration and Customs Enforcement agency had set up road blocks around the city. Undocumented immigrants would be pulled from their cars, incarcerated, and then deported. The undocumented storytellers, who had trained to share their experiences with a large audience at the University of Miami, stayed home. Their stories, and the knowledge the stories contained, went untold. In Newark, New Jersey, nearly a year later, a well-known local undocumented advocate named Ravi Ragbir, whose portrait and story appeared in Newark's companion exhibit, opened the exhibit with his personal history, and his assessment of the challenges ahead. About a month after the exhibit closed in Newark, he was taken into detention. Though his detention lasted only a few weeks, ICE continued to pursue Ragbir's deportation years later.[77]

Local hosts were invited to identify local criminal justice questions – large or small – that were up for debate in their area during the time the exhibit was on view there. The exhibit then included a feature called "Shape the Debate," which posed an open question about the policy and invited people to respond, with votes and comments, via their phones or on the website. In New York, the exhibit was launching just as the Lippman Commission was beginning its work to map out how to close Rikers; it thus raised one of the Commission's central questions, asking: "Remembering lessons from Rikers Island, what should New York City's future detention facilities be like?"[78] In California, the exhibit arrived during debate on a budget resolution around funding to improve – but also expand – the state's jails; the question asked: "California has approved $2 billion for jail construction. How could the funds be used to keep people out of jails instead?"[79] In Rhode Island, a commission had just been established to review the merits of solitary confinement in the state; local hosts asked, "A new Rhode Island state commission will study solitary confinement. Do you think prisons should use solitary confinement?" [80] Visitors could then see the votes and comments aggregate and change in real time, to learn from what others said.

The policy questions featured in "Shape the Debate" were not theoretical; they were happening in real time and real life. They described immediate reforms to the existing system. Participating in shaping the outcomes of those policies would not address the fundamental structures of mass incarceration, the foundations of the carceral state, nor significantly expand anyone's moral imagination. But the questions did help further expose the minutiae of the carceral state's operations, by identifying the specific, somewhat wonky levers of change in the criminal justice system. In voting in "Shape the Debate" questions, participants learned about why a particular budget line, or little-known appointed position in the legal system, or seemingly neutral employment mechanism, had significant sway over the fates of incarcerated people. They also learned how the policy would be decided and where real public input was invited. "Shape the Debate" provided an immediate avenue for engagement in specific decisions about to be made. In Ohio, Antioch College students created their portion of the exhibit with women serving life sentences at the Dayton Correctional Institution. In addition to their exhibit chapter, the team developed a policy platform for reforming state sentencing policies. Students were then trained in lobbying by local organizers, and presented the platform to state representatives reexamining sentencing guidelines.

The exhibit reached different audiences and promoted different public conversations on criminal justice policy depending on what kind of space it was displayed in. The most accessible space for most faculty was their campus gallery, which, though open to the public, attracted primarily campus audiences. These spaces could reach a ready audience ripe for conversation on incarceration, sparing local hosts significant time drumming up visitors, especially in contexts where few people ever ventured off campus. Yet campus galleries and their audiences did not, in the end, represent the majority of spaces where the exhibit traveled. In several cities, local teams installed the exhibit in major public libraries, where a wide cross-section of residents encountered the exhibit by chance, including returning citizens coming to public libraries for reentry services. The Riverside, California team opened the exhibit with a day-long summit on "Youth Justice in the Inland Empire," held at a local church that brought together dozens of different organizations to envision common strategies for confronting the criminalization of youth. In western Massachusetts, UMass's local collaboration of universities, public spaces, and advocacy organizations hosted over 50 public events over the course of a year at different spaces in the area, from academic lectures to Know Your Rights workshops to high school teacher training.

Some partners chose to stage the exhibition in mainstream cultural institutions whose primary audiences were far removed from the experience of mass incarceration, such as Ogden Museum of Southern Art in New Orleans. Placing the story in this space asserted to these audiences that the history and human expression of incarceration were of central cultural importance. In Newark, local hosts placed their exhibit in a skybridge connecting the train station with corporate office buildings, exposing it to tens of thousands of daily commuters. Newest Americans, a Rutgers University-Newark project working with documentary photographer Ed Kashi, placed Kashi's life-sized photos of people recently released from detention directly in commuters' path, accompanied by audio testimony accessible through their cell phones, making the formerly detained people's humanity and stories hard to avoid. The choice of exhibition space reflected different ideas of who were the most important people to reach – and who were key agents of change – in the specific context of each locality, in the specific moment of the exhibit's arrival.

The project made the most direct impact on university policies and practices. With their students, faculty, and administration now engaged in the issue of mass incarceration through the project, some university teams sought to open new examinations of their institutions' relationship with correctional institutions and how they could serve students inside. Brown University faculty consciously used the campus buzz around the project to revive a proposal for a prison education program. In Chicago, the Jane Addams Hull-House, the museum hosting the exhibit, organized a conference among area colleges on how and why to build programs in correctional institutions. The conference began with a visit to the exhibit. The collaboration between Johnson C. Smith University and the Village forged a new institutional partnership that made the foster care facility a quasi-campus entity and allowed Village residents to participate in campus life and learning.

UMass Amherst partners used the project to advocate for individual participants and call attention to the broader issue of discrimination in public higher education based on justice system involvement. One such participant was Israel Rivera, known to all as Izzy. Rivera attended community college and was a well-regarded community leader in the nearby city of Holyoke, which had one of the highest per capita incarceration rates in the state. Because of his leadership, Rivera, who had been incarcerated earlier in his life, was sought out by the staff of one of the organizations that planned to host the exhibit – Wisteriahurst, a city-run historic house museum and cultural center – to help shape the local exhibits and public programming. During the process, he applied to UMass – which required him to declare his criminal record – and was denied admission. When the Executive Director of Wisteriahurst learned of this, she reached out to the UMass SOI team in the history department to ask them to advocate for Izzy's case. After working with a historian-attorney – whom he met in the course of the UMass lectures – on his appeal, Rivera won admission. He later became program manager for Area Studies at UMass and ran for Holyoke City Council. "UMass Unboxed," a new campaign to remove the requirement for applicants to disclose criminal records, did not succeed in changing university policy. But Rivera's case and the year of events around SOI at UMass engaged more students and faculty in the movement, including spawning the UMass Prison Abolition Collective.

In Louisiana, the States of Incarceration exhibit came to New Orleans as the state legislature was debating whether to "ban the box." Louisiana, like many states across the country, required state college applicants to check the "Yes" or "No" box after the question, "have you ever been convicted of a felony?" While applicants who checked the box were not a priori denied admission, they suffered a distinct disadvantage. In Louisiana, where about 10% of the state's 33,000 incarcerated adults are 18–24 years old, and where 67% of all incarcerated people are Black, this created a huge barrier to entry for a vast proportion of African Americans from higher education.[81]

Advocates calculated that the legislature needed to hear from at least two key constituents on this issue: university presidents, and students. To get support for participating in States of Incarceration, UNO professor Molly Mitchell and her colleagues had already had to talk with UNO's president about Louisiana's unique place in mass incarceration's history, and the unique potential of UNO to shape public dialogue on its future. Investing in the exhibit, which was effectively a public statement on these points, helped pave the way for the president's public support for banning the box. Students and exhibit visitors had demonstrated public support for banning the box through responses to the team's Shape the Debate question: "Should your university or company have the right to ask about someone's prior convictions in their admission or job application?"[82] UNO visiting scholar Benjamin Weber shared the polling results with Syrita Steib-Martin and Annie Freitas of Operation Restoration, two of the leaders of the ban the box campaign, who brought them to the House Committee reviewing the bill, to demonstrate the support for it on campus. On June 16, 2017, Louisiana became the first state in the country to ban the box in public university applications.[83]

In several states, the project involved other public institutions: public libraries and public schools. For staff and leadership of these institutions, participating in the project inspired them to reflect on their institutions' roles in the carceral state. The director of the Forbes Library in Northampton, MA, which also hosted the exhibit and program, told Marla Miller, the UMass faculty lead, that she became "more conscious of 'the complexity and inherent flaws in the mass incarceration system in our country,' insights that now serve as 'a constant touch stone as I work through any interaction with the public that involves or has the potential to involve the police.'"[84] The library changed its employment policy to no longer automatically disqualify applicants based on their criminal records, and worked to make library resources more accessible to returning citizens by lifting ID and other requirements.

Some local hosts took the initiative to inspire their communities to push the boundaries of their moral imagination. University of New Orleans students conducted workshops with local middle and high school students around Angola's history and legacies of slavery for incarceration in Louisiana. Students were then invited to imagine a world without prisons, through visual art and poetry. Students' visions were displayed in the Odgen Museum of Southern Art, in tandem with the national traveling exhibit, as a companion exhibit titled "Picturing a World Without Prisons." Overall, however, abolitionist visions were the exception. The real – though incremental – policy victories in criminal justice reform taking place around this time, and the optimism of many advocates that more were possible, framed a focus on reform for most project partners.

States of Incarceration was intentionally designed to inspire participants – both students and exhibit visitors – to take action on criminal justice issues.

It did not make specific policy prescriptions, and, perhaps more significantly, did not explicitly define whether "action" meant policy reform, or prison abolition. Reform vs. abolition was not a debate the working group or any of the partners had in any depth. But influenced by the politics of most local partners and the project's corps of consulting experts – as well as the dominant discourse of criminal justice movements in the moment – the exhibition's central framing questions and tools for visitor interaction implicitly steered partners toward advocacy for local, incremental criminal justice policy change, as opposed to a total dismantling of the carceral state.

Notes

1 A wealth of scholarship on the US criminal justice system emerged in tandem with the public launch of States of Incarceration in 2016 and in the years that followed. Significant recent works that explore the intersectional histories of racialized criminalization and mass incarceration include: Elizabeth Hinton, *From the War on Poverty to the War on Crime: The Making of Mass Incarceration in America* (Cambridge: Harvard University Press, 2016); Heather Ann Thompson, *Blood in the Water: The Attica Prison Uprising of 1971 and Its Legacy* (New York: Pantheon Books, 2016); Kelly Lytle Hernández, *City of Inmates: Conquest, Rebellion, and the Rise of Human Caging in Los Angeles, 1771-1965* (Chapel Hill: The University of North Carolina Press, 2017); James Forman, Jr., *Locking Up Our Own: Crime and Punishment in Black America* (New York: Farrar, Straus and Giroux, 2017); Marc Mauer and Ashley Nellis, *The Meaning of Life: The Case for Abolishing Life Sentences* (New York: The New Press, 2018); Jackie Wang, *Carceral Capitalism* (South Pasadena: Semiotext(e), 2018); Shane Bauer, *American Prison: A Reporter's Undercover Journey Into the Business of Punishment* (New York: Penguin Press, 2018); Anne E. Parsons, *From Asylum to Prison: Deinstitutionalization and the Rise of Mass Incarceration after 1945* (Chapel Hill: The University of North Carolina Press, 2018); Emily Bazelon, *Charged: The New Movement to Transform American Prosecution and End Mass Incarceration* (New York: Random House, 2019); and Nicole R. Fleetwood, *Marking Time: Art in the Age of Mass Incarceration* (Cambridge: Harvard University Press, 2020).

2 University of California Riverside students Pamona Alexander, Mayela Caro, Marissa Friedman, Alice Lapoint, Max Loder, Alan Malfavon, Sonia Mehrmand, Grace Pankau, Christina Pappous, Clare Pope, and Meranda Roberts, and faculty lead Cathy Gudis, States of Incarceration, "California: In Detention: How have youth been criminalized?" https://statesofincarceration.org/states/california-detention

3 University of Texas at Austin students Sara Zavaleta, Jessica Carey-Webb, Andrew Leith, Joyce Hanlon, Katie Slusher, Sadie Dubicki, Maureen Anway, Josephine Hill, Claudia Rodriguez, Natalia Lopez, Anju Palta, and faculty lead Sarah Lopez, "Texas: Spatial Stories of Migration and Detention," States of Incarceration, https://statesofincarceration.org/states/texas-spatial-stories-migration-and-detention

4 Duke University students Amani Carson-Rose, Safiya Driskell, Elsa Gunnarsdottir, Georgia Hoagland, Cameron Hurley, Taylor Johnson, Shaun Jones, Meaghan Kachadoorian, Lauren Kelly, Robin Kirk, Leo Lou, Helen McGinnis, Carly Meyerson, Brenda Onyango, Morghan Phillips, Gayle Powell, Nivi Ram, Elsa Lilja, and faculty lead Jessica Namakkal, "North Carolina: Death and Life at Central Prison," States of Incarceration, https://statesofincarceration.org/states/north-carolina-death-and-life-central-prison

5 Arizona State University students Andrea Alonso, Kristina Clark, Ethan Clay, Judith Perera, Jacquelyn George, Scott Olsen, Heather Roehl, Kristen Rund,

Holly Solis, Samantha Vandermeade, Christen White, and faculty leads Mark Tebeau, Leah Sarat, and Kristine Navarro-McElhaney, "The Cost of Immigrant Detention," https://statesofincarceration.org/states/arizona-cost-immigrant-detention; University of North Carolina Greensboro students Alexis Lucas, Jessica O'Connor, Jessica Richmond, Joshua Dacey, Karen Ploch, Lance Wheeler, Leslie Leonard, Marick Lewis, Sonya Laney, Tamara Vaughan, and faculty leads Christopher Graham and Anne Parsons, "Voices from the Chain Gang," https://statesofincarceration. org/states/north-carolina-voices-chain-gang

6 Ryan Bourgeois, "Surveillance and the Expanse of Angola State Penitentiary," States of Incarceration, Fall 2015, student reflection held by Humanities Action Lab.

7 Ibid.

8 Danielle Kaeble and Lauren Glaze, "Correctional Populations in the United States, 2015," Bureau of Justice Statistics, U.S. Department of Justice, December 2016, https://bjs.ojp.gov/content/pub/pdf/cpus15.pdf

9 Bourgeois, "Surveillance and the Expanse of Angola State Penitentiary."

10 Douglas A. Blackmon, *Slavery by Another Name: The Re-Enslavement of Black Americans from the Civil War to World War II* (New York: Anchor Books, 2009). See also Talitha L. LeFlouria, *Chained in Silence: Black Women and Convict Labor in the New South* (Chapel Hill: The University of North Carolina Press, 2015) and Sarah Haley, *No Mercy Here: Gender, Punishment, and the Making of Jim Crow Modernity* (Chapel Hill: The University of North Carolina Press, 2016).

11 Andrea C. Armstrong, "Slavery Revisited in Penal Plantation Labor," *Seattle University Law Review* 835 (April 5, 2012): 871.

12 Ibid.

13 "Louisiana Profile," Prison Policy Initiative, https://www.prisonpolicy.org/ profiles/LA.html

14 Hannah Galloway, "Prisoner Life in Angola, Louisiana State Penitentiary," States of Incarceration, Fall 2015, student reflection held by Humanities Action Lab.

15 Armstrong, "Slavery Revisited."

16 Bryce Covert, "Louisiana Prisoners Demand an End to 'Modern-Day Slavery,'" *The Appeal*, June 8, 2018, https://theappeal.org/louisiana-prisoners-demand-an-end-to-modern-day-slavery/

17 University of Minnesota students, "Carceral Colonialism: Imprisonment in Indian Country," States of Incarceration, https://statesofincarceration.org/states/ minnesota-carceral-colonialism-imprisonment-indian-country

18 Karen Morgaine and Moshoula Capous-Desyllas, *Anti-Oppressive Social Work Practice: Putting Theory into Action* (Los Angeles: SAGE Publications, Inc., 2015), 36.

19 Stormy Ogden, as cited by University of Minnesota students in "Carceral Colonialism: Imprisonment in Indian Country," States of Incarceration, https:// statesofincarceration.org/states/minnesota-carceral-colonialism-imprisonment-indian-country.

20 Susan Sleeper-Smith, Juliana Barr, Jean M. O'Brien, Nancy Shoemaker, and Scott Manning Stevens, eds., *Why You Can't Teach United States History Without American Indians* (Chapel Hill: University of North Carolina Press, 2015).

21 Amber A. Annis, "This Is Indian Land: A Call to Museums in Addressing Mass Incarceration of American Indians," *Museums & Social Issues* 12, no. 1 (2017): 16.

22 Ibid.

23 Josh Olson, "Alcoholism v. Incarceration," States of Incarceration, Fall 2015, student reflection held by Humanities Action Lab.

24 "1% and yet 8%," States of Incarceration, Fall 2015, student reflection held by Humanities Action Lab.

25 Scott Russell, "Dakota Protesters Meet Sesquicentennial Wagon Train," Mendota Mdewakanton Dakota Tribal Community, May 10, 2008, https://mendotadakota.

com/mn/309/; Craig Stellmacher, "Dakota Activists Protest Fort Snelling Preservation," The UpTake, February 17, 2010, https://theuptake.org/2010/02/17/dakota-activists-protest-fort-snelling-preservation/; "Dakota Protest of Proposed FortSnellingFunding,"AsianAmericanPress,February 19,2010,http://aapress.com/social-issues/racism-hate/dakota-protest-of-proposed-fort-snelling-funding/

26 "The US-Dakota War of 1862," Historic Fort Snelling, Minnesota Historical Society, https://www.mnhs.org/fortsnelling/learn/us-dakota-war; "The Largest Mass Execution in US History," Death Penalty Information Center, https://deathpenaltyinfo.org/stories/the-largest-mass-execution-in-us-history

27 Coleman, "Elders Met Where Rivers Meet Genesis and Genocide are Whitewashed."

28 Dallas Ross, interviewed by Deborah Locke, May 5, 2011, transcript, U.S.-Dakota War of 1862 Oral History Project, Minnesota Historical Society, https://media.mnhs.org/things/cms/10248/284/AV2011_45_25_M.pdf

29 Carrie Schommer, interviewed by Deborah Locke, April 27, 2011, transcript, U.S.-Dakota War of 1862 Oral History Project, Minnesota Historical Society, http://collections.mnhs.org/cms/display.php?irn=11007780#transcript

30 "Aftermath," The US-Dakota War of 1862, Minnesota Historical Society, https://www.usdakotawar.org/history/aftermath

31 Jason Mack, "Bdote and Fort Snelling: A Place of Frame Disputes and Contested Meanings," MA Thesis, Minnesota State University-Mankato, 2015, https://core.ac.uk/download/pdf/214121167.pdf; Bdote Memory Map, Minnesota Humanities Center and Allies: media/art, https://bdotememorymap.org/memory-map/; Waziyatawin, *What Does Justice Look Like? The Struggle for Liberation in Dakota Homeland* (St. Paul: Living Justice Press, 2008).

32 https://www.house.leg.state.mn.us/comm/docs/uF6T2QsTX0eiqA9fV3vg Eg.pdf

33 Response to Joshua Lee, "The Deep Shadow of Our Concentration Camp," States of Incarceration, Fall 2015, student reflection held by Humanities Action Lab.

34 Response to David Eide, "Race and Incarceration," States of Incarceration, Fall 2015, student reflection held by Humanities Action Lab.

35 Detention Watch Network (DWN), as a public coalition of activists, lawyers, and citizens, publishes ICE spreadsheets which include a national list of ICE detention centers. Lopez's students eventually used such lists to cross-check their research, and added to DWN's list since they included immigration prisons and county jails that detained noncitizens. The lists are always being updated as facilities close and others open; see https://www.detentionwatchnetwork.org

36 John Nichols, "ALEC Exposed," *The Nation*, July 12, 2011, https://www.thenation.com/article/archive/alec-exposed/; Mike Elk and Bob Sloan, "The Hidden History of ALEC and Prison Labor," *The Nation*, August 1, 2011, https://www.thenation.com/article/archive/hidden-history-alec-and-prison-labor/

37 Eliza Berman, "Ava DuVernay on Her Oscar-Nominated Documentary *13th* and Resistance Through Art," *Time*, February 10, 2017, http://time.com/4662871/ava-duvernay-13th-documentary-interview/

38 "Detention of migrant children," States of Incarceration, Fall 2015, student reflection held by Humanities Action Lab.

39 Arthur C. Helton, "The Legality of Detaining Refugees in the United States," *New York University Review of Law & Social Change* 14, no. 2 (1986): 353–82.

40 See Timothy J. Dunn, *The Militarization of the U.S.-Mexico Border, 1978–1992: Low-Intensity Conflict Doctrine Comes Home* (Austin: Center for Mexican American Studies, University of Texas at Austin, 1996) and Mark Dow, *American Gulag: Inside U.S. Immigration Prisons* (Berkeley: University of California Press, 2004).

41 Doris Meissner, Donald M. Kerwin, Muzaffar Chishti, and Claire Bergeron, "Immigration Enforcement in the United States: The Rise of a Formidable

Machinery," Migration Policy Institute, January 2013, https://www.migrationpolicy. org/pubs/enforcementpillars.pdf

42 Ted Robbins, "Little-Known Immigration Mandate Keeps Detention Beds Full," NPR, November 19, 2013, https://www.npr.org/2013/11/19/245968601/ little-known-immigration-mandate-keeps-detention-beds-full. While ICE interpreted the policy as a directive to fill 34,000 immigration detention beds, immigrant rights activists have noted that the bill merely requires that 34,000 beds be funded. "Immigration Detention Bed Quotas: Private Prison Corporations, Government Collude to Keep Contracts Secret; Undue Corporate Influence Seen in FOIA Redactions, Attorneys Say," Center for Constitutional Rights, December 23, 2015, https://ccrjustice.org/home/press-center/press-releases/ immigration-detention-bed-quotas-private-prison-corporations

43 Monsy Alvarado et al., "'These People Are Profitable': Under Trump, Private Prisons Are Cashing in on ICE Detainees," USA Today, December 19, 2019, https://www.usatoday.com/in-depth/news/nation/2019/12/19/ice-detention-private-prisons-expands-under-trump-administration/4393366002/

44 Alison Parker, "Lost in Detention," The Marshall Project, March 4, 2015, https:// www.themarshallproject.org/2015/03/04/lost-in-detention

45 University of Texas at Austin students Sara Zavaleta, Jessica Carey-Webb, Andrew Leith, Joyce Hanlon, Katie Slusher, Sadie Dubicki, Maureen Anway, Josephine Hill, Claudia Rodriguez, Natalia Lopez, Anju Palta, and faculty lead Sarah Lopez, "Texas: Spatial Stories of Migration and Detention," States of Incarceration, https:// statesofincarceration.org/states/texas-spatial-stories-migration-and-detention

46 Ibid.

47 Josephine Hill, "Texas Detention Center Expansion Since 1984," https:// statesofincarceration.org/story/texas-detention-center-expansion-1984

48 Ibid.

49 Tom Dart, "More Than 20 Woman Detained in Texas Immigration Facility Begin Hunger Strike," The Guardian, October 29, 2015, https://www.theguardian. com/us-news/2015/oct/29/texas-immigration-detention-center-women-hunger-strike

50 Cristina Parker, "BREAKING: At Least 27 Women on Hunger Strike at the Hutto Detention Center," Grassroots Leadership, October 27, 2015, http:// grassrootsleadership.org/blog/2015/10/breaking-least-27-women-hunger-strike-hutto-detention-center-hutto27

51 University of Texas at Austin, "Texas: Spatial Stories of Migration and Detention."

52 Kate Livingston on behalf of ExposeYourMuseum LLC, "HAL States of Incarceration Visitor Evaluation," October 15, 2017, report held by Humanities Action Lab.

53 Mayela Caro and Marissa Friedman, "Public Histories of Incarceration: Reflecting on Museums and Social Change," Museums & Social Issues 12, no. 1 (2017): 50.

54 Ibid., 50.

55 Manuel Criollo, interviewed by Mayela Caro and Cathy Gudis, 2015, "Decriminalizing Students," States of Incarceration, https://statesofincarceration. org/story/decriminalizing-students

56 Ibid.

57 "Black, Brown, and Over-Policed in L.A. Schools," The Labor/Community Strategy Center, October 2013, https://www.njjn.org/uploads/digital-library/ CA_Strategy-Center_Black-Brown-and-Over-Policed-in-LA-Schools.PDF

58 Caro and Friedman, "Public Histories of Incarceration," 54.

59 "Targeting Gang Injunctions," States of Incarceration, https://statesofincarceration. org/story/targeting-gang-injunctions

60 Caro and Friedman, "Public Histories of Incarceration," 54.

61 "Fact Sheet: Incarcerated Women and Girls," The Sentencing Project, November 2020, https://www.sentencingproject.org/wp-content/uploads/2016/02/Incarcerated-Women-and-Girls.pdf

62 Ibid.

63 "Reforming Gender and the Carceral State," States of Incarceration, https://statesofincarceration.org/states/massachusetts-reforming-gender-and-carceral-state

64 Amy Halliday, Chel Rose (formerly Chelsea Miller), and Julie Peterson, "What Are Women's Prisons for?" *Museums & Social Issues* 12, no. 1 (2017): 57.

65 Bernard E. Harcourt, "Reducing Mass Incarceration: Lessons from the Deinstitutionalization of Mental Hospitals in the 1960s" (January 26, 2011). University of Chicago Law & Economics, Olin Working Paper No. 542, University of Chicago, Public Law Working Paper No. 335, available at SSRN: https://ssrn.com/abstract=1748796 or http://dx.doi.org/10.2139/ssrn.1748796. Thank you to Modupe Labode for this reference, and for advice on this section (any mistakes are mine).

66 James Austin and Lauren-Brooke Eisen, with James Cullen and Jonathan Frank, "How Many Americans Are Unnecessarily Incarcerated?" Brennan Center for Justice, https://www.brennancenter.org/sites/default/files/publications/Unnecessarily_Incarcerated_0.pdf

67 "The Treatment of Persons with Mental Illness in Prisons and Jails: A State Survey," Treatment Advocacy Center and National Sheriffs' Association, April 8, 2014, https://www.treatmentadvocacycenter.org/storage/documents/treatment-behind-bars/treatment-behind-bars.pdf. See also Darrell Steinberg, David Mills, and Michael Romano, "When Did Prisons Become Acceptable Mental Healthcare Facilities?" (Stanford Law School Three Strikes Project, 2015), https://law.stanford.edu/wp-content/uploads/sites/default/files/publication/863745/doc/slspublic/Report_v12.pdf

68 Austin and Eisen, "How Many Americans Are Unnecessarily Incarcerated?"

69 "The Treatment of Persons with Mental Illness in Prisons and Jails."

70 Darrin Wright, "Settlement for Prisoners with Mental Illness Seen as Victory," *WOWO Radio*, February 7, 2016, https://www.wowo.com/settlement-for-prisoners-with-mental-illnesses-seen-as-victory/

71 Emma Marston, "Reflections on Incarceration and Mental Illness," States of Incarceration, Fall 2015, student reflection held by Humanities Action Lab.

72 Vickie Stone, "THIS IS IMPORTANT! THIS IS A RESPONSIBILITY!" States of Incarceration, Fall 2015, student reflection held by Humanities Action Lab.

73 Winston Salem State University students, "Incarcerating Resistance in the Tar Heel State," States of Incarceration, exhibit panel text draft held by Humanities Action Lab.

74 Winston Salem State University students, "Political Prisoners and State Repression," States of Incarceration, exhibit panel text and photo captions draft held by Humanities Action Lab.

75 Johnson C. Smith University students, "Breaking the Chains between Foster Care and Incarceration," States of Incarceration, exhibit panel text draft held by Humanities Action Lab.

76 Ibid.

77 Ted Sherman, "High-Profile Immigration Activist Battles to Set Aside N.J. Fraud Conviction," NJ.com, January 30, 2018, https://www.nj.com/news/2018/01/nj_fraud_case_at_center_of_deportation_of_prominen.html; Amy Gottlieb, "I Thought Trump's Defeat Meant ICE Would Stop Targeting My Husband. Why Is It No Different Under Biden?" *Washington Post*, May 25, 2021, https://www.washingtonpost.com/opinions/2021/05/25/i-thought-trumps-defeat-meant-ice-would-stop-targeting-my-husband-why-is-it-no-different-under-biden/

78 "Remembering Lessons from Rikers Island, What Should New York City's Future Detention Facilities Be Like?" Shape the Debate, States of Incarceration, https://statesofincarceration.org/shape-the-debate/remembering-lessons-rikers-island-what-should-new-york-citys-future-detention

79 "California Has Approved $2 Billion for Jail Construction. How Could the Funds Be Used to Keep People Out of Jails Instead?" Shape the Debate, States of Incarceration, https://statesofincarceration.org/shape-the-debate/california-has-approved-2-billion-jail-construction-how-could-funds-be-used-keep

80 "A New Rhode Island State Commission Will Study Solitary Confinement. Do You Think Prisons Should Use Solitary Confinement?" Shape the Debate, States of Incarceration, https://statesofincarceration.org/shape-the-debate/new-rhode-island-state-commission-will-study-solitary-confinement-do-you-think

81 "2018 Status of State and Local Corrections Facilities and Program Report," Louisiana Commission on Law Enforcement and Administration of Criminal Justice, April 1, 2019, http://lcle.la.gov/programs/uploads/2018%20Status%20of%20State%20and%20Local%20Corrections%20Facilities%20and%20Program%20Reportrd.pdf

82 "Should Your University or Company Have the Right to Ask About Someone's Prior Convictions in Their Admission or Job Application?" Shape the Debate, States of Incarceration, https://statesofincarceration.org/shape-the-debate/should-your-university-or-company-have-right-ask-about-someones-prior-convictions

83 Gretel Kauffman, "College After Prison? New Louisiana Law Makes It Easier," *Christian Science Monitor*, July 5, 2017, https://www.csmonitor.com/EqualEd/2017/0705/College-after-prison-New-Louisiana-law-makes-it-easier

84 Marla Miller, "'In the Spaciousness of Uncertainty Is Room to Act': Public History's Long Game," *The Public Historian* 42, no. 3 (August 2020): 22.

PART IV

Climates of Inequality

11
HISTORICAL DENIAL AND THE CLIMATE CRISIS

The previous sections of this book explored two historical denials, operating on different scales, that have shaped US public policy: denial of a tiny "state of exception" at Guantánamo Bay that played an outsized role in defining the contours of American democracy; and denial of a carceral state that provides an invisible infrastructure for structural racism. This chapter addresses a third historical denial, perhaps the farthest reaching of all: denial of the existential threat to our planet, and to everyone in it, posed by climate change. The chapter will consider climate denial as a form of historical denial, largely driven by the US, rooted in this country's deep culture of refusing to acknowledge and assume accountability for its past actions, as explored in the two previous sections. Like the denial of the histories of Guantánamo and mass incarceration, this one has shaped public policy in significant ways, with disastrous consequences. Confronting it requires specific participatory public memory strategies, building on those discussed in previous chapters, but drawing new approaches from the environmental justice movement.

While climate change is, by definition, a historical phenomenon (describing change over time), in the 2010s it was popularly discussed in terms of anxiety about the future. Climate denial, meanwhile, was primarily diagnosed as denial of the science predicting that future. The denial of how human actions in the past have shaped the climate has thwarted regulation of human action in the present. And the denial of how histories of environmentally racist policies produced unequal impacts of climate change – and of frontline communities' environmental practices and strategies for resilience in the face of them – ensured that what environmental policies did pass left these inequalities intact or worsened them.

DOI: 10.4324/9781003185826-16

This chapter will begin by exploring the types of historical denial that have given rise to climate change: denial of human causality of "natural" phenomena; denial of the disproportionate impact of climate change on people of color and other marginalized people; and denial of the rich traditions of environmentalism in those communities. The section will then consider the opportunities and obligations this set of historical denials present for participatory public memory, and lessons to be drawn from the environmental justice movement for meeting them.

US Climate Denial

The US has been a world leader in denying the world's imminent demise. A study of public opinion in 23 nations conducted in 2019 found only Saudi Arabia and Indonesia had a greater percentage of respondents denying climate change and human responsibility for it.[1] So many Americans were disbelievers in 2016 that they elected Donald J. Trump, a president who had tweeted "Global warming is an expensive hoax!" and dismantled what feeble structures had been in place to prevent a further rise in temperature.[2] He also dismantled faith in facts among his base: belief that global warming is happening, and that it is human-caused, fell among Republican voters after 2016.[3]

Climate advocates have long interpreted climate denial as a denial of science: a refusal to believe the preponderance of data demonstrating the damage human action has caused. This scientific denial is often attributed to the machinations of the country's powerful fossil fuel industries, manipulating public understanding of science to protect their economic self-interest. As Naomi Oreskes and Erik M. Conway argued in their 2010 book *Merchants of Doubt*, these industries deliberately created a public discourse that distorted scientific understanding of climate, by running or funding think tanks and independent scientists, that promoted doubt about the scientific consensus on climate.[4] Diagnosing climate denial as a problem of knowledge and facts, a new profession of "climate communicators" poured energy into educating the public on climate science. This turned out not to work.[5] As polling by the Yale Program on Climate Change Communication (YPCCC) indicated, belief in climate change was not correlated with scientific knowledge, but with values, specifically as expressed through party affiliation and political identity, with conservatives far less likely to believe global warming is happening.[6] Nevertheless, by 2020, the tide had turned: a strong majority – 72% of poll respondents – finally believed in global warming.

But as American denial of climate change gets weaker, denial of America's historical responsibility for it remains strong, and it has crippled global efforts to fight climate change. Denial of climate change's history – and how to redress it – has long been US policy, even in eco-friendly administrations. The Obama administration, for example, promoted technical solutions to the climate crisis founded on the same refusal to look backward as he had with the issue of torture at Guantánamo. His administration saw an explosion of "green growth" policy proposals, based in what climate policy scholar Sonya Klinksy characterizes as "win-win narratives that highlight future well-being" and "forward-oriented momentum in efforts to address both poverty and climate change."[7] These proposals ignored the depth of Americans' possessive investment in the historical structures of consumption and extraction that drove climate change, which opponents defended as "the American way of life."[8]

International climate negotiations have long been stalled over the US's refusal to deal with historical responsibility. Obama sent US Special Envoy on Climate Change Todd Stern to the 2011 Durban climate negotiations with clear instructions not to acknowledge America's disproportionate historical role in the emissions that caused climate change, or to assume responsibility for paying for the damage. In the negotiations, Stern refused to engage with what he called an "ideological narrative of fault and blame," arguing that in any case you can't hold people accountable for something they didn't realize was harmful at the time, even when climate advocates pointed out that more than three quarters of emissions date from after rising CO2 levels were first observed.[9] Stern's bottom line, as he is reported to have said outside his official speeches, was "If equity's in, then we're out."[10]

As Stern shorthanded, reckoning with history required addressing inequality. Environmental degradation from climate change and pollution disproportionately impacts people of color and low-income people in the US and around the world. Race, even more than class, is the single strongest factor determining who lives near toxic facilities in the US.[11] Immigrant communities are also disproportionately affected, far more likely to be subject to environmental degradation or extreme weather events, and often have the least resources to protect themselves.[12]

The mainstream climate movement that shaped US climate policy itself has a long history of racism and exclusionary practices, embedded in the environmental movement from which it emerged. Many founding conservationists supported eugenics, in what *New Yorker* writer Jedediah Purdy described as "an unsettlingly short step from managing forests to managing the human gene pool."[13] Many US national parks were created by expelling or confining the Native Americans living there.[14] The post-war environmental movement cast overpopulation, especially of poor people of color, as its main enemy, in a practice Stevie Ruiz and Lisa Sun-Hee Park have labeled "nativist environmentalism," which shaped leading environmental organizations: for example, strong factions within the Sierra Club's membership organized against immigration.[15] The narrative that poor people of color *caused* environmental degradation erased long traditions of environmental organizing, sustainable practices, and recovery from environmental damage that many of these communities cultivated, while wealthier white Americans radically expanded their consumption and waste. As voters, people of color have been stronger and more active defenders of the environment than whites. In 2009, one poll found 61% of Black voters believed global warming was "extremely serious" or "very serious," while only 39% of whites did.[16] Yet the mainstream climate movement long ignored these communities as a constituency, believing that wealthier white Americans were more powerful agents of change, even though they had the greatest investment in maintaining the status quo.[17] The academic field of environmental history, which emerged from the environmental movement, mirrored the movement's focus on white activists in its first decade, inscribing its erasure of people of color in official history.[18]

These racist roots, and the aggressive historical denial, shaped a deep and lasting division between the mainstream climate movement, and the environmental justice (EJ) movement, which emerged from civil rights struggles led by people of color, and formally coalesced in the First People of Color Environmental Leadership Summit in 1991. The EJ movement differed from the environmental movement in its focus on human welfare, as opposed to that of landscapes and animal species, and in its analysis of housing segregation, labor abuses, air and water contamination, and fossil fuel extraction as interrelated harms caused by larger systems of exploitation. Its approach to the climate crisis foregrounded history, articulating climate change as a historical process inextricably intertwined with centuries-long histories of racism, colonialism, and other structural inequalities.[19] Surveying EJ leaders in 2009 on the state of the climate movement, a report summarized:

> most climate activists are primarily concerned with addressing the technological challenges of climate change. They frame climate change in terms of a scientific problem.... They tend to overlook the ways in which climate change is linked to historical exploitation and injustice.[20]

The EJ movement's frameworks for addressing the climate crisis recognized that change could only come through reckoning with and redressing past harms. The principles of environmental justice established at the 1991 Summit, recognized and referred to across the movement from then on, include the statement that "Environmental Justice protects the right of victims of environmental injustice to receive full compensation and reparations for damages as well as quality health care." The EJ movement's vision for tackling the climate crisis was through what it calls a Just Transition, a wholesale transformation of power structures to move from an extractive to a regenerative economic, social, and political system. As several coalitions of EJ organizations have articulated it, a Just Transition requires historical accountability. For the Indigenous Environmental Network, for instance, "The transition itself must be just and equitable; redressing past harms and creating new relationships of power for the future through reparations."[21] And for the groups assembled in the Climate Justice Alliance, this transformation required "reparations for land that has been stolen and/or destroyed by capitalism, colonialism, patriarchy, genocide and slavery."[22]

At the international level, where climate negotiations were blocked by the US's refusal to acknowledge its historical role so as not to be punished for it, some policy advocates turned to transitional justice, with its mechanisms for establishing historical responsibility without legal accountability.[23] During 2016, the Climate Strategies research network held a series of workshops to develop specific proposals, including a climate truth commission, in which testimonies of hunger, displacement, and illness would be publicly shared, accompanied by research clearly establishing the ways these human harms were caused by industrial activities of the Global North.[24] In return for public acknowledgment of responsibility and some form of symbolic reparations, polluters would be free from legal or financial penalty.[25]

As wealthy white Americans continued to be a weak constituency for climate action over the 2010s, the term "environmental justice" began to be adopted by many "Big Green" organizations, including those who had historically pursued racist environmental policies. The Sierra Club, for example, launched an environmental justice program; in parallel, the NAACP, a large mainstream civil rights organization which had not previously focused on climate, initiated a new program in Environmental and Climate Justice. In October 2018, environmental justice organizations came together with historically environmentalist organizations, including the Natural Resources Defense Council and the Sierra Club, as well as national policy organizations like the Center for American Progress and the League of Conservation Voters – to forge an alliance for an "Equitable and Just National Climate Platform." This platform was developed as an alternative to the various proposals circulating as the "Green New Deal," the best known of which was a congressional resolution introduced by New York Representative Alexandria Ocasio-Cortez and Massachusetts Senator Edward Markey and popularized by the Sunrise Movement, a youth-led activist group. EJ organizations critiqued the Green New Deal proposals, which included reducing US fossil fuel dependency and greenhouse gas emissions, providing good-paying clean energy jobs, and tackling income inequality and racial injustice, for not being informed or led by frontline communities and lacking deep substantive policy commitment to addressing inequities.[26] The embrace of the EJ mantle by mainstream climate organizations, however opportunistic, opened a new audience for confronting the climate crisis as a problem of history.

Participatory Public Memory for Climate Justice

In this context, in October 2017, nearly 50 historians, local environmental justice advocates, and public history faculty from 30 cities in the US, Latin America, and Europe came together to explore how to develop a participatory public history for climate justice. We gathered at the Rutgers University campus in Newark, NJ, the Humanities Action Lab's new home, a city whose post-war history was forged in environmental racism and local resistance to it. The result was Climates of Inequality: Stories of Environmental Justice. Like the other two Humanities Action Lab projects, this initiative was created through collaborations between universities and community organizations in each city, who produced a traveling exhibit and web platform integrating stories from all participating cities, paired with ongoing public dialogues and actions when each locality hosted it. It was managed by Aleia Brown, a scholar of Black women's material and digital culture created to advance black freedom struggles, who had recently co-founded #BlkTwitterstorians and #MuseumsRespondtoFerguson. Along the way, participants grappled with how a participatory public memory project could promote a frame for discourse and action on the climate crisis grounded in the terms, concerns, spaces, and histories of communities disproportionately affected by it.

Participants' local experiences demonstrated how the impact of climate change was grounded in histories of environmental racism and resistance to it. In Puerto Rico, Hurricane María's total devastation of the island's infrastructure in 2017, and the people's abandonment by the government, followed centuries of colonialism, which had also bred a long history of communal organizing that emerged from the wreckage to save thousands of lives. In Newark's Ironbound neighborhood, decades of toxic waste from the many industries housed there – including dioxin from Agent Orange, the chemical designed to decimate green landscapes in the Vietnam War – caused cancer to skyrocket and asthma rates three times higher than in the rest of the state. When Superstorm Sandy hit in 2012, this history of environmental racism rose up in the floodwaters, which inundated streets, playgrounds, and living rooms with the sediment from generations of dumping. In New Orleans, residents of Gordon Plaza, a development targeting Black homeowners that was built on top of a toxic dump in 1981, had already organized a movement to demand the city relocate them, when Hurricane Katrina brought the waste bubbling back up from the ground in 2005. In all these cases, reminders of generations of environmental racism – histories buried under thin layers of denial and topsoil – surfaced to shape marginalized communities' experiences of climate change.

Environmental justice advocates brought strong and clear principles to the project, grounded in the history of the EJ movement, to frame what a participatory public memory project for climate justice should look like. The Jemez Principles for Democratic Organizing, authored in 1996 at a working group meeting of EJ advocates in Jemez, New Mexico, established an enduring framework for environmental justice work. They emerged from a recognition that the disparate organizations and communities coming together to fight for environmental justice needed to create "common understandings between participants from different cultures, politics and organizations," on how they would work together and for what purpose. The group that the Humanities Action Lab brought together – academics and organizers; white, Latinx, Indigenous, and Black; from Newark to New Orleans, Mayagüez, Puerto Rico to Minneapolis – deeply needed such grounding.

Putting Frontline Voices First

The Jemez principles include the exhortation to "Let people speak for themselves":

> We must be sure that relevant voices of people directly affected are heard. Ways must be provided for spokespersons to represent and be responsible to the affected constituencies.[27]

Applying this to a public memory project meant supporting frontline advocates and communities to play a much stronger and more consistent role in identifying and sharing their histories than they had in the two previous HAL projects. The project allocated significantly more funds to support community organizations to co-teach or otherwise co-create local chapters, and provided much greater scaffolding for universities and communities to design their collaborations, such as models, protocols, planning worksheets, and facilitated co-design sessions. Equally important, the project sought out students living in frontline communities, whose lives had been shaped by struggles for environmental justice.

In Newark, almost all the students in HAL's "Environmental Justice in the Ironbound" class had grown up in Greater Newark. Remembering their own histories, student after student spoke about asthma. That semester, one in four residents of the Ironbound had asthma, three times the average rate in the rest of the state, caused by the toxic underbellies of systems serving the New York City region, including incinerating New York's garbage, and delivering goods via hundreds of trucks spewing exhaust.[28] The class was co-taught by advocate Maria Lopez-Nuñez of the Ironbound Community Corporation (ICC), and filmmaker Julie Winokur, who would go on to make a documentary with Maria called *Sacrifice Zone*. Coming up on a half-century of grassroots action, ICC had driven investigation of Diamond Alkali, the company that produced Agent Orange to decimate jungles for the war in Vietnam, while destroying Newark's soil and water with its toxic byproducts. ICC won acknowledgment and a start to remediation, by getting the massive contaminated area designated one of the largest superfund sites in US history, thereby securing government funding for cleanup efforts.[29] More recently, ICC had brought a lawsuit against the Covanta incinerator in Newark for spewing toxic iodine into the air.[30]

When Lopez-Nuñez and Winokur asked students at the outset of the class what environmental justice meant to them, students promoted recycling, changing light bulbs, and other acts of individual consumers. Despite growing up in an environmental justice community – characterized by extraordinary collective activism in response to egregious environmental burdens – the power of mainstream environmental discourse was such that it dominated students' framework, even as it was barely relevant to their own lives. Lopez-Nuñez and Winokur recognized the need to distinguish between environmentalism and environmental justice, by encouraging students to connect with the knowledge and experience from their own histories and that of their communities. Lopez-Nuñez introduced students to activists in the neighborhood, representing multiple generations of creative struggle for a healthy Ironbound through the ICC. One student realized she had seen the person she interviewed around the neighborhood but didn't know the woman had achieved so much for her community. For another, the experience made her realize: "We matter and if we continue to demand more we'll have better conclusions."[31]

Regenerative Relationships

Another core principle EJ organizers shared was to ensure that the relationships among people doing the work reflected the work's goals. Achieving a Just Transition – moving the world from an extractive to a regenerative economy – required moving from extractive to regenerative relationships. To apply this principle to a collaborative public memory project, partners had to resist the entrenched structures of university-community relationships, historically designed to support universities to extract data or real estate from their communities for their own gain. Although various efforts were being made in higher education to reject that dynamic, the administrative structures remained, and perhaps more powerfully, the frameworks and assumptions individuals brought to their work. For instance, "getting stories" by conducting oral histories remained a default public history mode, with the presumption that the most important audiences with whom to share frontline communities' stories were external, when in many cases storytellers would have benefited more from exchanging stories to mobilize and inspire people within their own communities.

In Puerto Rico, Professor Ricia Chansky and her students were reeling from the devastation of Hurricane María, a category 5 storm that tore through the island in September 2017. In the absence of state aid, she had spent the first months feeding her students and neighbors over a propane stove by candlelight, and opening a space for people to share stories, survival tips, and emotional support. Together they identified as "citizen responders," which she and her team later defined as "the everyday, average person who is prepared and equipped to care for themselves and their community in a time of crisis." Their definition included a practice of mutually supportive storytelling, a trauma-informed, participatory public memory process that integrated the exchange of narratives, food, and survival strategies. Once back in the classroom, Chansky mobilized over 150 University of Puerto Rico students to interview people in their communities, as well as share their own stories of surviving the hurricane, in a project called "Mi María."[32] The Mi María project gave students agency and community as citizen responders using the tool of storytelling. By inviting people to exchange and record what they had seen and experienced, the project provided a multi-layered resource, including healing from trauma; circulating vital information for survival; citizen science documentation of impacts and needs; and organizing to demand justice. Students exposed an abandoned warehouse of donations that had never been distributed; created and circulated information booklets; and began building a multi-media archive of stories of survival.

Mobilizing Frontline Communities

In contrast to States of Incarceration, where participating criminal justice reform organizations believed the project should engage both directly impacted and uninformed audiences, the environmental justice organizations participating in Climates of Inequality prioritized engaging their own communities. University partners whose students were not from frontline communities needed to adjust to a theory of change in which they were not the most important actors. They also learned new forms of action. Partnerships included exchanges that integrated histories of environmental racism with civic education on the mechanisms for resisting it. As the Kheprw Institute in Indianapolis later wrote,

> By collaborating with IUPUI students, we built relationships that allowed both the students and our youth leaders to get experience in leadership development and deep listening. Our members asked critical questions, gave the students a historical context of race and displacement, and connected students with community organizing efforts.[33]

For their part, students reflected that

> The issues in this exhibit became personal as we realized that we live in some of the communities and areas affected by environmental injustices in Indianapolis... By attending [Kheprw Institute] meetings and engaging with members, we learned how small steps can lead to powerful changes in our city.[34]

Translocal Organizing

Climates of Inequality emerged in the context of a tremendous flowering of translocal organizing for the climate crisis that built on models created by the EJ movement. In contrast to national organizing, in which people across the country all came together around the same, centrally defined campaign, translocal organizing was rooted in the distinct experiences of diverse local communities, bringing them together into a coalition of campaigns linked by common structural problems. The EJ movement had long recognized that nation states would not save the planet and would not advocate for the welfare of poor communities of color. It had therefore organized translocally, through coalitions such as the Indigenous Environmental Network, the Grassroots Global Justice Alliance, the Environmental Justice Climate Change Initiative, and the Just Transition Alliance. These groups helped shape the Climate Justice Alliance, formally organized in 2013; by the time of Trump's election, the group could activate a powerful and broad network of organizers and platforms for mobilization to design specific resistance to what was to come. As environmental justice scholar and advocate Ana Baptista argues, "These translocal alliances demonstrate how locally impacted, marginalized communities situated in different cultural and social contexts can leverage multiple sources of expertise to make critical discursive and productive networked actors on a global scale."[35]

Trump's withdrawal of the US from the Paris Accords, the world's principal international treaty on climate change, and his abandonment of climate policy at home prompted municipalities and states, as well as private sector actors like corporations and universities, to push local policies and practices over which they had control. They also built networks of solidarity and shared practices across localities, in groups across the US such as the "We are Still In" coalition, including mayors, governors, universities, corporations, and faith institutions; or international groups like the Global Covenant of Mayors for Climate and Energy. Youth activists organized the Sunrise Movement as a network of locally led groups rallying around the Green New Deal.

In this context, participants in Climates of Inequality explored what a translocal participatory public memory movement for climate justice could look like. Whereas States of Incarceration deliberately defined its component histories by state, because criminal justice policy in the US is largely determined at the state level, Climates of Inequality's histories were hyperlocal, at the neighborhood level. And whereas the mass incarceration memory project focused on the US, to reckon with this country's distinctive history and commitment to mass incarceration, this project included communities in Mexico and South America. This map of environmental justice sought to disrupt mainstream climate justice narratives contrasting the privilege of the Global North with the suffering of the Global South. Instead, the project centered the stories of communities disproportionately impacted by climate change in both hemispheres, to emphasize the structures of environmental racism operating across countries. Seeking to build a coalition of public memory makers, the project hoped to open spaces for organizers from La Villita in Chicago to Gordon Plaza in New Orleans to the Ironbound in Newark to connect not only their local histories, but their strategies for activating histories for organizing.

The Climates of Inequality exhibit launched in Newark in October 2019, as the Ironbound Community Corporation and other New Jersey environmental justice advocates were in the final stages of a decade-long struggle to pass a groundbreaking environmental justice bill in the state.[36] Newark Mayor Ras Baraka welcomed students, organizers, and faculty from all 21 participating cities, to meet each other for the first time, share their stories, and plan how they would activate the exhibit when it traveled to their community. Less than six months later, the world changed. The COVID-19 pandemic tore through environmental justice communities with particular savagery, while uprisings for racial justice made these communities' experiences and demands the center of national discussion. The pandemic closed public spaces, canceling the exhibit indefinitely; the histories of environmental justice it contained got shut away in shipping containers stacked in storage. But those same histories of environmental justice fundamentally shaped participating communities' experience of COVID – both the impact and the response. Meanwhile, after centuries of silence in US government, 2020 saw an explosion of calls for reparations at the municipal, state, and federal level. In April 2021, HR 40, the bill to study the legacies of slavery and proposals for redress, passed out of the House Judiciary Committee. Paired with the introduction of a bill "urging the establishment of a Truth, Racial Healing, and Transformation Commission," the post-Trump state foregrounded a new definition of truth and its role in society and governance. As the next and final chapter will explore, this introduced a new era of organizing with profound implications for participatory public memory.

Notes

1 Oliver Milman and Fiona Harvey, "US Is Hotbed of Climate Change Denial, Major Global Survey Finds," *The Guardian*, May 8, 2019, https://www.theguardian.com/environment/2019/may/07/us-hotbed-climate-change-denial-international-poll

2 Dylan Matthews, "Donald Trump Has Tweeted Climate Change Skepticism 115 Times. Here's All of It," *Vox*, June 1, 2017, https://www.vox.com/policy-and-politics/2017/6/1/15726472/trump-tweets-global-warming-paris-climate-agreement; Nadja Popovich, Livia Albeck-Ripka, and Kendra Pierre-Louis, "The Trump Administration Rolled Back More Than 100 Environmental Rules. Here's the Full List," *New York Times*, January 20, 2021, https://www.nytimes.com/interactive/2020/climate/trump-environment-rollbacks-list.html

3 Anthony Leiserowitz, Edward Maibach, Connie Roser-Renouf, Seth Rosenthal, Matthew Cutler, and John Kotcher, Politics & Global Warming, October 2017, Yale University and George Mason University (New Haven, CT: Yale Program on Climate Change Communication, 2017), https://climatecommunication.yale.edu/publications/politics-global-warming-october-2017/

4 Naomi Oreskes and Erik M. Conway, *Merchants of Doubt: How a Handful of Scientists Obscured the Truth on Issues from Tobacco Smoke to Climate Change* (New York: Bloomsbury Press, 2010).

5 Susanne C. Moser, "Communicating Climate Change: History, Challenges, Process and Future Directions," *WIREs Climate Change* 1, no. 1 (January/February 2010), 38.

6 Anthony Leiserowitz, Edward Maibach, Connie Roser-Renouf, Seth Rosenthal, Matthew Cutler, and John Kotcher, Politics & Global Warming, October 2017, Yale University and George Mason University (New Haven, CT: Yale Program on Climate Change Communication, 2017), https://climatecommunication.yale.edu/publications/politics-global-warming-october-2017/

7 Sonja Klinsky, "An Initial Scoping of Transitional Justice for Global Climate Governance," *Climate Policy* 18, no. 6 (2018), 754.

8 Jean-Daniel Collomb, "The Ideology of Climate Change Denial in the United States," *European Journal of American Studies* 9, no 1 (2014).

9 Cited in Brian Tokar, "Climate Solutions and the Challenge of Local Solutions," *Globalism and Localization: Emergent Solutions to Ecological and Social Crises,* ed. Jeanine M. Canty (Taylor & Francis Group, 2019), 23.

10 Jonathan Pickering, Steve Vanderheiden, and Seumas Miller, "'If Equity's In, We're Out': Scope for Fairness in the Next Global Climate Agreement," *Ethics & International Affairs*, no. 4 (2012), 423.

11 Bryce Covert, "Race Best Predicts Whether You Live Near Pollution: Environmental racism extends far beyond Flint." *The Nation,* February 18, 2016, accessed at https://www.thenation.com/article/race-best-predicts-whether-you-live-near-pollution/

12 Jorge Madrid, *From a "Green Farce" to a Green Future: Refuting False Claims About Immigrants and the Environment* (Center for American Progress, October 2010), accessed at https://www.americanprogress.org/wp-content/uploads/issues/2010/10/pdf/immigration_climate_change.pdf

13 Jedediah Purdy, "Environmentalism's Racist History," *The New Yorker*, August 13, 2015, https://www.newyorker.com/news/news-desk/environmentalisms-racist-history

14 Isaac Kantor, "Ethnic Cleansing and America's Creation of National Parks," *Public Land & Resources Law Review* 28, no. 41 (2007); Betsy Hartmann, "Conserving Racism: The Greening of Hate at Home and Abroad," *Different Takes: A Publication of the Population and Development Program at Hampshire College* 27 (2004), 1–4; Brendan Coolsaet, ed., *Environmental Justice: Key Issues* (Milton, England: Taylor & Francis Group, 2020).

15 Hop Hopkins, "How the Sierra Club's History with Immigrant Rights is Shaping Our Future," November 2, 2018, https://www.sierraclub.org/articles/2018/11/how-sierra-club-s-history-immigrant-rights-shaping-our-future

16 E: David Metz and Lori Weigel,(Public Opinion Strategies), "Key Findings from National Voter Survey on Conservation Among Voters of Color," memorandum, 2009, as cited in Angela Park, *Everybody's Movement: Environmental Justice and Climate Change* (Washington, DC: Environmental Support Center, 2009), retrieved from http://envsc.org/esc-publications/everybodysmovement

17 Martin Melosi, "Environmental Justice, Ecoracism, and Environmental History," in *To Love the Wind and the Rain: African Americans and Environmental History*, eds. Dianne D. Glave and Mark Stoll (Pittsburgh PA: University of Pittsburgh Press, 2005), 125–6.

18 Melosi, "Environmental Justice, Ecoracism, and Environmental History," 121–2.

19 Esme G. Murdock, "A History of Environmental Justice: Foundations, Narratives, and Perspectives," in *Environmental Justice: Key Issues*, ed. Brendan Coolsaet (Taylor & Francis Group, 2020) In her tight but expansive article offering an overview of EJ history, Murdock includes a rich bibliography.

20 Park, *Everybody's Movement*, 11.

21 Indigenous Environmental Network, "Indigenous Principles of Just Transition," http://www.ienearth.org/wp-content/uploads/2017/10/IENJustTransition Principles.pdf

22 "What Do We Mean By Just Transition?" Climate Justice Alliance, https://climatejusticealliance.org/just-transition/

23 Sonja Klinsky and Jasmina Brankovic, *The Global Climate Regime and Transitional Justice* (Abingdon, England: Routledge, 2018).

24 Sonja Klinsky, "Truth Commissions in the Climate Context," Climate Strategies, 2016.

25 Klinsky and Brankovic, *The Global Climate Regime and Transitional Justice.*

26 Lisa Friedman, "What Is the Green New Deal? A Climate Proposal, Explained," *New York Times*, February 21, 2019, https://www.nytimes.com/2019/02/21/climate/green-new-deal-questions-answers.html

27 "Jemez Principles for Democratic Organizing," The Ruckus Society, https://ruckus.org/philosophy/jemez-principles-for-democratic-organizing/

28 US Environmental Protection Agency, "EPA Agreement with Port Authority and Port Terminal Operators Will Cut Harmful Pollution from Idling Trucks in Newark and Beyond," News Release, July 23, 2015, https://archive.epa.gov/epa/newsreleases/epa-agreement-port-authority-and-port-terminal-operators-will-cut-harmful-pollution.html

29 Erik Ortiz, "'We've Been Forgotten': In Newark, N.J., A Toxic Superfund Site Faces Growing Climate Threats," NBC News, October 1, 2020, https://www.nbcnews.com/news/us-news/we-ve-been-forgotten-newark-n-j-toxic-superfund-site-n1240706

30 Keith Rushing, "Ironbound Unyielding: A Newark Neighborhood takes on a Toxic Trash Incinerator," Earthjustice, January 22, 2021, https://earthjustice.org/features/ironbound-unyielding

31 "International Exchange Post 1 Spring 2019," student reflection held by Humanities Action Lab.

32 Ricia A. Chansky and Marci Denesiuk, *Mi María: Surviving the Storm: Voices from Puerto Rico* (New York: Haymarket Books, 2021). See also Mi María: Puerto Rico after the Hurricane, https://mimariapr.org/

33 Kheprw Institute team Imhotep Adisa, Paulette Fair, Leah Humphrey, Asli Mwaafrika, Aghilah Nadaraj, and Alvin Sangsuwangul, "Our Point of View," in *Inequity Along the White River: Local Advocacy for Change*, https://climatesofinequality.org/story/inequity-along-the-white-river-local-advocacy-for-change/

34 IUPUI students Topher Anderson, Alisha Baginski, Allison Baker, Carole Bostelman, Barbara S. Castellanos, Kyrra Clevenger, Erin Crowther, Alexis Davenport, Jace Dostal, Caitlin Downey, Evan Dulaney, Brianna Durkin, Jim Fuller, Farah Gerber, Chyan Gilaspy, Madison Hincks, Cody Hudson, Taylor Hull, Brianna Jackson, Beth Kehrwald, Karen Lampert, Abi Lindstedt, Hannah Lundell, Laura Markley, Sidney Moore, Megan Perry, Molly Reynowsky, Jacqueline Rooksberry, Kate Sanford, Hadia Shaikh, Sarah Shorter, Dallas Sims, Natalie Smith, Stasia Tanzer, Katherine Watson, Dan Will, and Eldon Yeakel, "Our Point of View," in *Inequity Along the White River: Local Advocacy for Change*, https://climatesofinequality.org/story/inequity-along-the-white-river-local-advocacy-for-change/

35 Ana Isabel Baptista, "The Evolution of the Environmental Justice Movement: Translocal Voices for Systemic Transformations," in *Globalism and Localization: Emergent Solutions to Ecological and Social Crises*, ed. Jeanine M. Canty (New York: Routledge, 2019), 139.

36 Samantha Maldonado, "How a Long-Stalled 'Holy Grail' Environmental Justice Bill Found Its Moment in New Jersey," *Politico,* August 27, 2020, https://www.politico.com/states/new-jersey/story/2020/08/27/new-jersey-legislature-sends-groundbreaking-environmental-justice-bill-to-governors-desk-1313030

CONCLUSION

Participatory Public Memory for Truth's New Era

Historical Denials and Their Participatory Public Memory Strategies in Review

Participatory public memory can inspire an active citizenry resisting historical denial and its hold on public policy, by continually exploring the roots of inequality where they live, and imagining new ways to redress it. But historical denial operates differently around different aspects of the past, and how it shapes the present, requiring different participatory public memory strategies. The type of denial depends on the contours of visibility and invisibility of the site or story: who can see what.

The US Naval Station at Guantánamo Bay was (and continues to be) a remote, inaccessible place for US residents and Cubans alike, whose most abusive policies and practices were clandestine, hidden even from much of the US government, let alone its people. The US carceral state, on the other hand, was omnipresent for a huge swath of the population, majority Black and brown, while most white people could remain blissfully ignorant of it, consuming instead the hypervisible media version. This historical denial was produced not by a small number of counterterrorism officials redacting documents, but by the much more powerful and enduring force of white supremacy that supported willful blindness. Climate change is all around all of us, literally the air we breathe. This is an existential crisis perpetuated by historical denial, by a denial of climate's very historicity. The mainstream environmental movement insisted on diagnosing climate change as a technical problem, and climate denial as a lack of scientific knowledge. This fostered domestic policies that left the root causes of climate change and its unequal impacts intact, and stalled international climate negotiations over America's refusal to acknowledge historical responsibility.

DOI: 10.4324/9781003185826-17

The strategies required for puncturing these different types of denial require tailored theories of change, with specific targets. States of Incarceration had a very different opportunity to drive change than did the Guantánamo Public Memory Project, with a different way in which changing popular narratives on the subject could change public policy. For many Americans, imagining a world without Guantánamo – and without the brutality that came to define it – was easy. But bringing that world into being was hard: specific policies around Guantánamo, from whether and how to relocate prisoners, to international conventions on torture, to redefining the US lease with Cuba, were out of the hands of most voters. On the other hand, imagining a world without prisons – as Angela Davis and others so long theorized – seemed nearly impossible. But in the mid-2010s, making small changes was within reach: the US criminal justice system was held together by an erector set of local policies that could be pulled apart at the nodes by small groups of advocates. States of Incarceration therefore focused on making individual local policies that supported mass incarceration visible and mobilizing people around changing them. The climate crisis was awash in micro, technical solutions; the group behind Climates of Inequality believed participatory public memory should instead target the overall framing of the issue. That meant redefining climate change as a historically determined justice issue, as opposed to a scientific one, and recentering environmental justice movements' calls for historical accountability.

Strategies must also identify the agents of change, and therefore the audience for the memory project. If GTMO thrived because no one could see anything that was happening there, and very few people had any direct experience to share, then the main goal should be to simply raise basic awareness among the least informed. But mass incarceration worked differently: the legions of people with direct experience were living among the population at large, just unseen. While Black activists and academics with deeper stakes in the issue had been fighting for prison and criminal justice reform for decades, they had not enjoyed the same level of support and attention as those with no personal experience in the system, disproportionately white. Here the main goal should have been to support the leadership and voice of returning citizens. Yet States of Incarceration initially used the same participatory memory strategy as worked for GTMO: it assumed that change would come if people who claimed to be unaware of the US carceral state as a system of racial control were simply made aware of it. Despite a rhetorical commitment to provide a space for those directly impacted by the system to "say it out loud," the project's university-"community" partnership structure, which invited students to learn about prisons from those who had been there, initially resulted in a memory strategy that focused on those with the privilege to be unaware, and relied on those with direct experience as educators of those perceived to be change agents. As the project evolved, though, so did organizers' approach, focusing more on organizing those with direct experience to speak to and support each other. This was based on a theory that while reaching uninformed audiences remained important, only when combined with healing and mobilizing those directly impacted were there real possibilities for change. Environmental Justice organizers working on Climates of Inequality, on the other hand, were much more focused on speaking to and mobilizing frontline communities. The exclusionary history of the mainstream environmental movement, and the demonstrated failure of wealthier white voters to drive climate action, made EJ communities the clear target participants for participatory public memory for climate justice.

Each project also required different ways to define and navigate who was a directly affected stakeholder versus an uninformed learner, who was an insider versus an outsider. The division between people with direct experience at GTMO and the wider public that had none was clear. GTMO's policies and practices impacted most people by implication, through the precedents they set. The US carceral state, on the other hand, touched people in myriad and overlapping ways. A student in a college history class might have a family member in prison, or have grown up with the threat of prison through constant police harassment, or live in a community economically supported by its local prison. Someone working in criminal justice reform, with deep knowledge of policy and history, might not have any experience with prisons in their personal life. A memory movement around mass incarceration needed to wrestle with what kind of awareness had to be raised among whom, and resist assuming people held certain categories of knowledge and experience simply by virtue of their institutional location (for instance, university or criminal justice reform organization), or their visible biography. In this context, a participatory public memory project needed to engage stakeholders across institutions and public profiles. Every single person on the planet is impacted by climate change; yet those who contributed the least to the crisis – marginalized communities with tiny carbon footprints – bear the greatest burden. This gave these communities the greatest stake in addressing the climate crisis, yet for decades the mainstream climate movement dismissed them as stakeholders. The participatory public memory strategy for the climate crisis needed to turn the mainstream climate movement's insider/outsider frame inside out, highlighting the long history of environmentalism and resilience among EJ communities and centering EJ activists as core climate leaders.

Tracing the distinct contours of historical denial operating on any particular issue, and thinking precisely and strategically about theories of change and agents of change required to address it, is key for ensuring a public memory project makes the impact its organizers intend. Measuring that impact requires applying the same precise analysis and strategic thinking; it is much more difficult to achieve clear results, but that makes it even more important to try.

Exploring Impacts of Participatory Public Memory

Participatory public memory is neither discrete nor static: it intentionally integrates larger ecosystems of knowledge production, pedagogy, civic engagement, and activism, in hyperlocal contexts and across translocal coalitions. In many ways, that coalition building, in and of itself, is its main impact. The coalition structure multiplies the contributions of each partner to exponentially increase their reach, resources, and influence – from a few hundred audience members to a few hundred thousand, from one neighborhood to 20 cities – well beyond what any single partner could have managed themselves. But the intersectional and distributed structure makes it extremely difficult to isolate the contributions of individual events or components of a collective project, to assess their impact on particular actors in particular areas. Our best attempt to navigate this challenge was to segment our analysis into three different areas of impact: on individual participants; on institutional participants; and on related policy. Chapters 7, 8, 10, and 11 offer more detailed descriptions of these impacts, including student testimonies, institutional changes, and the projects' relationship to policy change.

Individual impacts: Evaluations of student experiences explored how working on participatory memory projects built their civic capacity around project issues, in a variety of interlocking steps: student participants demonstrated more knowledge about the issue and their relationship to it; a greater commitment to addressing it; greater knowledge about what kinds of organizing were happening around the issue; and, most important, a sense of their own efficacy as civic actors. For States of Incarceration students, the majority of whom did not have direct connections to incarcerated people before the start of the project, the strongest outcome was new empathy, reported by 84% of the 91 respondents from 17 campuses (out of a total of more than 500 project participants). Nearly 80% reported developing new confidence, and 70% could identify new action to take to address mass incarceration. In SOI as well as the Guantánamo project, the elements students said made the greatest impact on them were 1) creating something around a contested social issue; and 2) creating something real for the public.[1]

Student respondents who participated in Climates of Inequality (73 respondents out of about 300 project participants), half of whom were BIPOC and many of whom grew up in the communities around their colleges, reported 1) a new understanding of their own communities ("I now realize how many people are impacted by these environmental justice problems in my community – including myself!") and 2) a new capacity for civic action ("I actually feel more comfortable in my own skin because I have the knowledge and capacity to speak up").[2]

Students across all HAL projects expressed a new understanding of public memory as a critical component of civic action, whether it was deployed in museums, or in sectors like government or philanthropy.[3] That indicated progress toward our goal of ensuring that future generations would recognize the importance of confronting deep historical roots of current problems and mobilizing memory to make change from whatever field they wind up pursuing.

Institutional impacts: Institutions that partnered in participatory public memory projects were often able to leverage the local energy and national support these projects generated to embrace new partnerships and practices. As explored in Chapter 10, at universities participating in States of Incarceration, these ranged from new prison education programs; new ongoing partnerships with local community organizations; admission of formerly incarcerated students; or new curricula and pedagogies connecting heritage and public history with contemporary social issues. Community organizations reached new audiences for their work and issues, including new volunteers.

Policy impacts: As described in Chapter 4, my colleagues at the International Coalition of Sites of Conscience and I worked hard to determine how to assess the relationship between a single museum visit and larger shifts in policy or political culture. The Guantánamo Public Memory Project did not close Guantánamo; but through new courses at dozens of universities and public events held nearly every week in cities across the country for years, it sustained public attention on GTMO and fought the amnesia that enabled continued abuses there. New public attention to Rikers' history did not alone force New York City Mayor Bill de Blasio to commit to closing the jails; but, as detailed in Chapter 9, activists recognized that memory was essential to the #CLOSErikers movement's integrated strategy. The States of Incarceration project alone did not "ban the box" in Louisiana. But, as explored in Chapter 10, the project forced education and engagement with the issue of mass incarceration from one university's president, faculty, and students, resulting in one more letter of support and a collection of testimonies contributing to the combined pressure on the Louisiana legislature. Participatory public memory projects can add wind to movements' sails by creating new narrative frames that help people understand an issue in a different way, and by creating more spaces and opportunities for people to actively engage in the issue and participate in shaping it.

Participatory Public Memory for US Reparations and Truth Commissions

When I first heard 2020 Democratic presidential candidates pledging their support for reparations to Black Americans, I nearly fell off my chair.[4] If you've gotten through this whole book, you can understand why: in my 25 years of struggling to engage diverse people in confronting historical harms and their contemporary legacies, my government was extraordinary in its refusal to reckon. I watched the US refuse to participate in the International Criminal Court; the "Bush Truth Commission" crash and burn; and President Obama threaten to walk away from climate talks if they involved taking responsibility for history. So I had completely written off the possibility that the US state would ever take comprehensive responsibility for its abuses. This was despite centuries of citizen demands, and pioneering precedents like the Greensboro Truth and Community Reconciliation Project, initiated in 1999, and the Maine Wabanaki-State Child Welfare Truth and Reconciliation Commission, starting in 2013.[5] But over the past decade, the extraordinary uprisings of the Black Lives Matter movement in almost every city and town across the country broke the dam on reparations.

In April 2021, HR 40, the federal bill to study the legacies of slavery and proposals for redress, passed out of the House Judiciary Committee. This was after over 200 years of advocacy, starting with 18th-century formerly enslaved people who documented and demanded their rights to reparations, through social movements led by Marcus Garvey to Martin Luther King Jr., to the founding of the National Coalition of Blacks for Reparations in America in 1987, to the Movement for Black Lives' creation of a "Reparations Now" toolkit to support communities in their own campaigns.[6] HR 40 had been introduced and rejected every year since 1989, even outliving its original champion, John Conyers, carried on by Sheila Jackson Lee. For the first time, it was accompanied by a parallel Senate bill, introduced by New Jersey Senator Cory Booker. And it was joined by a new House bill, proposing a Truth, Racial Healing, and Transformation (TRHT) Commission. Where reparations bills demanded material redress and accountability; the TRHT bill focused on acknowledgment and healing. The TRHT bill expanded beyond slavery and its legacies to encompass the generations of "government actions directed against populations of color," including deliberately discriminatory policies of the FHA, Social Security Administration, and the GI bill.[7] Other federal initiatives focused on Indigenous historical trauma, such as the Department of Interior's Federal Indian Boarding School Initiative, which included examination of the DOI itself and its participation in establishing Indian Boarding Schools.[8]

The federal bills were symbolically striking, but the real action was at the local level. Dozens of government initiatives for truth commissions or reparations sprang up around the country, from municipal efforts like that in Evanston, Illinois, making reparations for housing discrimination, to state-level initiatives, like California's state Reparations Task Force.[9] In June 2021, eleven mayors from Los Angeles to Providence pledged to launch reparations projects in their cities.[10] Though some local initiatives remained at the level of a task force to study the issue, others went straight to compensation. And while many focused on distant historical violence, like the Maryland Lynching Truth and Reconciliation Commission, others took on more recent government actions, like Evanston's focus on the Federal Housing Administration's discriminatory policies starting in the 1930s.[11]

As initiatives sanctioned by the state, these bills represented a new vision for the place of historical reckoning in policy and governance. But as anyone who has worked for transitional justice in other countries can tell you, state participation opens as many pitfalls as it does possibilities.[12] On the one hand, only the state can take responsibility for its own abuses, giving it an irreplaceable role in repairing the harms it inflicted. On the other hand, state involvement risks co-opting or diluting the aims for which civil society advocates have fought for generations. State mechanisms for historical accountability, like truth commissions and reparations bills, may also be too limited in scope and duration to be able to fully break historical patterns of state oppression. It's memory advocates' job to ensure time-limited state accountability mechanisms have a lasting legacy, preventing historical abuses from reappearing in other forms.

The new engagement of the government in defining and pushing for historical truth and accountability presents critical new questions for participatory public memory work in the US. What does an integrated approach to reparations, that combines narrative and material change, look like for pedagogy, public policy, and public history practice in the US? What does a participatory public memory for reckoning with white supremacy look like? Who do we believe are the key agents of change, and how should they be involved? How can we foreground the leadership, voices, and deep activist experience of those historically harmed by white supremacy, while engaging people who have historically benefitted from white supremacy in grappling with their histories and their responsibilities for redress? What kind of partnerships and pressure should civil society movements bring to the state, to most effectively wrest lasting redress? Finally, how can we ensure that a focus on redress – with its frame of returning something to a past state – does not limit our imagination for a completely different future?

We stand at a moment of great possibility, brought about by centuries of work by thousands of people, and yet, like so many such moments, it can be easily lost. I hope this time we can seize this truth and hold on tight.

Notes

1 "Guantánamo Public Memory Project Student Participant Evaluations," Kate Livingston on behalf of ExposeYourMuseum LLC, "HAL States of Incarceration Student Evaluation," November 5, 2017, Humanities Action Lab files.
2 "Climate and Environmental Justice Student Post-Course Survey," Humanities Action Lab files.
3 "Guantánamo Public Memory Project Student Participant Evaluations"; Kate Livingston on behalf of ExposeYourMuseum LLC, "HAL States of Incarceration Student Evaluation," November 5, 2017; "Climate and Environmental Justice Student Post-course Survey," Humanities Action Lab files.

4 P. R. Lockhart, "The 2020 Democratic primary debate over reparations, explained,"
   Vox, June 19, 2019, https://www.vox.com/policy-and-politics/2019/3/11/18246741/
   reparations-democrats-2020-inequality-warren-harris-castro; "Reparations for
   Slavery: Where Democrats Stand," *Washington Post*, https://www.washingtonpost.
   com/graphics/politics/policy-2020/economic-inequality/reparations/

5 Lisa Magarrell and Joya Wesley, *Learning from Greensboro: Truth and Reconciliation
   in the United States* (Philadelphia: University of Pennsylvania Press, 2008); Daniel
   Posthumus and Kelebogile Zvobgo, "Democratizing Truth: An Analysis of Truth
   Commissions in the United States," *The International Journal of Transitional Justice*
   (2021).

6 Nkechi Taifa, "Reparations – Has the Time Finally Come?" ACLU News and Commentary, May 26, 2020, https://www.aclu.org/news/racial-justice/reparations-
   has-the-time-finally-come/; Andrea Ritchie, Deirdre Smith, Janetta Johnson,
   Jumoke Ifetayo, Marbre Stahly-Butts, Mariame Kaba, Montague Simmons, Nkechi
   Taifa, Rachel Herzing, Richard Wallace, and Taliba Obuya, "Movement for Black
   Lives Reparations Now Toolkit," Movement for Black Lives, 2019, https://m4bl.
   org/wp-content/uploads/2020/05/Reparations-Now-Toolkit-FINAL.pdf

7 "H.Con.Res.100 – Urging the Establishment of a United States Commission on
   Truth, Racial Healing, and Transformation," Congress.gov, June 4, 2020, https://
   www.congress.gov/bill/116th-congress/house-concurrent-resolution/100/text

8 "Secretary Haaland Announces Federal Indian Boarding School Initiative,"
   U.S. Department of the Interior, Press Release, June 22, 2021, https://www.
   doi.gov/pressreleases/secretary-haaland-announces-federal-indian-boarding-
   school-initiative

9 "Evanston Local Reparations," City of Evanston, https://www.cityofevanston.org/
   government/city-council/reparations; "AB 3121: Task Force to Study and Develop
   Reparation Proposals for African Americans," State of California Department of
   Justice, Office of the Attorney General, https://oag.ca.gov/ab3121

10 "11 U.S. Mayors Commit to Developing Pilot Projects for Reparations," NPR,
    June 18, 2021, https://www.npr.org/2021/06/18/1008242159/11-u-s-mayors-commit-
    to-developing-pilot-projects-for-reparations; Mayors Organized for Reparations
    and Equity, https://moremayors.org/

11 Maryland Lynching Truth and Reconciliation Commission, https://msa.maryland.
    gov/lynching-truth-reconciliation/index.html; Morris (Dino) Robinson, Jr., and
    Jenny Thompson, "Evanston Policies and Practices Directly Affecting the African
    American Community, 1900-1960 (and Present)," City of Evanston, https://www.
    cityofevanston.org/home/showpublisheddocument/59759/637382881295170000

12 Sebastian Brett, Louis Bickford, Liz Ševčenko, and Marcela Rios, "Memorialization
    and Democracy: State Policy and Civic Action," International Center for Transitional
    Justice, June 2007, https://www.ictj.org/publication/memorialization-and-
    democracy-state-policy-and-civic-action

APPENDIX

For Doers: Practical Questions for Building Translocal Participatory Public Memory

I hope the stories in this book, in their successes and their failures, can offer helpful insights for the exponentially growing numbers of people in the US propelling campaigns for historical truth and accountability, or for those supporting social movements – whether against police violence, for climate justice, or other issues – whose vision for the future insists on acknowledging the past. The cases I describe in the book are most relevant for people organizing public memory movements through translocal coalitions – whether across neighborhoods or continents. I believe this will be an increasingly common, and increasingly effective, mode for collective reckoning and radical imagining. I hope the stories here also contain lessons for people confronting contested histories in more traditional structures, like working in small historic sites or creating a single exhibit for a local museum, though there are many more resources out there to guide that work.[1]

This section gets into the weeds. Translocal participatory public memory is a mode that draws as many strategies from movement organizing as from public history; weaving these together into new synthetic approaches poses a variety of challenges. This section does not presume to offer a detailed how-to, or offer worksheets or other tools. Instead, I share some of the key strategic questions participants struggled with on a day-to-day basis, ones that anyone pursuing this mode would need to address for themselves, with reflections on our learning.

When Is the Time for Participatory Public Memory Projects? Reading and Seizing the Moment

Campaign organizers know how to spot a political opening and leverage it. They also know how fast political openings can close. A constellation of factors can come together to crack open a window onto new discourse and policy. Participatory memory projects can be most effective when they read the discursive, policy, and organizing landscape – what social movement theorists call the "political opportunity structure" – and find strategic ways to connect to existing movements.[2] For example, the mid-to-late 2000s saw growing national outrage over torture and detention at GTMO, but widespread ignorance of its long history, causing a misdiagnosis of the problem and how to address it. A public memory project could build on existing organizing, audiences, and appetite for engaging with the issue, while introducing new strategies based on historical understanding. The mid-2010s witnessed remarkable bi-partisan consensus that recognized and rejected mass incarceration, but deep divisions on how to remedy it, based in deep divisions around race, crime, and punishment. A public memory project could expose the roots of mass incarceration in systems of racial control for those insulated from the carceral state, and create more platforms for returning citizens to define narratives and policy solutions. In connecting with social movements, participatory public memory projects can ask, who are the people best positioned to drive change on this issue? This is not always "policy makers" or "people in power"; while local elected officials might be the main levers of change in some contexts, those most directly impacted, who have been historically excluded from traditional mechanisms of power but have deep histories of organizing, may make the strongest and most sustained impact. For these potential change-makers, what stories and experiences are least understood, or least validated? How can looking at the issue historically, and sharing memories, amplify and strengthen these stories into a broader and deeper collective consciousness?

When and Why Practice Public Memory through Coalition?

What Does Coalition Look Like, and What Are the Advantages and Disadvantages?

There's a difference between a project that is created collaboratively and one that is created in coalition. Choosing when to pursue a project in coalition depends on the project's strategic objectives. The Rikers Public Memory Project was founded by a partnership between three organizations; dozens of criminal justice organizations hosted story collecting days; and the interpretive framework was developed through ongoing consultation with an advisory committee of people who were incarcerated at Rikers or had family that were. As collaborative as it was, it's not a coalition. Creative control was not distributed: participating individuals and organizations did not each "own" a distinct piece of the Project that they were responsible for creating. Perhaps because the #CLOSErikers campaign was a coalition, the memory project that supported it did not need to be. Further, the managing team did not have the capacity to coordinate a coalition.

There's a difference between a network or a membership organization and a coalition. Networks provide opportunities for members to exchange knowledge and skills around shared concerns. But members of the network are not working in concert on a common project. In my experience, peer learning is stronger and more focused when participants are comparing apples to apples in real time – when everyone is trying to do the same thing, but in their own way.

The coalitions described in this book brought together individual institutions in a variety of contexts not only to pursue a shared mission, but to pursue it in a shared structure, with each institution innovating and exchanging distinct ways of filling that frame. In the Sites of Conscience coalition, that structure was a shared methodology of connecting past and present, facilitating open dialogue, and fostering action; members from Bangladesh to Buenos Aires were regularly accredited to ensure they met those common methodological commitments, but encouraged to meet them in their own ways, to generate as many different models for the movement as possible. In the Humanities Action Lab coalitions, the structure was a common project participants made together. Participants agreed to complete the project according to a shared set of frames – intellectual, ethical, design (more on those below) – but had independent creative authority within those frames. Coalitions can work together in an ongoing way, or come together around a single initiative and disband when it's over. Sites of Conscience recommitted annually; different members participated in different activities at different times. Participants in the Humanities Action Lab all came together around a specific project to work intensively for a circumscribed period of time, creating what amounted to separate coalitions for each public memory initiative. When participants' work concluded on the Guantánamo Public Memory Project, for instance, they could decide to help build the next one, States of Incarceration; or sit that one out and come back for the following. Each project had a core group of "veterans" who could guide and support new participants.

The advantage of coalitions is that they harness combined power through collective coordination while maintaining the creative energy and diversity of perspectives that come from local autonomy. They increase the number of people who have a serious stake in a project's outcome. They bring a diversity of knowledge, skills, and perspectives to bear on a common problem. They solidify the legitimacy of the common cause, and its individual adherents, to external skeptics.

For public memory movements that seek to foster a collective reckoning with historical harm and establish collective responsibility for redressing it, translocal coalitions are a particularly effective mode. On a variety of issues, translocal organizing has become a dominant mode: from the Sunrise Movement to Black Lives Matter, from the Slow Cities movement to Sanctuary Cities, social movements are increasingly linking local efforts into collective resistance to state violence, globalization, and authoritarian national governments.[3] As environmental justice scholar and activist Ana Baptista argues, "translocal, justice-centered networks may be the most viable and vibrant alternatives to address the ecological and social crisis of contemporary globalization."[4] In the context of public memory, translocal projects can mobilize people around the places and stories that are most immediate and meaningful to them, connecting people to what they can actually see, "bringing home" broader historical narratives and arguments that might otherwise feel abstract. For instance, the fundamental historical argument of climate justice – that those who have contributed least to global warming are bearing the greatest impact – can be much better understood by studying toxic histories and big weather events in one's own neighborhood. By linking local narratives together, projects can build solidarity and strength among people with parallel experiences, demonstrate how local experiences are part of a larger historical structure or policy system operating on a national or global scale – such as mass incarceration or environmental racism – that can only be changed through collective action. What "local" looks like depends on the issue the project is addressing, where its policy is controlled, and where the organizing is happening. As discussed earlier, States of Incarceration focused on states, since that was the unit with the most influence over criminal justice policy; Climates of Inequality focused on neighborhoods, since that was the best way to map environmental discrimination, and because that's where the energy for climate justice organizing was strongest.

Coalitions magnify participants' time, talent, and money. Alone, local teams with a small budget are most likely only to be able to produce a one-off exhibition. Working together and pooling their money, individual local teams and a small coordinating staff can produce a professionally designed, internationally traveling show, displayed in major public spaces, that lasts for years. Local creators' voices have a much broader reach for a longer time in spaces that attract a larger audience than they could build alone.

The main risks of coalition are dilution of specific arguments or perspectives. Coalitions can agree to adhere to common principles and approaches to the historical subject – for example, that a project on climate justice should focus on the stories of frontline communities, or that narratives on GTMO do not call into question what torture is or that it took place there – but the point is to allow each partner to bring their own voice and experience to the common project. If project organizers deem that the project's historical narratives and approach need to be singular and tightly controlled, working in coalition would invite too many variables.

Which Kinds of Institutions and Groups Make the Best Partners and Leaders for Any Given Public Memory Coalition?

If participatory public memory combines heritage and human rights, scholarship and social movement, where does it live? There are distinct opportunities and challenges of working with and within universities, museums/heritage bodies, or advocacy organizations; state entities or grassroots groups. Coalition structures, because they are about connecting the inherent strengths of diverse participants, do not require too much from any of its individual members, allowing even the scrappiest, leanest, and least-tested organizations to participate alongside larger and more established organizations. Working in coalition is an extension of the familiar collaborative model that defines most public humanities work, except it usually brings in even more diverse perspectives or a fresh set of eyes when needed. It can facilitate network building and resource sharing between well-funded institutions and small non-profit organizations in ways that can increase accessibility for many communities.

Any coalition will likely involve combinations of institutions of all shapes and sizes, but what role each type of institution plays depends on the goals and activities of the coalition. The Sites of Conscience coalition was founded primarily to establish human rights-oriented public memory as a universal good, across geographic and political contexts, and to prove the concept by elaborating specific and diverse methodological models. To achieve this aim, we needed to bring together the widest variety of institutions and sectors possible, from huge state entities like the US National Park Service to oppositional grassroot movements that wouldn't take a penny from their governments. Because they came together primarily to exchange strategy and collectively advocate, and did not actually have to collaborate, the huge differences in their institutional structures were nothing but a strength.

For coalitions in which participants are actually making something together – like the Humanities Action Lab – diversity needs to be balanced with compatibility, and power dynamics need to be attended to much more closely. These types of coalitions are best built by creatively connecting work people are already doing, requiring as little new work as possible. To identify coalition partners, the key thing is to find organizations that are not only already aligned in mission, but also already have structures and activities in place that can be reoriented to support the common initiative. The Guantánamo Public Memory Project, which gave rise to the other Humanities Action Lab initiatives, decided to base its work in universities in large part because university public history and museum studies courses provided a ready-made structure through which to work on public history projects with young people; many already had small amounts of funding for this purpose that could be pooled. Coalition partners should also be uniquely positioned to make an impact on the target issue. Given the political climate in which the GPMP began, few history museums or their funders would have agreed to undertake a project on Guantánamo. Building the GPMP as a "class project" created by students in institutions ostensibly devoted to academic freedom opened the space for the project to happen. The project was organized with universities as the lead partners in each locality, the main point of contact with the HAL organizing hub. Universities were responsible for identifying and coordinating partnerships with issue organizations relevant to their "chapter," and with the public space where the exhibit would be displayed when it came to their city.

In the development of the subsequent HAL projects, as equitable collaborations with issue organizations became a central priority, the prominent role of universities posed more challenges to the project aims. The projects were designed around university timetables and administrative structures, such as semester-long courses with final assignments. Because they were the ones who contributed funds for their "chapter" of the exhibition, universities had the greatest stake and accountability for the project's completion – faculty who solicited funds from their deans needed to show they had produced what they said they would with the money. Participating criminal justice and environmental justice organizations were deeply invested in the memory projects' aims, but they did not have pre-existing structures that could be neatly repurposed to participate in creating public memory projects. Their core work often focused on large public actions, or painstaking one-on-one engagements with individual elected officials; the outputs of oral histories, exhibits, and public programs definitely supported this work, but their organizational structures did not easily support creating them. The timelines were different, too: issue organizations' work was responsive and immediate, triggered by unpredictably timed events like a police shooting or a flood, on extremely fast timetables that were impossible to plan for; universities had to plan out students' activities up to a year in advance. The HAL Hub supported local issue organization staff with funds to compensate for the time away from their core work to participate. This was helpful, but even as the proportion of the budget increased from modest honoraria to fellowships that could replace salary for periods of time, it still was something organizations needed to make room for.

Moving forward, we are asking ourselves: what are the existing structures and activities in all the types of institutions we want to involve, and where do they connect?

What Does It Look Like to Actually "Make History" Together? Frames for Collaborative Curation

Creating public memory collectively doesn't happen naturally, but requires carefully designed and rigorously maintained frames into which diverse and dispersed participants place their varied contributions to create a coherent common project. These include frames for the collaboration itself, determining the roles and authority of all stakeholders; values and methodological frames, providing common principles and approaches that each partner can pursue in their own context; intellectual frames, providing common research questions that each partner can explore in its own locality; and design/media frames, such as templates for exhibit modules or formats for audio essays.

These frames also need to be collaboratively created, by a smaller group of people that represent the perspectives the project wants to combine. These voices and perspectives must be at the table and engaged from the earliest discussions. It is exceedingly difficult to integrate new voices later. As described in Chapter 7, when majority-white scholars created States of Incarceration's initial timeline for the history of mass incarceration in the US, somehow slavery wasn't on it. And when "student-community" collaborations were designed for the majority of students insulated from the impacts of incarceration, they focused on raising awareness among the uninformed more than opening space for healing or solidarity.

Organizational and Financial Frames

Coalitions require some central coordination and funding, with as much transparency as possible about what is expected of the central office versus coalition members. HAL was held together with detailed memoranda of understanding between the university hosting the HAL "Hub" (coordinating office), and partner universities.

HAL "Hub" staff raised money for staff, overhead, and partner convenings from external funders like the Institute for Museum and Library Services and the Andrew W. Mellon Foundation. These central costs were also borne by the university housing the "Hub": first The New School in New York City, followed by Rutgers University in Newark. But the cost of the element that most benefited partners – the design and production exhibition their students and communities created – was shared equally by the universities who co-created it, through contributions of $5,000 each. Many participating universities already had budgets for student projects, but at a scale that would only allow for something temporary and not well designed. Here universities contributed what many would have spent on a small-scale student project, but received a professionally designed exhibition that would travel their students' work around the country. This cost-sharing model ensured the centerpiece of everyone's work together would be paid for, and ensured that the leadership of participating institutions would be aware of and accountable to the project's success. But it excluded universities without access to those kinds of funds. And it gave universities who did pay a greater stake and authority in the projects than their non-university partners, who did not. As HAL recommitted to changing its composition and power structure, we worked to cover the cost of partners that represented particular priority skills and perspectives, and increased the central budget for community partners.

Frames for Goals and Values: What Are We All Holding Ourselves Accountable to?

The projects described in this book began by bringing stakeholders together to establish the goals and values that all participants would agree to follow and uphold as they pursued their work in their own context. The Guantánamo Public Memory Project's founding principles were more about the scope of overall content, which was deeply contentious in and of itself: this included to "involve the entire history of the site, not only its recent use in the 'War on Terror,' grounded in rigorous scholarship," and to "include multiple voices and perspectives such as recent and past detainees, military personnel, Cuban workers, Third Country Nationals and others, aiming to restore the dignity of all as human beings with complex individual histories and backgrounds."[5] Climates of Inequality, on the other hand, focused on cohering the values participants would uphold as they pursued their projects, with little framing of historical content: this included centering frontline communities, creating equitable partnerships, and defining and maintaining accountability to the various partners in the project.[6]

Intellectual Frames: How Can We Balance Individual Expression and Collective Coherence?

Projects began with scholars and stakeholders identifying the overall historical scaffolding into which individual partner's local stories would fit. The scaffolding could be chronological: in the case of the Guantánamo Public Memory Project, historians suggested a set of key periods in the base's history – the War of 1898, the Cold War, Haitian refugees – with a few sentences about why they were important and what questions they raised. Each local team then chose a period to concentrate on, and was free to explore and interpret it however their stakeholder group saw fit. The scaffolding could be thematic: in States of Incarceration, scholars and stakeholders identified four key thematic questions, and invited partners to identify a site or story in their locality that would address one of them. Specifically, local teams were invited to find a history unique or distinctive to their locality that had something specific to teach the rest of the country. Local stories were then grouped under each of these overarching historical themes.

Giving local teams freedom to voice their stories doesn't mean that any story goes. Local teams' freedom was balanced with feedback and fact checking from a central team, set up by the coordinating hub, with diverse expertise. This included academic historians with diverse regional and issue specialties, and national policy or advocacy experts with knowledge and sensibilities on communicating about the project's issue today, including people directly impacted. Each project included a style guide, to ensure terms were used consistently, but more importantly, that they reflected the project's shared values. For instance, States of Incarceration participants were required to use people-centered language, such as "formerly incarcerated person," instead of "inmate" or "criminal."[7] Finally, the design team and the coordinating hub team gave feedback on image choices, how to frame open-ended questions, and other interpretive questions; and ensured that partners' individual contributions did not repeat each other. At the beginning of the process, the hub team gave partners a chart showing which aspects of their work would be reviewed by which people; what kind of feedback they would give; and whether partners were expected to follow it (e.g. correcting a date or other basic inaccuracy) or take it under advisement.

It's a challenge to balance individual freedom and some central curation, to take advantage of the diversity of perspectives that can only arise organically, while ensuring stories are neither repeated nor excluded. In each HAL project, the group agreed to assume some collective responsibility for what emerged collectively. While each individual "chapter" did not need to address all vectors of experience, we committed to together ensure that when all the parts were assembled, key issues and their intersections – for instance, race and gender; incarceration and labor – were integrated. The HAL "Hub" coordinating office would look for gaps in the map, holes in the intellectual frame, and encourage local teams that had not yet decided on their focus to fill them. But no local team was forced to work on any particular topic.

This meant that diversity and intersectionality would be left to emerge organically, over time and space. This approach allowed each locality to find and speak from the experiences that felt the most urgent to them, without being forced to meet national demands. What was absent from the accounts of the first 20 teams might emerge from future localities. But leaving it up to the local partners risked that no one would choose to talk about certain issues, especially those that remained particularly marginalized, so silences would be replicated and reinforced. For example, the HAL Hub did not insist that any States of Incarceration local team focus on LGBTQ experiences, which represents a fundamental branch of the history of criminalization as social control, and a major issue in the contemporary carceral state. As a result, though, with the notable exception of UMass's work with OutNow, LGBTQ experiences remain almost entirely absent from the digital and physical exhibit. To date, none of the new partners have elected to explore it in their localities.

Perspectival Frames: How Do We Decide Whose Voices to Include and What's Up for Debate?

The role of dialogue and multiple perspectives depends on what a project is trying to achieve, and the political context in which it's working. The goal of the Guantánamo Public Memory Project was to open national dialogue on GTMO's history and current implications. It included the perspectives of people who served and lived at GTMO, as well as those held there against their will. This strategy was based on a theory of change that building a culture of human rights, one that would reject reserving a space for indefinite detention outside of US laws, required not just declaring that torture was wrong, but fostering a democratic practice of questioning and open debate, by fostering multiple perspectives and engaging conflicting perspectives in dialogue. Speaking from only one perspective risked "preaching to the converted," replacing one dogma with another, and stunting the movement. This didn't mean leaving everything up for debate; the project needed to establish clear boundaries of what would and would not be posed as an open question (e.g. whether torture took place at GTMO and whether torture was ever justified).

The Rikers Public Memory Project, on the other hand, was deliberate in its exclusive focus on people who were incarcerated at Rikers and their families. "Directly impacted" people, in the project's framework, did not include corrections officers. Unlike GTMO, this project's theory of change held that a culture of human rights needed to first acknowledge and redress the power relationships undergirding how the stories of the place had been told. The voices of corrections officers and other people who worked at Rikers did not exist on an equal plane as those of people who had been incarcerated there; placing stories of COs side by side with those of returning citizens would obfuscate that inequality. Until the power structures of the carceral state that excluded or distorted the voices of incarcerated people were addressed, the project needed to do its own work to redress and reverse it, by carving out uninterrupted space and time for their stories to speak and be heard. There was no fear of "preaching to the converted," since the goal here was not primarily to convert anyone, but to strengthen and mobilize directly impacted people, who in project organizers' experience had the greatest capacity to effect change.

For both public historians and advocates, creating a dialogic project based on questions, as opposed to a didactic one based on declarative statements, goes against all our training and instincts. The Guantánamo Public Memory Project and States of Incarceration exhibits were each organized as a series of questions: each local team framed their "chapter" not with a title that described their topic or argument, but with a question their piece of the history raised. The question was to be derived from the history, but applicable to the present day; it was to be open-ended, not rhetorical – something the team legitimately felt was open to debate and difficult to answer. Crafting these few words was the most challenging part of the entire exhibition. The struggle over crafting the question revealed how deeply the assignment conflicted with the skills students – and faculty too – had been taught to value as historians, even as public historians. The job of the historian was to make an argument. The job of the public historian was to communicate that argument to a broader public outside the university. Serving as effective facilitators – charged with soliciting arguments from others – was not something they had been trained for, nor was it something on which they could establish the same feeling of pride, recognition, or authority. Doing dialogic public history requires significant time and training around crafting open-ended questions, and investment in the value and expertise of facilitation.

Pedagogical and Process Frames: How Do We Break Down the Steps of Co-Creation?

The collaborations in the Humanities Action Lab projects took place across localities, as well as within them. Local teams were made up of university faculty and students; community organization leaders; and staff of exhibiting spaces, like public libraries and museums. But each local team had a different mix of participants collaborating in different ways. The Humanities Action Lab hub shared options for local collaborations along a spectrum, from consultation to co-creation, to encourage local partners to be intentional and transparent with each other about what they were able and willing to do. For example, in a consultation model, one partner is the decision-maker and creative director of the project, but solicits input from others, that the partner can either incorporate or ignore. On the other end of the spectrum is a co-creation model, in which each party separately creates components that are then combined, or parties work together and share creative control at every stage, including signing off on final text or other details. In between might be a collaboration in which partners share creative control of high-level decisions – for instance, the central theme of the exhibit and the stories and issues to foreground, and the values to work from – but the granular details that take the most time, such as writing and final approval of captions, is left to only one of the partners. Frames for collaboration included financial ones: over the course of its three projects, the Humanities Action Lab devoted a larger and larger proportion of its budget to compensating community organization partners for their time and expertise.

Understanding that collaborations can take different forms, along a spectrum of intensity, can make collaboration feel less daunting: it's not a choice between collaborating or not collaborating, but a choice of how to collaborate around which elements of one's project, always in keeping with the capacities of everyone involved. The important thing is for partners to be transparent with each other and with their external audiences about the specifics of their shared authority. Partners should make a clear agreement with each other, through a memorandum of understanding or something else everyone can see and refer back to, about the scope of each partner's authority. Collaborations should not be oversold to an external public to falsely legitimize a project through an inaccurate depiction of whose voices it represents.

Design Frames: How Do We Ensure Individual Contributions Fit Together?

For each project, the Humanities Action Lab "Hub" coordinating office hired one design team to lead the design and production of the physical and digital exhibits. Designers were charged with creating templates that would allow individual contributions to be integrated into a coherent whole. Designers conceived of the physical exhibit as a series of panels, each dedicated to one "chapter," of the story, authored by one local team. Each panel was made up of parallel components: for instance, a framing question, introductory text of specific length, a signature image, and supporting images and captions. The projects needed to create a continuous and coherent visitor experience, while demonstrating clearly that each "chapter" was separately authored, and, specifically, authored by non-experts. The team's authorship was clearly indicated, through a section in each panel titled "Our Point of View," in which students were asked to reflect on their positionality, personal history, or other context and how it informed their approach. This was critical to each project's ability to inspire public openness to the possibility of learning something new through the exhibit – by foregrounding the curiosity and discovery of the students, the projects hoped to predispose their visiting public to approach the subject with the same spirit.

The design frame also needed to balance between collective and individual contributions from each local team. Students on each campus were required to work together to produce one exhibit panel that spoke for all of them, that somehow represented a collective take, theoretically informed by a common local context. This required students to make difficult curatorial choices that forced them to grapple with the even more difficult political and ethical issues underlying those choices. To balance this consensus-driven process, and to generate more interpretive material outside the very limited confines of a single exhibit panel, the project invited students to produce individually authored pieces for the website. These could be a node on the timeline; a location on the map; or a "story" of someone with direct experience, through a video interview or audio slideshow. Each had a standard format, ensuring they could be integrated seamlessly onto the site. But each also was clearly identified as authored by a different student, with name and university affiliation attached.

How Do We Balance Process and Product?
Which Is Which? Why Are Each Necessary?

For a methodology so focused on process, it might come as a surprise that we focused so much on creating an exhibit. Exhibits are normally understood as products, and are often valued over the process of making them. In the context of participatory memory projects, the main purpose of an exhibit is to provide a frame or container for engagement among the people who create it, and secondarily, among the people who later view it. Exhibits are valuable to participatory memory projects only insofar as they catalyze a process of engagement with the past and with each other that fosters attitudinal, narrative, institutional, and/or policy change.

HAL's exhibits were designed to try to make the process visible to visitors, and allow them to connect with the discussions that developed the final product: for instance, by clearly marking each exhibit chapter as authored by students and stakeholder partners; including "our point of view" statements from local teams to be transparent about their subjective authorship; or by posing questions local teams had grappled with. But these elements were buried within an installation most visitors still viewed as a traditional, didactic exhibit. The most important parts of the project – the relationships built, knowledge exchanged, civic action inspired – could not be represented.

If the process is the only point, why spend the time and money to make an exhibit at all? Our evaluations suggested that for participants, the mandate to create something tangible that expresses the stories participants want to share, that others can see, and, most importantly, where participants can witness the impact their stories are making on others, was what drove the learning, relationships, and civic capacity. So many participants said their main takeaway was "I can do this!" because they saw something they did and could be proud of. While all the projects have included robust digital platforms, the real catalyst came from creating something that brought people together in physical space, at a particular moment in time. Although the projects in this book worked in traditional exhibit formats, a physical installation or performance could take many forms. It just needs a sense of "event" to create urgency and timeliness; and the chance for participants to see real people interact with the installation and with each other, allowing them to directly witness the project's impact in a way anonymous digital comments posted on a website did not. The product is both beside the point and the anchor for everything.

How should we prioritize process versus product when they come into conflict? The process was based in students and stakeholders finding their own way through their local histories and their implications, and deciding together what was most important to share with the outside world. The product – an exhibition for an outside public – needed to be historically accurate, legible to exhibition visitors, and completed by a deadline. To achieve these goals, as the production deadlines drew near, some local teams' contributions needed to be edited more heavily than others, which infringed on their agency and voice. We mitigated against this by warning people it might happen: establishing clear parameters and criteria for content and design at the outset, and identifying who would be reviewing contributions against them. But it could be painful in the moment.

How Can Participatory Public Memory Projects Last?

Participatory public memory products, unlike traditional exhibits, need to be conceived as lasting infrastructure for an ongoing movement that can respond to changing policy and political realities. Constantly promoting, updating, and maintaining an exhibit would require an enormous amount of time and resources if it were the sole responsibility of a central curator. Instead, Humanities Action Lab projects built sustainability into their structure. All of the HAL exhibits were iterative, inviting new communities to add new modules, addressing new issues and histories. The Guantánamo Public Memory Project exhibit launched with nine partners, scheduled to travel to their cities over one year; it grew to travel to 22 cities over the next three years. Welcoming more partners not only provides more exposure and reach for the issues the project raises, but also allows the information and perspectives to be continually refreshed. As the States of Incarceration exhibit traveled, and each new partner added its own state's story and hosted local events and actions, it became a sort of palimpsest, containing its own public historiography: stories of mass incarceration from 2015 stood next to others from 2021, a radically different moment in the public conversation on race, policing, and prisons. Shortly after the Climates of Inequality exhibit opened, the pandemic hit, and hit the communities featured in the exhibit hardest. As it traveled, local partners added new stories of their experiences in the pandemic, and how these stories were rooted in the histories of environmental racism they created for the original exhibit. Projects also created platforms for addressing evolving crises in individual locations. The University of Puerto Rico's "Mi María" project, included in Climates of Inequality, created a story-sharing process embedded in and supporting mutual aid after hurricane María, that served as a healing and organizing space. When this disaster was followed in short order by earthquakes and a devastating pandemic, the process was there. Mi María pivoted and expanded to organize story exchanges for community support around these new disasters. This endeavor, like all good participatory public memory projects, provided a framework for an active citizenry – ready to resist historical denial through documentation and mutual support, actively exploring the roots of inequality in a localized context, and imagining novel ways to redress it.

Notes

1 Several museum collectives and organizations provide expansive ideas of what communal education venues and dialogic public history can look like, and they provide rubrics and toolkits for practitioners. In addition to the International

Coalition of Sites of Conscience's toolkits and resources, https://www. sitesofconscience.org/en/resources/rc/, other useful sources include the MASS Action (Museum as Site for Social Action) Toolkit, https://www.museumaction.org/ resources; The Empathetic Museum's Maturity Model, http://empatheticmuseum. weebly.com/maturity-model.html; Museums & Race's Museum Report Card, https://museumsandrace.org/2020/01/01/report-card/; and the American Association for State and Local History's (AASLH) Technical Leaflet series, https:// learn.aaslh.org/technical-leaflets. Useful tools can also be found in previous publications on Sites of Conscience, such as my "Dialogue as a Resource for Heritage Management: Stories from Sites of Conscience," in *Consensus Building, Negotiation, and Conflict Resolution for Heritage Place Management: Proceedings of a Workshop Organized by the Getty Conservation Institute, Los Angeles, California, December 1-3, 2009*, eds. David Myers, Stacie Nicole Smith, and Gail Ostergren (Los Angeles: The Getty Conservation Institute, 2016), https://www.getty.edu/conservation/ publications_resources/pdf_publications/consensus_building.html

2 Sidney G. Tarrow, *Power in Movement: Social Movements and Contentious Politics.* Rev. & updated 3rd ed. (Cambridge: Cambridge University Press, 2011).

3 Jeanine M. Canty, Introduction, and Brian Tokar, "Climate Solutions and the Challenge of Local Solutions," in *Globalism and Localization: Emergent Solutions to Ecological and Social Crises*, ed. Jeanine M. Canty (New York: Routledge, 2019), 25–7; T. Linstroth and R. Bell, eds., *Local Action: The New Paradigm in Climate Change Policy* (Burlington, VT: University of Vermont Press, 2007).

4 Ana Isabel Baptista, "The Evolution of the Environmental Justice Movement: Translocal Voices for Systemic Transformations," in *Globalism and Localization: Emergent Solutions to Ecological and Social Crises*, ed. Jeanine M. Canty (New York: Routledge, 2019), 143.

5 Liz Ševčenko and Bix Gabriel, with Jonathan Hansen, Jana Lipman, Stephen Schwab, and Michael Strauss, "Project Blueprint," Guantánamo Public Memory Project (International Coalition of Sites of Conscience, September 2011), document held by Humanities Action Lab.

6 "Project Values and Expressions," Climates of Inequality: Stories of Environmental Justice, document held by Humanities Action Lab.

7 At the time of the project, there were few published resources or research on the issue. We worked from an unpublished 2013 paper by Eddie Ellis, President of the Center for NuLeadership on Urban Solutions, called "Words Matter: Another Look at the Question of Language," which he later published as an open letter (see https://static1.squarespace.com/static/58eb0522e6f2e1dfce591dee/t/596e13f 48419c2e5a0e95d30/1500386295291/CNUS-language-letter-2016.pdf). Now we have the benefit of work like: Alexandra Cox, "The Language of Incarceration," *Incarceration* 1, no. 1 (July 2020): 1-13; Nguyen T. Tran, Stéphanie Baggio, Angela Dawson, Éamonn O'Moore, Brie Williams, Precious Bedell, Olivier Simon, Willem Scholten, Laurent Getaz, and Hans Wolff, "Words Matter: A Call for Humanizing and Respectful Language to Describe People Who Experience Incarceration," *BMC International Health and Human Rights* 18, no. 1 (November 2018): 41.

INDEX